Autodesk Fusion 360

Black Book

(V 2.0.6508) Part 2

By
Gaurav Verma
Matt Weber
(CADCAMCAE Works)

ISBN # 978-1-988722-71-9

NOTICE TO THE READER

DEDICATION

To teachers, who make it possible to disseminate knowledge
to enlighten the young and curious minds
of our future generations

To students, who are the future of the world

THANKS

To my friends and colleagues

To my family for their love and support

Table of Contents

Part 2
Chapter 12 : Sculpting

Chapter 16 : Generating Milling Toolpaths - 1

Chapter 17 : Generating Milling Toolpaths - 2

Chapter 21 : Simulation Studies in Fusion 360

Chapter 22 : Sheetmetal Design

Part 1

Chapter 1: Starting with Autodesk Fusion 360

Chapter 2 : Sketching

Chapter 3 : 3D Sketch and SolidModeling

Chapter 6 : Solid Editing

Chapter 7 : Assembly Design

Chapter 11 : Drawing

Preface

Autodesk Fusion 360 is a product of Autodesk Inc. Fusion 360 is the first of its kind software which combine 3D CAD, CAM, and CAE tool in single package. It connects your entire product development process in a single cloud-based platform that works on both Mac and PC. In CAD environment, you can create the model with parametric designing and dimensioning. The CAD environment is equally applicable for assembly design. The CAE environment facilitates to analysis the model under real-world load conditions. Once the model is as per your requirement then generate the NC program using the CAM environment.

The **Autodesk Fusion 360 Black Book** (V 2.0.6508) is third edition of our series on Autodesk Fusion 360. The book is updated on Autodesk Fusion 360 Ultimate, Student V 2.0.6508. With lots of features and thorough review, we present a book to help professionals as well as beginners in creating some of the most complex solid models. The book follows a step by step methodology. In this book, we have tried to give real-world examples with real challenges in designing. We have tried to reduce the gap between educational use of Autodesk Fusion 360 and industrial use of Autodesk Fusion 360. This edition of book, includes latest topics on Sketching, 3D Part Designing, Assembly Design, Rendering & Animation, Sculpting, Mesh Design, CAM, Simulation, Sheetmetal, 3D printing, 3D PDFs, and many other topics. The book covers almost all the information required by a learner to master the Autodesk Fusion 360. The book starts with sketching and ends at advanced topics like Manufacturing, Simulation, and Animation. Some of the salient features of this book are :

In-Depth explanation of concepts

Every new topic of this book starts with the explanation of the basic concepts. In this way, the user becomes capable of relating the things with real world.

Topics Covered

Every chapter starts with a list of topics being covered in that chapter. In this way, the user can easy find the topic of his/her interest easily.

Instruction through illustration

The instructions to perform any action are provided by maximum number of illustrations so that the user can perform the actions discussed in the book easily and effectively. There are about **1930** small and large illustrations that make the learning process effective.

Tutorial point of view

At the end of concept's explanation, the tutorial make the understanding of users firm and long lasting. Almost each chapter of the book has tutorials that are real world projects. Moreover most of the tools in this book are discussed in the form of tutorials.

Project

Free projects and exercises are provided to students for practicing.

For Faculty

If you are a faculty member, then you can ask for video tutorials on any of the topic, exercise, tutorial, or concept.

Formatting Conventions Used in the Text

All the key terms like name of button, tool, drop-down etc. are kept bold.

Free Resources

Link to the resources used in this book are provided to the users via email. To get the resources, mail us at ***cadcamcaeworks@gmail.com*** with your contact information. With your contact record with us, you will be provided latest updates and informations regarding various technologies. The format to write us mail for resources is as follows:

Subject of E-mail as ***Application for resources of _____ book***.
Also, given your information like
Name:
Course pursuing/Profession:
E-mail ID:

Note: We respect your privacy and value it. If you do not want to give your personal informations then you can ask for resources without giving your information.

About Authors

The author of this book, Gaurav Verma, has authored and assisted in more than 16 titles in CAD/CAM/CAE which are already available in market. He has authored **AutoCAD Electrical Black Books** which are available in both **English** and **Russian** language. He has also authored books on various modules of Creo Parametric and SolidWorks. He has provided consultant services to many industries in US, Greece, Canada, and UK. He has assisted in preparing many Government aided skill development programs. He has been speaker for Autodesk University, Russia 2014. He has assisted in preparing AutoCAD Electrical course for Autodesk Design Academy. He has worked on Sheetmetal, Forging, Machining, and Casting designs in Design and Development departments of various manufacturing firms.

If you have any query/doubt in any CAD/CAM/CAE package, then you can contact the authors by writing at cadcamcaeworks@gmail.com

For Any query or suggestion

If you have any query or suggestion, please let us know by mailing us on *cadcamcaeworks@gmail.com*. Your valuable constructive suggestions will be incorporated in our books.

Chapter 12

Sculpting

Topics Covered

The major topics covered in this chapter are:

- *Plane*
- *Cylinder*
- *Quadball*
- *Face*
- *Loft*
- *Edit Form*
- *Merge Edge*
- *Weld Vertices*
- *Fill Hole*
- *Crease and Uncrease*
- *Pull and Flatten*
- *Freeze and UnFreeze*

INTRODUCTION

Sculpting is a workspace that offers tools to push, pull, grab, or pinch objects to modify their shapes. In this chapter, we will learn various commands and tool of **FORM** mode which are used to create or modify the object.

OPENING THE FORM MODE

The components or parts created in Form mode are easily converted in solid bodies. Generally, the **FORM** mode is not a workspace so it will not be available in **Change Workspace** drop-down. It is displayed in **DESIGN** workspace. The procedure to activate this mode is discussed next.

- Click on the **DESIGN** option from **Change Workspace** drop-down. The **DESIGN** workspace will be displayed in **Autodesk Fusion 360** window.
- Click on **Create Form** tool of **CREATE** drop-down from **Toolbar**; refer to Figure-1. The **FORM** mode will be displayed with updated **Toolbar**; refer to Figure-2.

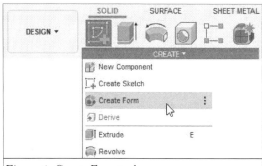

Figure-1. Create Form tool

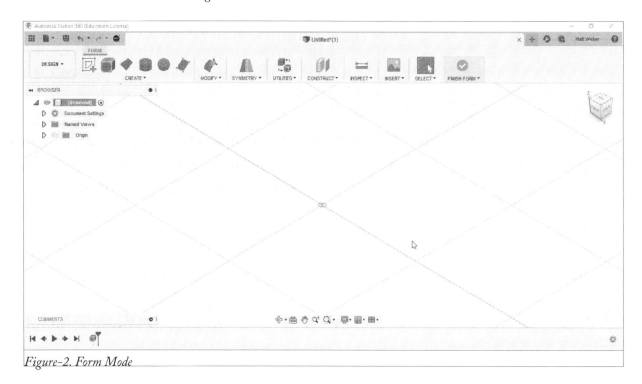

Figure-2. Form Mode

CREATION TOOLS

In this section, we will discuss the creation tools used to create form.

Box

The **Box** tool is used to create a rectangular body on the selected plane or face. The procedure to use this tool is discussed next.

- Click on the **Box** tool of **CREATE** drop-down from **Toolbar**; refer to Figure-3. The **BOX** dialog box will be displayed; refer to Figure-4.

Figure-3. Box tool

Figure-4. BOX dialog box

- You will be asked to select the plane or face. Click to select plane or face.
- Select **Center** option from **Rectangular Type** drop-down if you want to create a center rectangle as reference for box.
- Select **2-Point** option from **Rectangular Type** drop-down if you want to create a 2-Point rectangle as a reference for creating box. In our case, we are selecting the **Center** option.
- Specify the desired parameters in **Direction** and **Operation** drop-down as discussed earlier in **DESIGN Workspace**.
- Click on the screen to specify the center point of rectangle.
- Enter the desired dimension of length and width in the respective floating window and click on the screen. The updated **BOX** dialog box will be displayed; refer to Figure-5.

Figure-5. Updated BOX dialog box

- If you want to change the length of box then click in the **Length** edit box and enter the desired value.
- Click in the **Length Faces** edit box of **BOX** dialog box and enter the number of faces in which surface of box will be divided along the length.
- If you want to change the width of plane then click in the **Width** edit box and enter the desired value.
- Click in the **Width Faces** edit box of **BOX** dialog box and enter the number of faces in which surface of box will be divided along the width.
- Click in the **Height** edit box and enter the desired value of height of box.
- Click in the **Height Faces** edit box and enter the number of faces in which height of plane will be divided along the height.
- Select the **Mirror** option from **Symmetric** drop-down if you want to create a symmetric box. On selecting the **Mirror** option the updated dialog box will be displayed; refer to Figure-6.

Figure-6. Updated BOX dialog box on selecting Mirror Symmetry

- Select the **Length Symmetry** check box if you want to apply mirror symmetry along length of sculpt object; refer to Figure-7.

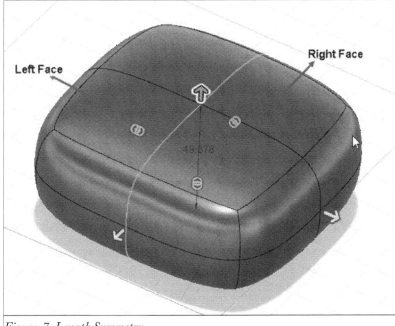

Figure-7. Length Symmetry

- Select the **Width Symmetry** check box if you want to apply mirror symmetry along width of sculpt object; refer to Figure-8. Note that later while editing, if you will move one face then the other symmetric face will also move accordingly.

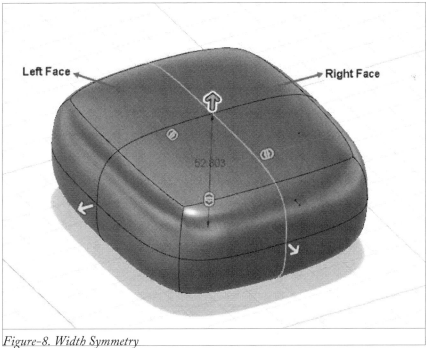

Figure-8. Width Symmetry

- Select the **Height Symmetry** check box if you want to apply mirror symmetry between upper and lower faces of sculpt object; refer to Figure-9.

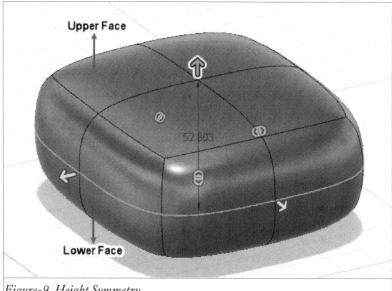

Figure-9. Height Symmetry

- Specify the desired parameters in **Direction** and **Operation** drop-down as discussed earlier in **DESIGN Workspace**.
- Note that you can also change shape of box by using the drag handles. After specifying the parameters, click on **OK** button from **BOX** dialog box to complete the process.

Plane

The **Plane** tool is used to create T-Spline plane. The procedure to use this tool is discussed next.

- Click on the **Plane** tool from **CREATE** drop-down; refer to Figure-10. The **PLANE** dialog box will be displayed; refer to Figure-11.

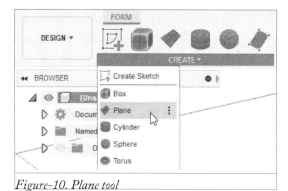

Figure-10. Plane tool

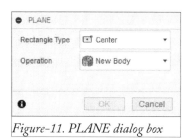

Figure-11. PLANE dialog box

- The options of **Rectangular Type** drop-down from **PLANE** dialog box are same as discussed earlier in last section.

- Click on the screen to specify the center point.
- Enter the desired dimension of length and width in respective input boxes. The updated **PLANE** dialog box will be displayed; refer to Figure-12.

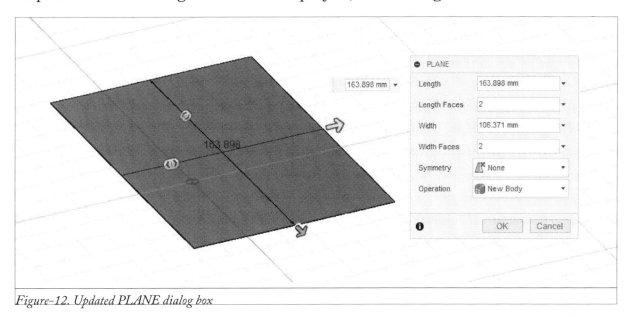

Figure-12. Updated PLANE dialog box

- If you want to change the length of plane then click in the **Length** edit box and enter the desired value or use drag handles.
- Click in the **Length Faces** edit box of **PLANE** dialog box and enter the number of faces in which surface of plane will be divided along the length.
- If you want to change the width of plane then click on the **Width** edit box and enter the desired value.
- Click in the **Width Faces** edit box of **PLANE** dialog box and enter the number of faces in which surface of plane will be divided along the width.
- After specifying the parameters, click on the **OK** button from **PLANE** dialog box to complete the process of creating plane. The plane will be displayed; refer to Figure-13.

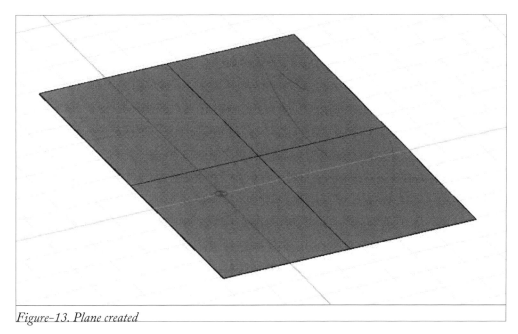

Figure-13. Plane created

Cylinder

The **Cylinder** tool is used to create a cylindrical body by defining diameter and depth. The procedure to use this tool is discussed next.

*   Click on the **Cylinder** tool from **CREATE** drop-down; refer to Figure-14. The **CYLINDER** dialog box will be displayed; refer to Figure-15.

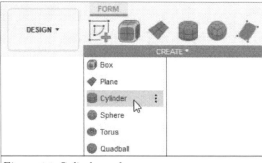

Figure-14. Cylinder tool

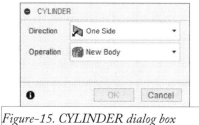

Figure-15. CYLINDER dialog box

*   You need to select the base plane or face to create the cylinder. Click on the plane to select.
*   Click on the screen to specify the center point and enter the desired radius of cylinder; refer to Figure-16.

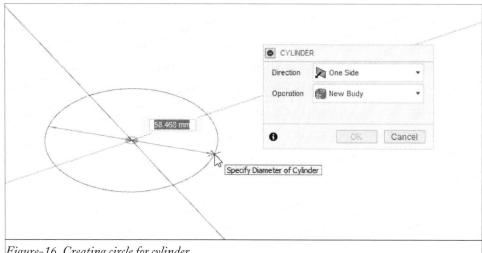

Figure-16. Creating circle for cylinder

*   After specifying the diameter, click on the screen. The updated **CYLINDER** dialog box will be displayed; refer to Figure-17.

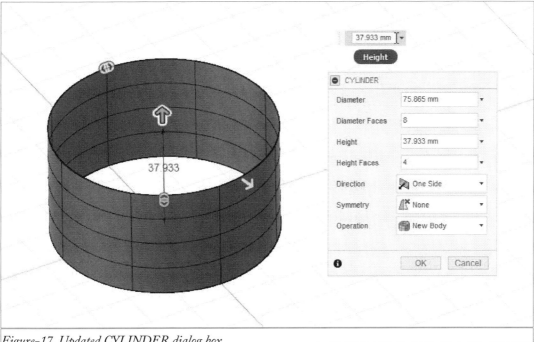

Figure-17. Updated CYLINDER dialog box

- If you want to change the diameter of cylinder then click on the **Diameter** edit box of **CYLINDER** dialog box and enter the desired diameter.
- Click in the **Diameter Faces** edit box and enter the number of faces in which the round surface of cylinder will be divided.
- Click in the **Height** edit box and enter the desired value of height of cylinder.
- Click in the **Height Faces** edit box and enter the number of faces in which height of cylinder will be divided along the height.
- The options in the **Direction** drop-down have been discussed earlier.
- Select **Circular** option from **Symmetry** drop-down if you want to apply circular symmetry between the faces of sculpt object.
- Click on the **Symmetric Faces** edit box and enter the desired value of circular symmetry on round surface.
- After specifying the parameters, click on the **OK** button from **CYLINDER** dialog box to complete the process.

Sphere

The **Sphere** tool is used to create a T-Spline sphere. The procedure to use this tool is discussed next.

- Click on the **Sphere** tool from **CREATE** drop-down; refer to Figure-18. The **SPHERE** dialog box will be displayed; refer to Figure-19.

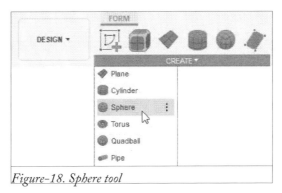

Figure-18. Sphere tool

Figure-19. SPHERE dialog box

- You are asked to select the base plane to create the sphere. Click on the plane/ face where you want to place the sphere.
- You are asked to specify centerpoint of the sphere. Click on the desired location to specify the center point. The preview of sphere will be displayed along with updated **SPHERE** dialog box; refer to Figure-20.

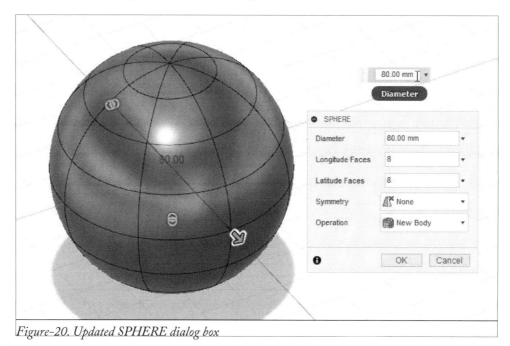

Figure-20. Updated SPHERE dialog box

- Click in the **Diameter** edit box and enter the desired value of sphere diameter.
- Click in the **Longitude Faces** edit box and enter the desired number of faces displayed on longitude of sphere.
- Click in the **Latitude Faces** edit box and enter the desired number of faces displayed on latitude of sphere.
- The options of **Symmetry** drop-down have been discussed earlier in **Box** and **Cylinder** tools.
- After specifying the parameters, click on the **OK** button from **SPHERE** dialog box to complete the process.

Torus

The **Torus** tool is used to create a T-Spline torus. The procedure to use this tool is discussed next.

- Click on the **Torus** tool from **CREATE** drop-down; refer to Figure-21.The **TORUS** dialog box will be displayed; refer to Figure-22.

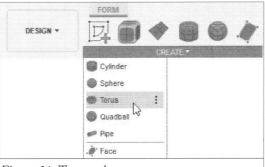

Figure-21. Torus tool

Figure-22. TORUS dialog box

- You need to select the base plane to create the torus. Click on the screen to select.
- Click on the screen to specify the center point and enter the desired diameter of torus in the input box. The preview of torus will be displayed along with updated **TORUS** dialog box; refer to Figure-23.

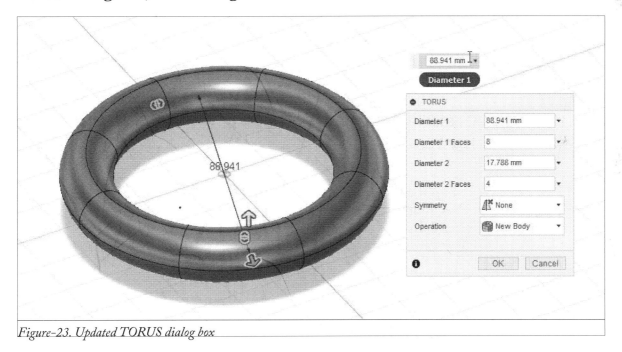

Figure-23. Updated TORUS dialog box

- Click in the **Diameter 1** edit box of **TORUS** dialog box and enter the desired value of diameter for center circle of torus.
- Click in the **Diameter 1 Faces** edit box and enter the number of faces in which round torus will be divided horizontally.
- Click in the **Diameter 2** edit box and enter the diameter of torus tube.
- Click in the **Diameter 2 Faces** edit box and enter the number of faces in which round torus will be divided vertically.
- After specifying the parameters, click on the **OK** button from **TORUS** dialog box.

Quadball

The **Quadball** tool is used to create a T-Spline quadball. The procedure to use this tool is discussed next.

- Click on the **Quadball** tool from **CREATE** drop-down; refer to Figure-24. The **QUADBALL** dialog box will be displayed; refer to Figure-25.

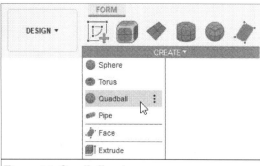

Figure-24. Quadball tool

Figure-25. QUADBALL dialog box

- You need to select the base plane to create the quadball. Click on the desired face/plane to select.
- Click on the screen to specify the center point. The preview of quadball will be displayed along with updated **QUADBALL** dialog box; refer to Figure-26.

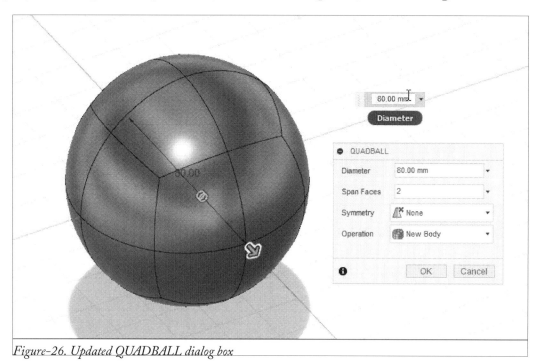

Figure-26. Updated QUADBALL dialog box

- Click in the **Diameter** edit box and enter the desired value of quadball diameter.
- Click in the **Span Faces** dialog box and enter the number of faces in which quadball will be divided.
- The options of **Symmetry** and **Operation** drop-down were discussed earlier.
- After specifying the parameters, click on **OK** button from **QUADBALL** dialog box. The quadball will be displayed; refer to Figure-27.

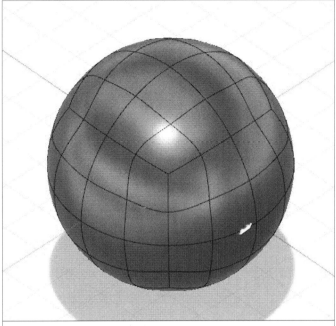

Figure-27. Quadball created with 4 span faces

Pipe

The **Pipe** tool is used to create complex pipe based on selected sketch. The procedure to use this tool is discussed next.

- Click on the **Pipe** tool from **CREATE** drop-down; refer to Figure-28. The **PIPE** dialog box will be displayed; refer to Figure-29.

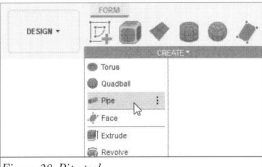

Figure-28. Pipe tool

Figure-29. PIPE dialog box

- The **Path** selection button is active by default. Click on the path to select. You can select sketch lines/curves or edges of the model. You can also use window selection to create pipe.
- Select the **Chain selection** check box if you want to select the nearby geometries in chain while selecting the one.
- On selection of sketch, the preview of pipe will be displayed; refer to Figure-30.

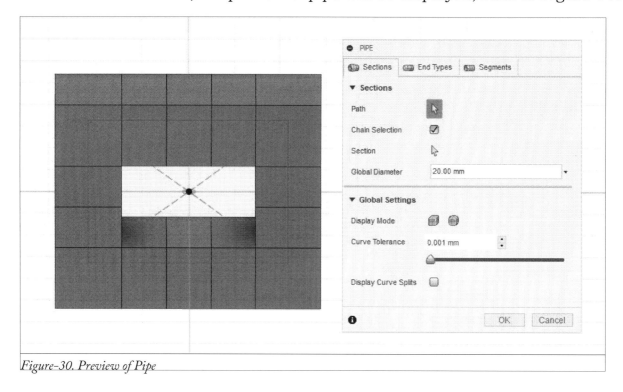

Figure-30. Preview of Pipe

- Click on the **Section** button of **Sections** tab if you want to modify the sections of pipe. On selecting the button, the sections of pipe will be displayed; refer to Figure-31.

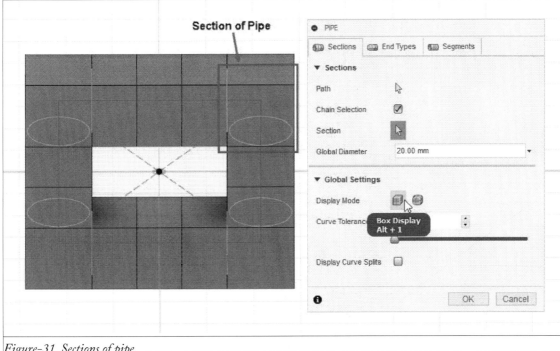

Figure-31. Sections of pipe

- Click on the desired section to change the diameter, angle, and position.
- Click on the **Diameter** edit box and enter the desired value of particular section diameter; refer to Figure-32.

Figure-32. Section options in PIPE dialog box

- Similarly, specify the value of **Angle** and **Position** in their respective edit box as desired. You can also move the arrow displayed on the selected section to specify the value.
- Click on the **Reset Section** button to reset all the changed value of sections.
- Click on the **Remove Section** button to remove the selected section.
- Click on **Box Display** button of **Display Mode** options from **Global Settings** section to display the rectangular T-Spline pipe of the selected sketch.
- Select **Smooth Display** button of **Display Mode** option from **Global Settings** section to display a smooth circular pipe; refer to Figure-33.

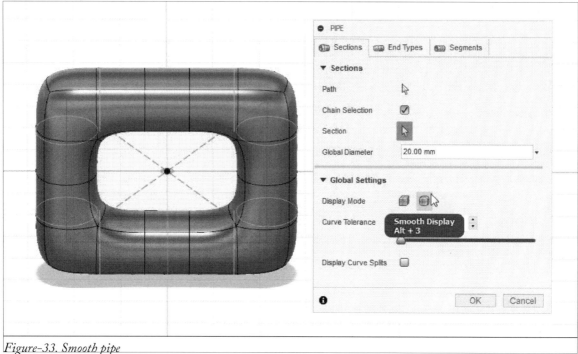

Figure-33. Smooth pipe

- Click in the **Curve Tolerance** edit box and enter the value of pipe tolerance. You can also set the tolerance by adjusting the **Curve Tolerance** slider.
- Select the **Display Curve Splits** check box if you want to see the curve splits of pipe; refer to Figure-34.
- Click on the **End Types** tab in the dialog box. The **Handle** selection button of **End Types** section from **End Types** tab is active by default and you are asked to select the end handle of pipe to modify its shape.
- Select the desired end handle from the model. Select **Open** option of **End Type** section from **End Types** tab if you want to keep all the ends of pipe open.

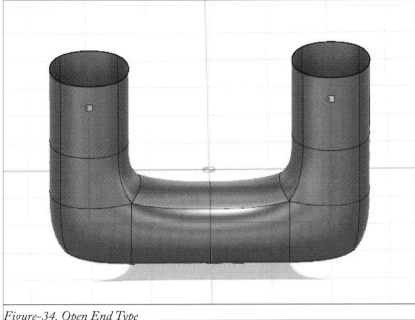

Figure-34. Open End Type

- Select **Square** option of **End Type** section from **End Types** tab if you want to close all the ends of pipe in square like structure; refer to Figure-35.

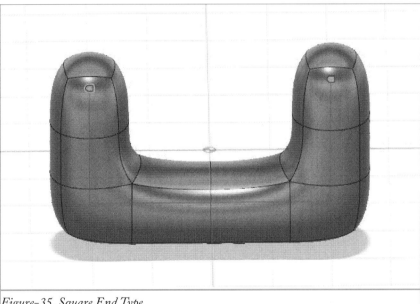

Figure-35. Square End Type

- Select **Spike** option of **End Type** section from **End Types** tab if you want to close all the ends of pipe in spike like structure; refer to Figure-36.

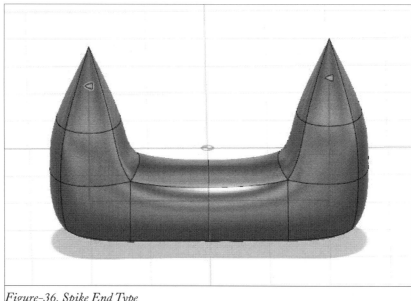

Figure-36. Spike End Type

- Click on the **Segments** tab in the dialog box. The **Segment** selection button of **Segments** section from **Segments** tab is active by default.
- Move the **Density** slider to increase or decrease the density of pipe segment.
- After specifying the parameters, click on the **OK** button from **PIPE** dialog box to complete the process.

Face

The **Face** tool is used to create individual faces. The procedure to use this tool is discussed next.

- Click on the **Face** tool from **CREATE** drop-down; refer to Figure-37. The **FACE** dialog box will be displayed; refer to Figure-38.

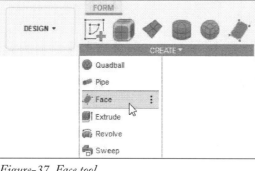

Figure-37. Face tool

Figure-38. FACE dialog box

Creating Face using Simple button

- Select **Simple** button of **Mode** option from **FACE** dialog box if you want to create a simple face by selecting four vertices on a specific plane.

- On selecting the **Simple** button, you need to select plane for creating the face. Click to select the plane.
- Now, specify the four corner on the plane as desired; refer to Figure-39.

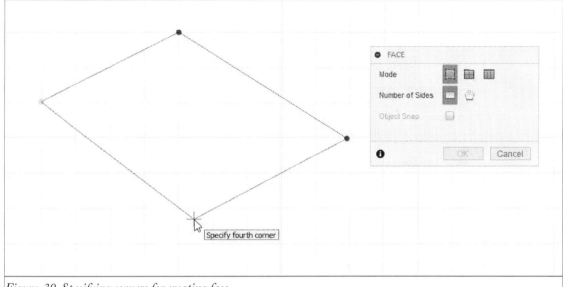

Figure-39. Specifying corners for creating face

- On selecting the fourth corner, the face will be created; refer to Figure-40.

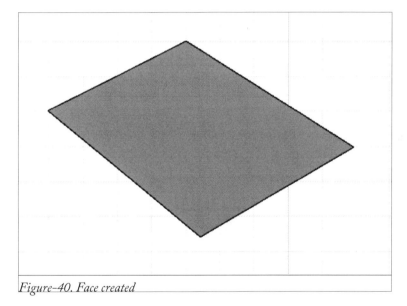

Figure-40. Face created

Creating Face using Edge button

The **Edge** button is used to create a face by selecting a edge. The procedure is discussed next.

- Click on the **Edge** button of **Mode** option from **FACE** dialog box. You need to select the edge an object.
- Now, you need to select the plane on which you want to create a face. Click to select the plane.
- Click on the screen to specify third and fourth corner.
- On creating fourth corner, the face will be created; refer to Figure-41.

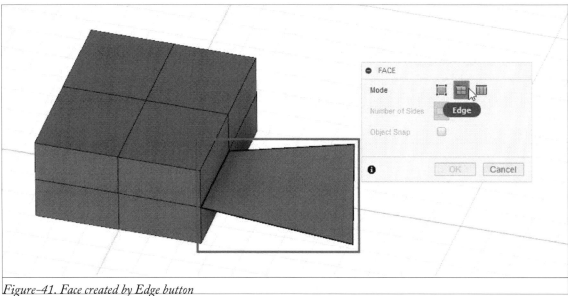

Figure-41. Face created by Edge button

Creating Chain of Faces using Edges

The **Chain** button is used to create multiple faces continuously. The procedure is discussed next.

- Click on the **Chain** button of **Mode** option from **FACE** dialog box. You will be asked to select an edge for creating face.
- Select the desired edge. Now, you need to select the plane on which you want to create a face. Click to select the plane.
- Specify third and fourth corner to create first face; refer to Figure-42.

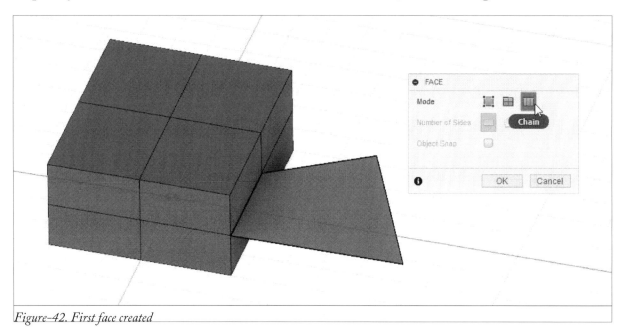

Figure-42. First face created

- After creating first face, specify third and fourth corner to create second face.
- On creating second face, click on the screen to create next faces as desired; refer to Figure-43.

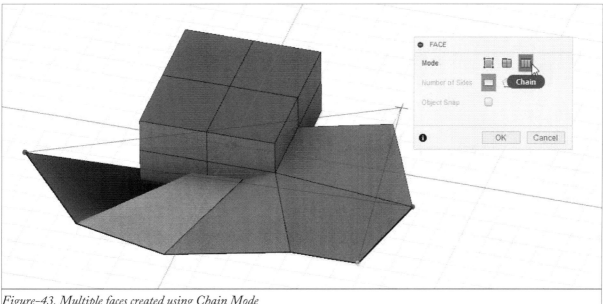
Figure-43. Multiple faces created using Chain Mode

- After creating desired number of faces, click on the **OK** button from **FACE** dialog box to complete the process.

Extrude

The **Extrude** tool is used to extrude the selected sketch up to the desired depth or height. The procedure to use this tool is discussed next.

- Click on the **Extrude** tool from **CREATE** drop-down; refer to Figure-44. The **EXTRUDE** dialog box will be displayed; refer to Figure-45.

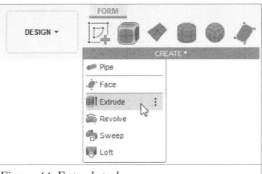
Figure-44. Extrude tool

Figure-45. EXTRUDE dialog box

- The **Profile** option of **EXTRUDE** dialog box is active by default. You are asked to select the sketch for extrude. On selecting the sketch; the updated **EXTRUDE** dialog box will be displayed; refer to Figure-46.

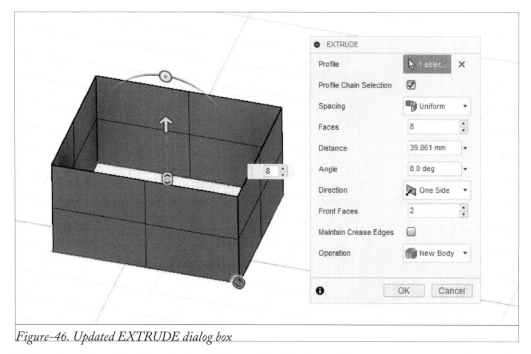

Figure-46. Updated EXTRUDE dialog box

- Select the **Profile Chain Selection** check box if you want to select the nearby geometries.
- Select **Uniform** button from **Spacing** drop-down if you want to position the faces evenly around the profile.
- Select **Curvature** button from **Spacing** drop-down if you want to position the faces based on the curvature of the profile. The more the curvature area more the faces.
- Click in the **Faces** edit box and enter the desired number of faces in which curvature of extruded sketch will be divided.
- Click in the **Distance** edit box and enter the distance for extrusion.
- Click in the **Angle** edit box and enter the desired angle of extrusion.
- Click in the **Front Faces** edit box and enter the desired number of faces in which surface of extrude will be divided along the height.
- Select the **Maintain Crease Edges** check box from **EXTRUDE** dialog box if you want to keep the crease at merged edges.
- After specifying the parameters, click on the **OK** button from **EXTRUDE** dialog box to complete the extrusion process. Note that you can also select face of any other sculpt body to extrude but some of the options in this dialog box will not be available in that case.

Revolve

The **Revolve** tool is used to create a revolve feature by sweeping the selected sketch around the selected axis. The procedure to use this tool is discussed next.

- Click on the **Revolve** tool from **CREATE** drop-down; refer to Figure-47. The **REVOLVE** dialog box will be displayed; refer to Figure-48.

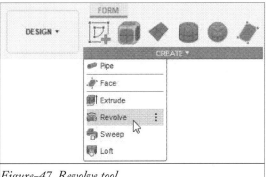
Figure-47. Revolve tool

Figure-48. REVOLVE dialog box

- The **Profile** option of **REVOLVE** dialog box is active by default. Click on the sketch to apply revolve feature.
- Click on **Select** button of **Axis** option and select the axis of rotation of sketch; refer to Figure-49.

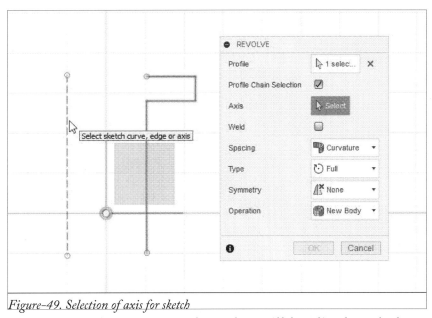
Figure-49. Selection of axis for sketch

- On selecting the axis, the preview of revolve will be displayed along with updated **REVOLVE** dialog box; refer to Figure-50.

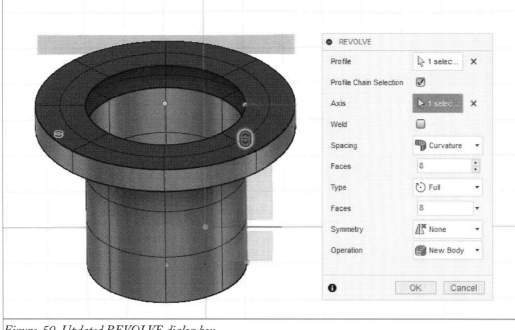

Figure-50. Updated REVOLVE dialog box

- Click in the **Faces** edit box below **Spacing** option and enter the desired number of faces in which curvature of revolved sketch will be divided along flat faces; refer to Figure-51.

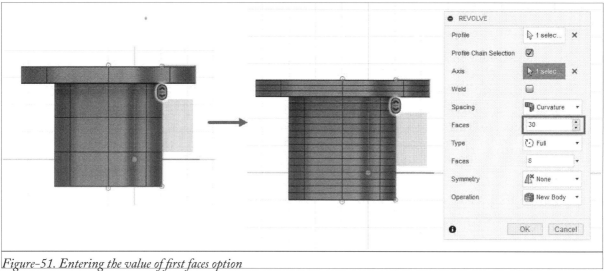

Figure-51. Entering the value of first faces option

- Click in the **Faces** edit box below **Type** option and enter the desired number of faces in which curvature of revolved sketch will be divided along round faces; refer to Figure-52.

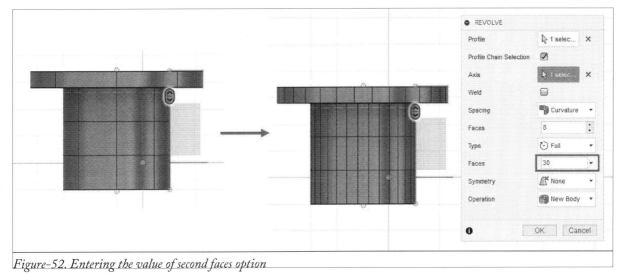

Figure-52. Entering the value of second faces option

- After specifying the parameters, click on the **OK** button from **REVOLVE** dialog box to complete the process.

Similarly, you can use other tools of **CREATE** drop-down as discussed in **DESIGN Workspace**.

MODIFYING TOOLS

Till now, we have learned about various tools to create the sculpt object. In this section we will learn various tools for modifying the sculpt object.

Edit Form

The **Edit Form** tool is used to move, scale, or rotate the selected geometry. The procedure to use this tool is discussed next.

- Click on the **Edit Form** tool of **MODIFY** drop-down; refer to Figure-53. The **EDIT FORM** dialog box will be displayed; refer to Figure-54.

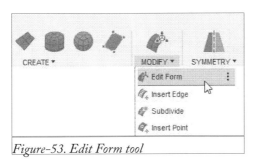

Figure-53. Edit Form tool

Figure-54. EDIT FORM dialog box

- The **Select** button of **T-Spline Entity** is active by default. Click on any face of the sculpt object to edit.
- Click on **Multi** button from **Transform Mode** option to edit the face with the help of 3D Manipulator; refer to Figure-55.

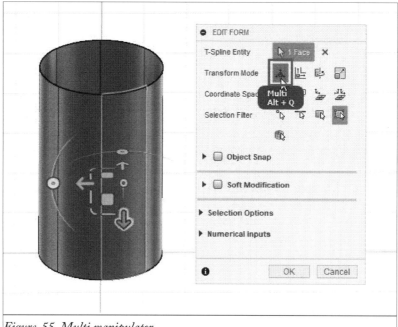

Figure-55. Multi manipulator

- Click on **Translation** button from **Transform Mode** option to edit the face with the help of translation manipulator; refer to Figure-56.

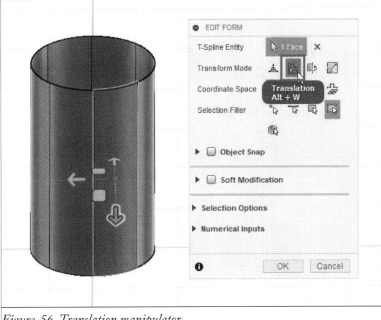

Figure-56. Translation manipulator

- Click on **Rotation** button from **Transform Mode** option to edit the face with the help of rotation manipulator; refer to Figure-57.

Figure-57. Rotation manipulator

- Click on **Scale** button from **Transform Mode** option to edit the face with the help of scale manipulator; refer to Figure-58.

Figure-58. Scale manipulator

- Select the **World Space** button from **Coordinate Space** option to orient the manipulator relative to the origin of model.
- Select the **View Space** button from **Coordinate Space** option to orient the manipulator relative to the current view of model.
- Select the **Selection Space** button from **Coordinate Space** option to orient the manipulator relative to the selected face.
- Select the **Local Per Entity** button from **Coordinate Space** option to orient the manipulator relative to the selected object.
- Select **Vertex** button from **Selection Filter** option to select the vertex of object for editing purpose. On selecting this button, only vertices will available for selection.
- Select **Edge** button from **Selection Filter** option to select the edge of object. On selecting this button, only edges of object will be available for selection.
- Select **Face** button from **Selection Filter** option to select the face of object. On selecting this button, only faces of object will be available for selection.
- Select **All** button from **Selection Filter** option to select the edge, vertex, or face from a object. On selecting this button edge, vertex, and face will available for selection.
- Select **Body** button from **Selection Filter** option to select the body for editing.
- Select the **Object Snap** check box and specify the desired value in the **Offset** edit box to specify the limit within which the selected vertex can move.

Soft Modification

Select the **Soft Modification** check box if you want to control the influence of changes on the surrounding area of object. On selecting the check box, the updated **EDIT FORM** dialog box will be displayed; refer to Figure-59.

Figure-59. Updated EDIT FORM dialog box

- When selected, the vertices of body is visually represented with red and white vertices highlighting that can be adjusted with the gradient slider.
- Select **Distance** button from **Extent** option to specify the distance in the **Distance** edit box for controlling the influence of round region. With the help of vertices displayed on object, you can control the amount of change they undergo and the shape of the affected region.
- Select **Face Count** button from **Extent** option to specify the number of faces far from selected object.
- Select **Rectangular Face Count** button from **Extent** option to specify the number of width and length faces.
- Select the desired shape of the affected region from **Transition** option.
- Click in the **Weight** edit box and enter the value of amount of influence applied in the affected region. The value of weight will be in between -1 to 1. You can also adjust the value of weight by moving the **Weight** slider.

Selection Options

- Click on the **Selection Options** node from **EDIT FORM** dialog box. The options of **Selection Options** node will be displayed; refer to Figure-60.

Figure-60. Selection Options

- The **Grow/Shrink** option is used to contract and expand the selected region.
- The **Loop Grow/Shrink** option is used to expand and contract the selected loop for the current location.
- The **Ring Grow/Shrink** option is used to expand and contract the ring after selecting the adjacent edge of the selected edge.
- The **Select Next** button is used to move the selected vertex, edge, or face to the next adjacent object. The movement to adjacent faces is based upon the current camera position.
- The **Feature Selection** button is used select all the faces of a strut or a hole.
- The **Invert Selection** button is used for reverse the selection. It means all the selected object will be deselected and deselected will be selected.
- The **Range Selection** button is used to select all the faces between two selected faces.
- The **Display Mode** option is used to select **Box display**, **Control Frame display**, and **Smooth Display** mode for the object.

Numerical Inputs

- Click on the **Numerical Inputs** node from **EDIT FORM** dialog box to enter the numerical value of various parameters, refer to Figure-61.

Figure-61. Numerical Inputs

- After specifying the various parameters, click on **OK** button from **EDIT FORM** dialog box to complete the process.

Insert Edge

The **Insert Edge** tool is used to insert an edge at a specified distance from the selected edge. The procedure to use this tool is discussed next.

- Click on the **Insert Edge** tool from **MODIFY** drop-down; refer to Figure-62. The **INSERT EDGE** dialog box will be displayed; refer to Figure-63.

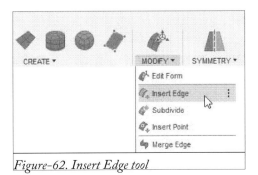

Figure-62. Insert Edge tool

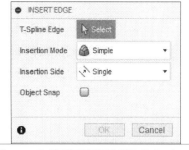

Figure-63. INSERT EDGE dialog box

- The **Select** button of **T-Spline Edge** option is active by default. Click on the edge from model to select. The preview of inserted edge will be displayed in green color; refer to Figure-64.

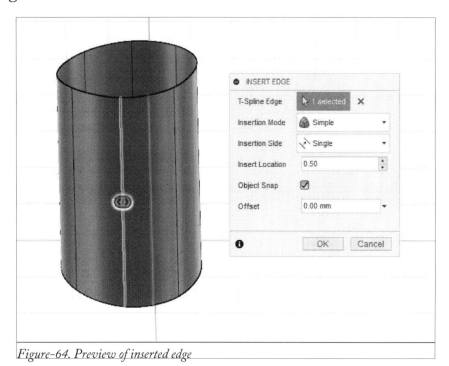

Figure-64. Preview of inserted edge

- Select **Simple** option from **Insertion Mode** drop-down if you do not want to move any point but may be it change the surface shape.
- Select **Exact** option from **Insertion Mode** drop-down to maintain the exact surface shape by adding points.
- Select **Single** option from **Insertion Side** drop-down to insert the edge in only one side to the selected edge.
- Select **Both** option from **Insertion Side** drop-down to insert the edge on both side to the selected edge.
- Click in the **Insert Location** edit box and enter the value of location for inserting edge. The value of **Insert Location** lie between 0 to 1.
- Select the **Object Snap** check box to move the new vertices to the closest point. These vertices can snap to solid, surface, and mesh bodies.
- Click in the **Offset** edit box and enter the desired value.
- After specifying the parameters, click on the **OK** button from **INSERT EDGE** dialog box to complete the process.

Subdivide

The **Subdivide** tool is used to divide selected face in four or more faces. The procedure to use this tool is discussed next.

- Click on the **Subdivide** tool from **MODIFY** drop-down; refer to Figure-65. The **SUBDIVIDE** dialog box will be displayed; refer to Figure-66.

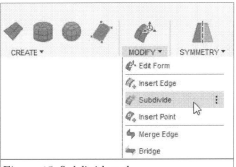

Figure-65. Subdivide tool

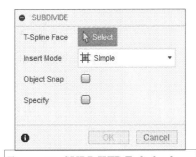

Figure-66. SUBDIVIDE dialog box

- The **Select** button of **T-Spline Face** option is active by default. Click on the face from model to select. Selected face will be divided into four face; refer to Figure-67.

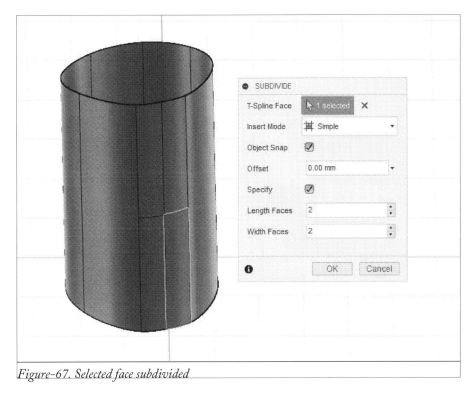

Figure-67. Selected face subdivided

- Select **Simple** option from **Insert Mode** drop-down to add the minimum number of control points to the subdivide face.
- Select **Exact** option from **Insert Mode** drop-down if you do not want to change the surface body and maintain the extra shape control points are added.
- Select the **Object Snap** check box to move the new vertices to the closest point. These vertices can snap to solid, surface, and mesh bodies.
- Click in the **Offset** edit box and enter the desired value.
- Select the **Specify** check box to enter the number of faces along length and width of the selected face.
- After specifying the parameters, click on the **OK** button from **SUBDIVIDE** dialog box to complete the process.

Insert Point

The **Insert Point** tool is used to insert control points at the selected locations. The procedure to use this tool is discussed next.

- Click on the **Insert Point** tool from **MODIFY** drop-down; refer to Figure-68. The **INSERT POINT** dialog box will be displayed; refer to Figure-69.

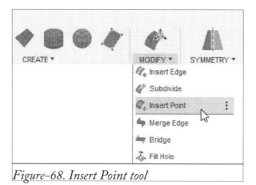

Figure-68. Insert Point tool

Figure-69. INSERT POINT dialog box

- The **Insertion Point** button is active by default. You need to click on the edge of the model to insert point; refer to Figure-70.

Figure-70. Inserting point

- The options of **Insertion Mode** and **Object Snap** were discussed earlier in this book.
- After specifying the parameters, click on the **OK** button from **INSERT POINT** dialog box to complete the process.

Merge Edge

The **Merge Edge** tool is used to connect two bodies by joining their edges. The procedure to use this tool is discussed next.

- Click on the **Merge Edge** tool from **MODIFY** drop-down; refer to Figure-71. The **MERGE EDGE** dialog box will be displayed; refer to Figure-72.

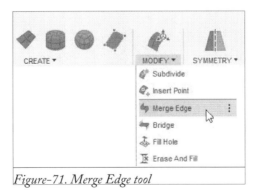
Figure-71. Merge Edge tool

Figure-72. MERGE EDGE dialog box

- The **Select** button of **Edge Group One** option is active by default. You need to select the edges or boundaries of a body.
- Click on the **Select** button of **Edge Group Two** option and select the boundary of other group; refer to Figure-73.
- Double-click on the edge of a face to select the adjacent edges also.

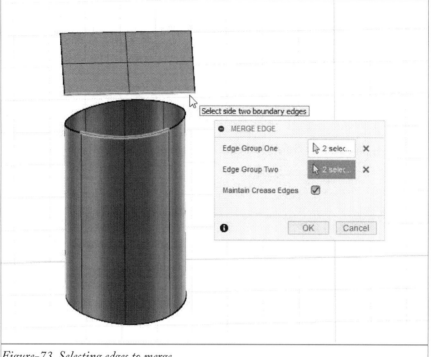

Figure-73. Selecting edges to merge

- Select the **Maintain Crease Edges** check box from **MERGE EDGE** dialog box to keep the crease at the merged edges.
- After specifying the parameters, click on the **OK** button from **MERGE EDGE** dialog box to complete the process; refer to Figure-74.

Figure-74. Edges merged

Bridge

The **Bridge** tool is used to connect two bodies by adding their intermediate faces. The procedure to use this tool is discussed next.

- Click on the **Bridge** tool from **MODIFY** drop-down; refer to Figure-75. The **BRIDGE** dialog box will be displayed; refer to Figure-76.

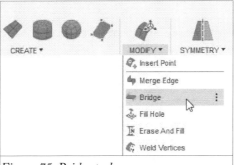

Figure-75. Bridge tool

Figure-76. BRIDGE dialog box

- Click on the **Side One** button from **BRIDGE** dialog box and select the desired faces.
- Click on the **Side Two** button from **BRIDGE** dialog box and select the faces from the model to join.
- Click on the **Follow Curve** button from **BRIDGE** dialog box and select a curve for the bridge to follow.
- Select the **Preview** check box to display a mesh preview of the bridge from the selected faces; refer to Figure-77.

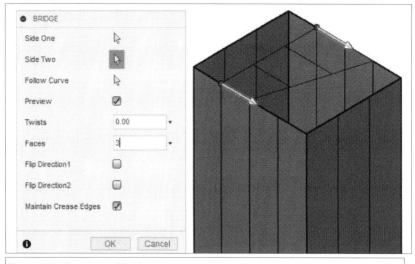

Figure-77. Preview of bridge

- Click in the **Twists** edit box and specify the number of rotation of bridge between two selected different faces (side one and side two).
- Click in the **Faces** edit box and specify the number of faces created between two selected sides.
- Select the **Flip Direction1** check box to flip the bridge direction of side one.
- Select the **Flip Direction2** check box to flip the bridge direction of side two.
- Select the **Maintain Crease Edges** check box from **BRIDGE** dialog box to keep the crease at the merged edges.
- After specifying the parameters, click on the **OK** button from **BRIDGE** dialog box to complete the process; refer to Figure-78.

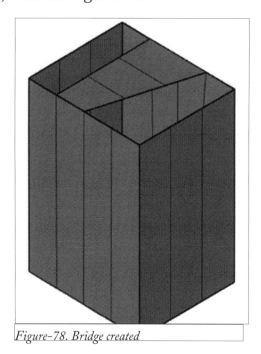

Figure-78. Bridge created

Fill Hole

The **Fill Hole** tool is used to close the opening of a T-Spline model. The procedure to use this tool is discussed next.

- Click on the **Fill Hole** tool from **MODIFY** drop-down; refer to Figure-79. The **FILL HOLE** dialog box will be displayed; refer to Figure-80.

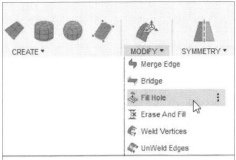

Figure-79. Fill Hole tool

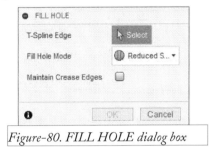

Figure-80. FILL HOLE dialog box

- The **Select** button of **T-Spline Edge** option is active by default. Click on the edge of hole to select. A preview will be displayed; refer to Figure-81.

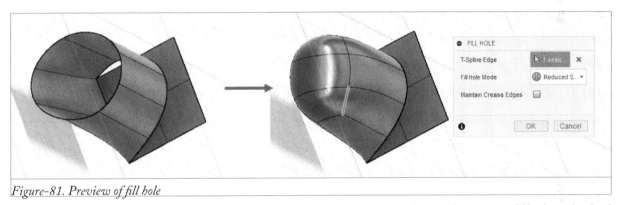

Figure-81. Preview of fill hole

- Select **Reduced Star** option from **Fill Hole Mode** drop-down to fill the hole by adding minimum number of star points of face.
- Select **Fill Star** option from **Fill Hole Mode** drop-down to fill the hole using single face. Due to this option the star points will created at each vertex; refer to Figure-82.

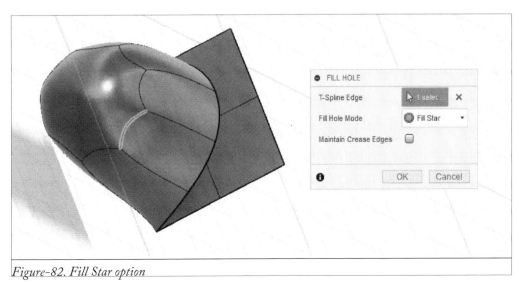

Figure-82. Fill Star option

- Select **Collapse** option from **Fill Hole Mode** drop-down to fill the hole by collapsing all the vertices of selected edge to the center point of hole face; refer to Figure-83.

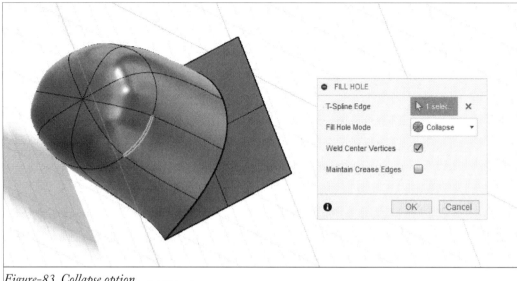

Figure-83. Collapse option

- Select the **Weld Center Vertices** check box from **FILL HOLE** dialog box to weld the vertices at the center of hole face. The **Weld Center Vertices** option is available when **Collapse** option is selected in the **Fill Hole Mode** drop-down.
- After specifying the parameters, click on the **OK** button from **FILL HOLE** dialog box to complete the process.

Erase And Fill

The **Erase And Fill** tool is used to delete a part of T-Spline geometry and fill new gaps with faces. The procedure to use this tool is discussed next.

- Click on the **Erase And Fill** tool from **MODIFY** drop-down; refer to Figure-84. The **ERASE AND FILL** dialog box will be displayed; refer to Figure-85.

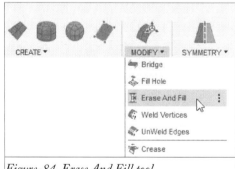

Figure-84. Erase And Fill tool

Figure-85. ERASE AND FILL dialog box

- The **Select** button of **T-Spline Faces** option is active by default. Select the faces to be erased and filled; refer to Figure-86.

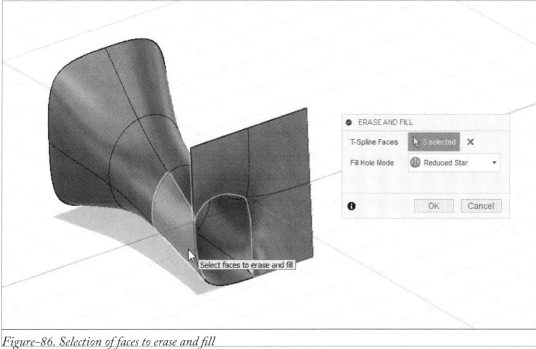

Figure-86. Selection of faces to erase and fill

- Select **Reduced Star** option from **Fill Hole Mode** drop-down to create the faces using minimum number of star points.
- Select **Fill Star** option from **Fill Hole Mode** drop-down to fill the hole with a single face. This tool creates star points at each vertex.
- After specifying the parameters, click on the **OK** button from **ERASE AND FILL** dialog box to complete the process; refer to Figure-87.

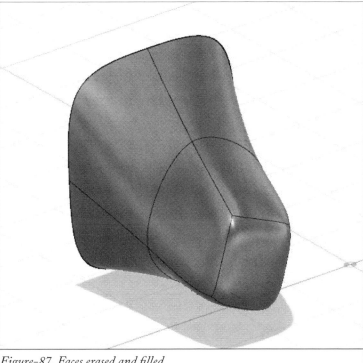

Figure-87. Faces erased and filled

Weld Vertices

The **Weld Vertices** tool is used to join two vertices into single vertex. The procedure to use this tool is discussed next.

- Click on the **Weld Vertices** tool from **MODIFY** drop-down; refer to Figure-88. The **WELD VERTICES** dialog box will be displayed; refer to Figure-89.

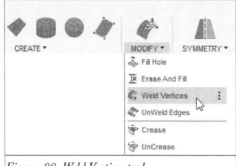

Figure-88. Weld Vertices tool

Figure-89. WELD VERTICES dialog box

- The **Select** button of **T-Spline Vertices** option is active by default. Click on the vertices to join together; refer to Figure-90.

Figure-90. Selecting vertices

- Select **Vertex to Vertex** option from **Weld Mode** drop-down to move the first vertex to the second vertex.
- Select **Vertex to Midpoint** option from **Weld Mode** drop-down to move the two vertices to the midpoint of the selections.
- Select **Weld to Tolerance** option from **Weld Mode** drop-down to weld all the visible and invisible vertices together with in a specified tolerance.
- Click in the **Weld Tolerance** edit box and enter the value of tolerance as required.
- After specifying the parameters, click on the **OK** button from **WELD VERTICES** dialog box to complete the process; refer to Figure-91.

Figure-91. Vertices welded

UnWeld Edges

The **UnWeld Edges** tool is used to detach an edge or loop. The procedure to use this tool is discussed next.

- Click on the **UnWeld Edges** tool from **MODIFY** drop-down; refer to Figure-92. The **UNWELD EDGES** dialog box will be displayed; refer to Figure-93.

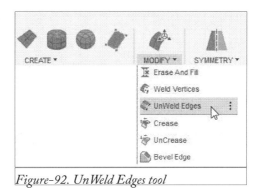

Figure-92. UnWeld Edges tool

Figure-93. UNWELD EDGES dialog box

- The **Select** button of **T-Spline Edges** option is active by default. Click on the edge or loop to select; refer to Figure-94. Double-click on the edge to select the loop.

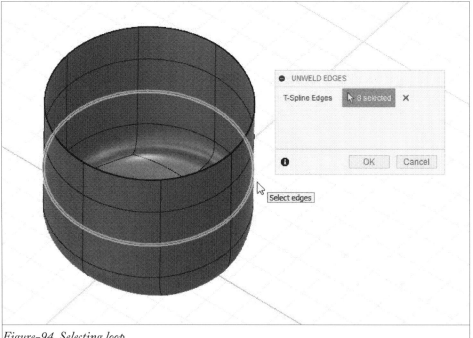

Figure-94. Selecting loop

- After selecting the edge or loop, click on the **OK** button from **UNWELDED EDGES** dialog box to complete the process; refer to Figure-95.

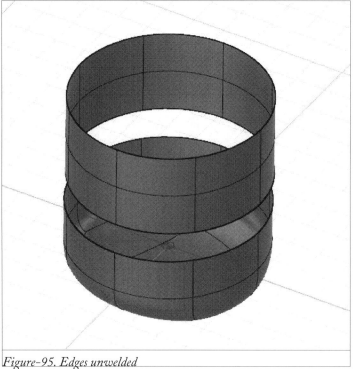

Figure-95. Edges unwelded

Crease

The **Crease** tool is used to add a sharp crease on the selected T-Spline body. The procedure to use this tool is discussed next.

- Click on the **Crease** tool from **MODIFY** drop-down; refer to Figure-96. The **CREASE** dialog box will be displayed; refer to Figure-97.

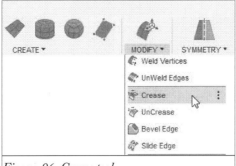

Figure-96. Crease tool

Figure-97. CREASE dialog box

- The **Select** button of **T-Spline Vertices or Edges** option is active by default. Click to select the edge. You can also use window selection to select multiple edges; refer to Figure-98.

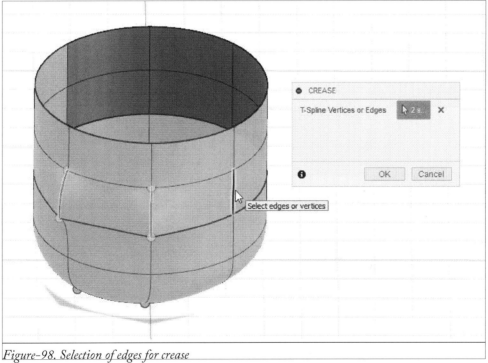

Figure-98. Selection of edges for crease

- After selection of edges for crease, click on **OK** button from **CREASE** dialog box. The selected edges will be converted into creased edges; refer to Figure-99.

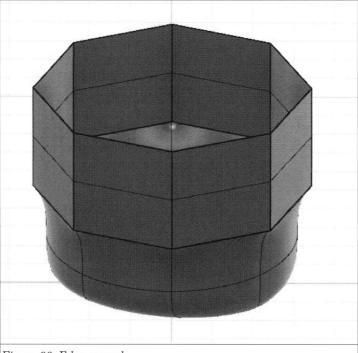

Figure-99. Edges creased

UnCrease

The **UnCrease** tool is used to remove crease from the selected body, edge, or vertex. The procedure to use this tool is discussed next.

- Click on the **UnCrease** tool from **MODIFY** drop-down; refer to Figure-100. The **UNCREASE** dialog box will be displayed; refer to Figure-101.

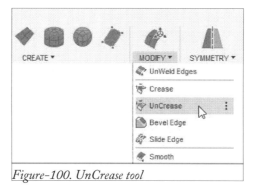

Figure-100. UnCrease tool

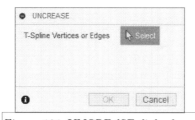

Figure-101. UNCREASE dialog box

- The **Select** button of **T-Spline Vertices or Edges** option is active by default. Click to select the edge. You can also use window selection to select multiple edges; refer to Figure-102.

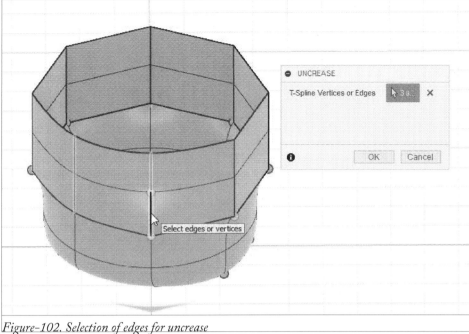

Figure-102. Selection of edges for uncrease

- After selection of edges for uncrease, click on **OK** button from **UNCREASE** dialog box to complete the process; refer to Figure-103.

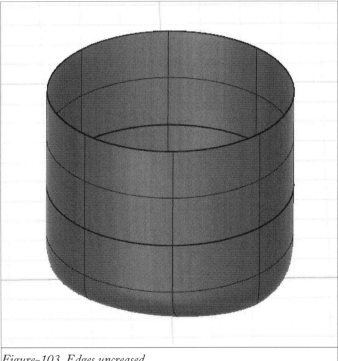

Figure-103. Edges uncreased

Bevel Edge

The **Bevel Edge** tool is used to flatten the area of body by selecting a specific edge. The procedure to use this tool is discussed next.

- Click on the **Bevel Edge** tool from **MODIFY** drop-down; refer to Figure-104. The **BEVEL EDGE** dialog box will be displayed; refer to Figure-105.

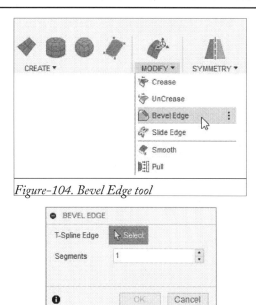

Figure-104. Bevel Edge tool

Figure-105. BEVEL EDGE dialog box

- The **Select** button of **T-Spline Edge** option is selected by default. Click on the edge of a body to select; refer to Figure-106.

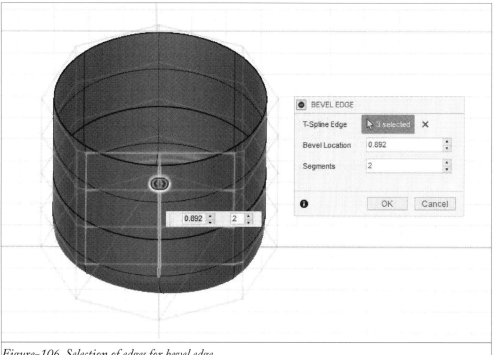

Figure-106. Selection of edges for bevel edge

- Click in the **Bevel Location** edit box and enter the value to position the new edge in decimal percentage. You can also set the value of **Bevel Location** option by moving the manipulator displayed on the selected edge.
- Click in the **Segments** edit box and enter the desired number of faces to be inserted in between new edges.
- After specifying the parameters, click on the **OK** button from **BEVEL EDGE** dialog box. The selected edge will be flattened; refer to Figure-107.

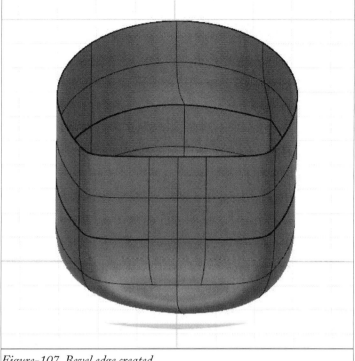

Figure-107. Bevel edge created

Slide Edge

The **Slide Edge** tool is used to move two edges closer together or farther apart. The procedure to use this tool is discussed next.

*   Click on the **Slide Edge** tool from **MODIFY** drop-down; refer to Figure-108. The **SLIDE EDGE** dialog box will be displayed; refer to Figure-109.

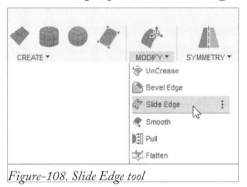

Figure-108. Slide Edge tool

Figure-109. SLIDE EDGE dialog box

*   The **Select** button of **T-Spline Edge** option is selected by default. Click on the edge of a body to select; refer to Figure-110.

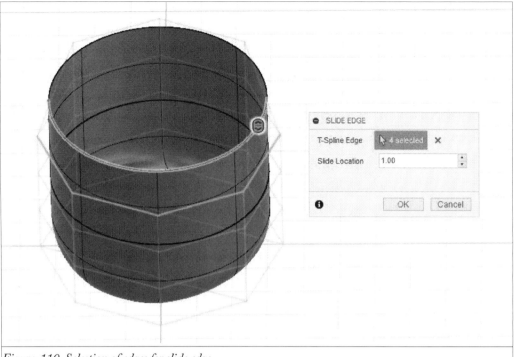

Figure-110. Selection of edges for slide edge

- Click in the **Slide Location** edit box and enter the value to position the new edge in decimal percentage. You can also set the value of **Slide Location** option by moving the manipulator displayed on the selected edge.
- After specifying the parameters, click on the **OK** button from **SLIDE EDGE** dialog box. The slide edge will be created; refer to Figure-111.

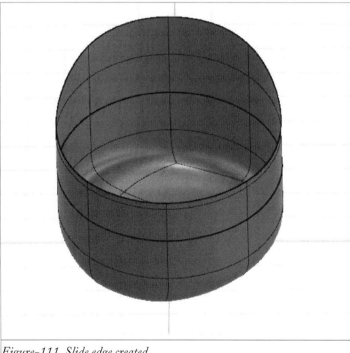

Figure-111. Slide edge created

Smooth

The **Smooth** tool is used to smooth an area of the T-Spline geometry by selecting the desired faces. The procedure to use this tool is discussed next.

- Click on the **Smooth** tool from **MODIFY** drop-down; refer to Figure-112. The **SMOOTH** dialog box will be displayed; refer to Figure-113.

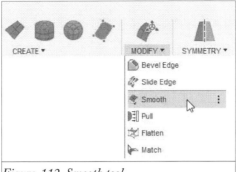

Figure-112. Smooth tool

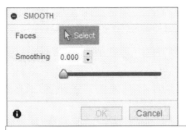

Figure-113. SMOOTH dialog box

- The **Select** button of **Faces** option is active by default. Select the faces around the desired area; refer to Figure-114.

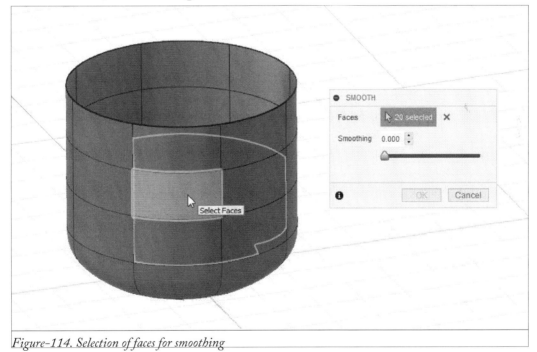

Figure-114. Selection of faces for smoothing

- Click in the **Smoothing** edit box and enter the value of smoothing rate from 0 to 1. You can also set the value of **Smoothing** option by moving the slider.
- After specifying the parameters, click on the **OK** button from **SMOOTH** dialog box to complete the process; refer to Figure-115.

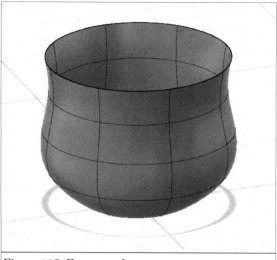

Figure-115. Faces smoothen

Pull

The **Pull** tool is used for moving the selected vertices to the target body. The procedure to use this tool is discussed next.

- Click on the **Pull** tool from **MODIFY** drop-down; refer to Figure-116. The **PULL** dialog box will be displayed; refer to Figure-117.

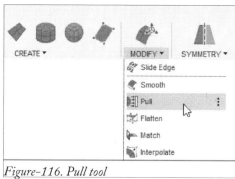

Figure-116. Pull tool

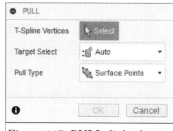

Figure-117. PULL dialog box

- The **Select** button of **T-Spline Vertices** option is active by default. You need to click on the specific vertex to pull the vertex upto the targeted body; refer to Figure-118.

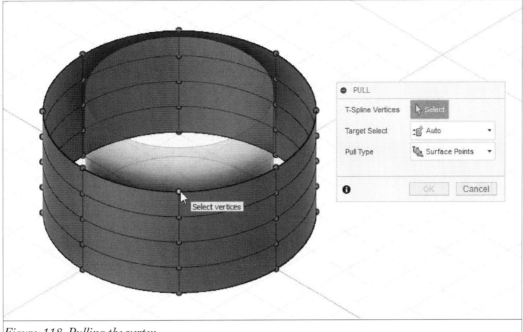

Figure-118. Pulling the vertex

- Select **Auto** option from **Target Select** drop-down to automatically pull the selected vertex.
- Select the **Select Targets** option from **Target Select** drop-down to manually select the target body. The updated **PULL** dialog box will be displayed; refer to Figure-119.

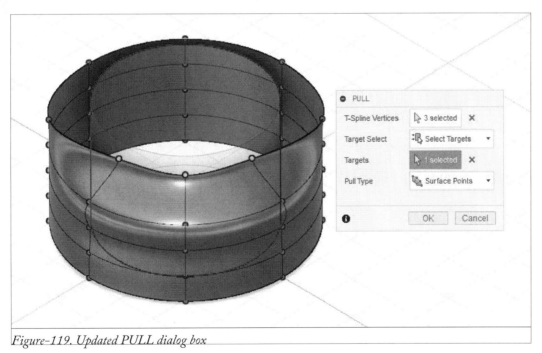

Figure-119. Updated PULL dialog box

- The **Select** button of **Targets** option is active by default. You need to click on the target body to pull the selected vertex.
- Select **Surface Points** option from **Pull Type** drop-down to move the surface points to the target body.
- Select **Control Points** option from **Pull Type** drop-down to move the control points to the target body.
- After specifying the parameters, click on the **OK** button from **PULL** dialog box to complete the process.

Flatten

The **Flatten** tool is used for moving the selected control point to the plane for flatten the selected surface. The procedure to use this tool is discussed next.

- Click on the **Flatten** tool from **MODIFY** drop-down; refer to Figure-120. The **FLATTEN** dialog box will be displayed; refer to Figure-121.

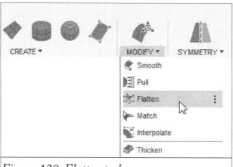

Figure-120. Flatten tool

Figure-121. FLATTEN dialog box

- The **Select** button of **T-Spline Vertices** option is active by default. Select the vertices of the face which you want to flatten; refer to Figure-122.

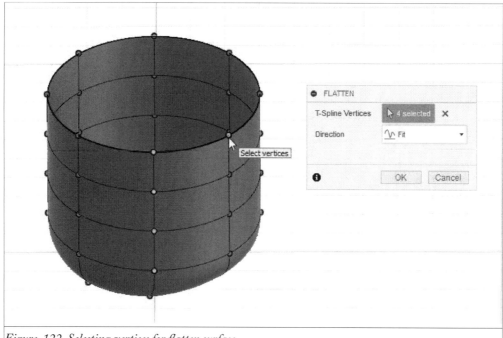

Figure-122. Selecting vertices for flatten surface

- On selecting all the vertices, the preview of flatten surface will displayed; refer to Figure-123.

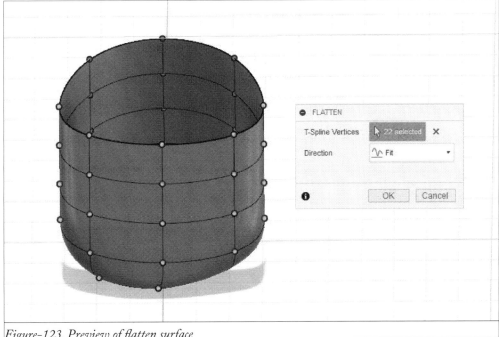

Figure-123. Preview of flatten surface

- Select **Fit** option from **Direction** drop-down to select the best fit plane for flatten the selected surface.
- Select **Select Plane** option from **Direction** drop-down to manually select the plane to flatten all control points. You are required to select the plane.
- Select **Select Parallel Plane** option from **Direction** drop-down to move the control points to the selected parallel plane. You are required to select the plane.
- After specifying the parameters, click on the **OK** button from **FLATTEN** dialog box to complete the process.

Match

The **Match** tool is used to align the selected T-Spline edge with a sketch, face, or edge. The procedure to use this tool is discussed next.

- Click on the **Match** tool from **MODIFY** drop-down; refer to Figure-124. The **MATCH** dialog box will be displayed; refer to Figure-125.

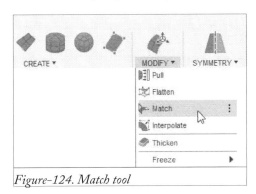

Figure-124. Match tool

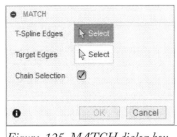

Figure-125. MATCH dialog box

- The **Select** button of **T-Spline Edges** option is active by default. You need to select the edge. You can also select the loop by double clicking on the edge; refer to Figure-126.

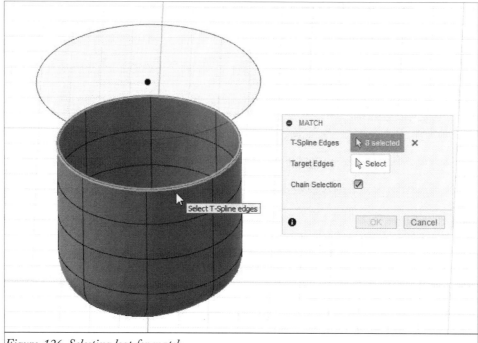

Figure-126. Selecting loop for match

- Click on the **Select** button of **Target Edges** option and select the target edge or sketch.
- On selecting, the preview of alignment will be displayed along with updated **MATCH** dialog box; refer to Figure-127.

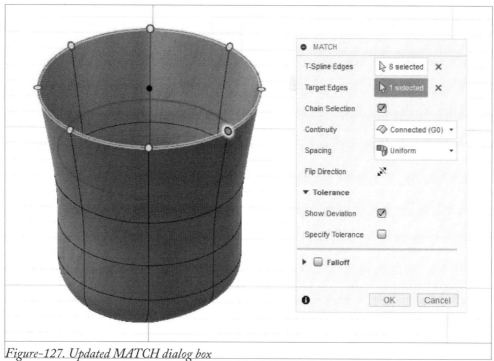

Figure-127. Updated MATCH dialog box

- Click on the **Flip Direction** button from **MATCH** dialog box to flip the direction of alignment; refer to Figure-128.

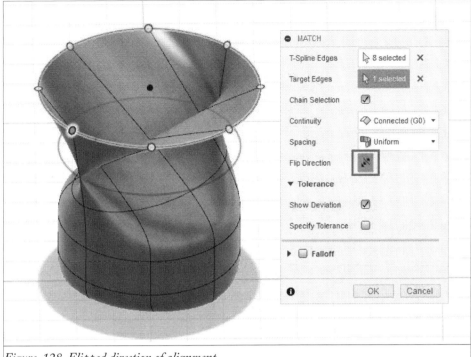

Figure-128. Flipped direction of alignment

- Select the **Show Deviation** check box from **Tolerance** node to display the amount and location of maximum deviation.
- Select the **Specify Tolerance** check box from **Tolerance** node to specifies the value of how close the T-Spline edges need to be to the target edge.
- Select the **Falloff** check box from **MATCH** dialog box to determine the value of surface affected by the match.
- Click in the **Falloff Range** edit box and enter the value of surface affected by the match.
- After specifying the parameters, click on the **OK** button from **MATCH** dialog box to complete the process.

Interpolate

The **Interpolate** tool is used to move the T-Spline control points or surface points for improving fitting. The procedure to use this tool is discussed next.

- Click on the **Interpolate** tool from **MODIFY** drop-down; refer to Figure-129. The **INTERPOLATE** dialog box will be displayed; refer to Figure-130.

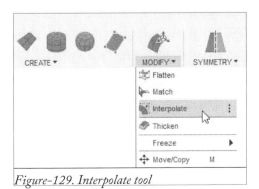

Figure-129. Interpolate tool

Figure-130. INTERPOLATE dialog box

- The **Select** button of **T-Spline Body** option is active by default. Click on the body to select; refer to Figure-131.

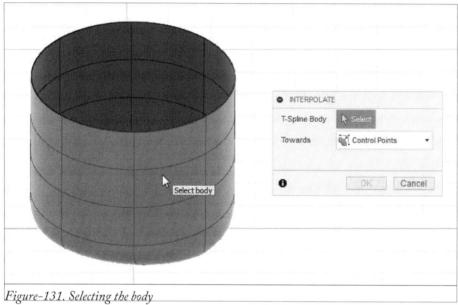

Figure-131. Selecting the body

- On selecting the body, the preview will be displayed; refer to Figure-132.

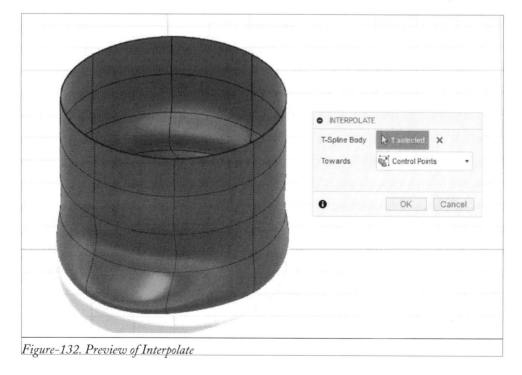

Figure-132. Preview of Interpolate

- Select **Surface Points** from **Towards** drop-down to move the control points towards the surface.
- Select **Control Points** from **Towards** drop-down if you want to fit the surface through existing control points.
- After specifying the parameters, click on the **OK** button from **INTERPOLATE** dialog box to complete the process.

Thicken

The **Thicken** tool is used to apply thickness to the sculpt faces. The procedure to use this tool is discussed next.

- Click on the **Thicken** tool from **MODIFY** drop-down; refer to Figure-133. The **THICKEN** dialog box will be displayed; refer to Figure-134.

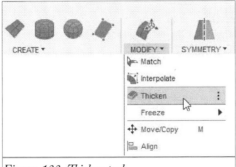

Figure-133. Thicken tool

Figure-134. THICKEN dialog box

- The **Select** button of **T-Spline Body** option is active by default. Click on the body to select. The updated **THICKEN** dialog box will be displayed.
- Click in the **Thickness** edit box and enter the desired thickness. You can also move the arrow displaying on the selected model to adjust the thickness; refer to Figure-135.

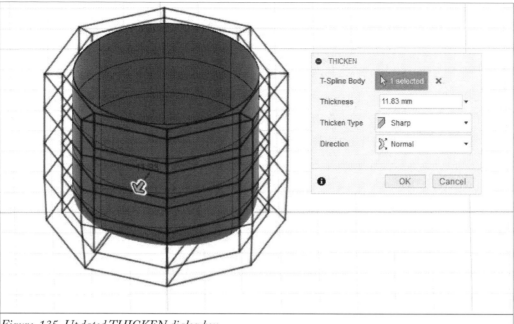

Figure-135. Updated THICKEN dialog box

- Select the **Sharp** button from **Thicken Type** drop-down to connect the surface with the straight face.
- Select the **Soft** button from **Thicken Type** drop-down to connect the surface with the round face.
- Select the **No Edge** button from **Thicken Type** drop-down to not connect the surfaces.
- Select **Normal** button from **Direction** drop-down to create a new surface perpendicular to the selected surface.
- Select **Axis** button from **Direction** drop-down to create a new surface perpendicular to a selected axis.
- After specifying the parameters, click on the **OK** button from **THICKEN** dialog box. The selected body will be thicken; refer to Figure-136.

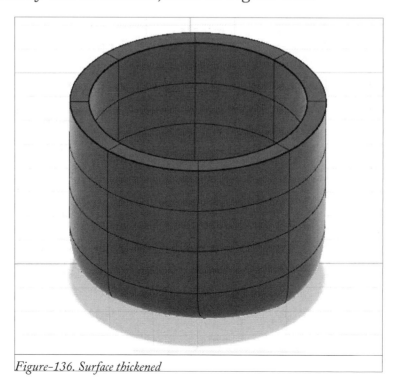

Figure-136. Surface thickened

Freeze

The **Freeze** tool is used to freeze the selected edges or faces to prevent changes. The procedure to use this tool is discussed next.

- Click on the **Freeze** tool of **Freeze** cascading menu from **MODIFY** drop-down; refer to Figure-137. The **FREEZE** dialog box will be displayed; refer to Figure-138.

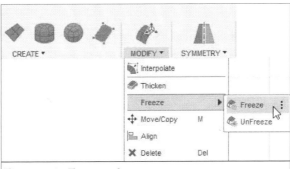

Figure-137. Freeze tool

Figure-138. FREEZE dialog box

- The **Select** button of **T-Spline Faces/Edges** option is active by default. Click on the edges/ faces to select; refer to Figure-139.

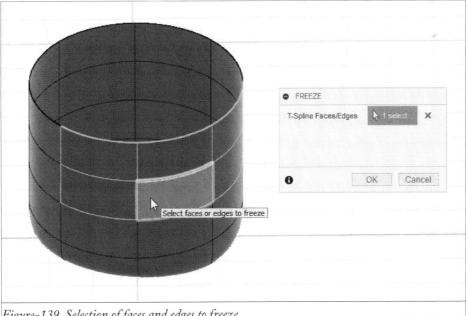

Figure-139. Selection of faces and edges to freeze

- After selection of edges, click on the **OK** button from **FREEZE** dialog box. The selected edges or faces will be frozen; refer to Figure-140.

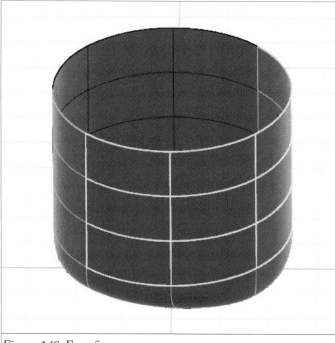

Figure-140. Faces frozen

UnFreeze

The **UnFreeze** tool is used to unfreeze the frozen edges of faces. The procedure to use this tool is discussed next.

*   Click on the **UnFreeze** tool of **Freeze** cascading menu from **MODIFY** drop-down; refer to Figure-141. The **UNFREEZE** dialog box will be displayed; refer to Figure-142.

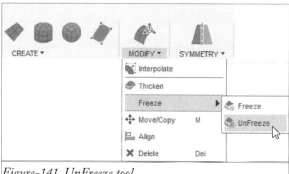

Figure-141. UnFreeze tool

Figure-142. UNFREEZE dialog box

*   The **Select** button of **T-Spline Faces/Edges** option is active by default. Click on the edges/faces to unfreeze; refer to Figure-143.

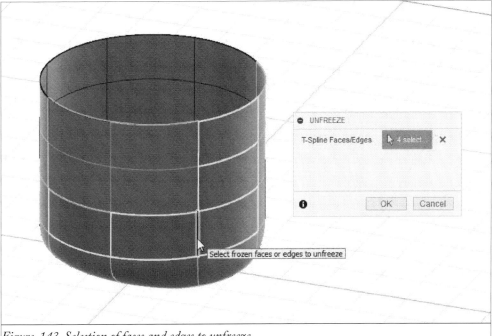

Figure-143. Selection of faces and edges to unfreeze

- After selecting, click on the **OK** button from **UNFREEZE** dialog box. The frozen edges will be unfreeze; refer to Figure-144.

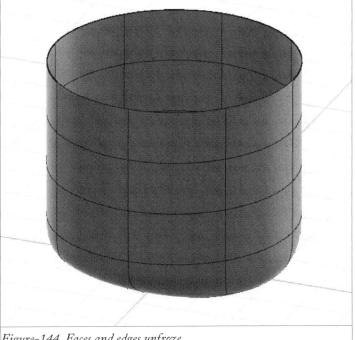

Figure-144. Faces and edges unfroze

PRACTICAL

In this practical, we will create the model shown in Figure-145.

Figure-145. Model for Practical1

Creating Sketch

- Open the **FORM** mode as discussed earlier.
- Click on the **Create Sketch** tool from **CREATE** drop-down in the **Toolbar** and select a plane on which you want to create sketch.
- Click on the **Center Rectangle** tool of **Rectangle** cascading menu from **CREATE** drop-down and create a rectangle as shown in Figure-146.

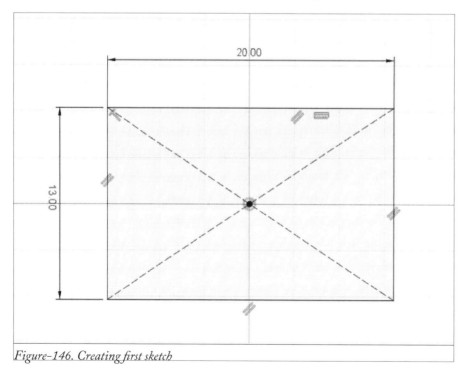

Figure-146. Creating first sketch

- Click on the **Fillet** tool of **MODIFY** drop-down from **Toolbar** and apply the fillet of 3 as shown in Figure-147.

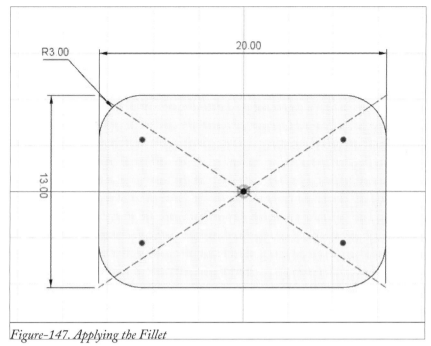

Figure-147. Applying the Fillet

- Click on the **Finish Sketch** button from **Toolbar** to exit the sketch.

Creating plane

- Click on the **Offset Plane** tool of **CONSTRUCT** drop-down from **Toolbar**. The **OFFSET PLANE** dialog box will be displayed.
- The **Select** button of **Plane** option is active by default. You need to select the recently created sketch plane as reference; refer to Figure-148.

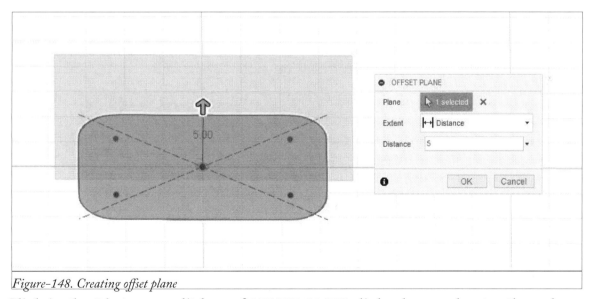

Figure-148. Creating offset plane

- Click in the **Distance** edit box of **OFFSET PLANE** dialog box and enter the value as **5**.
- After specifying the parameters, click on the **OK** button from **OFFSET PLANE** dialog box. The plane will be created and displayed above the first sketch.

Creating second sketch

- Click on the **Create Sketch** tool from **CREATE** drop-down in the **Toolbar** and select the recently created plane as reference to create sketch.

- Click on the **Center Rectangle** tool of **Rectangle** cascading menu from **CREATE** drop-down and create a sketch as shown in Figure-149.

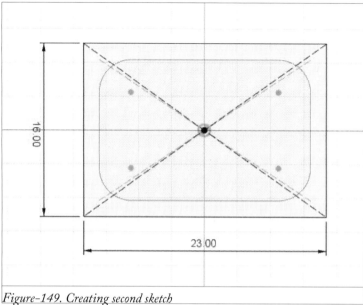

Figure-149. Creating second sketch

- Click on the **Fillet** tool of **MODIFY** drop-down from **Toolbar** and apply the fillet of 4 as shown in Figure-150.

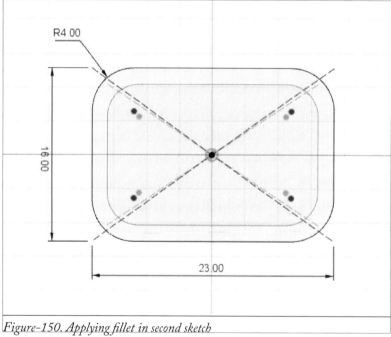

Figure-150. Applying fillet in second sketch

- Click on the **Finish Sketch** button from **Toolbar** to exit the sketch.

Creating Loft Feature

- Click on the **Loft** tool of **CREATE** drop-down from **Toolbar**. The **LOFT** dialog box will be displayed.
- Click on the **Chain Selection** check box of **LOFT** dialog box to select the edges in chain.
- Select the first and second created sketch to select in **Profiles** section; refer to Figure-151.

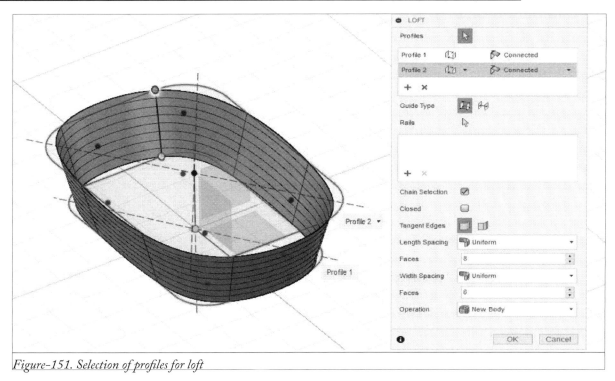

Figure-151. Selection of profiles for loft

- After specifying the parameters displayed on above figure, click on the **OK** button from **LOFT** dialog box.

Applying Fill Hole

- Click on the **Fill Hole** tool of **MODIFY** drop-down from **Toolbar**. The **FILL HOLE** dialog box will be displayed.
- Select the edge from the model as displayed; refer to Figure-152.

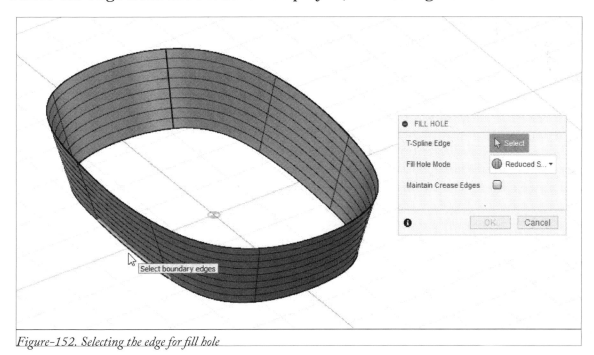

Figure-152. Selecting the edge for fill hole

- The selected hole will be filled.
- Click on the **PIPE** tool of **CREATE** drop-down from **Toolbar**. The **PIPE** dialog box will be displayed.
- Click on the edges of model as shown in figure to select as a path for pipe; refer

to Figure-153.

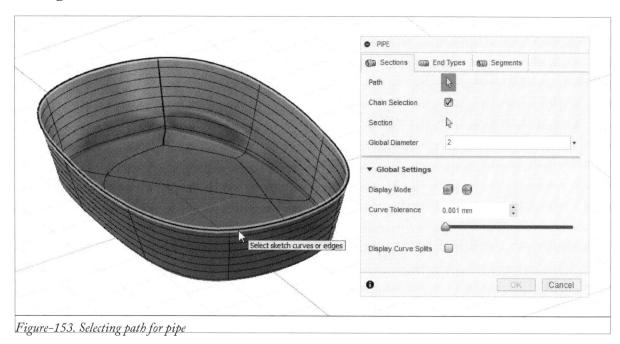

Figure-153. Selecting path for pipe

*   Click on the **Smooth Display** button of **Display Mode** option in **Global Settings** option from **Sections** tab of **PIPE** dialog box and enter the parameters as displayed in above figure.
*   After specifying the parameters, the model will be displayed as shown in Figure-154.

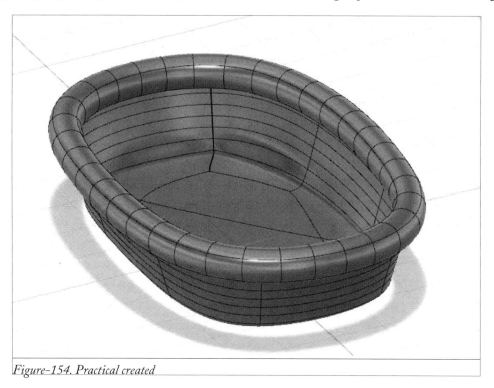

Figure-154. Practical created

SELF ASSESSMENT

Q1. What is Sculpting?

Q2. Select the .... check box if you want to see the curve splits of pipe.

Q3. The .... button is used to create multiple faces continuously.

Q4. What is the use of **Edit Form** tool?

Q5. The Feature selection button is used to select all the faces of a selected hole. (T/F)

Q6. The **Merge Edge** tool is used to connect two bodies by joining their edges. (T/F)

PRACTICE 1

Create a wooden tool as displayed in Figure-155 and Figure-156. As a primitive structure, use the Sculpt cylinder.

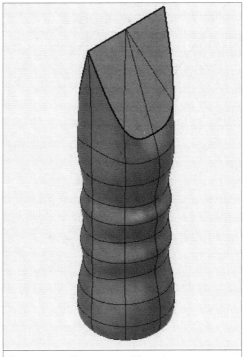

Figure-155. First view of Practice1

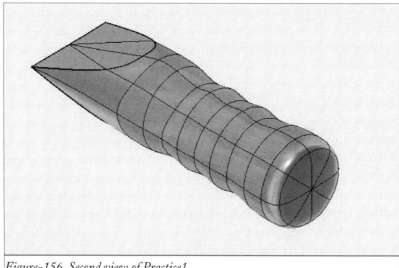

Figure-156. Second view of Practice1

PRACTICE 2

Create the model as shown in Figure-157 and Figure-158 by using the tools of **FORM** mode.

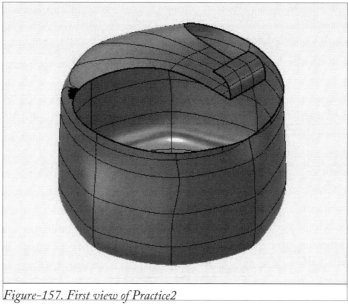

Figure-157. First view of Practice2

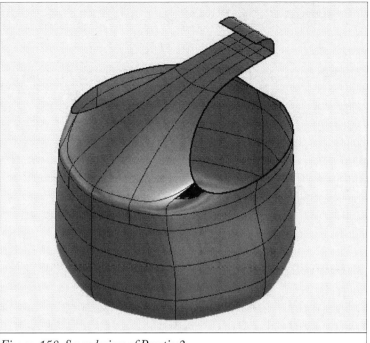

Figure-158. Second view of Practice2

FOR STUDENT NOTES

FOR STUDENT NOTES

Chapter 13

Sculpting-2

Topics Covered

The major topics covered in this chapter are:

- *Mirror Tools*
- *Duplicate Tools*
- *Utility Tools*
- *Repair Mode*
- *Convert Tools*

INTRODUCTION

In the last chapter, we have learned to create and modify the sculpt object by using various tools. In this chapter, we will discuss the symmetry and utilities tool used in **FORM** mode.

SYMMETRY TOOLS

Symmetry tools are used to create symmetric copies of the selected sculpt features in the **FORM Mode**. These tools are discussed next.

Mirror - Internal

The **Mirror - Internal** tool is used to create an internal mirror symmetry in the T-Spline body on selecting an edge, face, and vertex. The procedure to use this tool is discussed next.

- Click on the **Mirror - Internal** tool from **SYMMETRY** drop-down; refer to Figure-1. The **MIRROR - INTERNAL** dialog box will be displayed; refer to Figure-2.

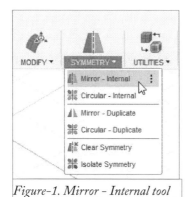

Figure-1. Mirror - Internal tool

Figure-2. MIRROR- INTERNAL dialog box

- The **Select** button of **Select Face** section is active by default. Click on the face from master side; refer to Figure-3.

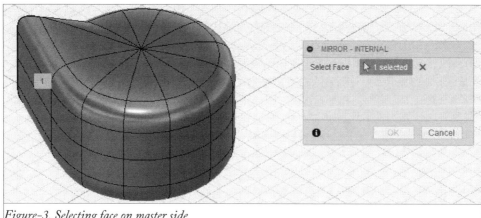

Figure-3. Selecting face on master side

- Click on the face to be made mirror symmetric. The preview of mirror will be displayed; refer to Figure-4.

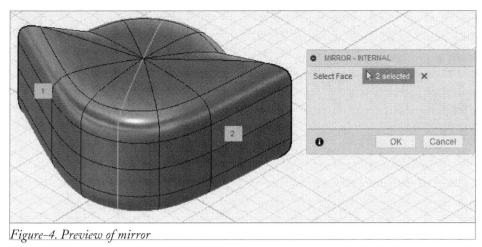

Figure-4. Preview of mirror

- If the preview of mirror symmetry is as required then click on the **OK** button from **MIRROR - INTERNAL** dialog box to complete the process.

Circular - Internal

The **Circular - Internal** tool is used to create an internal circular symmetry based on selected face, edge, or vertex. The procedure to use this tool is discussed next.

- Click on the **Circular - Internal** tool from **SYMMETRY** drop-down; refer to Figure-5. The **CIRCULAR - INTERNAL** dialog box will be displayed; refer to Figure-6.

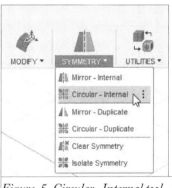

Figure-5. Circular- Internal tool

Figure-6. CIRCULAR- INTERNAL dialog box

- The **Select** button of **Select Face** section is active by default. Click on the face to select for symmetry; refer to Figure-7.

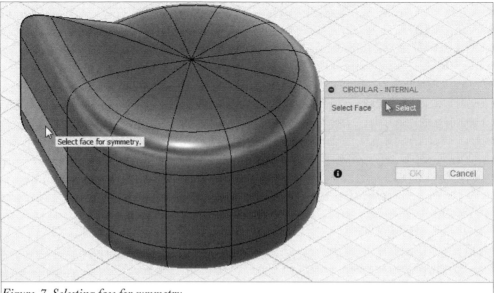

Figure-7. Selecting face for symmetry

- After selecting, the updated **CIRCULAR - INTERNAL** dialog box will be displayed along with the preview; refer to Figure-8.

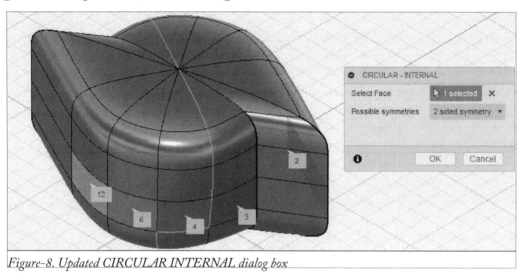

Figure-8. Updated CIRCULAR INTERNAL dialog box

- Select the desired option from **Possible symmetries** drop-down to define number of symmetric sections and click on the **OK** button from **CIRCULAR - INTERNAL** dialog box to complete the process; refer to Figure-9.

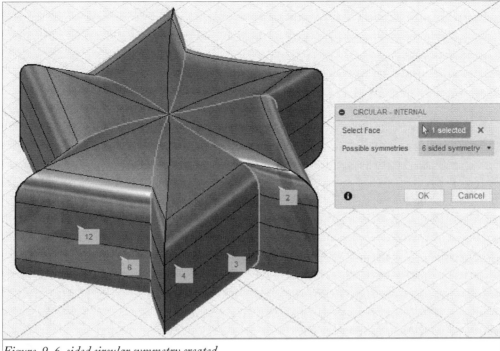

Figure-9. 6-sided circular symmetry created

Mirror - Duplicate

The **Mirror - Duplicate** tool is used to create a new T-Spline body or surface based on the selected plane or face. The procedure to use this tool is discussed next.

• Click on the **Mirror - Duplicate** tool from **SYMMETRY** drop-down; refer to Figure-10. The **MIRROR - DUPLICATE** dialog box will be displayed; refer to Figure-11.

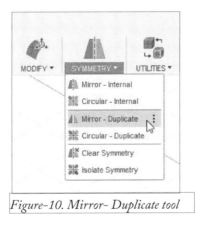

Figure-10. Mirror- Duplicate tool

Figure-11. MIRROR- DUPLICATE dialog box

- The **Select** button of **T-Spline Body** section is active by default. Click on the sculpt body whose mirror copy is to be created; refer to Figure-12.

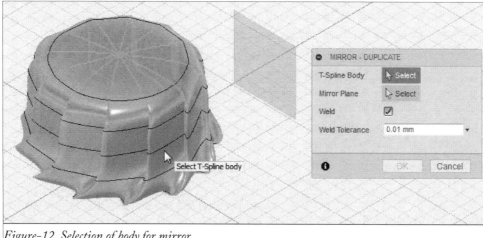

Figure-12. Selection of body for mirror

- Now, click on the **Select** button of **Mirror Plane** section and select the desired plane to mirror the selected body. The preview of mirror will be displayed; refer to Figure-13.

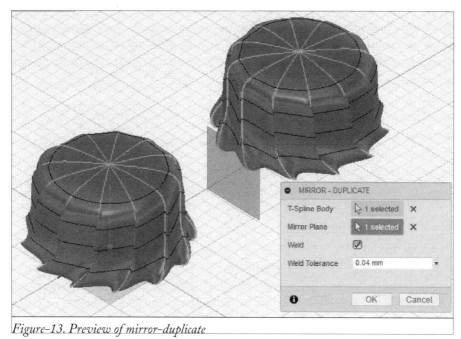

Figure-13. Preview of mirror-duplicate

- Select the **Weld** check box from **MIRROR - DUPLICATE** dialog box to weld the symmetric edges together.
- Click in the **Weld Tolerance** edit box and enter the desired value of tolerance.
- After specifying the parameters, click on the **OK** button from **MIRROR - DUPLICATE** dialog box to complete the process.

Circular - Duplicate

The **Circular - Duplicate** tool is used to create circular symmetric copies of the selected body around an axis. The procedure to use this tool is discussed next.

- Click on the **Circular - Duplicate** tool from **SYMMETRY** drop-down; refer to Figure-14. The **CIRCULAR - DUPLICATE** dialog box will be displayed; refer to Figure-15.

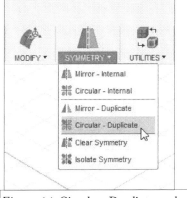

Figure-14. Circular- Duplicate tool

Figure-15. CIRCULAR- DUPLICATE dialog box

- The **Select** button of **T-Spline Body** section is active by default. Click on the body from canvas to select.
- Click to select the axis; refer to Figure-16.

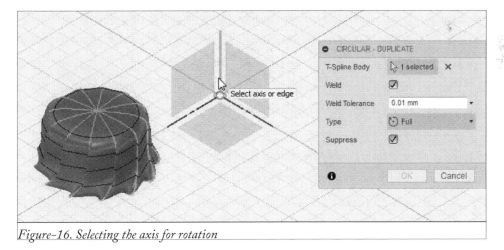

Figure-16. Selecting the axis for rotation

- Select the **Weld** check box if required.
- Click in the **Quantity** edit box and enter the desired number of duplicate copies you want to create; the preview of duplicate copies will be displayed; refer to Figure-17.

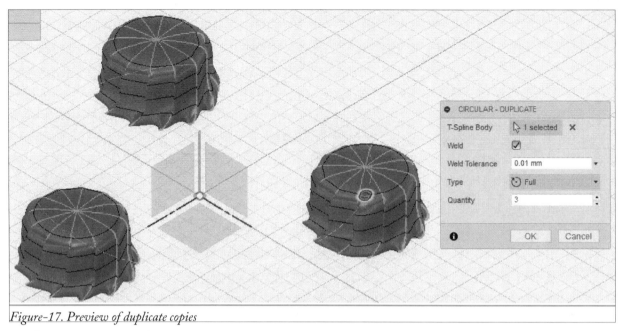

Figure-17. Preview of duplicate copies

- After specifying the parameters, click on the **OK** button from **CIRCULAR -DUPLICATE** dialog box to complete the process.

Clear Symmetry

The **Clear Symmetry** tool is used to delete the symmetry created earlier on the body. The procedure to use this tool is discussed next.

- Click on the **Clear Symmetry** tool from **SYMMETRY** drop-down; refer to Figure-18. The **CLEAR SYMMETRY** dialog box will be displayed; refer to Figure-19.

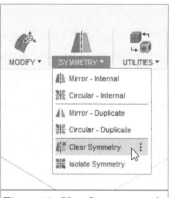

Figure-18. Clear Symmetry tool

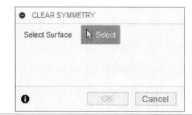

Figure-19. CLEAR SYMMETRY dialog box

- The **Select** button of **Select Surface** option is active by default. Click on the symmetry bodies for removing the symmetry constraint; refer to Figure-20.

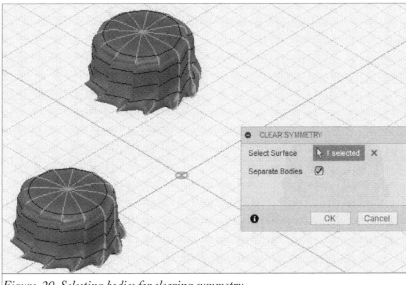

Figure-20. Selecting bodies for clearing symmetry

- Select the **Separate Bodies** check box to create a new bodies for disjointed surface.
- After specifying the parameters, click on the **OK** button from **CLEAR SYMMETRY** check box to complete the process; refer to Figure-21.

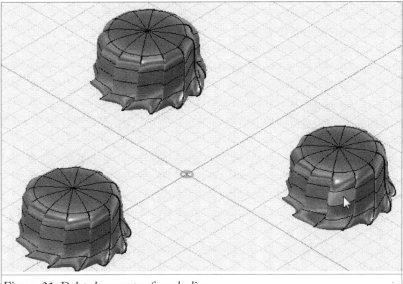

Figure-21. Deleted symmetry from bodies

Isolate Symmetry

The **Isolate Symmetry** tool is used to remove the symmetry condition from the selected face, edge, or vertex but the selected geometry will still symmetric to the other duplicate bodies. The procedure to use this tool is discussed next.

- Click on the **Isolate Symmetry** tool from **SYMMETRY** drop-down; refer to Figure-22. The **ISOLATE SYMMETRY** dialog box will be displayed; refer to Figure-23.

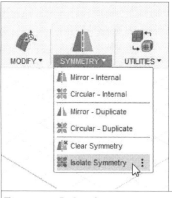

Figure-22. Isolate Symmetry tool

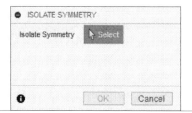

Figure-23. ISOLATE SYMMETRY dialog box

- The **Select** button of **Isolate Symmetry** section is active by default. Click on the symmetry to select; refer to Figure-24.

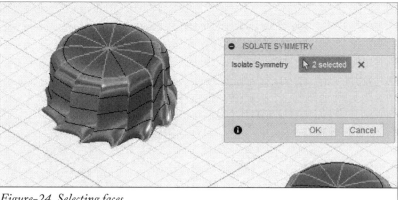

Figure-24. Selecting faces

- After specifying the parameters, click on the **OK** button from **ISOLATE SYMMETRY** dialog box to complete the process.
- If you edit or modify the isolated face, the symmetry faces will modified accordingly; refer to Figure-25.

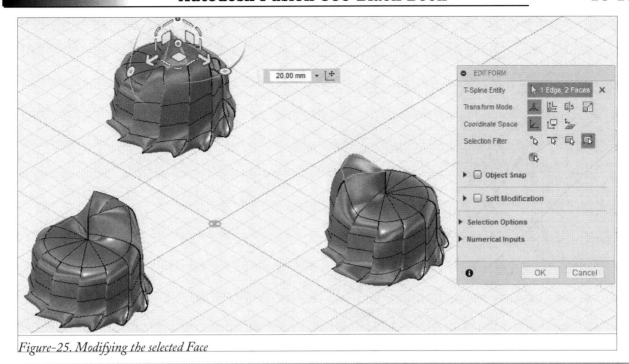

Figure-25. Modifying the selected Face

UTILITIES

Till now, we have discussed various symmetric tool. In this section we will discuss various utility tools used in **FORM** Mode.

Display Mode

The **Display Mode** tool is used to switches the view of selected body to box or smooth display. The procedure to use this tool is discussed next.

- Click on the **Display Mode** tool from **UTILITIES** drop-down; refer to Figure-26. The **DISPLAY MODE** dialog box will be displayed; refer to Figure-27.

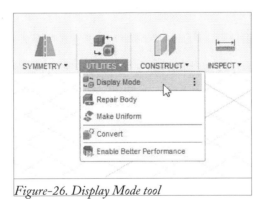

Figure-26. Display Mode tool

Figure-27. DISPLAY MODE dialog box

- The **Select** button of **T-Spline Entity** is active by default. You need to select the face, edge, body or vertex. You can also use window selection for selecting the whole geometry; refer to Figure-28.

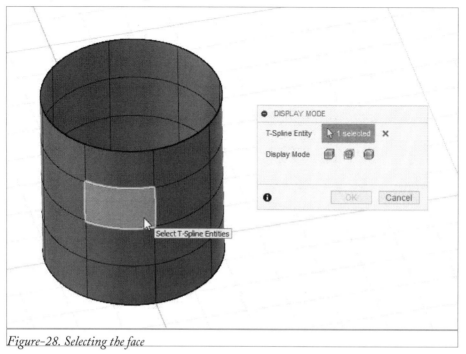

Figure-28. Selecting the face

- Select **Box Display** button from **Display Mode** section to display the control points of the T-Spline body.
- Select **Control Frame Display** button from **Display Mode** section to display the rounded frame body with the control frame around it.
- Select **Smooth Display** button from **Display Mode** section to display the rounded shape of the T-Spline body.
- After selecting the required display, click on the **OK** button from **DISPLAY MODE** dialog box to complete the process; refer to Figure-29.

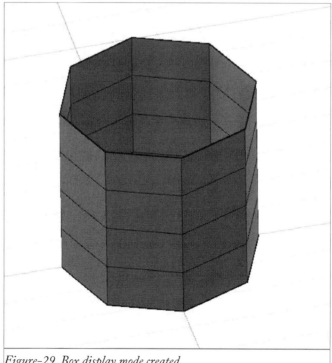

Figure-29. Box display mode created

Repair Body

The **Repair Body** tool is used for displaying the information about the mesh of sculpt body. This tool also repairs error star points and error T points. The procedure to use this tool is discussed next.

- Click on the **Repair Body** tool from **SYMMETRY** drop-down; refer to Figure-30. The **REPAIR BODY** dialog box will be displayed; refer to Figure-31.

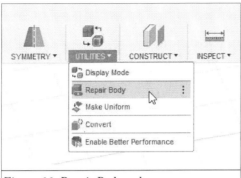

Figure-30. Repair Body tool

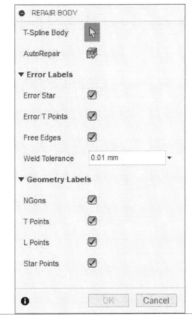

Figure-31. REPAIR BODY dialog box

- The **Select** button of **T-Spline Body** section is active by default. Click on the body to select.
- Click on the **AutoRepair** button from **REPAIR BODY** dialog box to repair error star points, error T points, and free edges.
- Select the **Error Star** check box of **Error Labels** section to display a red star on star points with an error.
- Select **Error T Points** check box of **Error Labels** section to display a red T on T point with an error.
- Select **Free Edges** check box to highlight the open edges on the body.
- Click in the **Weld Tolerance** edit box and specify the distance between edges to weld when using **AutoRepair** button.

- Select the **NGons** check box from **Geometry Labels** section to display the NGons with the number of edges on the selected model. NGons are faces which less than or more than 4 edges.
- Select the **T Points** check box to display a yellow T on T points of model.
- Select the **L Points** check box to display a yellow L on L Points of the selected model.
- Select the **Star Points** check box to display a yellow star on star points of model.
- After specifying the parameters, click on the **OK** button from **REPAIR BODY** dialog box to complete the process.

Make Uniform

The **Make Uniform** tool is used to create uniform surface of the selected body. This tool is used for making all the knots interval of selected body uniform. The procedure to use this tool is discussed next.

- Click on the **Make Uniform** tool from **UTILITIES** drop-down; refer to Figure-32. The **MAKE UNIFORM** dialog box will be displayed; refer to Figure-33.

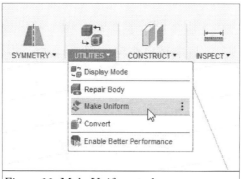
Figure-32. Make Uniform tool

Figure-33. MAKE UNIFORM dialog box

- The **Select** button of **T-Spline Body** section is active by default. Click on the body to select and click on the **OK** button. The tool will be applied.

Convert

The **Convert** tool is used to convert a sculpt object into other forms. The type of body created depends on selected body. The procedure to use this tool is discussed next.

- Click on the **Convert** tool from **UTILITIES** drop-down; refer to Figure-34. The **CONVERT** dialog box will be displayed; refer to Figure-35.

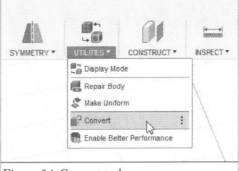

Figure-34. Convert tool

Figure-35. CONVERT dialog box

- Select **T-Splines to BRep** option from **Convert Type** drop-down to convert a T-Spline body into solid body.
- Select **BRep Face to T-Splines** option from **Convert Type** drop-down to convert a surface/face into sculpt.
- Select **Quad Mesh to T-Splines** option from **Convert Type** drop-down to convert a mesh body to a T-Spline body (sculpt).
- In our case, we are converting a T-Spline body to a solid body. The **Select** button of **Selection** section is active by default. Click on the sculpt body to convert; refer to Figure-36.

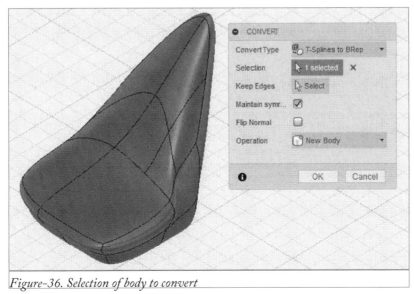

Figure-36. Selection of body to convert

- Click on the **Select** button from **Keep Edges** section and select the required edges to maintain the selected edges in converted body.

- Select the **Maintain symmetry** check box from **CONVERT** dialog box to maintain the symmetry of T-Spline body after conversion.
- Select the **Flip Normal** check box to change the normal direction of selected bodies.
- After specifying the parameters, click on the **OK** button from **CONVERT** dialog box; refer to Figure-37. The converted body will be displayed in **DESIGN Workspace**.

Figure-37. Converted body

Enable Better Performance

The **Enable Better Performance** tool is used to toggle between better performance or better display. The better display shows the bodies at highest quality and better performance calculates modification by applying G0 conditions at star points.

SELF ASSESSMENT

Q1. Which of the following tools is used to replicate changes made in one side of sculpt body to another side?

a. Mirror - Duplicate   b. Mirror - Internal
c. Isolate Symmetry   d. Circular - Internal

Q2. Which of the following tool is used to create replica of sculpt body with respect to a plane?

a. Mirror - Duplicate   b. Mirror - Internal
c. Isolate Symmetry   d. Circular - Internal

Q3. Which of the following tool is used to create symmetrical copies of selected sculpt body about an axis?

a. Mirror - Duplicate   b. Mirror - Internal
c. Circular Duplicate   d. Circular - Internal

Q4. Which of the following tool is used to remove symmetric conditions applied selected faces of sculpt body?

a. Clear Symmetry   b. Make Uniform
c. Isolate Symmetry   d. Erase and Fill

Q5. Which of the following tool is used to check geometry labels of sculpt mesh like L points, T points, and Star points?

a. Display Mode   b. Repair Body
c. Make Uniform   d. Enable Better Performance

FOR STUDENT NOTES

Chapter 14

Mesh Design

Topics Covered

The major topics covered in this chapter are:

- *BRep to Mesh*
- *Make Closed Mesh*
- *Erase and Fill*
- *Plane Cut*
- *Reverse Normal*
- *Separate and Merge Bodies*

INTRODUCTION

A model of mesh consists of vertices, edges, and faces that use polygonal representation, including triangles and quadrilaterals, to define a 3D shape. Mesh models has no mass properties but they can be used as frame reference to create solid model with mass properties. Using mesh model, allows to use manipulation techniques that are not available in solid modeling like applying crease, split, smoothness level, and so on. Note that 3D printers use mesh model to create the 3D print.

OPENING THE MESH WORKSPACE

The tools in **MESH** workspace are used to create mesh models. At the time of writing this book, the Mesh workspace is available in Preview mode so, you need select the **Mesh Workspace** check box from **Preview** node in the **Preferences** dialog box; refer to Figure-1. The procedure to open Mesh workspace is discussed next.

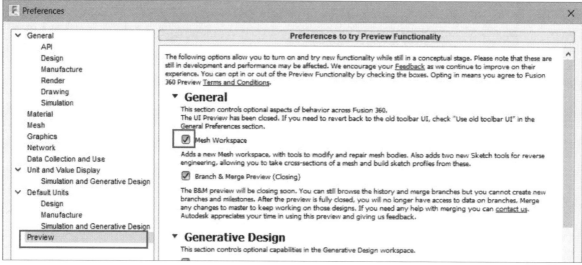

Figure-1. Mesh Workspace check box

• Click on the **DESIGN** option from **Change Workspace** drop-down. The **Design Workspace** will be displayed in **Autodesk Fusion 360** window.

• Click on **Create Mesh** tool from **CREATE** drop-down in the **Toolbar**; refer to Figure-2. The **MESH Workspace** will be displayed with **MESH PALETTE**; refer to Figure-3.

Figure-2. Mesh Workspace tool

- If **MESH PALETTE** is not displayed by default then select the **Mesh Palette** check box from **SELECT** drop-down in the **Toolbar** of Mesh environment. The tools in **MESH PALETTE** are used to manage selection range for mesh objects. Like increasing the brush size using **Brush Size** slider will expand the range of selection and allow selecting more mesh elements per click. Buttons in **Modify Selection** section are used to increase or decrease the number of elements in current selection.

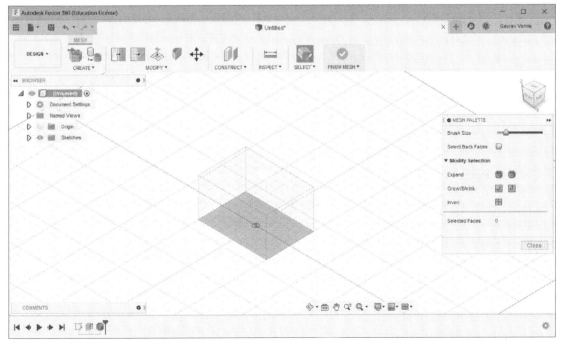

Figure-3. MESH Workspace window

INSERTING FILE

After starting Mesh workspace, the next step is to import a mesh model or convert an exiting solid to mesh model. In this section, we will learn to insert selected file into Mesh workspace and convert a solid model to mesh model.

Insert Mesh

The **Insert Mesh** tool is used for inserting a .OBJ or .STL mesh file into current design. The procedure to use this tool is discussed next.

*   Click on the **Insert Mesh** tool from **Create** drop-down; refer to Figure-4. The **Open** dialog box will be displayed; refer to Figure-5.

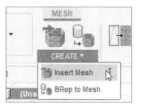

Figure-4. Insert Mesh tool

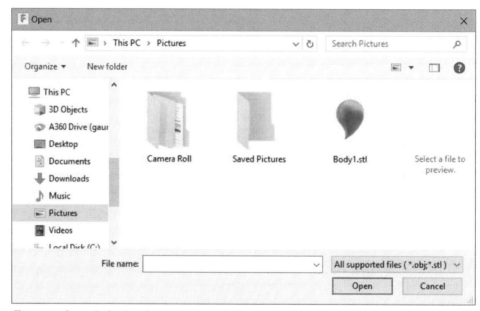

Figure-5. Open dialog box for inserting mesh file

*   Select the desired file and click on the **Open** button. The selected file will be displayed in the **MESH** workspace and the **INSERT MESH** dialog box will be displayed; refer to Figure-6.

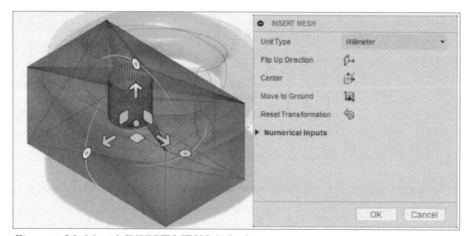

Figure-6. Model with INSERT MESH dialog box

*   Set the desired unit & orientation of model, and then click on the **OK** button from the dialog box to insert the mesh. You can also use the handles displayed on model to modify orientation of mesh model.

BRep to Mesh

The **BRep to Mesh** tool is used to convert the selected solid body into mesh body. A BRep (Boundary representation) method is the one in which object is defined by its boundary limits. In Solid modeling and CAD, Solids and surfaces are the generally created by BRep method. Sometimes solids and surfaces are collectively called BRep. The procedure to use this tool is discussed next.

- Make sure you have a solid/surface model created in **Design** workspace or open a model and then switch to **MESH Workspace** to convert the body to mesh body.
- Click on the **BRep to Mesh** tool from **CREATE** drop-down; refer to Figure-7. The **BREP TO MESH** dialog box will be displayed; refer to Figure-8.

Figure-7. BRep to Mesh tool

- The **Select** button of **Body** section is active by default. Click on the body to be converted to mesh; refer to Figure-9.

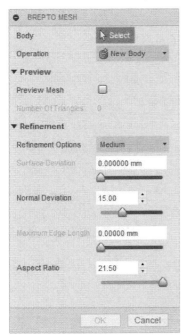
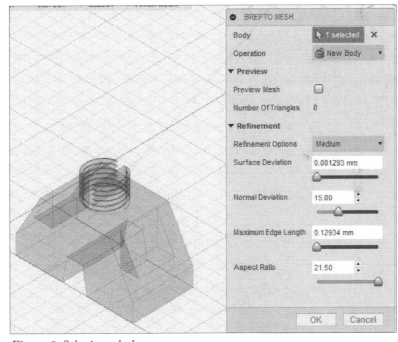

Figure-8. BREP TO MESH dialog box

Figure-9. Selecting a body

- Select the **Preview Mesh** check box under **Preview** node from **BREP TO MESH** dialog box to display the preview of mesh body of the selected solid body. The preview of mesh body will be displayed along with **Number of Triangles**; refer to Figure-10.

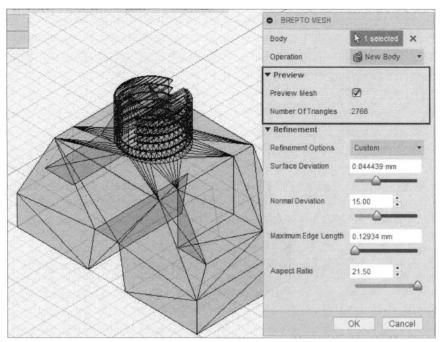

Figure-10. Preview of mesh body

- Select the **High**, **Medium**, or **Low** option from **Refinement Options** drop-down to set the refinement of mesh body automatically.
- If you want to set the refinement manually then click on the **Custom** option from **Refinement Options** drop-down.
- Move the **Surface Deviation**, **Normal Deviation**, **Maximum Edge Length**, and **Aspect Ratio** sliders to set the respective values.
- After specifying the parameters, click on the **OK** button from **BREP TO MESH** dialog box to complete the process; refer to Figure-11.

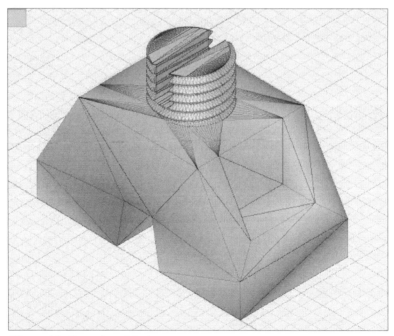

Figure-11. Created mesh body

MODIFICATION TOOLS

In this section, we will discuss various tools which are used to modify the mesh body.

Remesh

The **Remesh** tool is used to refine the selected mesh faces or body to form regular-shaped triangular faces. Note that in FEM there can be different shaped elements in a mesh like tetrahedra, hexahedra, and so on. The procedure to use this tool is discussed next.

* Click on the **Remesh** tool from **MODIFY** drop-down; refer to Figure-12. The **REMESH** dialog box will be displayed; refer to Figure-13.

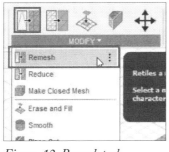

Figure-12. Remesh tool

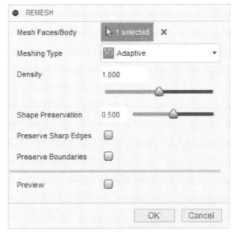

Figure-13. REMESH dialog box

* The **Select** button of **Mesh Faces/Body** section is active by default. Click on the faces to select. You can also drag the cursor to select multiple faces.
* Select **Uniform** option from **Meshing Type** drop-down for creating the similar size face on the entire selection. This option is used for keeping the face sizes even.
* Select **Adaptive** option from **Meshing Type** drop-down for smaller faces in the region of high detail and larger faces in the region of low detail. This option is used for preserving details on the selected model.
* Click in the **Density** edit box and enter the desired value of density. You can also specify the value of density by moving the **Density** slider from **REMESH** dialog box; refer to Figure-14. It controls the number of faces created.

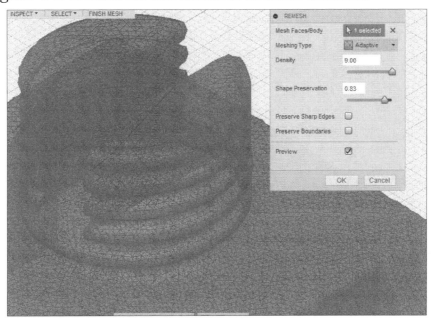

Figure-14. Specifying density

- Click in the **Shape Preservation** edit box and enter the value. You can also specify the value by moving the **Shape Preservation** slider. The value of **Shape Preservation** lies between 0 to 1. Note that this option will be available if you have selected **Adaptive** option from the **Meshing Type** drop-down in dialog box.
- Select the **Preserve Sharp Edges** check box from **REMESH** dialog box to preserve the sharp edges from the input mesh.
- Select the **Preserve Boundaries** check box from **REMESH** dialog box to make sure that any open boundaries of the selected model do not change shape. This option is useful if you have two separate bodies meeting at open boundaries that you wish to merge later.
- Select the **Preview** check box to view the mesh preview before it is created.
- After specifying the parameters, click on the **OK** button from **REMESH** dialog box. The created mesh body will be displayed; refer to Figure-15.

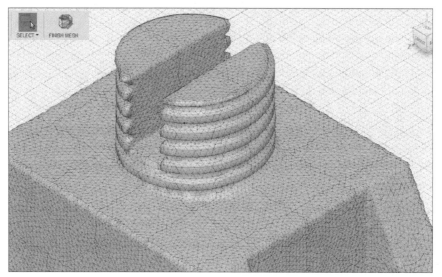

Figure-15. Created mesh body

Reduce

The **Reduce** tool is used to reduce the number of faces on your model while trying to maintain its shape. The procedure to use this tool is discussed next.

- Click on the **Reduce** tool from **MODIFY** drop-down; refer to Figure-16. The **REDUCE** dialog box will bc displayed; refer to Figure-17.

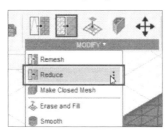

Figure-16. Reduce tool

Figure-17. REDUCE dialog box

- The **Select** button of **Mesh Faces/Body** section is active by default. Click on the mesh body from the **BROWSER** or select faces of mesh.

- Select the desired option from the **Reduce Target** drop-down to define which parameter is to be reduced.
- Move the slider to increase or decrease the value of parameter selected in **Reduce Target** drop-down; refer to Figure-18.

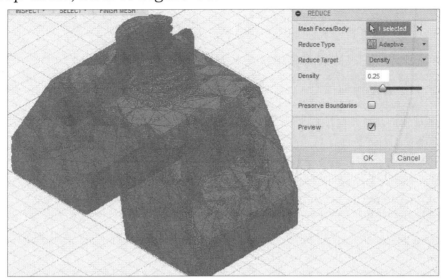

Figure-18. Adjusting the density of mesh body

- Select the **Preserve Boundaries** check box to retain the existing boundaries of body after modification.
- Select the **Preview** check box to view the mesh preview before it is created.
- After specifying the parameter, click on the **OK** button from **REDUCE** dialog box. The mesh body will be created; refer to Figure-19.

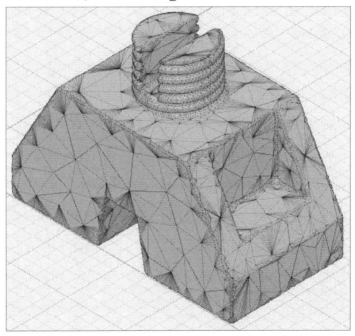

Figure-19. Created mesh body after Reduce tool

Make Closed Mesh

The **Make Closed Mesh** tool is used for rebuilding the selected mesh body as a new closed mesh. If there is any gap in your mesh part then it will be filled automatically to form a closed mesh. The procedure to use this tool is discussed next.

- Click on the **Make Closed Mesh** tool from **MODIFY** drop-down; refer to Figure-20. The **MAKE CLOSED MESH** dialog box will be displayed; refer to Figure-21.

Figure-20. Make Closed Mesh tool

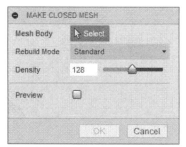

Figure-21. MAKE CLOSED MESH dialog box

- The **Select** button of **Mesh Body** section is active by default. Click on the body to be selected; refer to Figure-22. Note that if there is a single body then it will get selected automatically.
- Select **Standard** option from **Rebuild Mode** drop-down to rebuild the mesh with default behavior. This option provides a good balance of speed and accuracy, but sharp edges will become soft.
- Select **Preserve Sharp Edges** option from **Rebuild Mode** drop-down to rebuild the mesh similar to the **Standard** option but it will preserve sharp edges. In this option the mesh density is higher near the edge.
- Select **Accurate** option from **Rebuilds Mode** drop-down to create a closed mesh of the selected body with high accuracy. The performance will be slower than standard but accuracy may be improved.
- Select **Blocky** option from **Rebuilds Mode** drop-down to rebuild the model as simple cubes. This option does not provide an accurate approximation of the input shape, this is just intended to give your model a bulky aesthetic.
- Click in the **Density** edit box and enter the desired value. You can also specify the value of density by moving the **Density** slider.
- Select the **Preview** check box to view the mesh preview before it is created.
- After specifying the parameter, click on the **OK** button from **MAKE CLOSED MESH** dialog box. The mesh body will be created; refer to Figure-23.

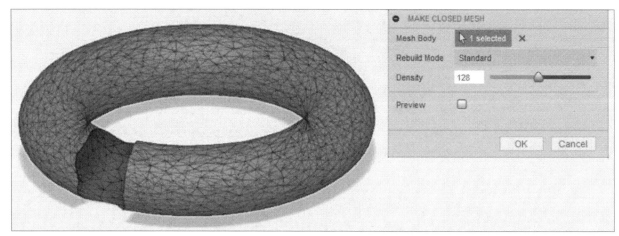

Figure-22. Selecting mesh body for creating closed mesh

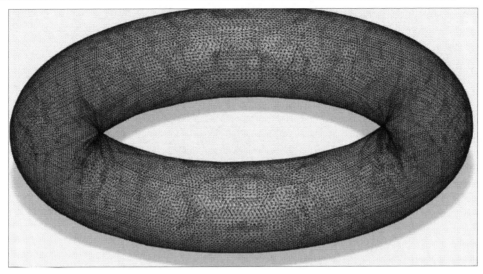

Figure-23. Created closed mesh body

Erase and Fill

The **Erase and Fill** tool is used to fill a hole or heal regions or defects on a mesh body. The procedure to use this tool is discussed next.

- Select the boundary of hole/cut in the mesh or select the complete mesh model to be filled or healed; refer to Figure-24.

Figure-24. Boundary of cut selected for healing

- Click on the **Erase and Fill** tool from **MODIFY** drop-down in the **Toolbar**; refer to Figure-25. The **ERASE AND FILL** dialog box will be displayed along with preview of fill feature; refer to Figure-26.

Figure-25. Erase and Fill tool

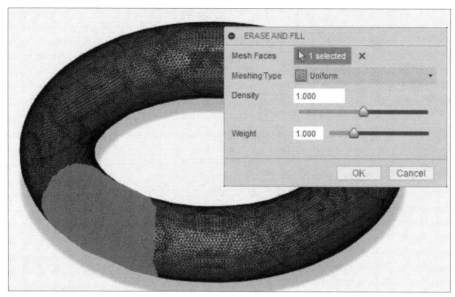

Figure-26. ERASE AND FILL dialog box

- Select **Uniform** option from **Meshing Type** drop-down to fill the selected region with regular shaped triangles. This option gives the smoothest and most reliable results.
- Select **Minimal** option from **Meshing Type** drop-down to uses the minimum number of faces to fill the selected hole.
- (For **Uniform** option) Click in the **Density** edit box and enter the desired value. You can also specify the value of density by moving the **Density** slider.
- (For **Uniform** option) Click in the **Weight** edit box and enter the weight mesh after filling. You can also specify the weight by moving the **Weight** slider. Note that weight defines the maximum deviation of new fill face from surrounding faces.
- After specifying the parameters, click on the **OK** button from **ERASE AND FILL** dialog box. The filled hole will be displayed; refer to Figure-27.

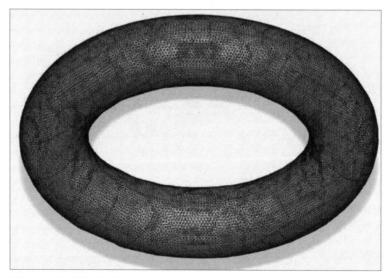

Figure-27. Filled hole

Smooth

The **Smooth** tool is used to smooth out uneven regions on the mesh. The procedure to use this tool is discussed next.

- Click on the **Smooth** tool from **MODIFY** drop-down; refer to Figure-28. The **SMOOTH** dialog box will be displayed; refer to Figure-29.

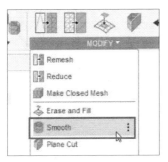

Figure-28. Smooth tool

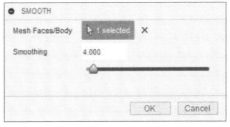

Figure-29. SMOOTH dialog box

- The **Select** button of **Mesh Faces/Body** section is active by default. Click on the body to select; refer to Figure-30.
- Click in the **Smoothing** edit box and enter the desired value for smoothing of mesh body. You can also move the **Smoothing** slider to specify the smoothing value.
- After specifying the parameters, click on the **OK** button from **SMOOTH** dialog box. The mesh body will be displayed; refer to Figure-31.

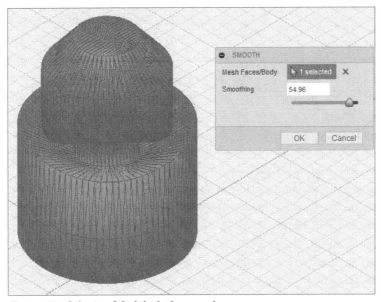

Figure-30. Selecting Mesh body for smooth

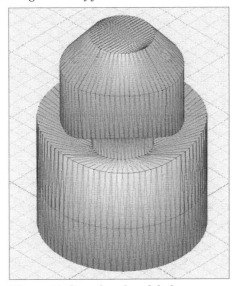

Figure-31. Smoothened mesh body

Plane Cut

The **Plane Cut** tool is used to cut the selected mesh body using a plane/face/surface. The procedure to use this tool is discussed next.

- Click on the **Plane Cut** tool from **MODIFY** drop-down; refer to Figure-32. The **PLANE CUT** dialog box will be displayed; refer to Figure-33.

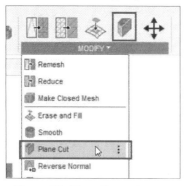

Figure-32. Plane Cut tool

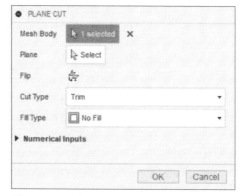

Figure-33. PLANE CUT dialog box

- The **Select** button of **Mesh Body** section is active by default. Click on the body to select. The manipulator will be displayed on the selected body; refer to Figure-34.

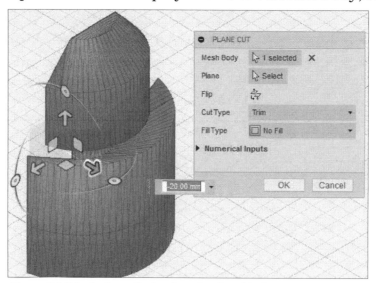

Figure-34. Manipulator displayed on the selected body

- Move the manipulator to split the body. To select desired cutting plane, click on the **Select** button of **Plane** section and select the required plane; refer to Figure-35. The preview of model cut by selected plane will be displayed.

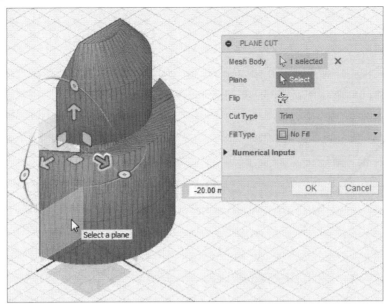

Figure-35. Selecting plane to split

- Click on the **Flip** button from **PLANE CUT** dialog box to flip the direction of split.
- Select **Trim** option from **Cut Type** drop-down to split the body into two sides and removes one of the sides.
- Select **Split Body** option from **Cut Type** drop-down to split the body to create two separate mesh body.
- Select **Split Faces** option from **Cut Type** drop-down to split the faces that intersect the plane but keep the body intact. This option will create a new face group on one side of the split.
- Select **No Fill** option from **Fill Type** drop-down if you want to leave open boundary at the cut.
- Select **Uniform** option from **Fill Type** drop-down if you want to fill the hole with new faces of regular shape.
- Select **Minimal** option from **Fill Type** drop-down of you want to fill the hole with minimal number of possible faces.
- Click on the **Numerical Inputs** node from **PLANE CUT** dialog box to manually enter the value of manipulator in respective edit box.
- After specifying the parameters, click on the **OK** button from **PLANE CUT** dialog box to split the model. The model will be displayed; refer to Figure-36.

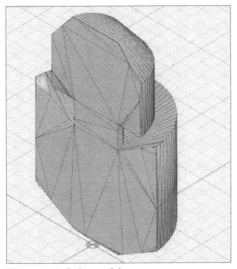

Figure-36. Split model

Reverse Normal

The **Reverse Normal** tool is used to flip the normal direction of the selected face. The procedure to use this tool is discussed next.

*   Click on the **Reverse Normal** tool from **MODIFY** drop-down; refer to Figure-37. The **REVERSE NORMAL** dialog box will be displayed; refer to Figure-38.

Figure-38. REVERSE NORMAL dialog box

Figure-37. Reverse Normal tool

*   The **Select** button of **Mesh Face** section is active by default. Click on the face of mesh body to select; refer to Figure-39

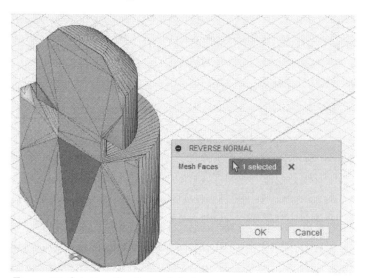

Figure-39. Selecting face for mesh body

*   You can also select multiple faces by clicking on them.
*   After selecting the required faces, click on the **OK** button from **REVERSE NORMAL** dialog box. The normal direction of selected face will be flipped; refer to Figure-40.

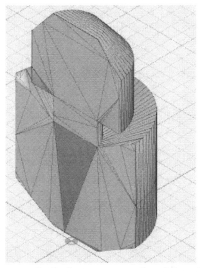

Figure-40. Applied reverse normal on Selected face

Delete Faces

The **Delete Faces** tool is used to remove selected face from the body. The procedure to use this tool is discussed next.

- Click on the **Delete Faces** tool from **MODIFY** drop-down; refer to Figure-41. The **DELETE FACES** dialog box will be displayed; refer to Figure-42.

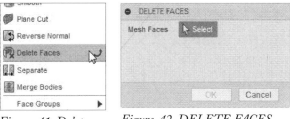

Figure-41. Delete Faces tool   *Figure-42. DELETE FACES dialog box*

- The **Select** button of **Mesh Faces** section is active by default. Click on the desired faces to select; refer to Figure-43.

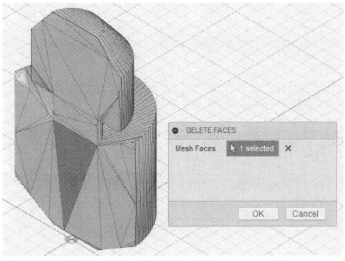

Figure-43. Selecting face to delete

*   Click on the **OK** button from **DELETE FACES** dialog box to delete the selected faces. The faces will be deleted; refer to Figure-44.

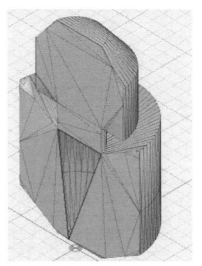

Figure-44. Deleted Face

Separate

The **Separate** tool is used to create a new mesh body from selected set of faces. The procedure to use this tool is discussed next.

*   Click on the **Separate** tool from **MODIFY** drop-down; refer to Figure-45. The **SEPARATE** dialog box will be displayed; refer to Figure-46.

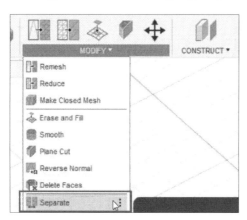

Figure-46. SEPARATE dialog box

Figure-45. Separate tool

*   The **Select** button of **Mesh Faces** section is active by default. Click on the face to select. You can also select multiple faces by holding the **CTRL** key; refer to Figure-47.

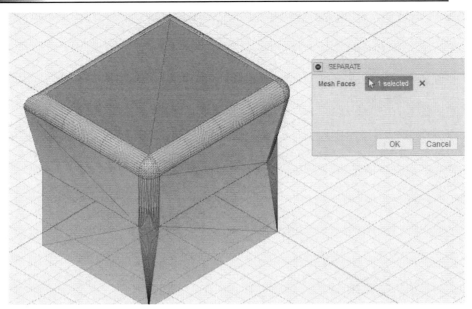

Figure-47. Selecting face for separate

- After selection of required faces, click on the **OK** button from **SEPARATE** dialog box. The selected face will be separated; refer to Figure-48.

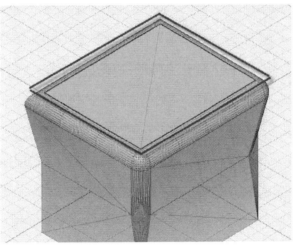

Figure-48. Separated face

Merge Bodies

The **Merge Bodies** tool is used to create a single body from multiple input bodies. If the input bodies have touching boundary edges then these edges will be stitched together. The procedure to use this tool is discussed next.

- Click on the **Merge Bodies** tool from **MODIFY** drop-down; refer to Figure-49. The **MERGE BODIES** dialog box will be displayed; refer to Figure-50

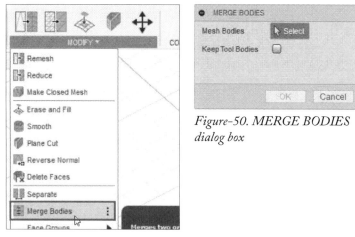

Figure-50. MERGE BODIES dialog box

Figure-49. Merge Bodies tool

- The **Select** button of **Mesh Bodies** section is active by default. Click on the bodies to be merged; refer to Figure-51.

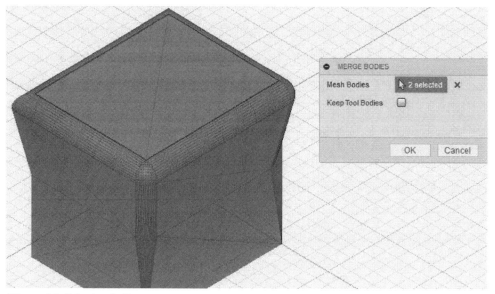

Figure-51. Selecting bodies to merge

- Select the **Keep Tool Bodies** check box from **MERGE BODIES** dialog box to keep the input bodies after merging operation as separate bodies.
- After specifying the parameter, click on the **OK** button from **MERGE BODIES** dialog box. The selected bodies will be merged; refer to Figure-52

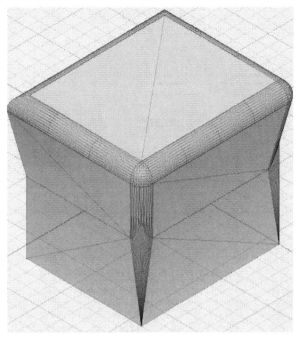

Figure-52. Merged bodies

Face Groups

The tools of **Face Groups** cascading menu are used to segment a mesh body into logical regions. The tools in this cascading menu are used to generate, clear, or create the face groups. Note that you can select the whole face group by double-clicking on one of its face.

Generate Face Groups

The **Generate Face Groups** tool is used to divide faces of the selected mesh body into groups based on normal angles of their faces or the origination of faces in the mesh body. The procedure to use this tool is discussed next.

- Click on the **Generate Face Groups** tool of **Face Groups** cascading menu from **MODIFY** drop-down; refer to Figure-53. The **GENERATE FACE GROUPS** dialog box will be displayed; refer to Figure-54.

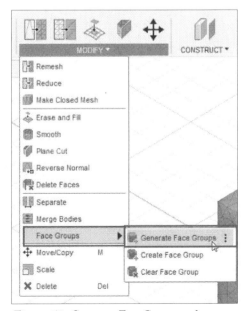

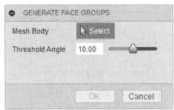

Figure-54. GENERATE FACE GROUPS dialog box

Figure-53. Generate Face Groups tool

- The **Select** button of **Mesh Body** section is active by default. Click on the mesh body to select; refer to Figure-55.

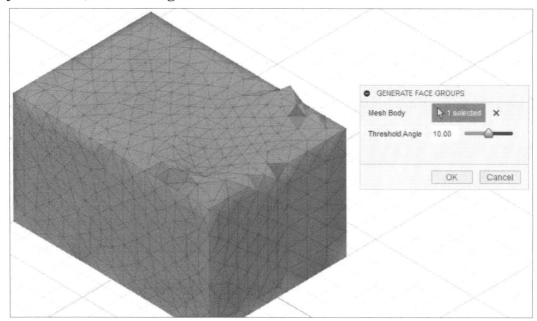

Figure-55. Selecting mesh body for generating face groups

- Click in the **Threshold Angle** edit box and enter the value of angle for faces at which they will be counter in different groups. Example: suppose, there are 20 faces which have angle of inclination from 0 to 10 then they will be counted in one type of group. There are another group of faces which have angle value from 11 to 20 then they will become another face group.

- After specifying the parameters, click on the **OK** button from **GENERATE FACE GROUPS** dialog box. The generated face groups will be displayed; refer to Figure-56.

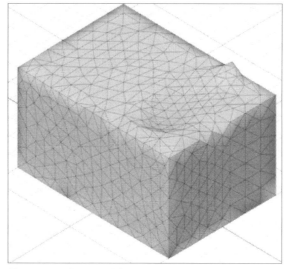

Figure-56. Generated face groups

Create Face Group

The **Create Face Group** tool is used to create a new face group from a selected set of faces. The procedure to use this tool is discussed next.

- Click on the **Create Face Group** tool of **Face Groups** cascading menu from **MODIFY** drop-down; refer to Figure-57. The **CREATE FACE GROUP** dialog box will be displayed; refer to Figure-58.

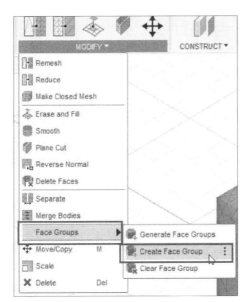

Figure-58. CREATE FACE GROUP dialog box

Figure-57. Create Face Group tool

• The **Select** button of **Mesh Faces** section is active by default. Click on the desired face to select; refer to Figure-59.

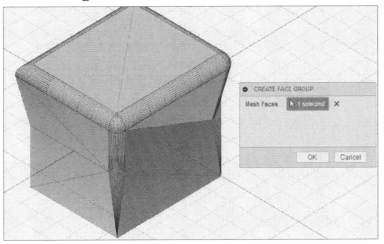

Figure-59. Selection of faces for creating face group

• After selection of required faces, click on the **OK** button from **CREATE FACE GROUP** dialog box. The created face group will be displayed; refer to Figure-60.

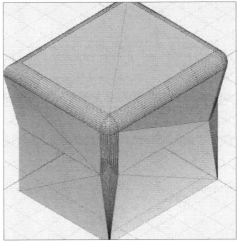

Figure-60. Created face group

Clear Face Group

The **Clear Face Group** tool is used to clear any existing face group from selected body. The procedure to use this tool is discussed next.

- Click on the **Clear Face Group** tool of **Face Groups** cascading menu from **MODIFY** drop-down; refer to Figure-61. The **CLEAR FACE GROUP** dialog box will be displayed; refer to Figure-62.

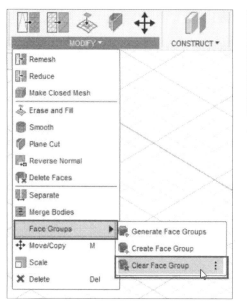

Figure-62. CLEAR FACE GROUP dialog box

Figure-61. Clear Face Group tool

- The **Select** button of **Mesh Faces/Body** section is active by default. Click on the existing face groups to be cleared or select the whole mesh body; refer to Figure-63.

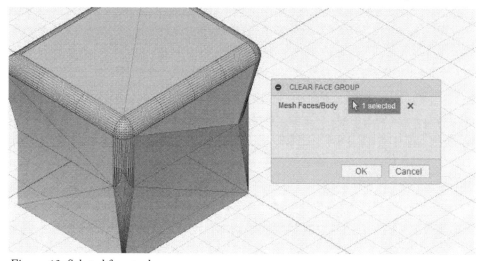

Figure-63. Selected faces to clear

- After selection of faces, click on the **OK** button from **CLEAR FACE GROUP** dialog box. The selected face will be cleared; refer to Figure-64.

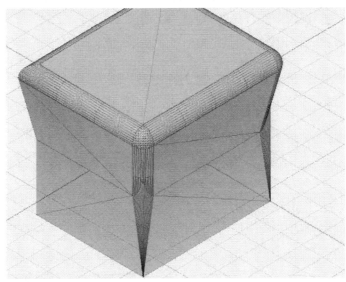

Figure-64. Cleared face group

- Others tools of **MODIFY** drop-down are same as discussed earlier in this book.
- After creating or modifying the mesh body, click on the **FINISH MESH** button from **Toolbar** to exit the **MESH Workspace**.

PRACTICAL

Create the mesh model as shown in Figure-65.

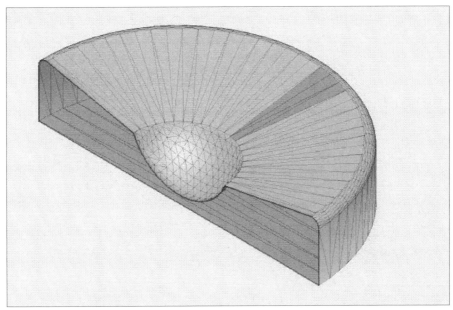

Figure-65. Final model

Converting model into mesh

Before modifying the mesh file, we need to convert the model into mesh file.

- Create or open the model of this practical in the **MODEL Workspace**. The file is available in the resource kit of this book.
- Click on the **Create Mesh** tool from **CREATE** drop-down in **SOLID** tab of **Toolbar**. The **MESH Workspace** will be displayed along with the model; refer to Figure-66.

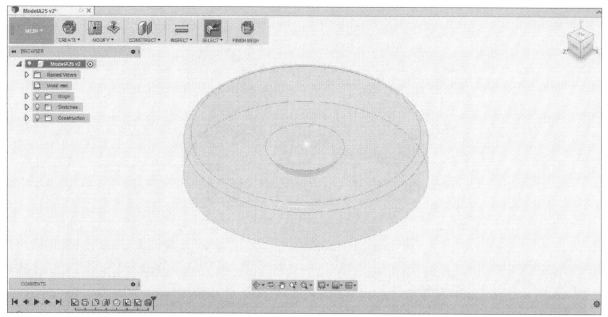

Figure-66. Added model into MESH Workspace

- Click on the **BRep to Mesh** tool of **CREATE** drop-down from **Toolbar**. The **BREP TO MESH** dialog box will be displayed.
- The **Select** button of **Body** option is active by default. Select the transparent model to convert it into mesh model and specify the parameters as shown in Figure-67.

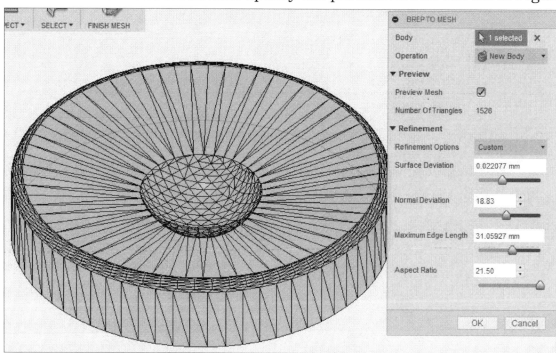

Figure-67. Specifying parameters for Creating mesh file

- After specifying the parameters, click on the **OK** button from **BREP TO MESH** dialog box. The mesh body will be created and displayed on the **MESH** workspace.

Reverse the face

- Click on the **Reverse Normal** tool of **Modify** drop-down from **Toolbar**. The **REVERSE NORMAL** dialog box will be displayed.
- Select the face as shown in Figure-68 and click on the **OK** button. The selected face will be reversed. You can also use window selection for selecting multiple faces.

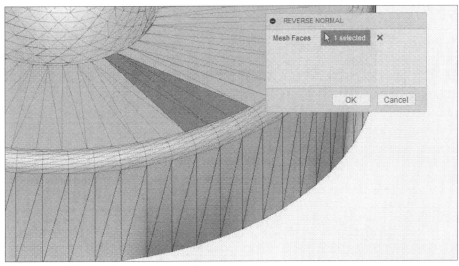

Figure-68. Selection for reverse normal

Plane Cut

- Click on the **Plane Cut** tool of **MODIFY** drop-down from **Toolbar**. The **PLANE CUT** dialog box will be displayed.
- The **Select** button of **Mesh Body** option is active by default. You need to select the model for plane cut. Click on the model to select.
- Click on the **Select** button of **Plane** option and select the YZ plane to cut the body; refer to Figure-69.

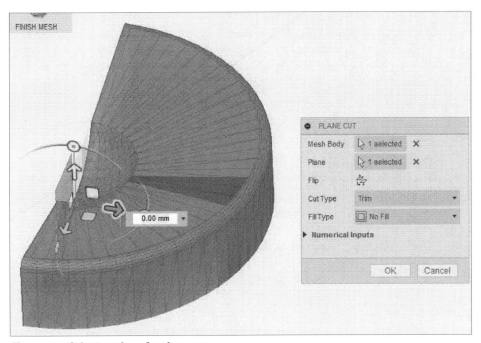

Figure-69. Selecting plane for plane cut

- Specify the parameters as shown in above figure and click on the **OK** button from **PLANE CUT** dialog box.
- After following all the steps discussed above, the model will be displayed as shown in Figure-70.

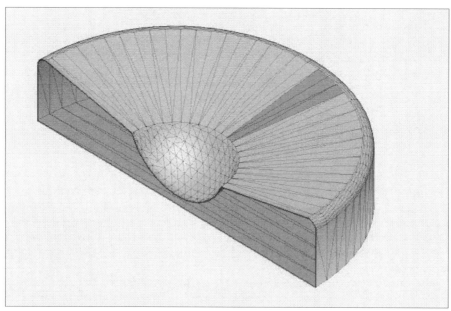

Figure-70. final model

PRACTICE

Create the model as displayed in the Figure-71.

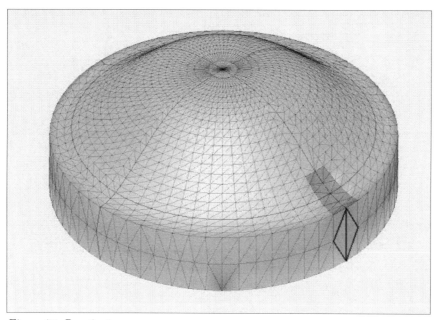

Figure-71. Practice 1

SELF ASSESSMENT

Q1. Which of the following are included in a mesh model?

a. Vertices   b. Edges
c. Faces   d. Surfaces
e. Hole features   f. Sketches

Q2. In Mesh workspace, selection brush is used instead of window selection to select elements (T/F).

Q3. Which of the following is not an object created by BRep method?

a. Sheetmetal model
b. Surface model
c. Solid model
d. Mesh model

Q4. In Autodesk Fusion 360, mesh model is combination of only triangulated faces. (T/F)

Q5. Which of the following tool is used to automatically fill all the holes and cuts in the selected mesh body?

a. Erase and Fill
b. Make Closed Mesh
c. Reduce
d. Remesh

FOR STUDENTS NOTES

Chapter 15

Manufacturing

Topics Covered

The major topics covered in this chapter are:

- *New Setup*
- *Milling Machine Setup*
- *Turning Machine Setup*
- *Milling and Turning Tools*
- *Creating new Mill and Turning tool*

INTRODUCTION

CAM stands for Computer Aided Manufacturing. CAM is a mode where you can convert the 3D model into a machine readable program codes used for the manufacturing process (usually G code). The some of the common manufacturing processes that are studied under CAM are Milling, Turning, Drilling, and Laser Cutting. In the CAM workspace of Autodesk Fusion, you will be able to generate high-quality toolpaths within minutes. Depending on the Fusion 360 version, you can create high quality 2D, 3D, 5-Axis milling, and turning toolpaths for high speed machining (HSM).

STARTING THE MANUFACTURE WORKSPACE

The tools in **MANUFACTURE** workspace are used to generate toolpaths for machining parts. The procedure to start **MANUFACTURE** workspace is discussed next.

- Click on the **MANUFACTURE** option of **Workspace** drop-down from current workspace; refer to Figure-1. The **MANUFACTURE** workspace will be displayed; refer to Figure-2.

Figure-1. MANUFACTURE workspace option

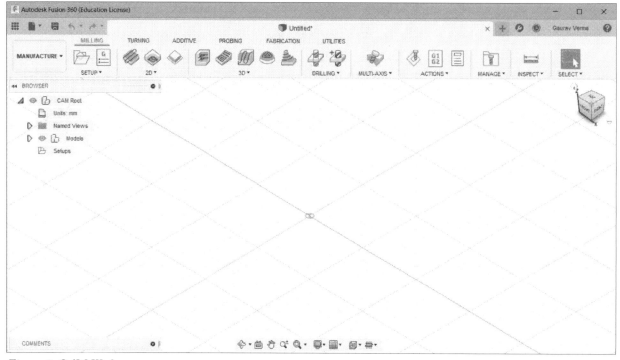

Figure-2. CAM Workspace

JOB SETUP

In this section, we will discuss the procedure of setting up the workpiece and create the required material stock for machining process. Job setup lets you define your stock for machining and machine type to be used like Milling or Turning. Stock is the workpiece out of which the final product will be produced after machining. The shape and size of stock depends upon the part which is to be created by machining.

New Setup

Before starting any machining project, you need to define a job setup to tell Autodesk Fusion 360 that the toolpaths will be generated for Milling machine or Turning machine. You also need to set the part zero location to be used as machining coordinates origin. You can also define any fixture components for machining. The procedure to setup the workpiece is discussed next.

- Click on the **New Setup** tool from **SETUP** drop-down; refer to Figure-3. The **SETUP** dialog box will be displayed along with the workpiece; refer to Figure-4.

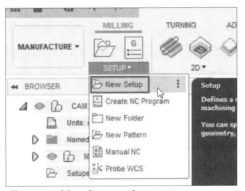

Figure-3. New Setup tool

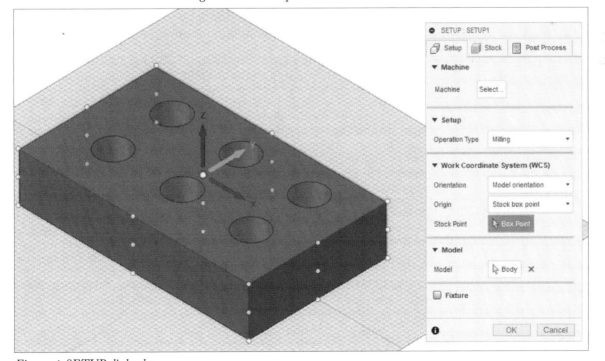

Figure-4. SETUP dialog box

Setting a Milling machine

The options in **Machine** node of **SETUP** dialog box deals with set up of machines. Depending on your requirement, you can select a machine or you can add a new entry of your machine in dialog box. Here, we will discuss the procedure of setting a milling machine and later we will discuss the procedure of setting a turning machine.

Setup

- Click on the **Select** button in **Machine** section of the dialog box to select predefined machine or specify machine related parameters. The **Machines** dialog box will be displayed; refer to Figure-5.

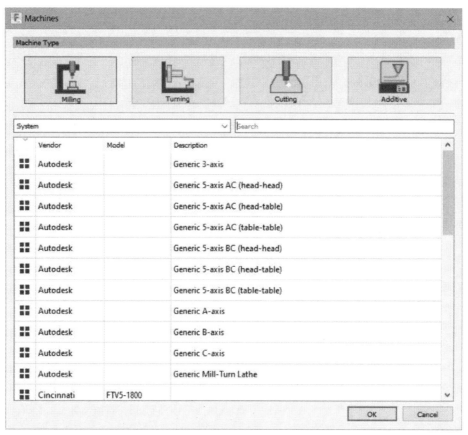

Figure-5. Machines dialog box

- Select the desired machine type and then machine from the dialog box and click on the **OK** button. The **Machine** node will be modified in the **SETUP** dialog box.
- Click on the **Edit** button to modify the parameters of the selected machine. The **Machine Configuration** dialog box will be displayed; refer to Figure-6.

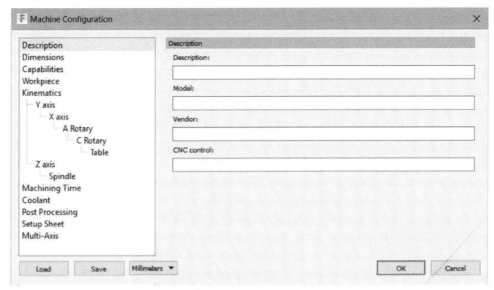

Figure-6. Machine Configuration dialog box

Machine Configuration

- Click on the **Load** button at the bottom left corner of the dialog box to set the parameters as per pre-defined machines. The **Open Machine Configuration** dialog box will be displayed; refer to Figure-7.

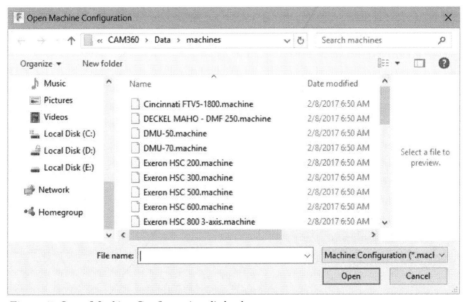

Figure-7. Open Machine Configuration dialog box

- Select the desired configuration file and click on the **Open** button from the dialog box. The parameters will be updated automatically in **Machine Configuration** dialog box.
- If you want to define each of the machine configuration parameter manually, then specify the desired parameters in the **Machine Configuration** dialog box and click on the **Save** button from the dialog box. The **Save Machine Configuration** dialog box will be displayed. Save the machine configuration at desired location and then click on the **OK** button from the **Machine Configuration** dialog box.

Operation Type

- Select the **Milling** option from the **Operation Type** drop-down in **Setup** section of **Setup** tab for setting up a milling operation. Note that if you have not defined machine then you can select the desired option from **Operation Type** drop-down but if you have select a machine in the **Machine** section of this dialog box then the option will be automatically selected in the **Operation Type** drop-down based on your machine.

Setting Work Coordinate System

• Select **Model Orientation** option in **Orientation** section from **Work Coordinate System (WCS)** to automatically set the orientation of coordinate system on workpiece for machining.

• Select the **Select Z axis/plane & X axis** option of **Orientation** section of **Work Coordinate System (WCS)** node to select the Z axis and X axis for setting the orientation of workpiece; refer to Figure-8. The updated **WCS** section will be displayed along with axis or face selection on part; refer to Figure-9

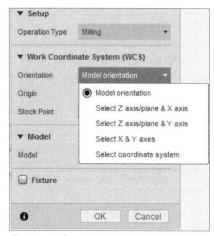

Figure-8. Orientation

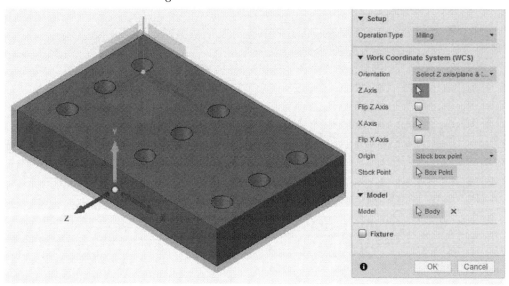

Figure-9. Updated WCS section of dialog box

• Click on the **Select Z axis/plane & Y axis** option of **Orientation** section of **Work Coordinate System (WCS)** to select the Z axis and Y axis for setting the orientation to reflect the machining plane.

• Click on the **Select X & Y axes** option of **Orientation** section of **Work Coordinate System (WCS)** to select the X axis and Y axis for setting the orientation to reflect the machining plane. You need to select a face or an edge of model to define the X and Y axis.

- Click on the **Select Coordinate System** option of **Orientation** section of **Work Coordinate System (WCS)** to define a user defined coordinate system in the model to set the WCS orientation.
- Click on the **Z Axis** button from **Work Coordinate System (WCS)** section and click on the desired axis or plane from Origin node in the **Browser** to define the Z axis. The Z axis should be perpendicular to machining plane.
- Select the **Flip Z Axis** check box to flip the selected direction of Z axis at 180 degree.
- The **X Axis** button is active by default. Click on the axis or plane to define the X axis; refer to Figure-10. The X axis will be defined perpendicular to the selected plane.

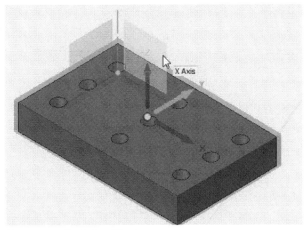

Figure-10. Defining X axis

- Select the **Flip X Axis** check box to flip the selected direction of X axis at 180 degree.
- Select **Model Origin** option of **Origin** drop-down from **Work Coordinate System (WCS)** section to uses the coordinate system (WCS)origin of the current part for the WCS origin.
- Select the **Selected Point** option of **Origin** drop-down to select a vertex or an edge for the WCS origin and click on the desired vertex or edge to define the WCS origin from model.
- Select **Stock box point** option of **Origin** drop-down from **Work Coordinate System (WCS)** section to define WCS origin by selecting a point on the stock bounding box. The **Stock Point** button of **Origin** section will be activated. Click on the stock point from workpiece to define WCS origin; refer to Figure-11.

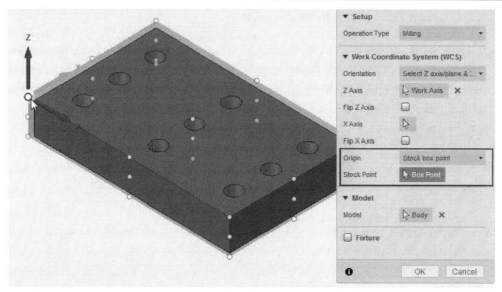

Figure-11. Defining stock box point

- Select **Model Box Point** option of **Origin** drop-down from **Work Coordinate System (WCS)** section to define a point for WCS origin by selecting a point on the model bounding box. The **Model Point** selection button for **Stock Point** section is active by default. Click at the desired box point of model to define the WCS origin.

Model Body Selection

- The body/model which is considered for generating toolpaths is active by default in **Model** section from **Setup** tab. If there are multiple solid model in file then it is recommended to select the required model for machining process.

Fixture Selection

- Select the **Fixture** check box from **SETUP** dialog box to define the fixture for the workpiece.
- The **Fixture** selection button is active by default on selecting the **Fixture** check box. You need to select the component/body to defined fixture; refer to Figure-12. Note that components defined as fixture will be avoided by tool while cutting.

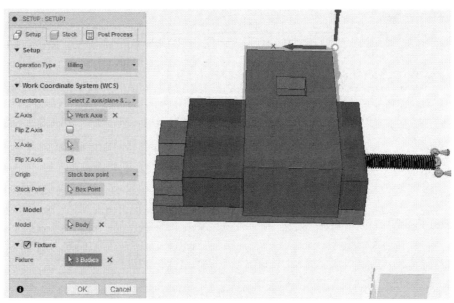

Figure-12. Selecting Fixture

Stock tab

- Click on the **Stock** tab of **SETUP** dialog box to define the workpiece dimensions. The **Stock** tab will be displayed; refer to Figure-13.

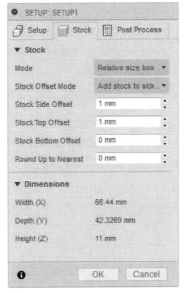

Figure-13. Setup tab

Fixed size box

- Select **Fixed size box** option from the **Mode** drop-down in **Setup** tab to create a rectangular stock body of defined parameter. The updated **Stock** tab will be displayed; refer to Figure-14.

Figure-14. Fixed size box options

- Click in the **Width (X)** edit box and specify the width of the stock body.
- Select the **Offset from left side (-X)** option of **Model Position** drop-down from **Stock** section to offset the stock to the left side of model.
- Click in the **Offset** edit box and enter the required value; refer to Figure-15.

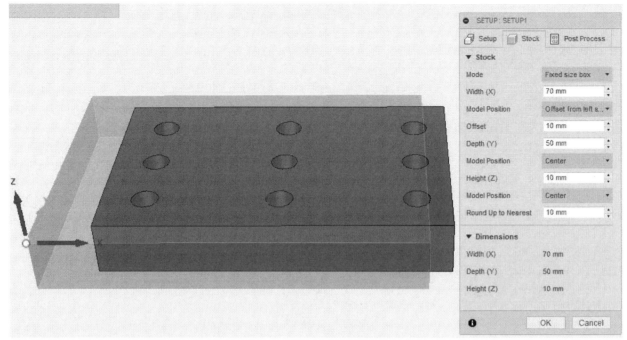

Figure-15. Offset from left side

- Select **Center** option of **Model Position** drop-down from **Stock** section to place the stock on the center of model.
- Select the **Offset from right side (+X)** option of **Model Position** drop-down from **Stock** section to offset the stock to the right side of model.
- Click in the **Offset** edit box and enter the required value. In our case we are selecting the **Center** option.
- Click in the **Depth (Y)** edit box and enter the required depth of the stock.
- Click in the **Height (Z)** edit box and enter the required height of stock.
- Click in the **Round Up to Nearest** edit box and enter the round of increment of the stock size.

Relative Size Box

- Select the **Relative Size Box** option from **Mode** drop-down in **Stock** tab to create a rectangular stock body larger then the model by specifying the required values. The updated **SETUP** dialog box will be displayed; refer to Figure-16.
- Select the **No additional stock** option of **Stock Offset Mode** drop-down from **Stock** section to not add any offset value to the stock size.
- Select the **Add stock to the sides and top-button** option of **Stock Offset Mode** drop-down to add symmetric values to all side of stock and unique values to top and button offsets.
- Click in the respective offset edit box and enter the value as desired.
- Select the **Add stock to all sides** option of **Stock Offset Mode** drop-down if you want to enter the specific the values for all offset directions of stock.
- Click in the respective offset edit box and enter the value as desired.

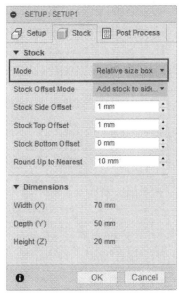

Figure-16. Relative size box option

Fixed size cylinder

- Select the **Fixed size cylinder** option of **Mode** drop-down from **Stock** section to create a fixed size cylinder stock body. The updated **SETUP** dialog box will be displayed; refer to Figure-17.
- The **Axis** button of **Setup** section is active by default. You need to select the axis from model; refer to Figure-17.

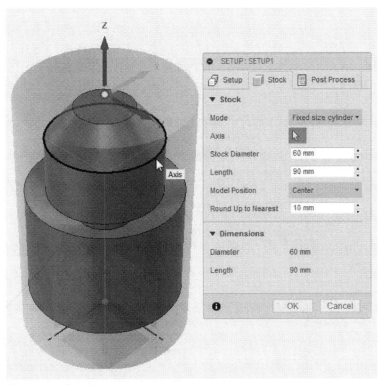

Figure-17. Selecting axis

- Click in the **Stock Diameter** edit box from **Stock** section and enter the desired diameter of stock.
- Click in the **Length** edit box and enter the desired length of stock.

Relative size cylinder

- Select **Relative size cylinder** option of **Mode** drop-down from **Stock** section to create the larger stock body. Specify the required values. The updated **SETUP** dialog box will be displayed; refer to Figure-18.

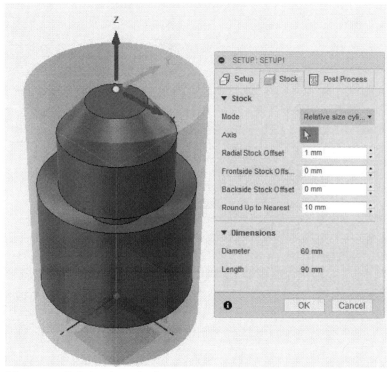

Figure-18. Relative size cylinder option

- The **Axis** button is active by default. Click on the axis from model to select.
- Click in the **Radial Stock Offset** edit box and enter the value of radial offset of the stock.
- Click **Frontside Stock Offset** edit box and specify the distance to machine beyond the front side of the model.
- Click in the **Backside Stock Offset** edit box and specify the distance to machine beyond the backside of the model.

Fixed size tube

- Select **Fixed size tube** option of **Mode** drop-down from **Stock** section to create a tube stock body of fixed size. The updated **SETUP** dialog box will be displayed; refer to Figure-19.

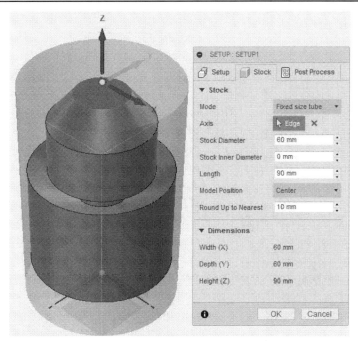

Figure-19. Fixed size tube option

- The **Axis** button is active by default. Click on the axis from model to select.
- Click in the **Stock Diameter** edit box from **Stock** section and enter the desired diameter of stock.
- Click in the **Stock Inner Diameter** edit box and enter the inner diameter of stock; refer to Figure-20.

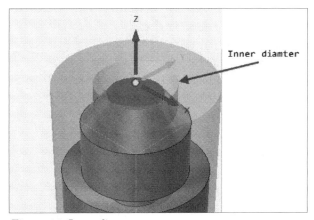

Figure-20. Inner diameter

- Click in the **Length** edit box and enter the desired length of stock.
- Select **Offset from front** option of **Model Position** drop-down from **Stock** section to offset the stock to the front side of model; refer to Figure-21.

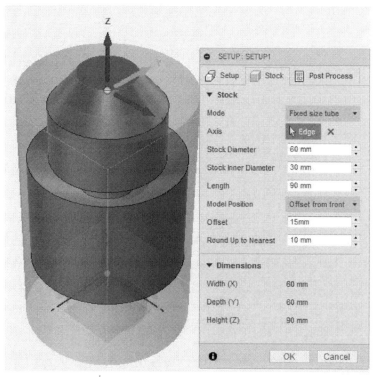

Figure-21. Offset from front option

- Click in the **Offset** edit box and enter the required value.
- Select the **Center** option of **Model Position** drop-down from **Stock** section to place the stock at the center of model.
- Select **Offset from back** option of **Model Position** drop-down from **Stock** section to offset the stock to the back side of model.

Relative size tube

- Select the **Relative size tube** option of **Mode** drop-down from **Stock** section to create the larger stock body then model by specifying the required values. The updated **SETUP** dialog box will be displayed; refer to Figure-22.

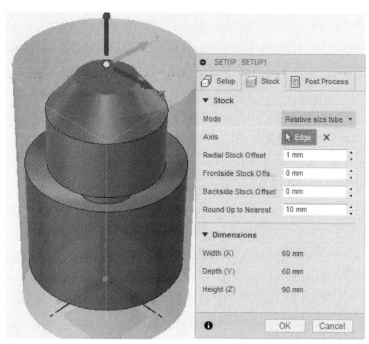

Figure-22. Relative size tube

- The edit boxes of **Relative size tube** were discussed in **Relative size cylinder** option of this tool.

From solid

- Select **From solid** option of **Mode** drop-down from **Stock** section to create a stock by selecting a solid body in a multi-body part or from a part file in an assembly. The updated **SETUP** dialog box will be displayed; refer to Figure-23.

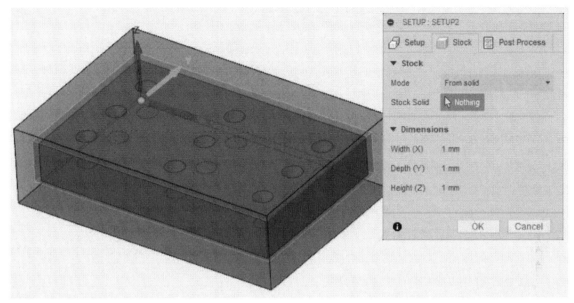

Figure-23. From solid option

- Click on the **Nothing** button of **Stock Solid** option and click on the body to be used as stock; refer to Figure-24.

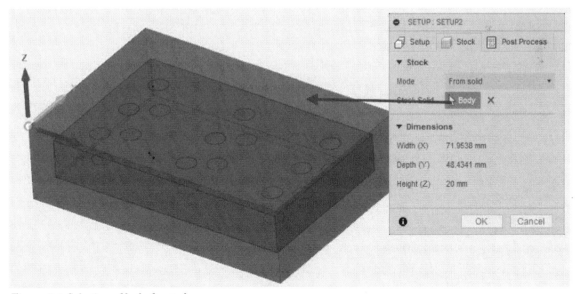

Figure-24. Selection of body for stock

- Click on the **Dimensions** node of **Stock** tab from **SETUP** dialog box to check the exact dimensions of the stock.

Post Process tab

- Click on the **Post Process** tab from **SETUP** dialog box to define post processing parameters. The **Post Process** tab will be displayed; refer to Figure-25

Figure-25. Post Process tab

- Click in the **Program Name/Number** edit box of **Post Process** tab from **Setup** dialog box to define the NC program name/number. This number is output at the start of the NC program code as the "0" number. It is also used as a storage name on the CNC controller storage.
- Click in the **Program Comment** edit box and enter the desired comment. The comment text will not be read by CNC control but it will be displayed in program.
- Click on the **WCS Offset** edit box of **Machine WCS** section from **Post Process** tab to select the work offset used in the NC machine to provide tool compensation. The output in the NC program is generally produced by G54 through G59 codes, but will vary between various NC Controls/Machines. Zero (0) in WCS Offset will output the first available fixture offset and 1 will output the 2nd available offset.
- Click in the **Probe WCS override** edit box of **Machine WCS** section to enter the value of offset for probe while checking coordinates in CMM or any probe installed in your machine.
- Select the **Multiple WCS Offsets** check box if there are multiple work pieces on the machine bed and WCS offset is to be duplicated for each of them.
- The **Operation Order** drop-down of **Multiple WCS Offsets** check box is used to specifies the ordering of the individual operations.
- Select **Preserve Order** option from **Operation Order** drop-down to the features which are machined in the order in which they are selected.
- Select **Order by Operation** option from **Operation Order** drop-down to specify the ordering of the individual operations.
- Select **Order by tool** option from **Operation Order** drop-down to specify the ordering of operations by tool.
- After specifying the desired parameters, click on the **OK** button from **SETUP** dialog box. The **Setup1** will be added in **Browser**; refer to Figure-26.
- If you want to edit the earlier created stock or setup parameter then right click on the **Setup** option from **Setups** node of **BROWSER** and click on **Edit** button from marking menu; refer to Figure-27. The **SETUP** dialog box will be displayed.

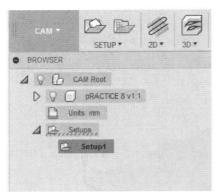

Figure-26. Setup1 in BROWSER

Figure-27. Edit stock

Turning Machine Setup

In this section, we will discuss about the procedure of setting machine for **Turning** operation. The procedure is discussed next.

• Click on the **Turning or mill/turn** option from **Operation Type** drop-down in **SETUP** dialog box. The options used in turning process will be displayed along with the model; refer to Figure-28. You can also select a turning machine by using **Select** button in **Machine** section of this dialog box. The procedure is same as for milling machine.

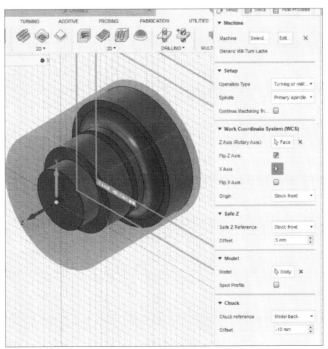

Figure-28. Turning or mill turn option

- Select **Primary spindle** or **Secondary spindle** option from **Spindle** drop-down in **Setup** section to specify the spindle to be used if your machine has two spindles.
- Select the **Continue Machining from Previous Setup** check box from **Setup** section if you want to use the machine setup earlier created.
- Click on the **Z Axis (Rotary Axis)** button of **Work Coordinate System (WCS)** section from **SETUP** dialog box and select the Z axis as required; refer to Figure-29.

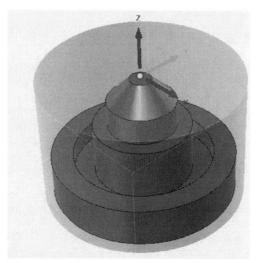

Figure-29. Selecting Z axis for turning

- Select the **Flip Z Axis** check box to flip the selected direction of Z axis at 180 degree.
- The **X Axis** button is active by default. Click on the axis or plane to define the X axis.
- Select the **Flip X Axis** check box to flip the selected direction of X axis at 180 degree.
- The **Origin** drop-down will define where zero position will be located on the part. Click on the **Origin** drop-down from **Work Coordinate System (WCS)** section and select the desired option to set origin.
- Click in the **Safe Z Reference** drop-down and select the desired reference for safe Z position where tool should move after making cutting passes.
- Click in the **Offset** edit box of **Safe Z** node in the dialog box and specify the distance of safe Z location from selected reference.
- Select the **Spun Profile** check box of **Model** section from **Setup** tab to generate profile for turning. If you are going to mill-turn a part which has irregular surface then you should select this check box to avoid accident.
- Click in the **Spun Profile Tolerance** edit box of **Model** section and enter the desired value of tolerance
- Select the **Spun Profile Smoothing** check box to smooth the profile.
- Select the desired reference for defining position of check from the Chuck reference drop-down.
- Click in the **Offset** edit box of the **Chuck** node and specify the desired value of distance at which chuck should be placed from the selected reference.

The tools of **Stock** and **Post Process** tab have been discussed earlier in **Milling** section.

• After specifying the parameters, click on the **OK** button from **SETUP** dialog box to complete the process of creating stock and defining machine parameters.

Cutting Machine Setup

In this section, we will discuss the procedure of setting up a cutting machine. This machine can be water jet machine, laser/plasma cutting machine, and so on. The procedure is discussed next.

• Click on the **Cutting** option of **Operation Type** drop-down from **SETUP** dialog box. The options used in cutting process will be displayed; refer to Figure-30.

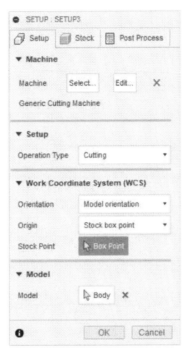

Figure-30. SETUP dialog box for Cutting operation

• Set the orientation and zero point for cutting operation from **SETUP** dialog box.
• The other options in the dialog box have been discussed earlier.
• After specifying the parameters, click on the **OK** button from **SETUP** dialog box.

Additive Manufacturing Machine Setup

In this section, we will setup a 3D printing machine. The procedure is given next.

• Select an additive manufacturing machine by using the **Select** button from the **Machine** node in the **SETUP** dialog box (like Aconity3D). The options will be displayed as shown in Figure-31.

Figure-31. SETUP dialog box for
additive manufacturing

- Make sure the **Additive** option is selected in the **Operation Type** drop-down of Setup node.
- Select the **Automatic** check box from the **Arrangement** node to automatically place all the parts on the machine bed.
- After specifying the parameters, click on the **OK** button from **SETUP** dialog box.

TOOL SELECTION

Before proceeding towards the tools used to generate 2D and 3D path, you need to know various types of tools used in machining and their selection criteria. For this we need to discuss the **Select Tool** dialog box; refer to Figure-32. To display this dialog box, click on the **2D Adaptive Clearing** tool from the **2D** drop-down in the Toolbar. A dialog box will be displayed. Click on the **Select** button for **Tool** section in the **Tool** node of the dialog box. The **Select Tool** dialog box will be displayed. Note that in this chapter, we will discuss about cutting tools only. In next chapter, we will discuss the toolpaths.

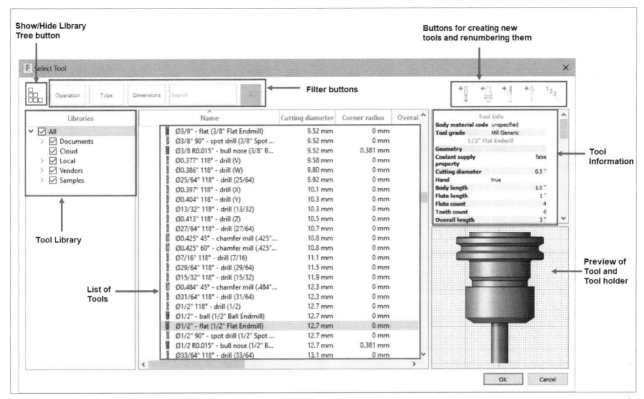

Figure-32. Select Tool dialog box

- The **Show/Hide Library** button of **Select Tool** dialog box is used to display or hide the Tool Library.
- The **Operation** button is used to display the list of tools based on operations selected. Click on the **Operation** button from **Select Tool** dialog box. The list of operations will be displayed; refer to Figure-33. Select the desired operation from the list by which you want to filter the tools. Note that on selecting the option from Operations list, the **Type** button is modified displaying the tools available for selected operation. If you want to erase the selection then click on the **Clear** button from bottom in the **Operations** list. The selected tool will be cleared.
- Click on the **Type** button from the dialog box to filter the list of tools based on selected type of tool. Like, you can filter list to only flat mills or ball mills. The list of tools will be displayed accordingly; refer to Figure-34.

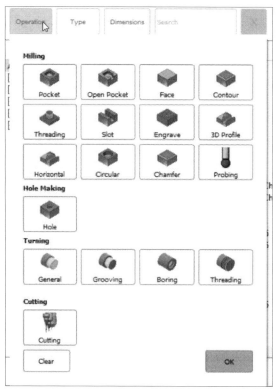

Figure-33. List of operations for filtering

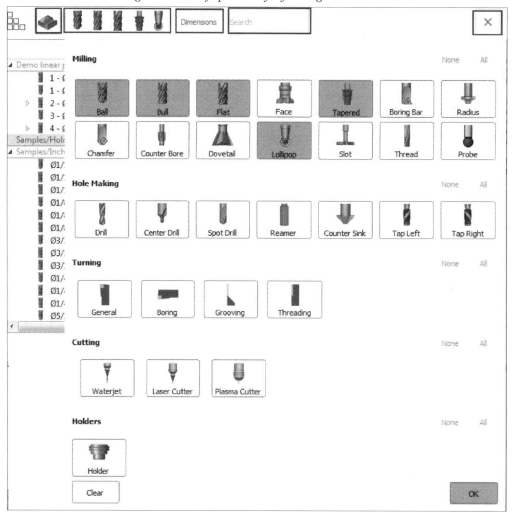

Figure-34. Tools selection list

- If you want to filter the tools according to the parameter like flute length, diameter, number of flutes, and so on then click on the **Dimensions** button from **Select Tool** dialog box. The **Dimensions** filter box will be displayed; refer to Figure-35.

Figure-35. Dimension box

- Select the desired parameter check boxes from **Dimension** box and enter the desired values in respective edit boxes to define filter parameters.
- After specifying the parameters, click on the **OK** button from **Dimension** box. The tools of selected parameter will be displayed.
- If you want to search the tool by its name/keywords then click in the **Search** box from **Select Tool** dialog box and type the required keywords. The tools with typed keywords will be displayed in table.
- If you want to erase all the applied filters for tool selection, click on the **Clear All Filter** button from **Select Tool** dialog box.

TOOLS USED IN CNC MILLING AND LATHE MACHINES

The tools used in CNC machines are made of cemented carbide, High Speed Steel, Tungsten Alloys, Ceramics, and many other hard materials. The shapes and sizes of tools used in Milling machines and Lathe machines are different from each other. These tools are discussed next.

Milling Tools

There are various type of milling tools for different applications. These tools are discussed next.

End Mill

End mills are used for producing precision shapes and holes on a Milling or Turning machine. The correct selection and use of end milling cutters is paramount with either machining centers or lathes. End mills are available in a variety of design styles and materials; refer to Figure-36.

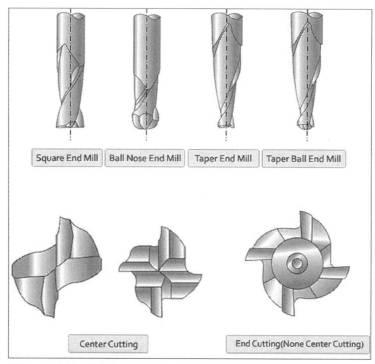

Figure-36. End Mill tool types

Titanium coated end mills are available for extended tool life requirements. The successful application of end milling depends on how well the tool is held (supported) by the tool holder. To achieve best results an end mill must be mounted concentric in a tool holder. The end mill can be selected for the following basic processes:

FACE MILLING - For small face areas, of relatively shallow depth of cut. The surface finish produced can be 'scratchy".

KEYWAY PRODUCTION - Normally two separate end mills are required to produce a quality keyway.

WOODRUFF KEYWAYS - Normally produced with a single cutter, in a straight plunge operation.

SPECIALTY CUTTING - Includes milling of tapered surfaces, "T" shaped slots & dovetail production.

FINISH PROFILING - To finish the inside/outside shape on a part with a parallel side wall.

CAVITY DIE WORK - Generally involves plunging and finish cutting of pockets in die steel. Cavity work requires the production of three dimensional shapes. A Ball type end mill is used for the finishing cutter with this application.

Roughing End Mills, also known as ripping cutters or hoggers, are designed to remove large amounts of metal quickly and more efficiently than standard end mills; refer to Figure-37. Coarse tooth roughing end mills remove large chips for heavy cuts, deep slotting and rapid stock removal on low to medium carbon steel and alloy steel prior to a finishing application. Fine tooth roughing end mills remove less material but the pressure is distributed over many more teeth, for longer tool life and a smoother finish on high temperature alloys and stainless steel.

Figure-37. Roughing End Mill

Bull Nose Mill

Bull nose mill look alike end mill but they have radius at the corners. Using this tool, you can cut round corners in the die or mold steels. Shape of bull nose mill tool is given in Figure-38.

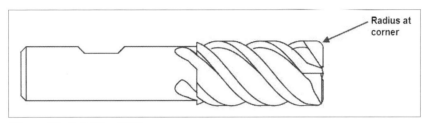

Figure-38. Bull Nose Mill cutter

Ball Nose Mill

Ball nose cutters or ball end mills has the end shape hemispherical; refer to Figure-36. They are ideal for machining 3-dimensional contoured shapes in machining centres, for example in moulds and dies. They are sometimes called ball mills in shop-floor slang. They are also used to add a radius between perpendicular faces to reduce stress concentrations.

Face Mill

The Face mill tool or face mill cutter is used to remove material from the face of workpiece and make it plane; refer to Figure-39.

Figure-39. Face milling tool

Radius Mill and Chamfer Mill

The Radius mill tool is used to apply round (fillet) at the edges of the part. The Chamfer mill tool is used to apply chamfer at the edges of the part. Figure-40 shows the radius mill tool and chamfer mill tool.

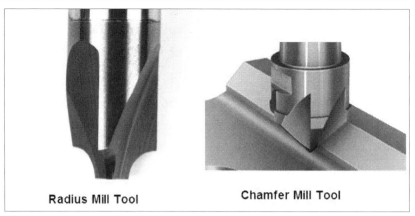

Figure-40. Radius mill and Chamfer mill tool

Slot Mill

The Slot mill tool is used to create slot or groove in the part metal. Figure-41 shows the shape of slot mill tool.

Figure-41. Slot mill tool

Taper Mill

In CNC machining, taper end mills are used in many industries for a large number of applications, such as walls with draft or clearance angle, tool and die work, mold work, even for reaming holes to make them conical. There are mainly two types of taper mills, Taper End Mill and Taper Ball Mill; refer to Figure-36.

Dove Mill

Dove mill or Dovetail cutters are designed for cutting dovetails in a wide variety of materials. Dovetail cutters can also be used for chamfering or milling angles on the bottom surface of a part. Dovetail cutters are available in a wide variety of diameters and in 45 degree or 60 degree angles; refer to Figure-42.

Figure-42. Dovetail milling cutters

Lollipop Mill

The Lollipop mill tool is used to cut round slot or undercuts in workpiece. Some tool suppliers use a name Undercut mill tool in place of Lollipop mill in their catalog. The shape of lollipop mill tool is given in Figure-43.

Figure-43. Lollipop mill tool

Engrave Mill

The Engrave mill tool is used to perform engraving on the surface of workpiece. Engraving has always been an art and it is also true for CNC machinist. You can find various shapes of engraving tool that are single flute or multi-flute; refer to Figure-44. You can use ball mill/end mill for engraving or you can use specialized engrave mill tool for engraving. This all depends on your requirement. If you want to perform engraving on softer materials or plastics then it is better to use ball end mill but if you want an artistic shade on the surface then use the respective engrave mill tool. Keep a note of maximum depth and spindle speed mentioned by your engrave mill tool supplier.

Figure-44. Engrave mill tools

Thread Mill

The Thread mill tool is used to generate internal or external threads in the workpiece. The most common question here is if we have Taps to create thread then why is there need of Thread mill tool. The answer is less machining time on CNC, tool cost saving, more parts per tool, and better thread finish. Now, you will ask why to use tapping. The answer is low machine cost. Figure-45 shows thread mill tools.

Figure–45. Thread Mill

Barrel Mill

Barrel Mill tool is the tool recently being highly used in machining turbine/impeller blades and other 5-axis milling operations. Barrel Mill has conical shape with radius at its end; refer toFigure-46. Note that earlier Ball mill tools were used for irregular surface contouring but Barrel Mill tools give much better surface finish so they are highly in demand for 5-axis milling now a days.

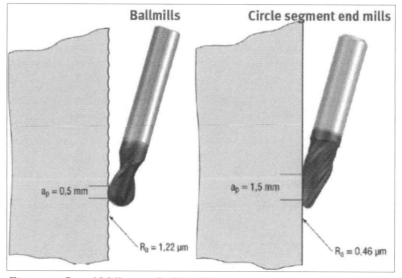

Figure–46. Barrel Mill versus Ball Mill Tool

Drill Bit

Drill bit is used to make a hole in the workpiece. The hole shape depends on the shape of drill bit. Drill bits for various purposes are shown in Figure-47. Note that drill is the machine or holder in which drill bit is installed to make cylindrical holes. There are mainly four categories of drill bit; Twist drill bit, Step drill bit, Unibit (or conical bit), and Hole Saw bit (Refer to Figure-48). Twist drill bits are used for drilling holes in wood, metal, plastic and other materials. For soft materials the point angle is 90 degree, for hard materials the point angle is 150 degree and general purpose twist drill bits have angle of 150 degree at end point. The Step drill bits are used to make counter bore or countersunk holes. The Unibits are generally used for drilling holes in sheetmetal but they can also be used for drilling plastic, plywood, aluminium and thin steel sheets. One unibit can give holes of different sizes. The Hole saw bit is used to cut a large hole from the workpiece. They remove material only from the edge of the hole, cutting out an intact disc of material, unlike many drills which remove all material in the interior of the hole. They can be used to make large holes in wood, sheet metal, and other materials.

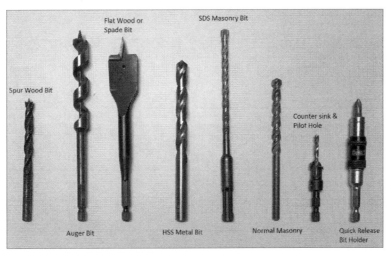

Figure-47. Drill Bits for different purposes

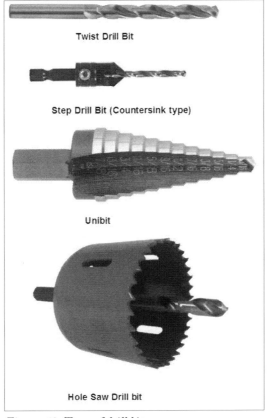

Figure-48. Types of drill bits

Reamer

Reamer is a tool similar to drill bit but its purpose is to finish the hole or increase the size of hole precisely. Figure-49 shows the shape of a reamer.

Bore Bar

Bore Bar or Boring Bar is used to increase the size of hole; refer to Figure-50. One common question is why to use bore bar if we can perform reaming or why to perform reaming when we have bore bar. The answer is accuracy. A reamer does not give tight tolerance in location but gives good finish in hole diameter. A bore bar gives tight tolerance in location but takes more time to machine hole as compared to reamer. The decision to choose the process is on machinist. If you need a highly accurate hole then perform drilling, then boring and then reaming to get best result.

Figure-50. Boring Bar

Figure-49. Reamer tool

Lathe Tools or Turning Tools

The tools used in CNC lathe machines use a different nomenclature. In CNC lathe machines, we use insert for cutting material. The Insert Holder and Inserts have a special nomenclature scheme to define their shapes. First we will discuss the nomenclature of Insert holder and then we will discuss the nomenclature of Inserts.

Insert Holders

Turning holder names follow an ISO nomenclature standard. If you are working on a CNC shop floor with lathes, knowing the ISO nomenclature is a must. The name looks complicated, but is actually very easy to interpret; refer to Figure-51.

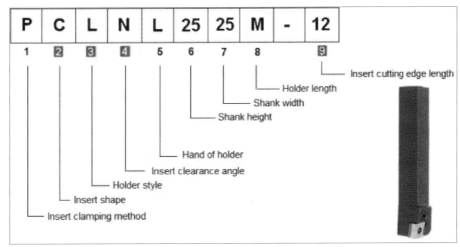

Figure-51. CNC Lathe Insert Holder nomenclature

When selecting a holder for an application, you mainly have to concentrate on the numbers marked in red in the above nomenclature. The others are decided automatically (e.g., the shank width and height are decided by the machine), or require less effort. In Figure-52, the rows with the question mark indicate the parameters that require the decision by machinist based on job.

	Parameter		How is this decided ?
1	Insert clamping method		Select based on cutting forces. Top clamping is the most sturdy, screw clamping the least.
2	Insert shape	?	Decided by the contour that you want to turn.
3	Holder style	?	Decided by the contour that you want to turn.
4	Insert clearance angle	?	Positive / Negative, based on application.
5	Hand of holder		Decided based on whether you want to cut towards the chuck or away from the chuck, and on turret position - turret front / rear
6	Shank height		Decided by holder size.
7	Shank width		Decided by machine.
8	Holder length		Decided by machine.
9	Insert cutting edge length	?	Decide based on depth of cut you want to use.

Figure-52. CNC Lathe Insert Holder nomenclature parameters

Figure-53 and Figure-54 show the options available for each of the parameters.

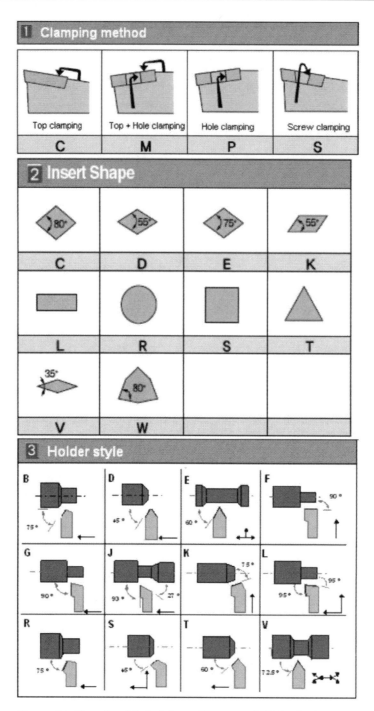

Figure-53. Clamping Method, Insert Shapes, and Holder Style

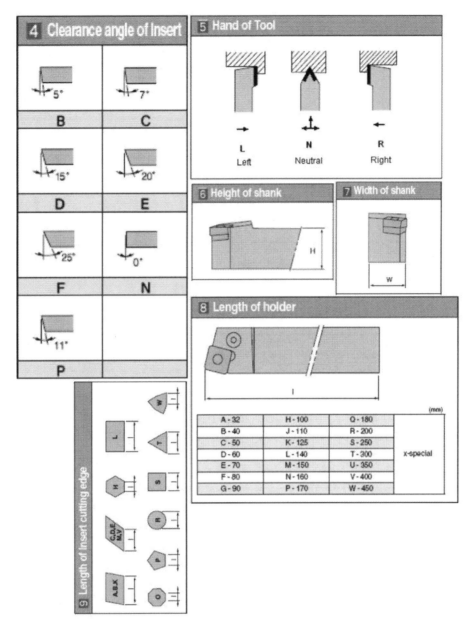

Figure-54. Insert Holder Parameters

CNC Lathe Insert Nomenclature

General CNC Insert name is given as

C	**N**	**M**	**G**	**12**	**04**	**08**
1	2	3	4	5	6	7

Meaning of each box in nomenclature is given next.

1 = Turning Insert Shape

The first letter in general turning insert nomenclature tells us about the general turning insert shape, turning inserts shape codes are like C, D, K, R, S, T, V, W. Most of these codes surely express the turning insert shape like

C = C Shape Turning Insert
D = D Shape Turning Insert

K = K Shape Turning Insert
R = Round Turning Insert
S = Square Turning Insert
T = Triangle Turning Insert
V = V Shape Turning Insert
W = W Shape Turning Insert

Figure-55 shows the turning inserts shapes.

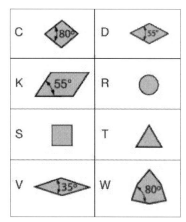

Figure-55. Turning Insert Shapes

The general turning insert shape play a very important role when we choose an insert for machining. Not every turning insert with one shape can be replaced with the other for a machining operation. As C, D, W type turning inserts are normally used for roughing or rough machining.

2 = Turning Insert Clearance Angle

The second letter in general turning insert nomenclature tells us about the turning insert clearance angle.

The clearance angle for a turning insert is shown in Figure-56.

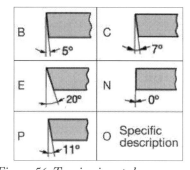

Figure-56. Turning insert clearance angle

Turning insert clearance angle plays a big role while choosing an insert for internal machining or boring small components, because if not properly chosen the insert bottom corner might rub with the component which will give poor machining. On the other hand a turning insert with 0° clearance angle is mostly used for rough machining.

3 = Turning Insert Tolerances

The third letter of general turning insert nomenclature tells us about the turning insert tolerances. Figure-57 shows the tolerance chart.

Code Letter	Cornerpoint (inches)	Thickness (inches)	Inscribed Circle (in)	Cornerpoint (mm)	Thickness (mm)	Inscribed Circle (mm)
A	.0002"	.001"	.001"	.005mm	.025mm	.025mm
C	.0005"	.001"	.001"	.013mm	.025mm	.025mm
E	.001"	.001"	.001"	.025mm	.025mm	.025mm
F	.0002"	.001"	.0005"	.005mm	.025mm	.013mm
G	.001"	.005"	.001"	.025mm	.13mm	.025mm
H	.0005"	.001"	.0005"	.013mm	.025mm	.013mm
J	.002"	.001"	.002-.005"	.005mm	.025mm	.05-.13mm
K	.0005"	.001"	.002-.005"	.013mm	.025mm	.05-.13mm
L	.001"	.001"	.002-.005"	.025mm	.025mm	.05-.13mm
M	.002-.005"	.005"	.002-.005"	.05-.13mm	.13mm	.05-.15mm
U	.005-.012"	.005"	.005-.010"	.06-.25mm	.13mm	.08-.25mm

Figure-57. Insert tolerance chart

4 = Turning Insert Type

The fourth letter of general turning insert nomenclature tells us about the turning insert hole shape and chip breaker type; refer to Figure-58.

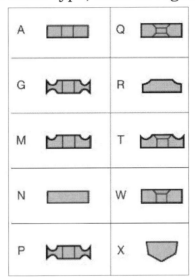

Figure-58. Turning Insert hole shape and chip breaker

5 = Turning Insert Size

This numeric value of general turning insert tells us the cutting edge length of the turning insert; refer to Figure-59.

Figure-59. Turning Insert Cutting Edge Length

6 = Turning Insert Thickness

This numeric value of general turning insert tells us about the thickness of the turning insert.

7 = Turning Insert Nose Radius

This numeric value of general turning insert tells us about the nose radius of the turning insert.

Code	=	Radius Value
04	=	0.4
08	=	0.8
12	=	1.2
16	=	1.6

You can learn more about machining tools from your tool supplier manual.

Creating New Mill Tool

You have learned to use an already available tool in the library but what if the tool is not available in library. The procedure to create a new mill tool is discussed next.

- Select **Library** option from **Local** node in the **Libraries** area of the **Select Tool** dialog box and click on the **New Mill Tool** button from the dialog box. The **Library** dialog box will be displayed; refer to Figure-60

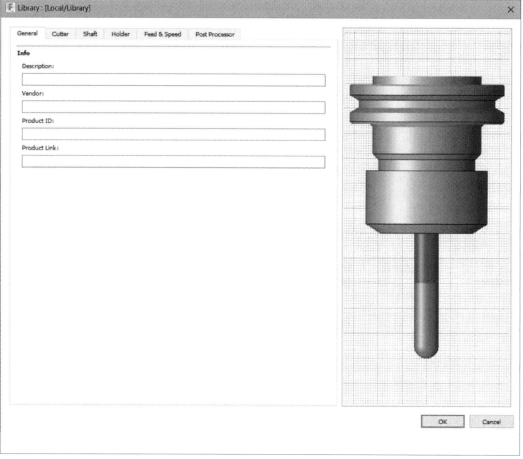

Figure-60. Library dialog box

- Specify the desired parameters in the edit boxes of the **General** tab in the dialog box like description of tool, name of vendor, and so on.
- Click on the **Cutter** tab in the dialog box. The options will be displayed as shown in Figure-61.

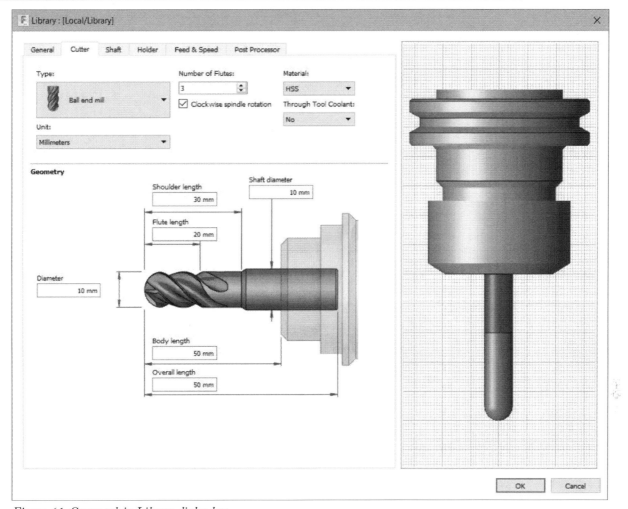

Figure-61. Cutter tab in Library dialog box

- Click on the **Type** drop-down of **Cutter** tab from **Library** dialog box and select the desired type of tool. The selected mill will be displayed in graphics section.
- Click on the **Material** drop-down and select the required material for tool.
- Click on the **Through Tool Coolant** drop-down from **Cutter** tab and select the desired option.
- Click on the **Unit** drop-down from **Cutter** tab and select the desired unit.
- Select the **Clockwise spindle rotation** check box to set the rotation of spindle to clockwise direction.
- Click in the **Number of flutes** edit box and enter the enter the desired value.
- Specify the information about the tool in **Info** section of **Cutter** tab in their respective edit box.
- Click in the **Diameter** edit box of **Cutting Edge** section and specify the diameter of tool.
- Click in the **Shaft diameter** edit box of **Cutting Edge** section and specify the diameter of shaft.
- Similarly, click in the other edit boxes and specify the desired parameters in **Geometry** area of **Cutter** tab.
- Click on the **Shaft** tab from **Library** dialog box. The **Shaft** tab will be displayed; refer to Figure-62

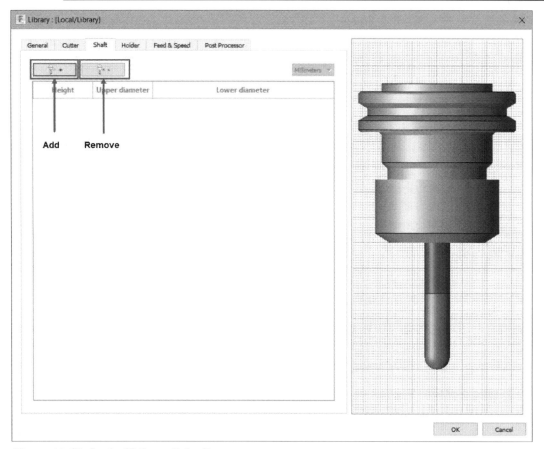

Figure-62. Shaft tab of Library dialog Box

- To add the shaft, click on the **Add** button and if you want to delete the created shaft then click on the **Remove** button from **Shaft** tab.
- After adding shaft, double-click on the shaft parameter to be changed from the table and specify the desired value to edit the dimension of created shaft; refer to Figure-63.

Figure-63. Editing the value of shaft

- Click on the **Holder** tab from **Library** dialog box to select the desired tool holder. The **Holder** tab will be displayed; refer to Figure-64.

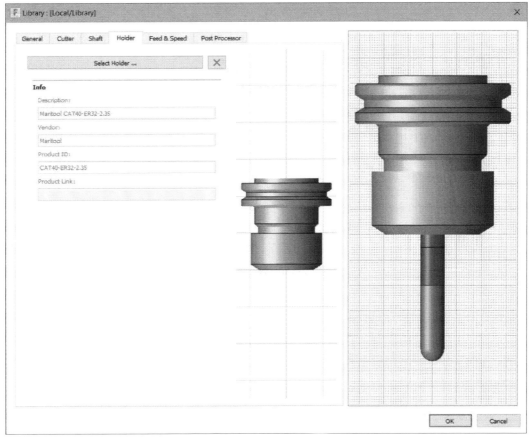

Figure-64. Holder tab

- Click on the **Select Holder** button from **Holder** tab. The **Select Holder** dialog box will be displayed; refer to Figure-65.

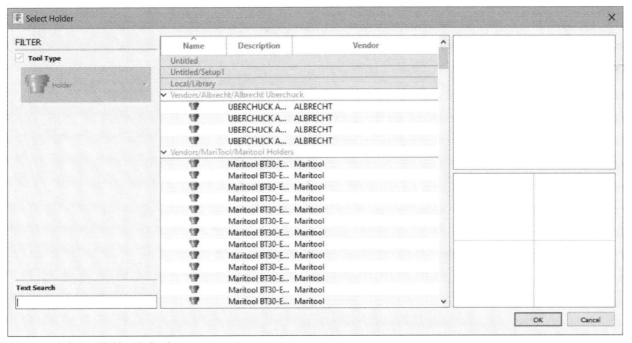

Figure-65. Select Holder dialog box

- Select the desired holder from table and click on the **OK** button from **Select Holder** dialog box. The selected holder will be displayed in **Holder** tab of **Library** dialog box.

- Click on the **Feed & Speed** tab of **Library** dialog box to set the feed and speed of tool. The **Feed & Speed** tab will be displayed; refer to Figure-66.

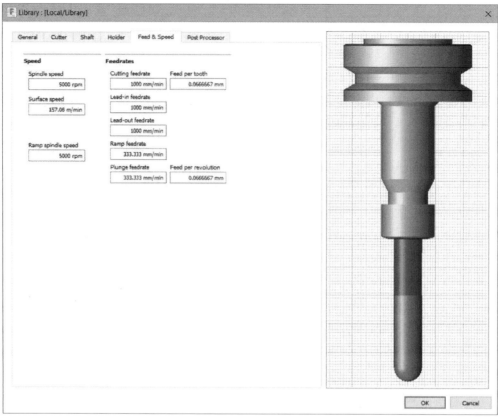

Figure-66. Feed & Speed tab

- Click in the edit boxes and specify the desired values to define speed and feed rates.
- Click in the **Post Processor** tab of **Library** dialog box to specify the post processor values of NC machining. The **Post Processor** tab will be displayed; refer to Figure-67.

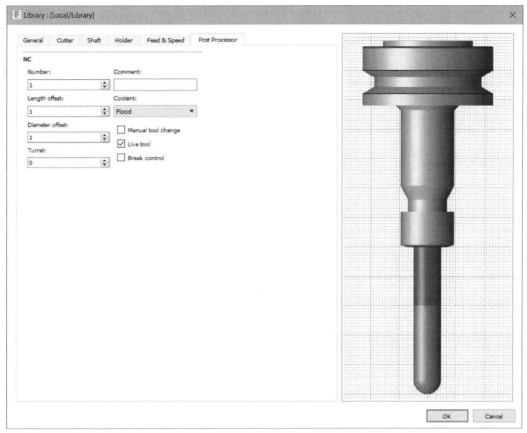

Figure-67. Post Processor tab

- Click in the edit boxes and specify the desired values for post processing.
- Click in the **Coolant** drop-down and select the desired coolant type for the tool.
- After specifying the parameters in **Library** dialog box, click on the **OK** button. The mill tool will be added in the tools list.

Creating New Holder

In this section, we will discuss about the procedure of creating new tool holder. The procedure is discussed next.

- Click on the **New Holder** button from **Select Tool** dialog box. The **Library** dialog box will be displayed; refer to Figure-49.

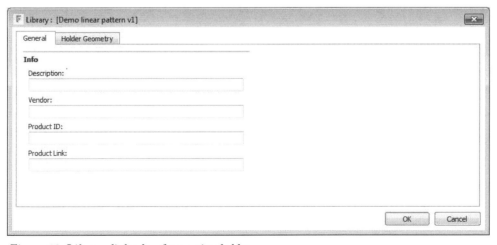

Figure-68. Library dialog box for creating holder

- Click in the edit boxes of **General** tab from **Library** dialog box and specify the information of holder as desired.
- Click in the **Holder Geometry** tab from **Library** dialog box to view or change the geometry of holder; refer to Figure-69.

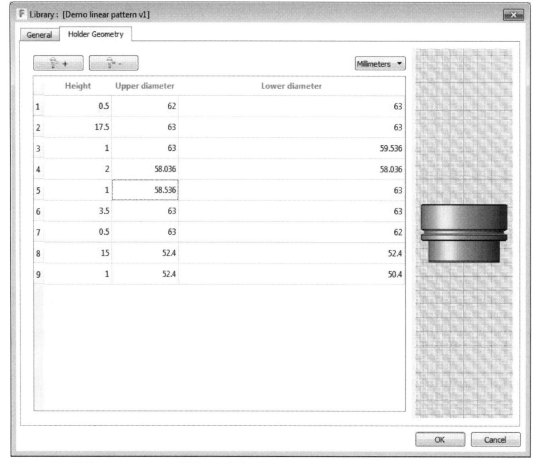

Figure-69. Holder Geometry tab of Library dialog box

- To change a parameter, double-click on it and specify the desired value. The holder in graphic window will be updated.
- After specifying the parameter, click on the **OK** button from **Library** dialog box. The created tool holder will be displayed in **Select Tool** dialog box.

Creating New Turning tool

In this section, we will discuss about the procedure of creating a new turning tool. The procedure is discussed next.

- Click on the **New Turning** tool from **Select Tool** dialog box. The **Library** dialog box will be displayed; refer to Figure-70.
- Specify the desired parameters in the dialog box.
- Click on the **Insert** tab from the dialog box. The dialog box will be displayed as shown in Figure-71.

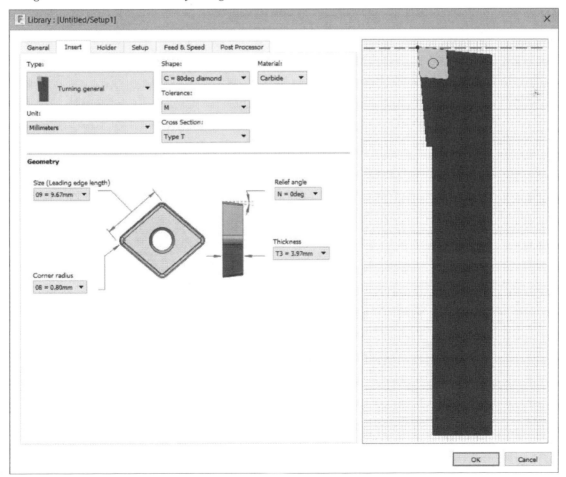

Figure-70. General tab in Library dialog box

Figure-71. Library dialog box for turning tool

- Click in the **Type** drop-down from **Insert** tab and select the desired turning tool type.
- Specify the desired information about the tool in **Geometry** section of **Insert** tab in various drop-downs.
- Click on the **Shape** drop-down and select the desired shape type for tool.
- Click on the **Relief angle** drop-down of **Insert** tab and select the desired option to define relief angle.
- Similarly, set the other options of turning tool in **Insert** tab.
- Specify the desired parameter of **Holder** tab in **Library** dialog box as discussed earlier.
- Click in the **Setup** tab from **Library** dialog box to setup the tool. The **Setup** tab will be displayed; refer to Figure-72.

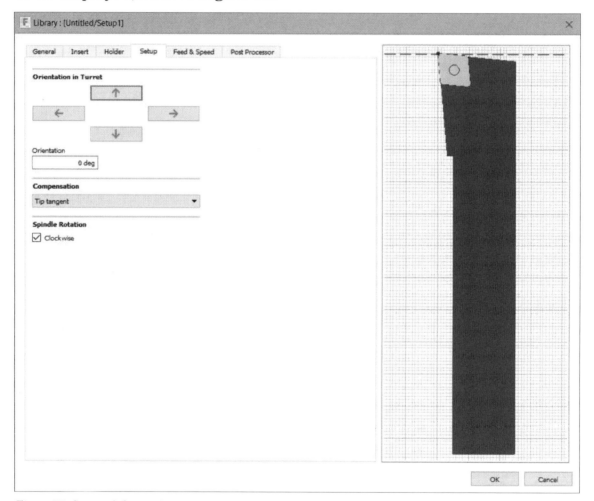

Figure-72. Setup tab for turning

- The four arrows keys are used to define the orientation of the tool in turret. This orientation defines which side of tool holder will be used for cutting. Click on the upper key to orient the tool's tip upward, left key to orient the tool to left side, right key to orient the tool to right side, and down key to orient the tool's tip downward. If you want to orient the tool at specified angle then click in the **Orientation** edit box and specify the angle.
- Click on the **Compensation** drop-down from **Setup** tab and select the desired option.
- Select the **Clockwise** check box from **Spindle Rotation** section to specify the rotation direction of spindle as clockwise.

- Set the parameters in other tabs of **Library** dialog box and click on the **OK** button. The new turning tool will be displayed in **Select Tool** dialog box.

Creating new tool for Waterjet/ Plasma Cutter/ Laser Cutter

In this section, we will discuss about the procedure of creating the Waterjet/Plasma Cutter/Laser Cutter tool. The procedure is discussed next.

- Click on the **Create new tool for waterjet, laser, and plasma cutting** tool from **Select Tool** dialog box. The **Library** dialog box will be displayed; refer to Figure-73.

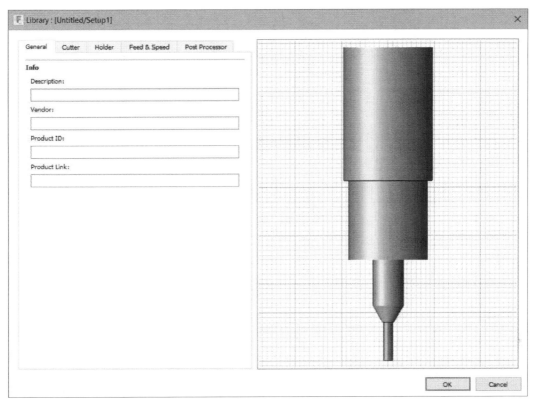

Figure-73. Library dialog box for waterjet

- The options of **Library** dialog box are similar as discussed earlier in **Creating New Mill tool** section of this chapter.
- After specifying the parameters, click on the **OK** button from **Library** dialog box. The created tool will be displayed in **Select Tool** dialog box.
- After selecting the required tool from **Select Tool** dialog box, click on the **OK** button. The tool will be selected for the required operation.

PRACTICAL

Create the stock of the given model Figure-74 and create the required milling tool.

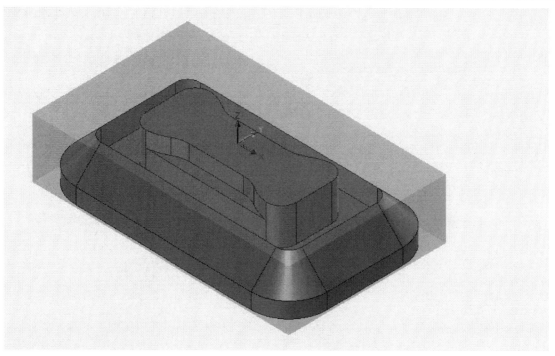

Figure-74. Practical 1

Opening Model in CAM

- Create and save the part in **DESIGN** workspace. The part file is also available in the chapter 15 folder of **Autodesk Fusion 360** resource kit so you can open it from there instead of creating.
- Click on the **MANUFACTURE** option from **Workspace** drop-down. The model will be displayed in the **MANUFACTURE** workspace; refer to Figure-75.

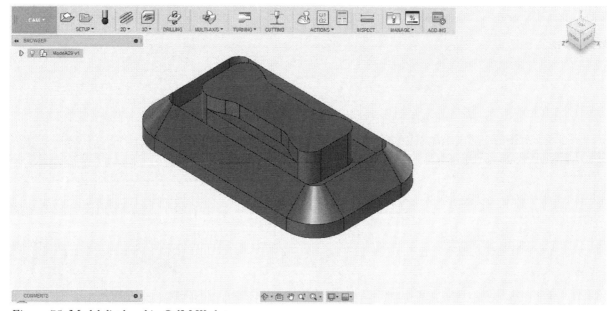

Figure-75. Model displayed in CAM Workspace

Creating Setup

- Click on the **New Setup** tool of **SETUP** drop-down from **Toolbar**. The **SETUP** dialog box will be displayed along with the setup; refer to Figure-76.

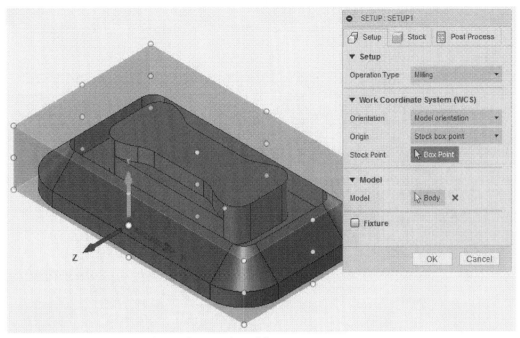

Figure-76. SETUP DIALOG box along with model

- Click on the **Milling** option of **Operation Type** drop-down from **Setup** tab to specify the type of operation.
- Click on the **Select Z axis/plane & X axis** option of **Orientation** drop-down from **Setup** tab and select the Z-axis for milling; refer to Figure-77.

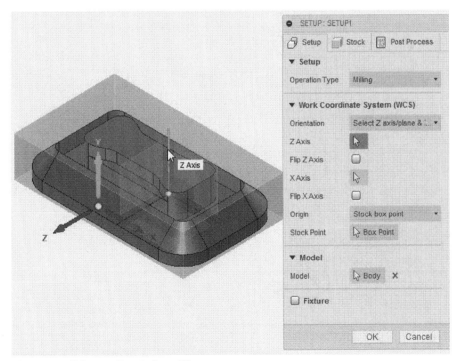

Figure-77. Selecting Z axis for milling

- The **Arrow** button of **X Axis** option is active by default. You need to click on the Z axis from origin to select as X axis.
- Click on the **Box Point** button of **Stock Point** option from **SETUP** tab and select the box point as displayed in the Figure-78.

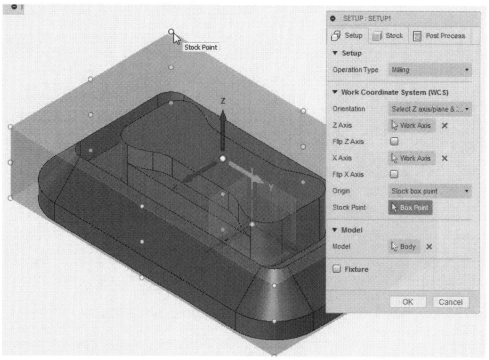

Figure-78. Selecting stock point

- Click on the **Relative Size Box** option of **Mode** drop-down from **Stock** tab and enter the parameters as shown in Figure-79.

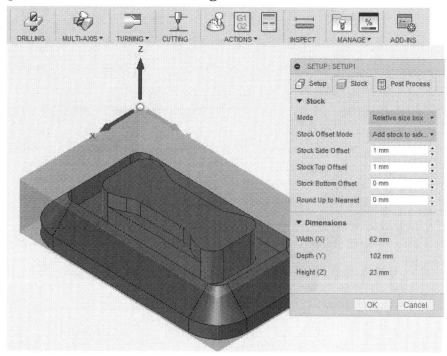

Figure-79. Specifying the parameters for creating stock

- After specifying the parameters of **SETUP** dialog box, click on the **OK** button from **SETUP** dialog box. The stock of model will be created.

Creating a new Milling tool

- Before creating a new tool, you need to know the inner and outer dimension of the model like height of pocket, radius, etc. Use the **Measure** tool in **INSPECT** drop-down of **Toolbar** to find out parameters.

- Click on the **Tool Library** tool of **MANAGE** drop-down from **Toolbar**. The **CAM Tool Library** dialog box will be displayed.
- Click on the **New Mill Tool** button of **CAM Tool Library** dialog box; refer to Figure-80. The **Library** dialog box will be displayed.

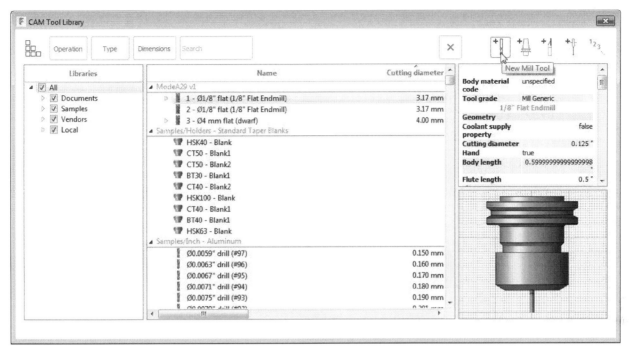

Figure-80. Creating new mill tool

- Enter the desired parameters in the **General** and **Cutter** tab of **Library** dialog box; refer to Figure-81.

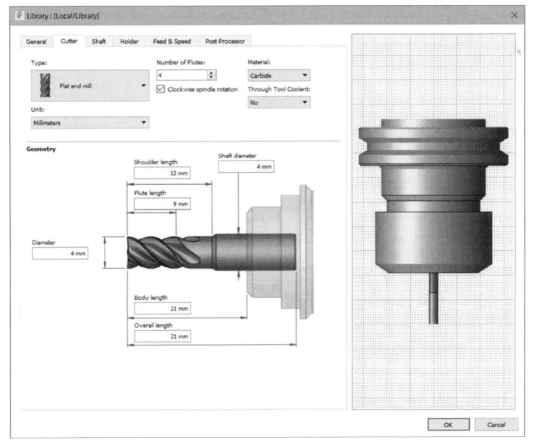

Figure-81. Cutter tab

- Click on the **Shaft** tab of **Library** dialog box and specify the parameters as displayed in Figure-82.

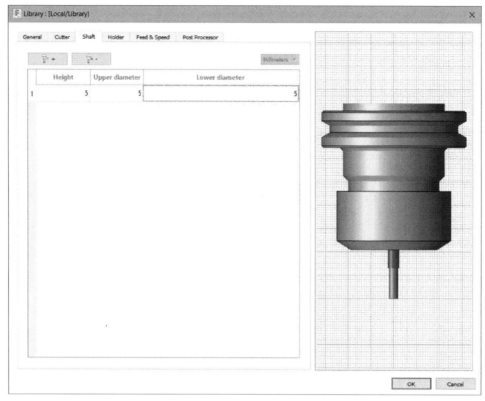

Figure-82. Shaft tab

- Click on the **Holder** tab of **Library** dialog box. The **Holder** tab will be displayed.
- Click on the **Select Holder** button of **Holder** tab. The **Select Holder** dialog box will be displayed.
- Select the holder as displayed in Figure-83 and click on **OK** button from **Select Holder** dialog box.

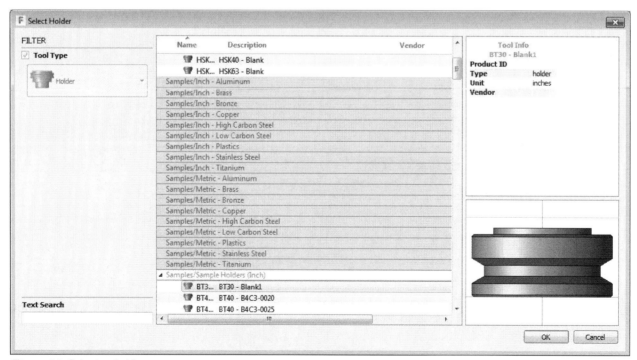

Figure-83. Selecting holder

- Click on the **Feed & Speed** tab of **Library** dialog box and specify the parameters as shown in Figure-84.

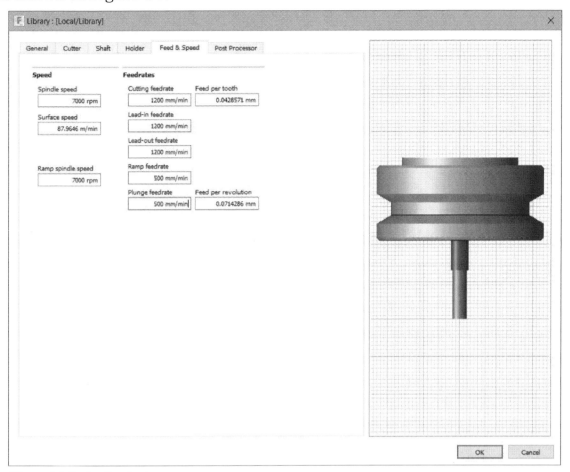

Figure-84. Feed & Speed tab

- After specifying the parameters, click on the **OK** button from **Library** dialog box. The tool will be created and displayed in the tool library.

PRACTICAL 2

Create the stock for lathe machining as shown in Figure-85.

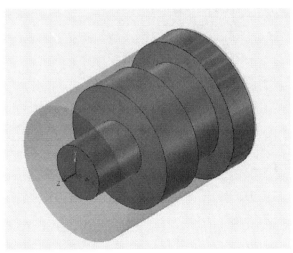

Figure-85. Practical 2

Adding model in CAM Workspace

- Create and save the part in **DESIGN** workspace. The part file is also available in the respective chapter folder of **Autodesk Fusion 360 Resources** folder.
- Click on the **MANUFACTURE** option from **Workspace** drop-down. The model will be displayed in the **MANUFACTURE** workspace; refer to Figure-86.

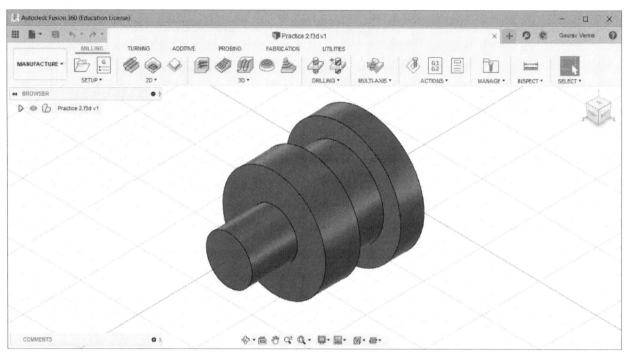

Figure-86. Model in CAM Workspace

Creating Setup

- Click on the **New Setup** tool of **SETUP** drop-down from **Toolbar**. The **SETUP** dialog box will be displayed along with the stock of model; refer to Figure-87.

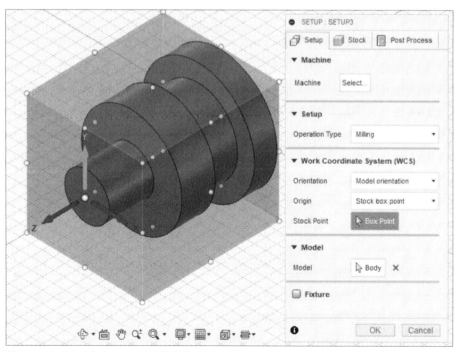

Figure-87. Model along with SETUP dialog box

- Click on the **Turning or mill/turn** option of **Operation Type** drop-down from **Setup** tab to specify the machining type.

- The **Arrow** button of **Z Axis(Rotary Axis)** option is active by default. Select the edge as displayed in Figure-88.

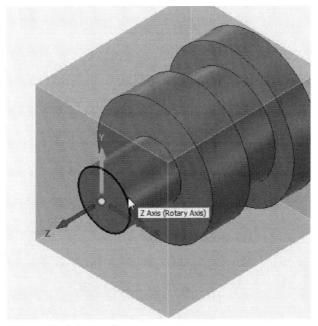

Figure-88. Selecting Z axis

- Click on the **Stock** tab of **SETUP** dialog box and specify the parameters as displayed in Figure-89.

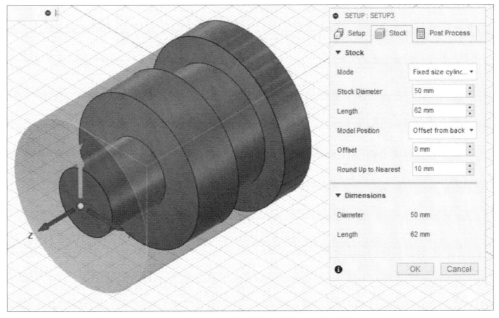

Figure-89. Specifying parameters in stock tab

- Click in the **Post Process** tab of **SETUP** dialog box and specify the parameters as displayed in Figure-90.

Figure-90. Post process tab of turning

- After specifying the parameters, click on the **OK** button from **SETUP** dialog box. The stock will be created and displayed on the model; refer to Figure-91.

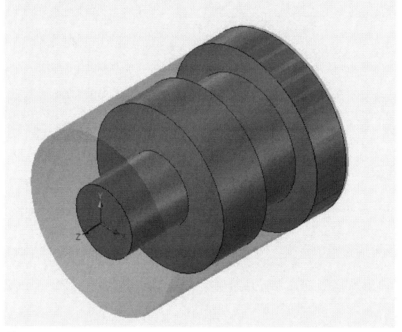

Figure-91. Practical 2

Creating new Turning tool

- Before creating a new tool, you need to know the dimensions of slot, radius of part, length of part, etc. Use the **Measure** tool in **INSPECT** drop-down to find out various parameters.
- Click on the **Tool Library** tool of **MANAGE** drop-down from **Toolbar**. The **CAM Tool Library** dialog box will be displayed.
- Click on the **New Turn Tool** button of **CAM Tool Library** dialog box; refer to Figure-92. The **Library** dialog box will be displayed.

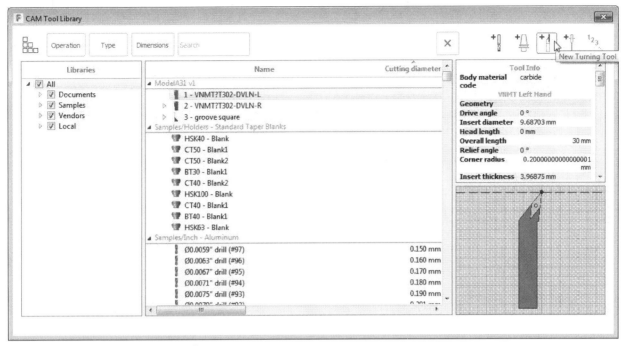

Figure-92. Creating new turning tool

- Specify the **Description** of tool as Roughing tool in the **General** tab of dialog box.
- Specify the parameters of **Insert** tab from **Library** dialog box as displayed in Figure-93.

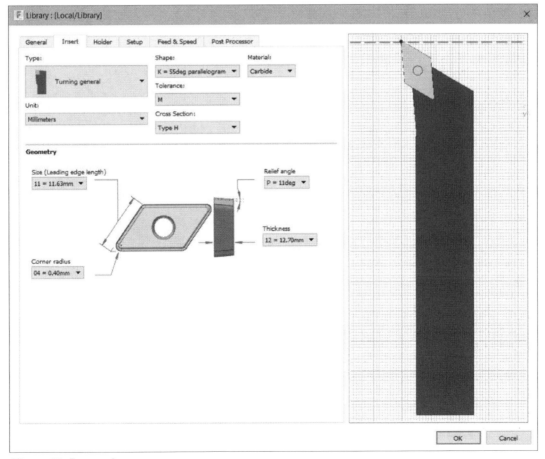

Figure-93. Insert tab

- Click on the **Holder** tab of **Library** dialog box and specify the parameters as displayed in Figure-94.

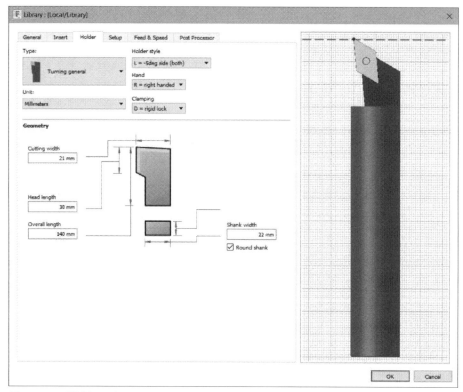

Figure-94. Holder tab

- Click on the **Feed & Speed** tab of **Library** dialog box and enter the parameters as displayed in Figure-95.

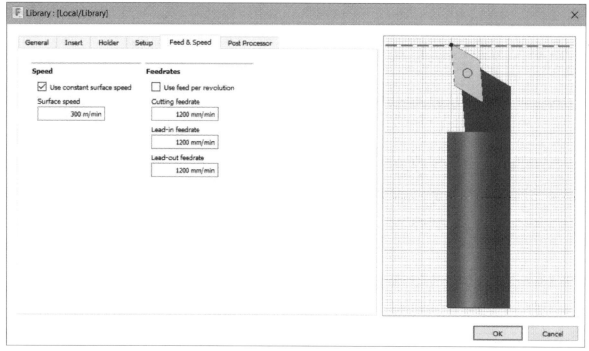

Figure-95. Feed & Speed tab

- After specifying the parameters, click on the **OK** button from **Library** dialog box. The tool will be created and displayed in the tool library.

SELF ASSESSMENT

Q1. Which of the following workspace is used to generate toolpaths for NC programs?

a. DESIGN   b. ANIMATION
c. SIMULATION   d. MANUFACTURE

Q2. The **New Setup** tool in **SETUP** panel can be used to prepare model for additive manufacturing. (T/F)

Q3. If the workpiece provided for machining your part has an irregular shape then which of the following stock mode should be used?

a. Relative size cylinder   b. Fixed size box
c. From Part   d. Fixed size tube

Q4. Generally in NC programming G54 through G59 codes are used to define work coordinate system offsets. (T/F)

Q5. Which of the following cutting tools can be used for pocket milling?

a. Spot Drill   b. Thread
c. Dovetail   d. Radius

Q6. Engrave mill tool is used to apply chamfer at the edges of part. (T/F)

PRACTICE

Create the stock of given part; refer to Figure-96.

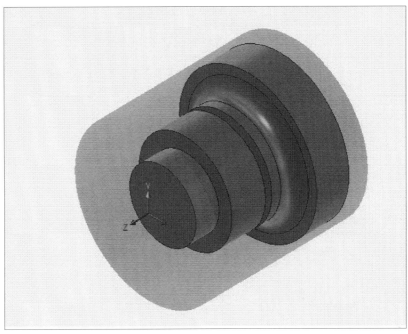

Figure-96. Practice

F<small>OR</small> S<small>TUDENT</small> N<small>OTES</small>

F<small>OR</small> S<small>TUDENT</small> N<small>OTES</small>

Chapter 16

Generating Milling Toolpaths - 1

Topics Covered

The major topics covered in this chapter are:

- *2D Pocket Toolpath*
- *2D Contour Toolpath*
- *Trace Toolpath*
- *Bore Toolpath*
- *Engrave Toolpath*
- *Adaptive Clearing Toolpath*
- *Parallel Toolpath*
- *Contour Toolpath*
- *Horizontal Toolpath*
- *Scallop Toolpath*

GENERATING 2D TOOLPATHS

Till now, we have discussed the procedure of creating the stock and placing the tool on the stock. In this section, we will learn to create the 2D toolpaths using tools in **2D** drop-down of **MILLING** tab in the **Toolbar**.

2D Adaptive Clearing

The **2D Adaptive Clearing** tool is used to create a machining operation on the part which uses the adaptive path as per the parts curvature to avoid abrupt direction changes. The procedure to use this tool is discussed next.

- Click on the **2D Adaptive Clearing** tool of **2D** drop-down from **Toolbar**; refer to Figure-1. The **2D ADAPTIVE** dialog box will be displayed; refer to Figure-2.

Figure-1. 2D Adaptive Clearing tool

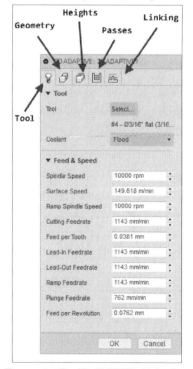

Figure-2. 2D ADAPTIVE dialog box

- Click on the **Select** button of **Tool** section from **2D ADAPTIVE** dialog box. The **Select Tool** dialog box will be displayed.

- Select dia. 3/16 - flat Endmill (High Carbon Steel) tool from the dialog box and click on the **OK** button.
- Specify the parameters as shown in Figure-2.

Geometry

In this section, we will discuss the procedure of selecting the geometry for removal of the extra material from workpiece. The procedure is discussed next.

- Click on the **Geometry** tab from **2D ADAPTIVE** dialog box. The geometry tab will be displayed; refer to Figure-3.

Figure-3. Geometry tab for 2D ADAPTIVE dialog box

- The **Nothing** selection button of **Pocket Selections** section in **Geometry** node is active by default. Click on the geometries of model to be machined as shown in Figure-4.

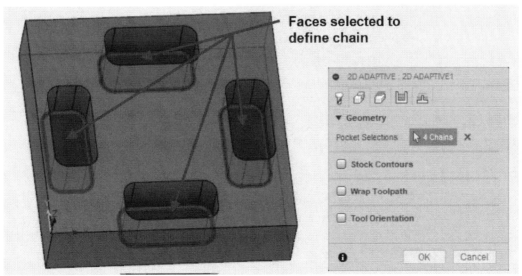

Figure-4. Selected geometry for 2D adaptive

- Select the **Stock Contours** check box of **Geometry** tab from **2D ADAPTIVE** dialog box to specify the boundaries of stock. After selecting this check box, select the edges to define boundaries of stock, the tool will not perform cutting move outside this boundary.
- Select the **Rest Machining** check box of **Geometry** tab from the dialog box to machine only left over material from previous tool. Specify the tool diameter and corner radius if previous tool for rest machining in the respective edit boxes of **Rest Machining** node.
- Select the **Wrap Toolpath** check box of **Geometry** tab from **2D ADAPTIVE** dialog box to wrap the toolpath around a cylinder. This check box is generally used in creating a toolpath for round shaped body.
- Select the **Tool Orientation** check box of **Geometry** tab from **2D ADAPTIVE** dialog box to override the orientation of tool earlier defined in setup. The procedure to orient the tool has been discussed earlier.

Heights

The **Heights** tab of the **2D ADAPTIVE** dialog box is used to set height of different planes for standard tool movement. The procedure to define these heights are discussed next.

- Click on the **Heights** tab of **2D ADAPTIVE** dialog box. The **Heights** tab will be displayed along with model; refer to Figure-5.

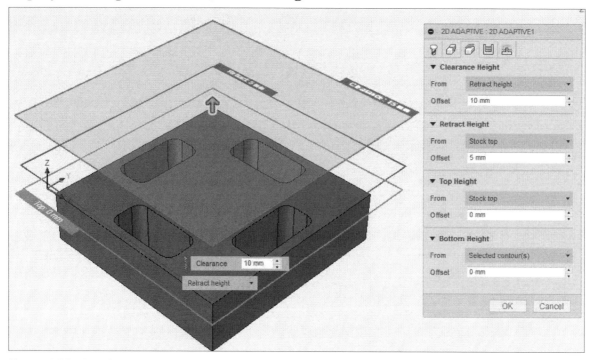

Figure-5. Heights tab

- The Clearance height is the distance between tool and workpiece at which the tool rapidly moves before the start of the toolpath for machining process.
- Click on the **From** drop-down of **Clearance Height** section from **Heights** tab and select the desired reference from which height will be measured.
- Click in the **Offset** edit box of **Clearance Height** section and specify the value of distance from selected reference.
- The Retract height is the distance at which tool moves upward after a cutting pass and before performing the next pass of machining or cutting. The Retract height should be set above the Feed Height and Top of workpiece.

- Click on the **From** drop-down of **Retract Height** section from **Heights** tab and select the desired parameter.
- Click in the **Offset** edit box of **Retract Height** section and specify the value of retract height from selected reference.
- The Top height is the term used to define the top of the cut.
- Click on the **From** drop-down of **Top Height** section from **Heights** tab and select the desired parameter.
- Click in the **Offset** edit box of **Top Height** section and specify height from selected reference.
- The Bottom Height is the term used to define the depth of the cut in a workpiece. If it is not defined in the dialog box then system will automatically assume the stock depth.
- Click on the **From** drop-down of **Bottom Height** section from **Heights** tab and select the desired parameter.
- Click in the **Offset** edit box of **Bottom Height** section and specify the distance from selected reference for bottom height.

Passes

The options in **Passes** tab are used to define various parameters related to cutting and non-cutting passes of tool. These options are discussed next.

Passes Options

- Click on the **Passes** tab of **2D ADAPTIVE** dialog box. The options of the tab will be displayed as shown in Figure-6.

Figure-6. Passes tab

- Click in the **Tolerance** edit box of **Passes** section from **Passes** tab and enter the desired value of deviation allowed between linear representation of curve and their original form while cutting. A lower value of tolerance can increase processing time or make the tool path impossible to cut by your tool if you are using a roughing tool.

- Click in the **Optimal Load** edit box of **Passes** section from **Passes** tab and enter the desired value to specify the amount of engagement the adaptive strategies should maintain. This is the amount of material being removed in one cutting pass while tool is in same XY plane. The Optimal load parameter is directly linked with tool diameter and strength.

- Select the **Both Ways** check box to allow cutting during both forward and return motion of tool. Note that using this option can increase the load on tool and workpiece so you should select it cautiously and only for soft materials. On selecting this check box, the **Optimal Load Other Way** and **Other Way Feedrate** edit boxes will be displayed below the check box. Specify the lower values of optimal load and feedrate in these edit boxes to reduce chances of accident.

- Click in the **Minimum Cutting Radius** edit box and enter the desired value minimum cutting radius that can be achieved while machining. If a corner on workpiece has fillet value lower than specified value then it will be ignored while machining.

- Select the **Use Slot Clearing** check box to start cutting from the middle of slot with plunge entry and continue a spiral motion for rest of the pocket; refer to Figure-7.

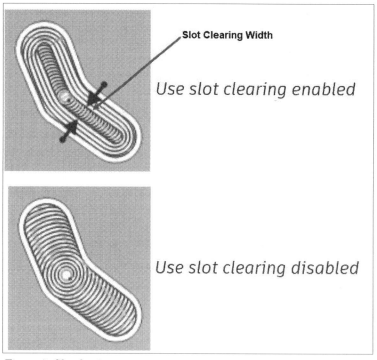

Figure-7. Slot clearing

- Click in the **Slot Clearing Width** edit box and enter the desired value of slot.

- Select **Conventional** option from **Direction** drop-down of **Passes** section to specify the material removal process by conventional milling. In **Conventional** milling, the cutting process is performed in opposite direction of tool movement which causes the tool to scoop up the material; refer to Figure-8. The cutting process is starts at zero thickness and increases up to maximum.

- Click on the **Climb** option of **Direction** drop-down from **Passes** section to specify the material removal process by climb milling. In climb milling, the cutting process starts by machining maximum thickness and then decreases to zero.

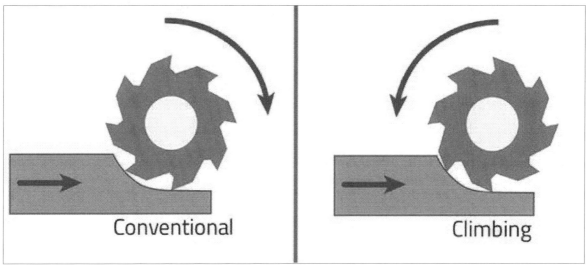

Figure-8. Conventional and climb machining

Multiple Depth Options

- Select the **Multiple Depths** check box from **Passes** tab to cut the material in multiple depths instead of cutting in one go. Note that every tool has a cutting length out of which it does not cut material. When the Multiple Depths check box is not selected then the tool will cut only upto the depth allowed by its cutting length.

- Click in the **Maximum Roughing Stepdown** edit box and enter the maximum value of step-down distance between two roughing depths.

- Select the **Order By Depth** check box to sequence machining by pockets based on their depths.

- Select the **Order By Area** check box to sequence machining by pockets based on their areas.

Stock To Leave Options

- Select the **Stock to leave** check box from **Passes** tab to define the amount of stock to leave on the workpiece after roughing. This stock will be removed in finishing pass.

- Click in the **Radial Stock to Leave** edit box of **Stock to Leave** section and enter the value of stock to remain along round face of part or side walls of the pockets.

- Click in the **Axial Stock to Leave** check box edit box of **Stock to Leave** section and enter the value of stock to remain on bottom flat surface/face of pocket.

Smoothing Options

- Select the **Smoothing** check box from **Passes** tab to smooth the toolpath by removing excessive points and fitting arcs within a specified tolerance. Selecting this check box can reduce the size of G-codes as it will convert multiple connected lines into arcs wherever possible and similarly, multiple consecutive points into a line.

- Click in the **Smoothing Tolerance** edit box of **Smoothing** section and enter the desired value of tolerance.

Feed Optimization Options

- Select the **Feed Optimization** check box of **Passes** tab to specify the reduced feed at corners and curves. Note that the feed optimization options will not be available if **Both Ways** check box is selected in the dialog box.

- Click in the **Maximum Directional Change** check box of **Feed Optimization** section and specify the maximum value of angle change allowed before feed rate is changed automatically to lower value.
- Click in the **Reduced Feed Radius** edit box and specify the value of minimum radius allowed before the feed is reduced.
- Click in the **Reduced Feed Distance** edit box and specify the value of distance before a corner to reduce the feed rate.
- Click in the **Reduced Feedrate** edit box and specify the value to specify the slower feed rate to be used when the tool is moving in X direction while cutting material.
- Select the **Only Inner Corners** check box of **Feed Optimization** section to reduce the feed rate at inner corners.

Linking

The options of **Linking** tab are used to define, how toolpath passes should be linked in different directions. The procedure to use this options is discussed next.

- Click on the **Linking** tab from **2D ADAPTIVE** dialog box. The options of **Linking** tab will be displayed; refer to Figure-9.

Figure-9. Linking tab

Linking Options

- Select **Full retraction** option of **Retraction Policy** drop-down to retract the tool up to retract height at the end of cutting pass before moving to the start of next machining pass.

- Select **Minimum retraction** option of **Retraction Policy** drop-down to move the tool up to the minimum retraction height from one cutting pass to other pass where the tool clears the workpiece.
- The **High Feedrate Mode** drop-down is used to specify the tool rapid movements which should be output as true rapid movement. Click on the **High Feedrate Mode** drop-down and select the desired option to define in which direction the rapid movement of tool will be retained during cutting.
- Select the **Allow Rapid Retract** check box from **Linking** tab to do the retracts as rapid movements. Clear the **Allow Rapid Retract** check box to force retract at lead-out feedrate.
- Click in the **Maximum Stay-Down Distance** edit box and enter the maximum value of distance between different cutting passes for which the tool stays down and does not retract.
- Click in the **Minimum Stay-Down Clearance** edit box and enter the radial clearance distance values for the stay down moves.
- Click on the **Stay-Down Level** drop-down of **Linking** section and select the desired option to control how much the tool will try to stay down around obstacles during cutting process.
- Click in the **Lift Height** edit box and enter the value of distance lift during reposition moves of the tool.
- Click in the **No-Engagement Feedrate** edit box of **Linking** section to specify the feedrate used for rapid movements where the tool is not in engagement with the material of workpiece during cutting pass.

Leads and Transitions

- The options of **Leads & Transitions** section of **Linking** tab is used to specify how leads and transitions should be generated at the time of tool entering or exiting the material.
- Click in the **Horizontal Lead In/Out Radius** edit box and enter the value of radius required for horizontal entry/exit.
- Click in the **Vertical Lead In/Out Radius** edit box and enter the value of radius required for vertical entry/exit.

Ramp Options

- The options in **Ramps** section of **Linking** tab are used to define how tool will entry into the material during its first cutting pass.
- Hover the cursor on the options of **Ramp Type** drop-down, the explanation of these options will be displayed on the screen. Select the option as required and specify related parameters.

Position Options

- The options of **Positions** section of **Linking** tab are used to specify the tool entry point and predrill positions if required.
- The **Nothing** selection button of **Predrill Positions** section is active by default. Click on the point in workpiece where drill has been done earlier so that the cutting tool can enter the material.
- Click on the **Nothing** selection button of **Entry Positions** section and click on the geometry near the location of workpiece where you want to enter the tool.
- After specifying the parameter for **2D ADAPTIVE** dialog box, click on the **OK** button. The toolpath will be created and displayed on the workpiece; refer to Figure-10.

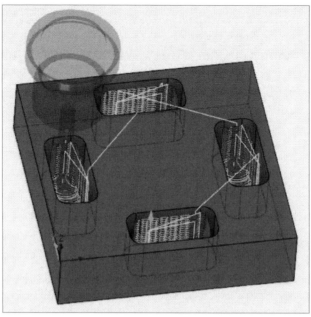

Figure-10. Toolpath created by adaptive clearing

- The option of the created toolpath will be added in **BROWSER**. Right-click on the toolpath. A shortcut menu will be displayed; refer to Figure-11.

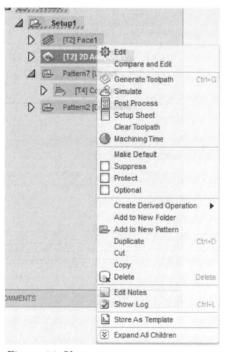

Figure-11. Shortcut menu

- If you want to edit the parameters then click on the **Edit** button from shortcut menu. The dialog box will be displayed of the selected toolpath.
- If you want to check the animation of material cutting by selected toolpath then click on the **Simulate** button. The **SIMULATE** dialog box will be displayed along with simulation keys. Click on the **Play** or **Pause** button as required.
- The other tools of this shortcut menu will be discussed later.

2D POCKET

The **2D Pocket** tool is used to remove the material from pockets in the model. The procedure to use this tool is discussed next.

- Click on the **2D Pocket** tool of **2D** drop-down in **MILLING** tab from **Toolbar**; refer to Figure-12. The **2D POCKET** dialog box will be displayed; refer to Figure-13.
- Click on the **Select** button of **Tool** section. The **Select Tool** dialog box will be displayed.
- Click on the required tool from the dialog box and click on the **OK** button from **Select Tool** dialog box. The tool will be selected and displayed in **Tool** section of **2D POCKET** dialog box.
- Click on the **Geometry** tab of **2D POCKET** dialog box. The **Geometry** tab will be displayed.
- The **Nothing** button of **Pocket Selections** section from **Geometry** tab is active by default. Click on the surface/edge of the model to select; refer to Figure-14.

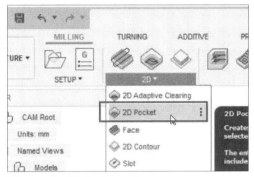

Figure-12. 2D Pocket tool

Figure-13. 2D POCKET dialog box

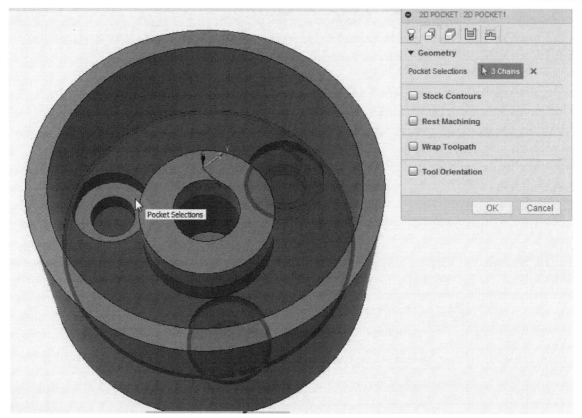

Figure-14. Pocket selections of model

- Select the desired option from the **Sideways Compensation** drop-down of **Passes** section in **Passes** tab to define the motion of tool with respect to walls.
- Select the **Finishing Passes** check box if you want to perform finishing pass. The options related to finishing pass will be displayed in the dialog box. Specify the desired parameters.
- Select the **Preserve Order** check box if you want to machine the part in same sequence as it was selected.
- Select the **Use Morphed Spiral Machining** check box from the dialog box to perform smoother machining.
- Select the **Allow Stepover Cusps** check box if you want to allow cusps being formed at corners while cutting material. Selecting this option decreases the machining time.
- For multiple depths pocket, the **Multiple Depths** check box should be selected from **Passes** tab.
- The other parameters have been discussed earlier in this chapter.
- After specifying the parameters, click on the **OK** button from **2D POCKET** dialog box. The toolpath will be generated and displayed on the model; refer to Figure-15.

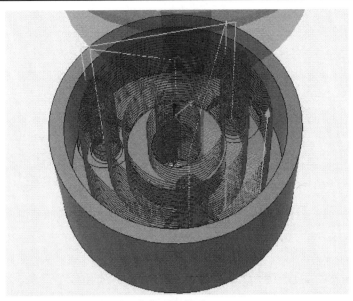

Figure-15. Created toolpath for 2D Pocket

Face

The **Face** tool is used to remove material from the face of the workpiece. In any machining sequence, this is generally the first toolpath to be generated for flat head workpiece. The procedure to use this tool is discussed next.

- Click on the **Face** tool of **2D** drop-down from **Toolbar**; refer to Figure-16. The **FACE** dialog box will be displayed; refer to Figure-17.

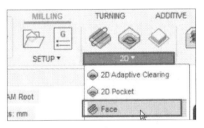

Figure-16. Face tool

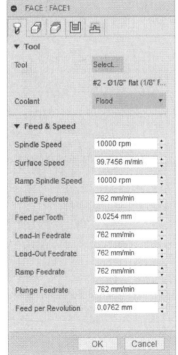

Figure-17. FACE dialog box

- Click on the **Select** button from **Tool** tab and select the required tool for facing according to your model from **Select Tool** dialog box. Generally, we use flat mill or face mill cutting tools for this operation.
- Click on the **Geometry** tab of **FACE** dialog box. The **Geometry** tab will be displayed.

- The **Nothing** selection button of **Stock Selections** section is active by default asking you to select the boundary of workpiece. Click on the outer edge of the model; refer to Figure-18.

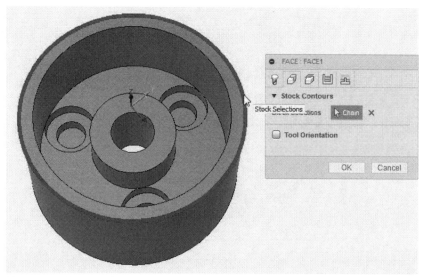

Figure-18. Selection for FACE dialog box

- Select the **Use Chip Thinning** check box from **Passes** tab of dialog box to make tool roll while cutting so that chips formed are thin.
- The other options of the dialog box have been discussed earlier.
- After specifying the parameters, click on the **OK** button from **FACE** dialog box. The toolpath will be created and displayed on workpiece; refer to Figure-19.

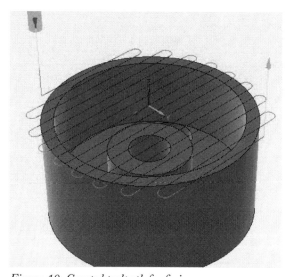

Figure-19. Created toolpath for facing

- Right-click on the recently created **Face** toolpath and click on the **Simulate** button to check the animation of facing operation.

2D Contour

The **2D Contour** tool is used to remove material by following the contour of the model. This tool is generally used to remove the material from outer/inner walls of the selected workpiece. You can use this toolpath for path roughing and finishing. The procedure to use this tool is discussed next.

- Click on the **2D Contour** tool of **2D** drop-down from **Toolbar**; refer to Figure-20. The **2D CONTOUR** dialog box will be displayed; refer to Figure-21.

Figure-20. 2D Contour tool

Figure-21. 2D CONTOUR dialog box

- Click on the **Select** button of **Tool** tab from **2D CONTOUR** dialog box and select the required tool according to your model from **Select Tool** dialog box.
- Click on the **Geometry** tab of **2D CONTOUR** dialog box. The **Geometry** tab will be displayed.
- The **Nothing** button of **Contour Selection** section is active by default. Click on the edges of model to select; refer to Figure-22.
- Click in the **Tangential Extension Distance** edit box of **Geometry** tab and enter the value of distance to extend the open contours tangentially.
- Select the **Separate Tangentially End Extension** check box to enable tangential extension at the end of cutting pass.

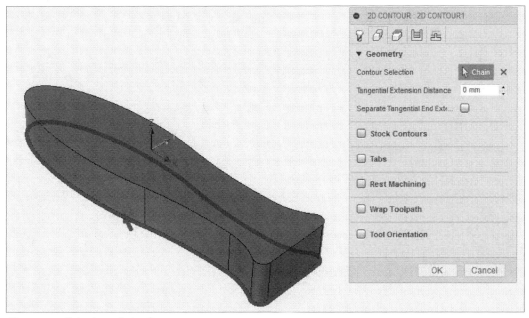

Figure-22. Selection of edge for contour

Tabs

The **Tabs** check box is used to define parameters for holding the workpiece when you are cutting a part from sheet. This option is generally used when you are working on a sheet and after operation the part will be detached from this sheet. The procedure is discussed next.

*   Click on the **Tabs** check box to enable options related to tab.
*   Select on the required shape of tab from **Tab Shape** drop-down.
*   Click in the **Tab Width** edit box and enter the value of width of tab.
*   Click in the **Tab Height** edit box and enter the value of height of tab.
*   Select the **By distance** option of **Tab Positioning** drop-down from **Tabs** section to position the tab around the workpiece by distance entered; refer to Figure-23.

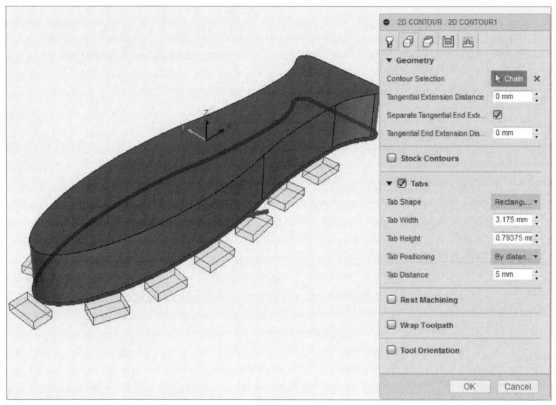

Figure-23. Tab positioning by distance

*   Select the **At points** option of **Tab Positioning** option from **Tabs** section to position the tab by selecting points on the edge of model; refer to Figure-24.

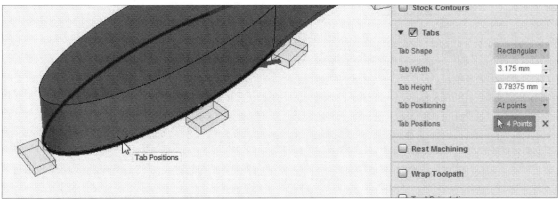

Figure-24. Positioning by points

- The other options of this dialog box are same as discussed earlier.
- After specifying the parameters, click on the **OK** button from **2D CONTOUR** dialog box. The toolpath will be generated and displayed on the model; refer to Figure-25.

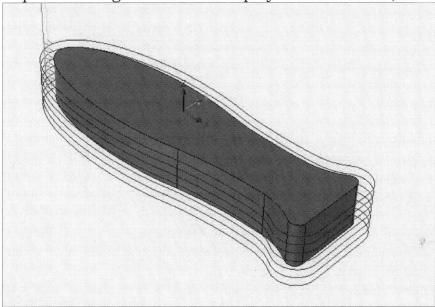

Figure-25. Created toolpath for solid

Slot

The **Slot** tool is used to remove the slot material from model. Note that this slot milling is governed in 2D plane so the depth of cut need to be specified explicitly. The procedure to use this tool is discussed next.

- Click on the **Slot** tool of **2D** drop-down from **Toolbar**; refer to Figure-26. The **SLOT** dialog box will be displayed; refer to Figure-27.
- Click on the **Select** button of **Tool** tab from **SLOT** dialog box. The **Select Tool** dialog box will be displayed. Select the tool as required.
- Click on the **Geometry** tab of **2D CONTOUR** dialog box. The **Geometry** tab will be displayed.
- The **Nothing** button of **Pocket Selections** section is active by default. You need to select the slot; refer to Figure-28.

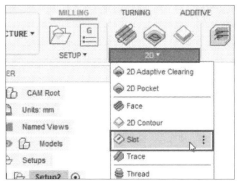

Figure-26. Slot Tool

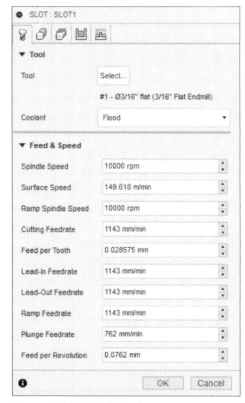

Figure-27. SLOT dialog box

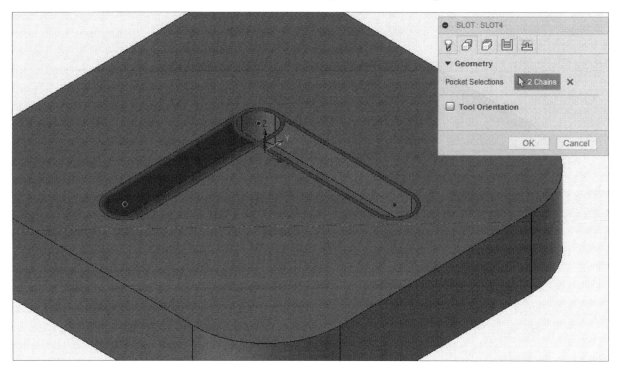

Figure-28. Selection for slot

- Select the desired option from the **Ramp Type** drop-down. In our case, we have applied **Plunge** option of **Ramp Type** drop-down from **Linking** tab for better generation of toolpath as tool entry is not available.
- Specify the desired parameters for ramp if asked based on selected option. The other options of this dialog box have been discussed earlier.
- After specifying the parameters, click on the **OK** button from **SLOT** dialog box. The toolpath will be generated and displayed on the model; refer to Figure-29.

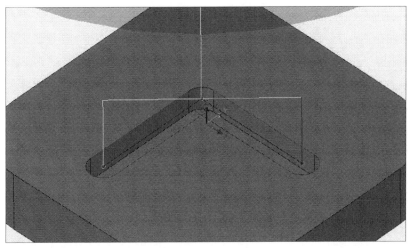

Figure-29. Generated toolpath for slot

Trace

The **Trace** tool is used to trace the selected path for machining. The procedure to use this tool is discussed next.

- Click on the **Trace** tool of **2D** drop-down from **Toolbar**; refer to Figure-30. The **TRACE** dialog box will be displayed; refer to Figure-31.
- Click on the **Select** button of **Tool** tab from **TRACE** dialog box. The **Select Tool** dialog box will be displayed. Select the tool as required.
- Click on the **Geometry** tab of **TRACE** dialog box. The **Geometry** tab will be displayed.

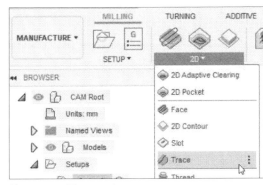

Figure-30. Trace tool

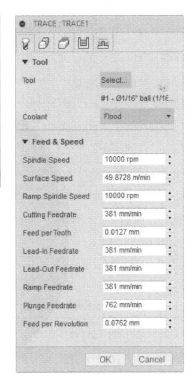

Figure-31. TRACE dialog box

- The **Nothing** button of **Curve Selections** section of **Geometry** tab is active by default. Select the geometry for trace; refer to Figure-32. You can also select sketch curves for this toolpath.

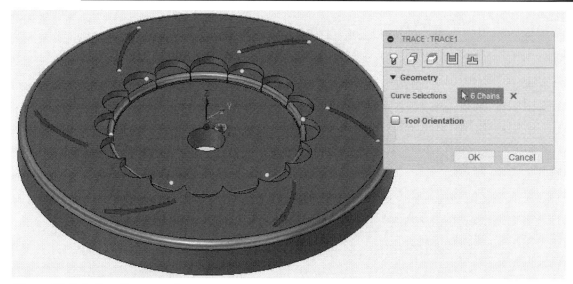

Figure-32. Selection of geometry for trace

- Click on the **Passes** tab of **TRACE** dialog box. The **Passes** tab will be displayed; refer to Figure-33.

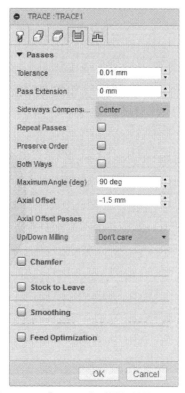

Figure-33. Passes tab of TRACE dialog box

- Click in the **Pass Extension** edit box and enter the value of distance to extend the toolpath along length.
- Select the **Repeat Passes** check box from **Passes** tab to perform an additional finishing pass with zero stock for better finish.
- Select the **Preserve Order** check box from **Passes** tab to specify that the geometry machined in the order in which they are selected.
- Select the **Both Ways** check box from **Passes** tab to use the climb and conventional machining to the open profile of the selected geometry.
- Click in the **Maximum Angle (deg)** edit box and specify the maximum plunge angle for machining.

- Click in the **Axial Offset** edit box and specify the value of axial offset for the toolpath of selected geometry.
- Select the **Axial Offset Passes** check box from **Passes** tab to enable multiple depths machining.
- Click on the **Up/Down Milling** drop down and select the required option.
- Select the **Chamfer** check box of **Passes** tab from **TRACE** dialog box to perform a chamfer operation on selected geometry. This option is available if you have selected chamfer mill as cutting tool.
- Click in the **Chamfer Width** edit box of **Chamfer** section from **Passes** tab and enter the value of width for machining of chamfer.
- Click in the **Chamfer Depth** box of **Chamfer** section from **Passes** tab and enter the value of depth of chamfer for machining.
- The other options of this dialog box are same as discussed earlier.
- After specifying the parameters, click on the **OK** button from **TRACE** dialog box. The toolpath will be generated and displayed on the model; refer to Figure-34.

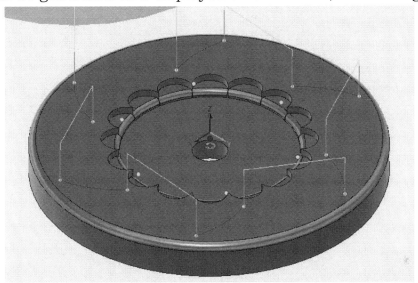

Figure-34. Created toolpath for trace

Thread

The **Thread** tool is used to create internal or external threads on the selected geometry. The procedure to use this tool is discussed next.

- Click on the **Thread** tool of **2D** drop-down from **Toolbar**; refer to Figure-35. The **THREAD** dialog box will be displayed; refer to Figure-36.
- Click on the **Select** button of **Tool** tab from **THREAD** dialog box. The **Select Tool** dialog box will be displayed. Select the tool as required.
- Click on the **Geometry** tab of **THREAD** dialog box. The **Nothing** button of **Circular Face Selections** option from **Geometry** tab is active by default.
- You need to click on the circular faces on which you want to create the threads; refer to Figure-37
- If you want to select all the faces which have same diameter for creating threads then select the **Select Same Diameter** check box and then select the round face of model. To further filter your selection, select the **Only Same Hole Depth** check to select only those holes which have same depth as the selected one and select the **Only Same Z Top Height** check box to select only those holes/boss features which have same height.

- Click on the selection button for **Containment Boundary** option and select the desired boundary chain within which the holes/boss features should be selected automatically.
- Set the other options as desired in the **Geometry** tab of dialog box.

Figure-35. *Thread tool*

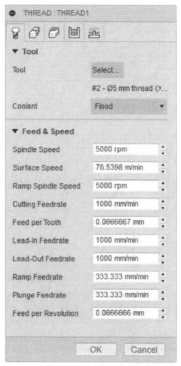

Figure-36. *THREAD dialog box*

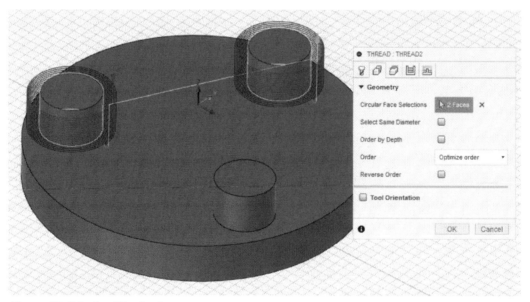

Figure-37. *Selecting Circular faces*

- Click on the **Passes** tab from **TREAD** dialog box. The **Passes** tab will be displayed; refer to Figure-38.
- Specify the desired value of thread entry angle in the **Start Angle** edit box.
- Select the **Right handed** option of **Threading Hand** drop-down from **Passes** tab to create a right handed thread direction. Select the **Left handed** option of **Threading Hand** drop-down from **Passes** tab to create a left handed thread direction.
- Click in the **Thread Pitch** edit box of **Passes** tab to enter the value of distance between two thread.

- Click in the **Pitch Diameter Offset** edit box of **Passes** tab to enter the value of difference between major and minor thread diameter.
- Select the **Do Multiple Threads** check box of **Passes** tab to create multiple threads and specify number of threads value in **Number of Threads** edit box. This will create a multi-start threading.
- Select the required option from **Compensation Type** drop-down to define the compensation type. Select the **In computer** option from the drop-down if you want to create the path which already accommodates compensation based on tool and toolpath. Select the **In control** option to insert G41/42 codes in NC program so that the operator can specify compensation while working on machine. Select the **Wear** option if you want to use benefit of both **In computer** and **In control** which means the compensation is provided in the toolpath itself and G41/42 codes are also provided in NC program for manual changes. Note that the wear compensation needs to be entered as negative if **Wear** option is selected. Select the **Inverse wear** option if you want to specify wear compensation in positive value and use all features **Wear** option.
- Select the **Multiple Passes** check box of **Passes** tab to enter a value for multiple depth cuts when thread milling. This option is used when you want to create deeper threads.
- Select the **Repeat Passes** option if you want to repeat the cutting passes once again for better finish.
- The other options of this dialog box have been discussed earlier.
- After specifying the parameters, click on the **OK** button from **THREAD** dialog box. The toolpath will be generated and displayed on the model; refer to Figure-39.

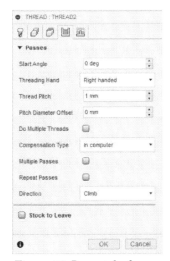

Figure-38. Passes tab of THREAD dialog box

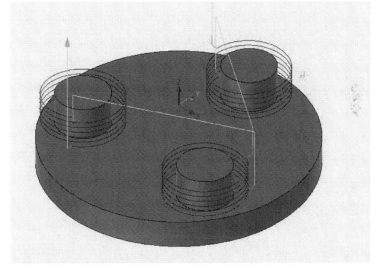

Figure-39. Generated Toolpath for thread

Bore

The **Bore** tool is used to increase the diameter of hole in tight tolerance. You can also finish cylindrical islands in the model by using this tool. The procedure to use this tool is discussed next.

- Click on the **Bore** tool of **2D** drop-down from **Toolbar**; refer to Figure-40. The **BORE** dialog box will be displayed; refer to Figure-41.

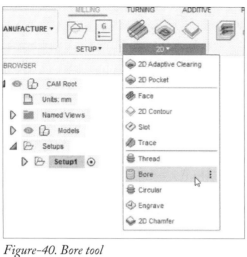

Figure-40. Bore tool

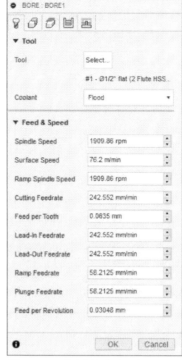

Figure-41. BORE dialog box

- Click on the **Select** button of **Tool** tab from **BORE** dialog box. The **Select Tool** dialog box will be displayed. Select the tool as required.
- Click on the **Geometry** tab of **THREAD** dialog box. The **Geometry** tab will be displayed.
- The **Nothing** button of **Circular Face Selections** option from **Geometry** tab is active by default. You need to click on the circular face of model which has been drilled earlier; refer to Figure-42.

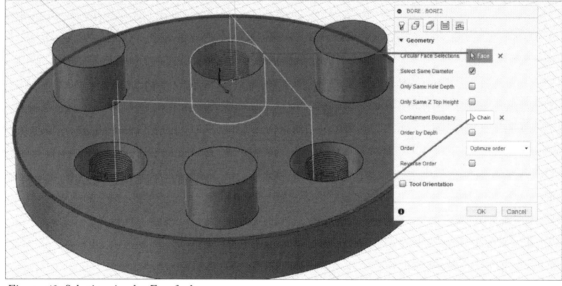

Figure-42. Selecting circular Face for bore

- The other options of the dialog box have been discussed earlier.
- After specifying the parameter, click on the **OK** button from **BORE** dialog box. The toolpath will be generated and displayed on the model.

Circular

The **Circular** tool is used for milling circular or round pocket/boss features. The procedure to use this tool is discussed next.

- Click on the **Circular** tool of **2D** drop-down from **Toolbar**; refer to Figure-43. The **CIRCULAR** dialog box will be displayed; refer to Figure-44.

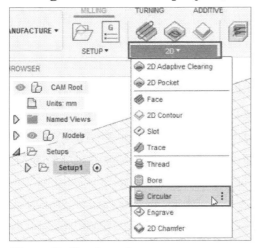

Figure-43. Circular tool

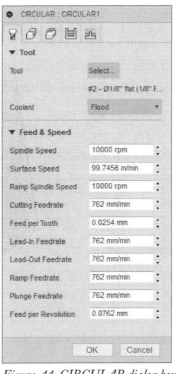

Figure-44. CIRCULAR dialog box

- Click on the **Select** button of **Tool** tab from **CIRCULAR** dialog box. The **Select Tool** dialog box will be displayed. Select the tool as required.
- Click on the **Geometry** tab of **CIRCULAR** dialog box. The **Geometry** tab will be displayed.
- The **Nothing** button of **Circular Face Selections** option from **Geometry** tab is active by default. You need to click on the circular face from model to select; refer to Figure-45.

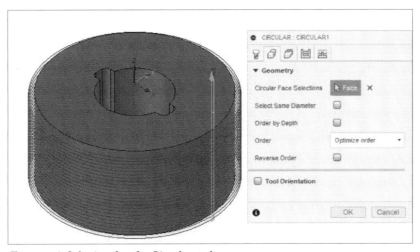

Figure-45. Selecting face for Circular tool

- The other options of the dialog box are same as discussed earlier.
- After specifying the parameters, click on the **OK** button from **CIRCULAR** dialog box. The toolpath will be generated and displayed on the model.

Engrave

The **Engrave** tool is used to create artistic machining over the workpiece. These toolpath are also used to print text on the press dies. The procedure to use this tool is discussed next.

- Click on the **Engrave** tool of **2D** drop-down from **Toolbar**; refer to Figure-46. The **ENGRAVE** dialog box will be displayed; refer to Figure-47.

Figure-46. Engrave tool

Figure-47. ENGRAVE dialog box

- Click on the **Select** button of **Tool** tab from **ENGRAVE** dialog box. The **Select Tool** dialog box will be displayed. Select the tool as required.
- Click on the **Geometry** tab of **ENGRAVE** dialog box. The **Geometry** tab will be displayed.
- The **Nothing** button of **Contour Selection** from **Geometry** tab is active by default. You need to select the contour for engraving; refer to Figure-48.
- The other options of the dialog box are same as discussed earlier.
- After specifying the various parameters, click on the **OK** button from **ENGRAVE** dialog box to complete the process. The toolpath will be generated and displayed on the model; refer to Figure-49.

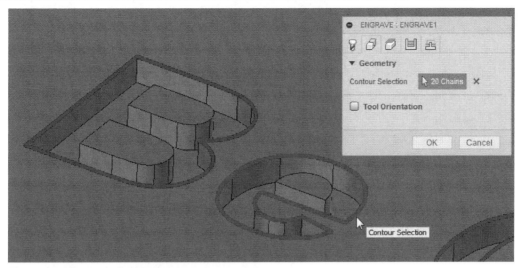

Figure-48. Contour selection for engraving

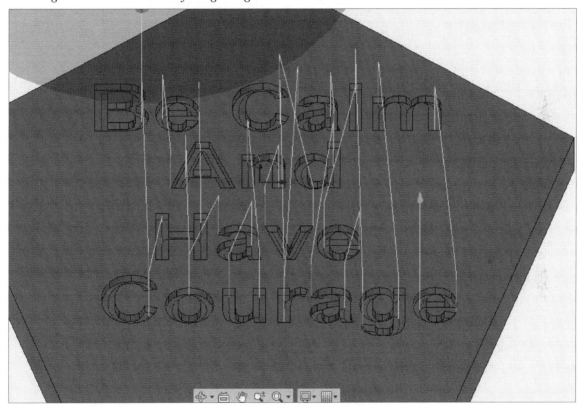

Figure-49. Generated toolpath for engrave

2D Chamfer

The **2D Chamfer** tool is used to create chamfer profile on the edge of model. The procedure to use this tool is discussed next.

- Click on the **2D Chamfer** tool of **2D** drop-down from **Toolbar**; refer to Figure-50. The **2D CHAMFER** dialog box will be displayed; refer to Figure-51.
- Click on the **Select** button of **Tool** tab from **2D CHAMFER** dialog box. The **Select Tool** dialog box will be displayed. Select the tool as required.

- Click on the **Geometry** tab of **2D CHAMFER** dialog box. The **Geometry** tab will be displayed.
- The **Nothing** button of **Contour Selection** section from **Geometry** tab is active by default. You need to select the edge for creating chamfer; refer to Figure-52.

Figure-50. 2D Chamfer tool

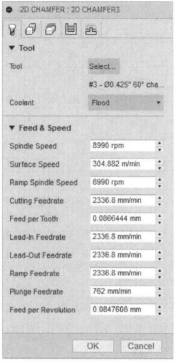

Figure-51. CHAMFER dialog box

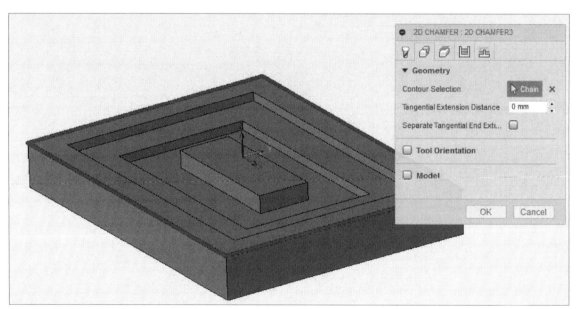

Figure-52. Selection of edge for chamfer

- Click in the **Passes** tab from **2D CHAMFER** dialog box. The options of **Passes** tab will be displayed; refer to Figure-53.
- Click in the **Chamfer Width** edit box of **Chamfer** section from **Passes** tab and enter the value of width of chamfer.
- Click in the **Chamfer Tip Offset** edit box of **Chamfer** section from **Passes** tab and enter the value of tip offset so that cut is not made from the tip but from the approximate middle of cutting edge of tool.

- Click in the **Chamfer Clearance** edit box of **Chamfer** section and enter the value of clearance from near by walls to avoid collision.
- The other tools of the dialog box are same as discussed earlier.
- After specifying the parameters, click on the **OK** button from **2D CHAMFER** dialog box. The toolpath is generated and displayed on the model; refer to Figure-54.

Figure-53. Passes tab 2D CHAMFER dialog box

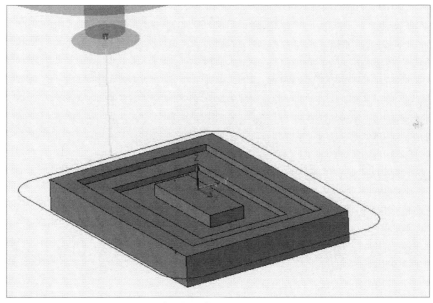

Figure-54. Toolpath generated for chamfer

GENERATING 3D TOOLPATH

Till now, we have discussed the procedure of generating the 2D Toolpaths. In this section, we will discuss the tools used to create 3D Toolpaths. 3D toolpaths enable simultaneous movement of tool in horizontal and vertical direction.

Adaptive Clearing

The **Adaptive Clearing** tool is used to remove the material in bulk from workpiece. It is generally a roughing process. It uses an advanced strategy of milling motion so that there is less load on the tool. The procedure to use this tool is discussed next.

- Click on the **Adaptive Clearing** tool of **3D** drop-down from **MILLING** tab in the **Toolbar**; refer to Figure-55. The **ADAPTIVE** dialog box will be displayed; refer to Figure-56.

Figure-55. Adaptive Clearing tool

Figure-56. ADAPTIVE dialog box

- Click on the **Select** button of **Tool** tab from **ADAPTIVE** dialog box. The **Select Tool** dialog box will be displayed. Select the tool as required.
- Select the **Shaft & Holder** check box of **Tool** tab from **ADAPTIVE** dialog box to specify how the shaft and holder of the tool is used to avoid collisions with stock or workpiece.
- Click on the **Shaft and Holder Mode** drop-down of **Shaft and Holder** section from **Tool** tab and select the desired option.
- Select the **Use Holder** check box of **Shaft and Holder Mode** to use holder of the selected tool in the toolpath calculation to avoid collisions.
- Click in the **Holder Clearance** edit box of **Shaft and Holder Mode** and enter the value of tool clearance to keep away the holder from the part.

Geometry

- Click on the **Geometry** tab of **ADAPTIVE** dialog box. The **Geometry** tab will be displayed; refer to Figure-57.
- Select the **None** option of **Machining Boundary** drop-down from **Geometry** tab to machine all the stock without limitation. The **None** option is not available for all machining strategies.
- Select the **Bounding Box** option of **Machining Boundary** drop-down from **Geometry** tab to machine the toolpath within a specified box defined by the maximum extents of the part viewed from the WCS.

- Select the **Silhouette** option of **Machining Boundary** drop-down from **Geometry** tab to machine the toolpath within a defined boundary by the geometry of part or model viewed from WCS. Note that on selecting this option, the curvature of part will also be taken into account while calculation stock for machining.

- Select the **Selection** option of **Machining Boundary** drop-down from **Geometry** tab to machine the toolpath within a region bound by selected boundary. You can also specify the position of tool with respect to boundary while cutting by using the options in **Tool Containment** drop-down.

- Select the **Stock Contours** check box from **Geometry** tab to select the geometry for machining.

- The **Nothing** button of **Stock Selection** section from **Stock Contours** check box is active by default. You need to select the geometry; refer to Figure-58.

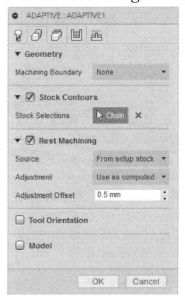

Figure-57. Geometry tab of ADAPTIVE dialog box

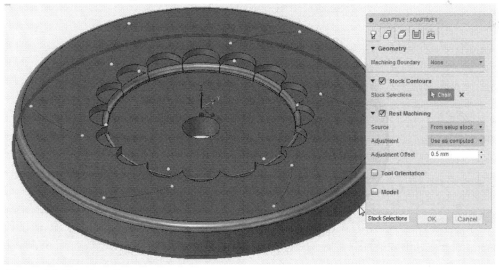

Figure-58. Selection of geometry

- Select the **Rest Machining** check box of **Geometry** tab to limit the operation to remove the material which is not removed by the previous tool.

- Click on the **Source** drop-down of **Rest Machining** section and select the required option to define source to be used for remaining stock calculation.

- Click on the **Adjustment** drop-down of **Rest Machining** section and select the required option. If you want to machine small cusps left by tool in previous operation then select **Machine Cusps** option. If you do not want to machine them then select the **Ignore Cusps** option. Selecting **Use as computed** option allows the system to automatically decide whether to remove cusps or not based on the value specified in **Adjustment Offset** edit box.

• Click in the **Adjustment Offset** edit box of **Rest Machining** check box and enter the value of stock to be removed, depending on the rest material adjustment setting.

Passes

• Click on the **Passes** tab of **ADAPTIVE** dialog box. The **Passes** tab will be displayed; refer to Figure-59.

Figure-59. Passes tab of ADAPTIVE dialog box

• Click in the **Tolerance** edit box of **Passes** tab and enter the value of tolerance for curves of model.
• Select the **Machine Shallow Areas** check box of **Passes** tab to remove the excessive cusps from the shallow areas of Z-level.
• Click in the **Optimal Load** edit box of **Passes** tab and enter the value of engagement which is followed by adaptive strategies.
• Click in the **Minimum Cutting Radius** edit box of **Passes** tab and enter the value of cutting radius.
• Select the **Machine Cavities** check box of **Passes** tab to machine the pockets of the model.
• Select the **Use Slot Clearing** check box of **Passes** tab to start pocket clearing with a slot along its middle, before continuing with a spiral motion towards the pocket walls.
• Select the **Fillets** check box of **Passes** tab to enter a value of fillet radius.
• The other options of the dialog box are same as discussed earlier.

- After specifying the parameters, click on the **OK** button of from **ADAPTIVE** dialog box. The toolpath will be generated and displayed on the model; refer to Figure-60.

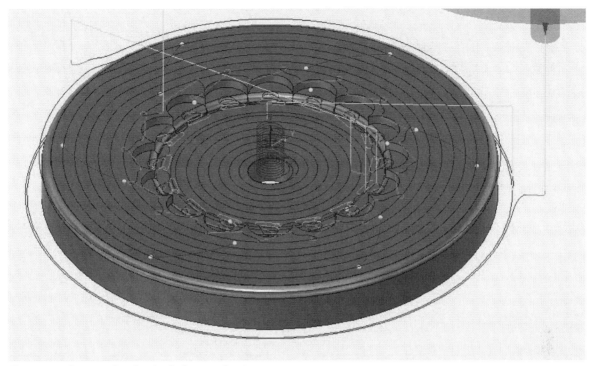

Figure-60. Generated toolpath of adaptive clearing

Pocket Clearing

The **Pocket Clearing** tool is mainly used for clearing large quantity of material in pockets of the model. The procedure to use this tool is discussed next.

- Click on the **Pocket Clearing** tool of **3D** drop-down from **Toolbar**; refer to Figure-61. The **POCKET** dialog box will be displayed; refer to Figure-62
- Click on the **Select** button of **Tool** tab from **POCKET** dialog box. The **Select Tool** dialog box will be displayed. Select the tool as required.
- The options of this dialog box are same as discussed earlier.
- After specifying the parameters, click on the **OK** button from **POCKET** dialog box. The toolpath will be generated and displayed on the model; refer to Figure-63.

Figure-61. Pocket Clearing tool

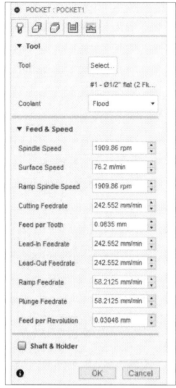

Figure-62. POCKET dialog Box

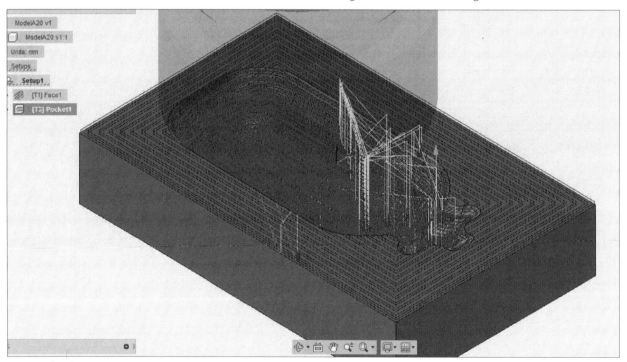

Figure-63. Generated toolpath for pocket

Steep and Shallow

As the name suggests, this tool is used to create toolpath for machining steep and shallow areas of part based on specified threshold. When the area to be machined is steep then contour passes are used and then the area is shallow then parallel passes are used for machining. The procedure to use this tool is given next.

- Click on the **Steep and Shallow** tool from the **3D** drop-down in the **Toolbar**; refer to Figure-64. The **STEEP AND SHALLOW** dialog box will be displayed refer to Figure-65.

Figure-64. Steep and Shallow tool

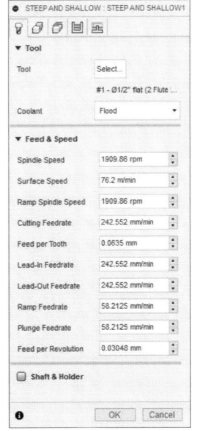

Figure-65. STEEP AND SHALLOW dialog box

- Specify the desired parameters in **Tool**, **Geometry**, **Heights**, and **Linking** tabs of dialog box as discussed earlier. Click on the **Passes** tab. The options will be displayed as shown in Figure-66.

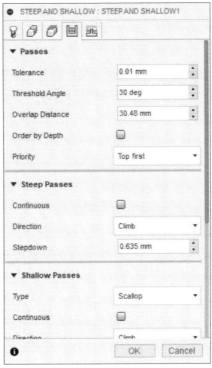

Figure-66. Passes tab

- Specify the desired value of angle in **Threshold Angle** edit box. The areas which have slope angle larger than this value with respect to horizontal line will be counted as shallow areas and below this value will be counted as steep areas.
- The value specified in **Overlap Distance** edit box is distance past the threshold angle line which will act as transitional area for blending steep and shallow areas.
- Select the desired option from the **Type** drop-down of **Shallow Passes** section to define parallel or scallop toolpaths for shallow areas.
- Set the other parameters as discussed earlier and click on the **OK** button from the dialog box. The toolpath will be generated; refer to Figure-67.

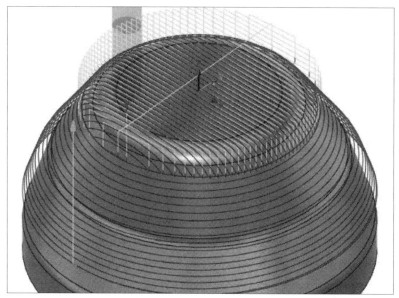

Figure-67. Steep and Shallow toolpath

Parallel

The **Parallel** tool is used mainly for finishing strategies. This toolpath is used when parallel cutting passes are needed to machine the workpiece. The procedure to use this tool is discussed next.

- Click on the **Parallel** tool of **3D** drop-down from **Toolbar**; refer to Figure-68. The **PARALLEL** dialog box will be displayed; refer to Figure-69.

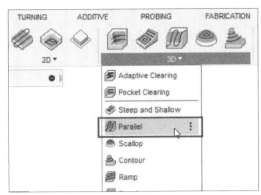

Figure-68. Parallel tool

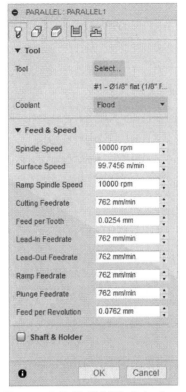

Figure-69. PARALLEL dialog box

- Click on the **Select** button of **Tool** tab from **POCKET** dialog box. The **Select Tool** dialog box will be displayed. Select the tool as required.
- Click on the **Geometry** tab of **PARALLEL** dialog box. The **Geometry** tab will be displayed; refer to Figure-70.

Figure-70. Geometry tab of PARALLEL dialog box

- Select the **Contact Point Boundary** check box of **Geometry** section to specify the boundary limits where the tool touches the surface of model rather than the tool center location.
- Select the **Contact Only** check box of **Geometry** section to not generate the toolpath on the model where the tool is not in contact with the machining surface.
- Select the **Slope** check box of **Geometry** tab to specify the range of slope within which the faces of part will be considered for machining.
- Click in the **From Slope Angle** edit box of **Slope** check box and enter the angular value greater than 0 degree.
- Click in the **To Slope Angle** edit box of **Slope** check box and enter the value less than 90 degree. Only area equal to or less then this values will be machined.
- Select the **Avoid/Touch Surface** check box of **Geometry** tab to define surfaces which will be avoided or touched while machining within a specified distance.
- The **Nothing** button of **Avoid/Touch Surfaces** node is active by default. You need to click on the surfaces to select.
- Click in the **Avoid/Touch Surface Clearance** edit box of **Avoid/Touch Surface** check box and enter the required value.
- Select the **Touch Surfaces** check box of **Avoid/Touch Surfaces** check box to invert the meaning of **Avoid/Touch Check Surface** check box.
- The other options of the dialog box are same as discussed earlier.
- After specifying the parameters, click on the **OK** button from **PARALLEL** dialog box. The toolpath will be generated and displayed on the model; refer to Figure-71.

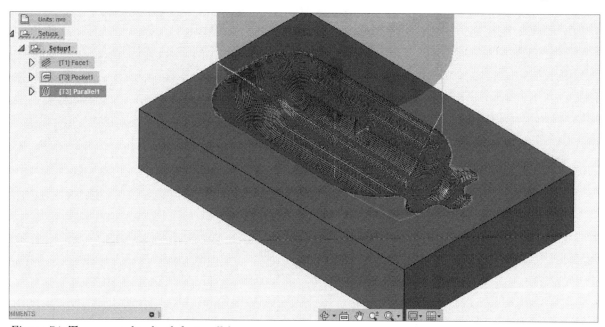

Figure-71. The generated toolpath for parallel

Scallop

The **Scallop** tool is used to finish round faces of the model with slopes. This tool can also be used to machine fillets. The procedure to use this tool is discussed next.

- Click on the **Scallop** tool of **3D** drop-down from **Toolbar**; refer to Figure-72. The **SCALLOP** dialog box will be displayed; refer to Figure-73.

Figure-72. Scallop tool

- Click on the **Select** button of **Tool** tab from **SCALLOP** dialog box. The **Select Tool** dialog box will be displayed. Select the tool as required.
- Click on the **Passes** tab of **SCALLOP** dialog box. The **Passes** tab will be displayed; refer to Figure-74.

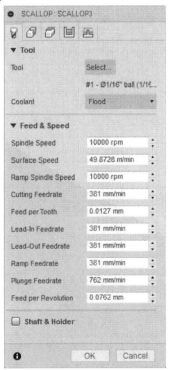

Figure-73. SCALLOP dialog box

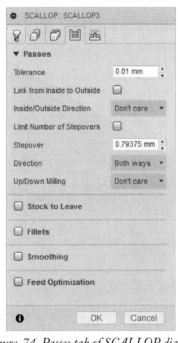

Figure-74. Passes tab of SCALLOP dialog box

- Select the **Link from Inside to Outside** check box of **SCALLOP** dialog box to specify that linking should be done by ordering from inside passes to outside passes.
- Click on the **Inside/Outside Direction** drop-down of **Passes** tab and select the desired option to define how cutting will progress on surface.
- Select the **Limit Number of Stepovers** check box of **Passes** tab to limit the number of steps of the tool so that the tool will not collapse with the surface of model.
- The options of the dialog box are same as discussed earlier.
- After specifying the parameters, click on the **OK** button from **SCALLOP** dialog box. The generated toolpath will be displayed on the model; refer Figure-75.

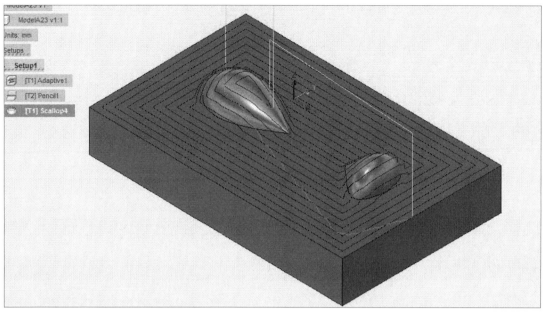

Figure-75. Generated toolpath of scallop tool

Contour

The **Contour** tool is generally used for finishing step walls. This tool can be used for machining vertical walls. The procedure to use this tool is discussed next.

- Click on the **Contour** tool of **3D** drop-down from **Toolbar**; refer to Figure-76. The **CONTOUR** dialog box will be displayed; refer to Figure-77.

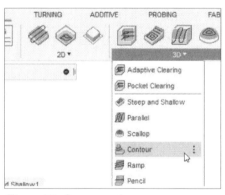

Figure-76. Contour tool

Figure-77. CONTOUR dialog Box

- Click on the **Select** button of **Tool** tab from **POCKET** dialog box. The **Select Tool** dialog box will be displayed. Select the tool as required.
- Click on the **Passes** tab of **CONTOUR** dialog box. The **Passes** tab will be displayed; refer to Figure-78
- Select the **Multi-Axis Tilting** check box of **Passes** tab from **CONTOUR** dialog box to enable multi axis tilting to avoid collision of model with tool holder when using short tools or machining complex areas.
- Click in the **Maximum Tilt** edit box of **Multi-Axis Tilting** check box and specify the maximum allowed tilt from the selected operation tool axis.
- Click in the **Maximum Segment Length** edit box of **Multi-Axis Tilting** check box and specify the length of a single segment for the generated toolpath.
- Click in the **Maximum Tool Axis Sweep** edit box of **Multi-Axis Tilting** check box and specify the value of maximum angle change in a single tool axis sweep for the generated toolpath.
- The other options of the dialog box are same as discussed earlier.
- After specifying the parameters, click on the **OK** button from **CONTOUR** dialog box. The toolpath will be generated and displayed on the model; refer to Figure-79

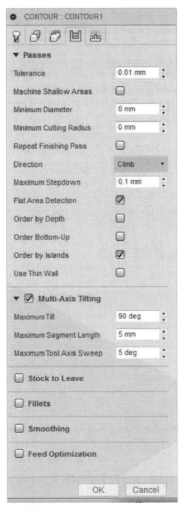

Figure-78. Passes tab of CONTOUR dialog box

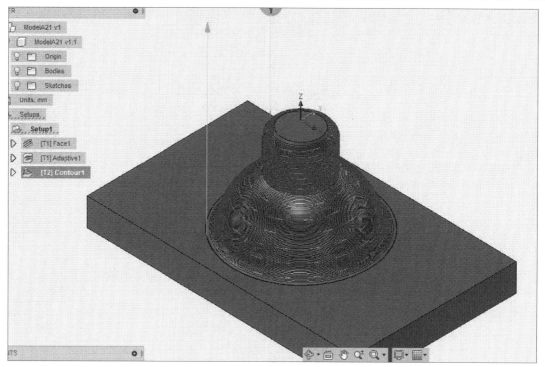

Figure-79. The generated toolpath for Contour tool

Ramp

The **Ramp** tool is used to create a finishing operation meant for step areas similar to Contour tool. The procedure to use this tool is discussed next.

- Click on the **Ramp** tool of **3D** drop-down from **Toolbar**; refer to Figure-80. The **RAMP** dialog box will be displayed; refer to Figure-81.

Figure-80. Ramp tool

Figure-81. RAMP dialog box

- Click on the **Select** button of **Tool** tab from **RAMP** dialog box. The **Select Tool** dialog box will be displayed. Select the tool as required.
- The other options of the dialog box are same as discussed earlier.

- After specifying the parameters, click on the **OK** button from **RAMP** dialog box. The generated toolpath will be displayed on the model; refer to Figure-82.

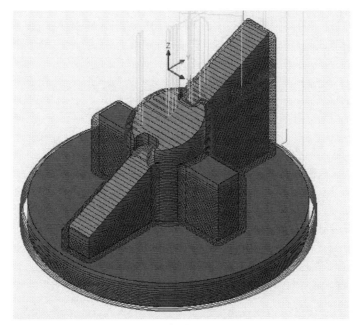

Figure-82. Generated toolpath for Ramp tool

Horizontal

The **Horizontal** tool is used for machining flat surfaces of model which are surrounded by other features. The procedure to use this tool is discussed next.

- Click on the **Horizontal** tool of **3D** drop-down from **Toolbar**; refer to Figure-83. The **HORIZONTAL** dialog box will be displayed; refer to Figure-84

Figure-83. Horizontal tool

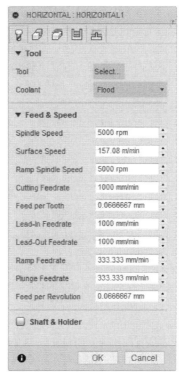

Figure-84. HORIZONTAL dialog box

- Click on the **Select** button of **Tool** tab from **HORIZONTAL** dialog box. The **Select Tool** dialog box will be displayed. Select the tool as required.
- The other options of the dialog box are same as discussed earlier.
- After specifying the parameters, click on the **OK** button from **HORIZONTAL** dialog box. The generated toolpath will be displayed on the model; refer to Figure-85.

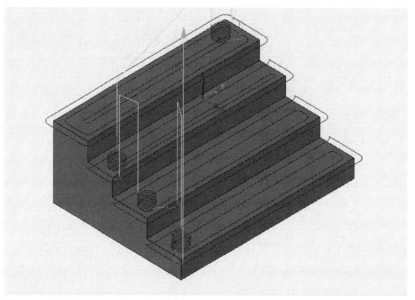

Figure-85. The generated toolpath for Horizontal tool

Pencil

The **Pencil** tool is used to create toolpaths along sharp internal corners with small radii tool. This tool is generally used to remove material where no other toolpath can work. The procedure to use this tool is discussed next.

- Click on the **Pencil** tool of **3D** drop-down from **Toolbar**; refer to Figure-86. The **PENCIL** dialog box will be displayed; refer to Figure-87

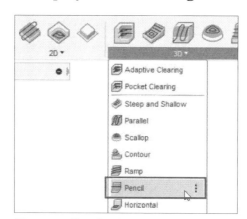

Figure-86. Pencil tool

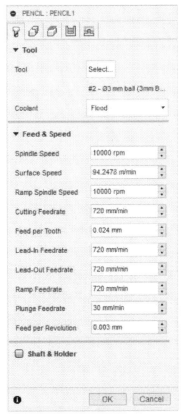

Figure-87. PENCIL dialog box

- Click on the **Select** button of **Tool** tab from **PENCIL** dialog box. The **Select Tool** dialog box will be displayed. Select the tool as required.
- The other options of the dialog box are same as discussed earlier.
- After specifying the parameters, click on the **OK** button from **PENCIL** dialog box. The generated toolpath will be displayed on the model; refer to Figure-88.

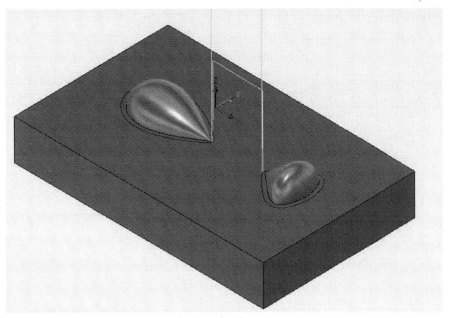

Figure-88. The generated toolpath for Pencil tool

PRACTICAL

Generate the toolpath of the given model shown in Figure-89 using 2D tools.

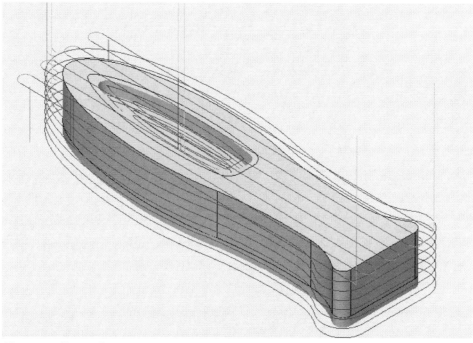

Figure-89. Practical

Adding Model to CAM

- Create and save the part in **DESIGN** workspace. The part file is available in the respective chapter folder of **Autodesk Fusion 360 Resources**.
- Click on the **MANUFACTURE** option from **Workspace** drop-down. The model will be displayed in the **MANUFACTURE** workspace; refer to Figure-90.

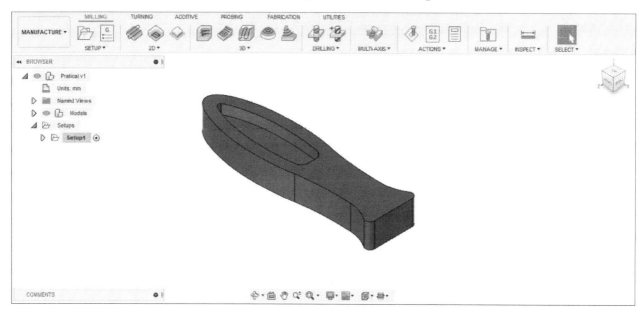

Figure-90. Practical1

Creating Stock

- Click on the **New Setup** tool of **SETUP** drop-down from **Toolbar**. The **SETUP** dialog box will be displayed along with the stock of model.

- Click on the **Setup** tab of **SETUP** dialog box and specify the parameters as displayed in Figure-91.

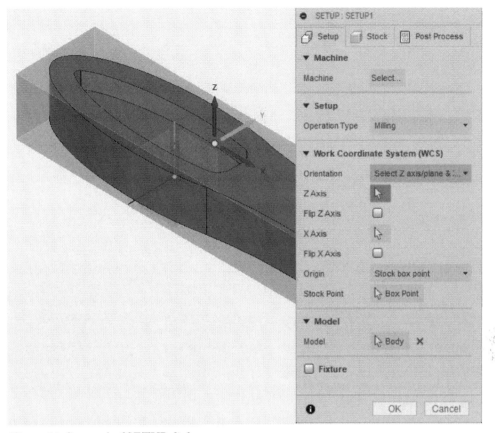

Figure-91. Setup tab of SETUP dialog

- Click on the **Stock** tab of **SETUP** dialog box and enter the parameters as displayed in Figure-92.

Figure-92. Stock tab of practical

- Click on the **Post Process** tab of **SETUP** dialog box and enter the parameters as displayed in Figure-93.

Figure-93. Post Process tab of SETUP dialog box

- After specifying the parameters, click on the **OK** button from **SETUP** dialog box. The stock will be created and displayed on the model.

Generating Face toolpath

- Click on the **Face** tool of **2D** drop-down from **Toolbar**. The **FACE** dialog box will be displayed.
- Click on the **Select** button of **Tool** option from **Tool** tab and select the tool from **Select Tool** dialog box as displayed; refer to Figure-94.
- After selecting the tool, click on the **OK** button from **Select Tool** dialog box. The tool will be selected for machining.
- Specify the parameters of **Tool** tab as displayed in Figure-95.

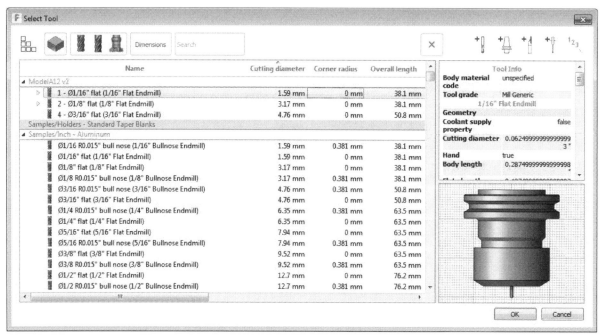

Figure-94. Selecting tool for facing

- Click in the **Passes** tab of **FACE** dialog box and specify the parameters as displayed in Figure-96.

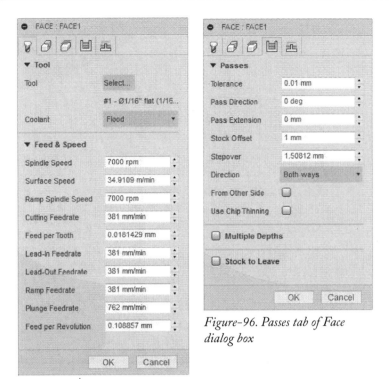

Figure-95. Tool tab

Figure-96. Passes tab of Face dialog box

- Click on the **Linking** tab of **FACE** dialog box and specify the parameters as displayed in Figure-97.

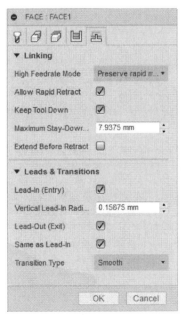

Figure-97. Linking Tab of FACE dialog box

- After specifying the parameters, click on the **OK** button from **FACE** dialog box. The toolpath will be generated and displayed on the model; refer to Figure-98.

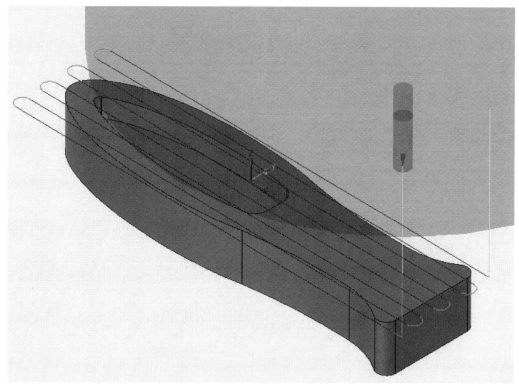

Figure-98. Created Face toolpath

Creating 2D Contour toolpath

- Click on the **2D Contour** tool of **2D** drop-down from **Toolbar**. The **2D CONTOUR** dialog box will be displayed.
- Click on the **Select** button of **Tool** option from **Tool** tab and select the tool as displayed from **Select Tool** dialog box; refer to Figure-99.

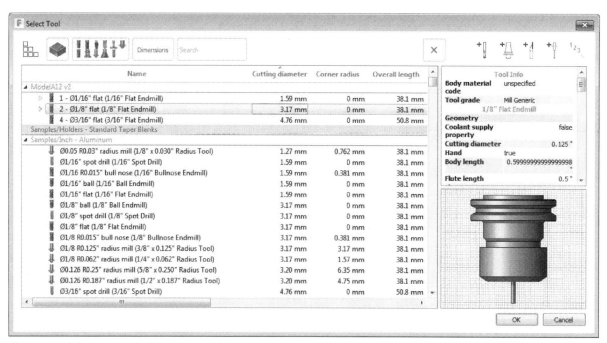

Figure-99. Selecting tool for 2D Contour

- After selecting desired tool, click on the **OK** button from **Select Tool** dialog box.
- Click on the **Geometry** tab of **2D CONTOUR** dialog box and specify the parameters as displayed in Figure-100.

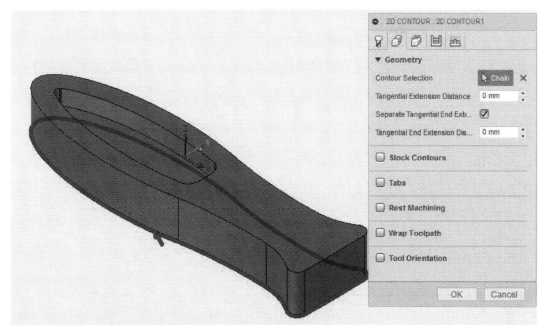

Figure-100. Geometry tab of 2D Contour

- Click in the **Passes** tab of **2D CONTOUR** dialog box and specify the parameters of **Passes** and **Multiple Depths** check box as displayed in Figure-101.
- Click on the **Linking** tab of **2D CONTOUR** dialog box and specify the parameters as displayed in Figure-102.

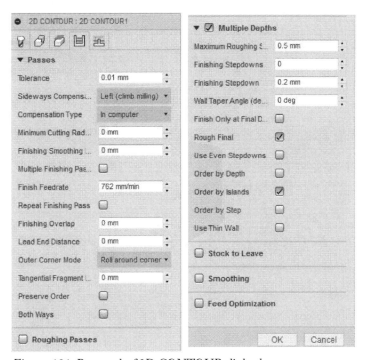

Figure-101. Passes tab of 2D CONTOUR dialog box

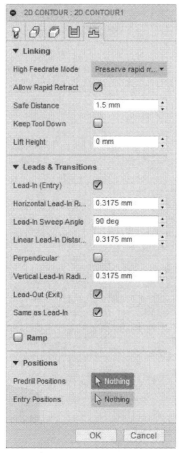

Figure-102. Linking tab of 2D CONTOUR dialog box

- After specifying the parameters, click on the **OK** button from **2D CONTOUR** dialog box. The toolpath will be generated and displayed on the model; refer to Figure-103.

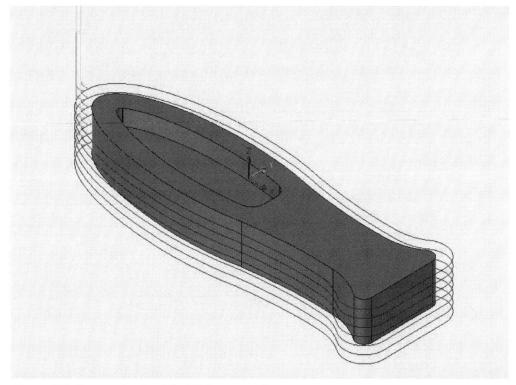

Figure-103. Generated toolpath for 2D Contour tool

Generating Pocket toolpath

- Click on the **2D Pocket** tool of **2D** drop-down from **Toolbar**. The **2D POCKET** dialog box will be displayed.
- Click on the **Select** button of **Tool** option from **Tool** tab and select the tool from **Select Tool** dialog box as displayed; refer to Figure-104.

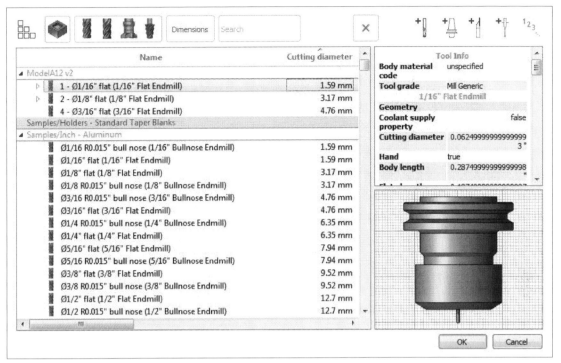

Figure-104. Selecting tool for pocket

- Specify the parameters of **Tools** tab as shown in Figure-105.

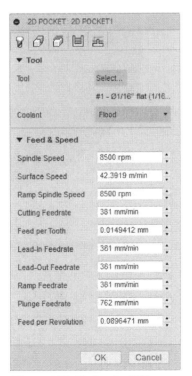

Figure-105. Tools tab of 2D POCKET dialog box

- Click on the **Geometry** tab of **2D POCKET** dialog box and specify the parameters as shown in Figure-106.

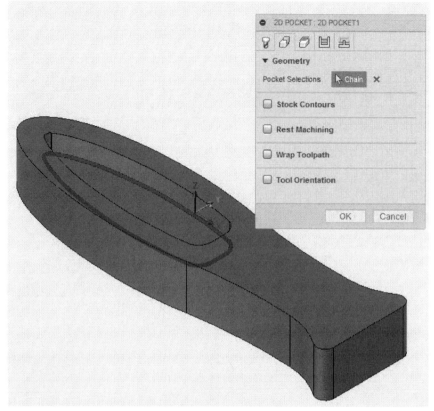

Figure-106. Geometry tab of 2D POCKET dialog box

- Click in the **Passes** tab of **2D POCKET** dialog box and specify the parameters as shown in Figure-107.
- Click in the **Linking** tab of **2D POCKET** dialog box and specify the parameters as shown in Figure-108.

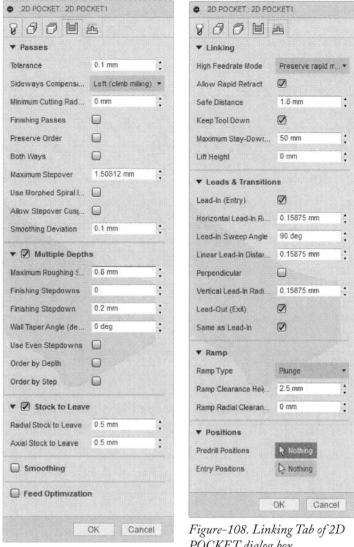

Figure-107. Passes tab of 2D POCKET dialog box

Figure-108. Linking Tab of 2D POCKET dialog box

- After specifying the parameters, click on the **OK** button from **2D POCKET** dialog box. The toolpath will be generated and displayed on the model; refer to Figure-109.
- After creating the required operations for a model, we need to simulate the generated toolpath.

Simulating the toolpath

- Click on the **Setup** option from **BROWSER** and right-click on it. A shortcut menu will be displayed.
- Click on the **Simulate** tool from shortcut menu. The **SIMULATE** dialog box will be displayed along with simulation keys; refer to Figure-110.

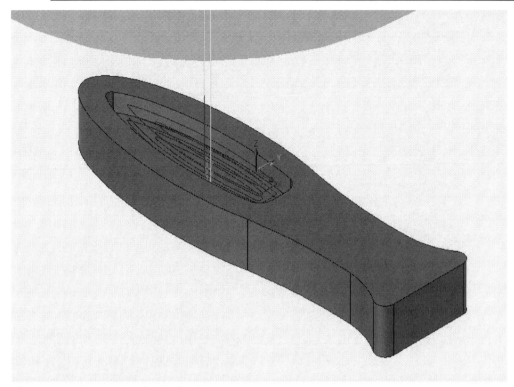

Figure-109. Generated toolpath of pocket

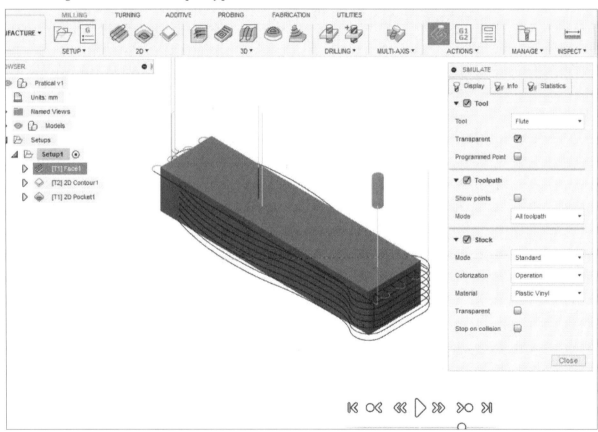

Figure-110. Simulating the model

- Click on the **Play** button to view the simulation process. One by one all generated toolpath will be applied to the model and at the end of simulation the part will display along with toolpaths on the model; refer to Figure-111. Note that till now only roughing toolpaths have been created. Create the finishing toolpaths as discussed earlier.

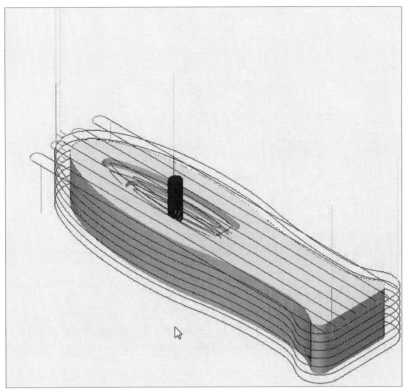

Figure-111. Running simulation process

PRACTICE 1

Machine the stock of diameter as 55 mm and length as 12 mm to create the part as shown in Figure-112. The pat file of this model is available in the respective folder of **Autodesk Fusion 360**.

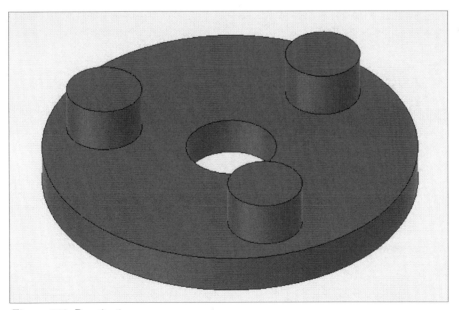

Figure-112. Practice 1

PRACTICE 2

Machine the stock of diameter as 55 mm and length as 8 mm to create the part as shown in Figure-113.

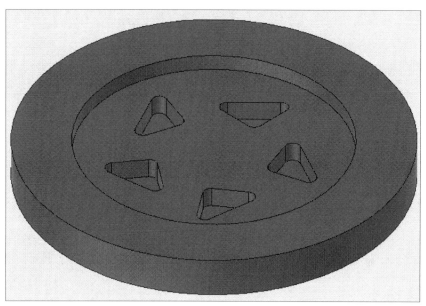

Figure-113. Practice 2

FOR STUDENT NOTES

FOR STUDENT NOTES

Chapter 17

Generating Milling Toolpaths - 2

Topics Covered

The major topics covered in this chapter are:

- *Spiral Toolpath*
- *Radial Toolpath*
- *Morphed Spiral Toolpath*
- *Project Toolpath*
- *Swarf Toolpath*
- *Multi-Axis Contour Toolpath*
- *Drilling Toolpath*

3D TOOLPATHS

In previous chapter, we have worked on 2D toolpaths and some 3D toolpaths available in **Toolbar**. In this chapter, we will discuss rest of the 3D toolpaths. Later, we will also work on multi-axis toolpaths and drilling operations.

Spiral

The spiral toolpath is used to cut material in spiral fashion. This toolpath is useful when you need to finish rough objects like shown in Figure-1. The procedure to use this tool is discussed next.

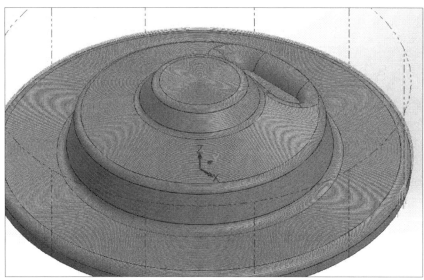

Figure-1. Spiral Toolpath

- Click on the **Spiral** tool of **3D** drop-down from **Toolbar**; refer to Figure-2. The **SPIRAL** dialog box will be displayed; refer to Figure-3.

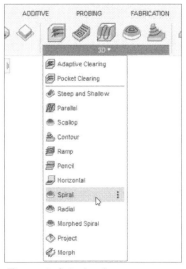

Figure-2. Spiral tool

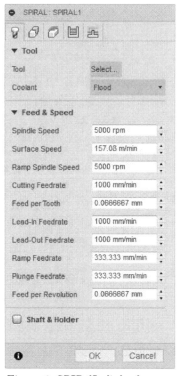

Figure-3. SPIRAL dialog box

- Click on the **Select** button of **Tool** section from **Tool** tab. The **Select Tool** dialog box will be displayed. Select the desired tool.
- Click on the **Passes** tab of **SPIRAL** dialog box. The **Passes** tab will be displayed; refer to Figure-4.

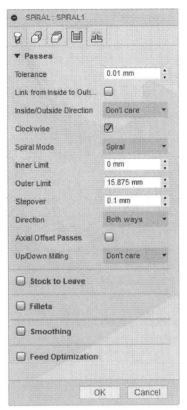

Figure-4. Passes tab of SPIRAL dialog box

- Select the **Clockwise** check box of **Passes** tab to set the direction of spiral to clockwise.
- Select the **Spiral** option from **Spiral** drop-down to create a spiral toolpath which starts from the center and ends at the outermost boundary.
- Select the **Spiral with circles** option from **Spiral** drop-down to create a circular toolpath at the minimum and maximum radius. This toolpath will only be created if the minimum radius is larger than zero and maximum radius is smaller than the radius of regulation boundary.
- Select the **Concentric circles** option from **Spiral** drop-down to create a concentric circle toolpath.
- Click in the **Inner Limit** edit box of **Passes** tab to set the minimum inner radius.
- Click in the **Outer radius** edit box of **Passes** tab to set the maximum outer radius.
- Click in the **Stepover** edit box of **Passes** tab and enter the value.
- The other options of the dialog box are same as discussed earlier.
- After specifying the parameters, click on the **OK** button from **SPIRAL** dialog box. The toolpath will be generated and displayed on the model; refer to Figure-5

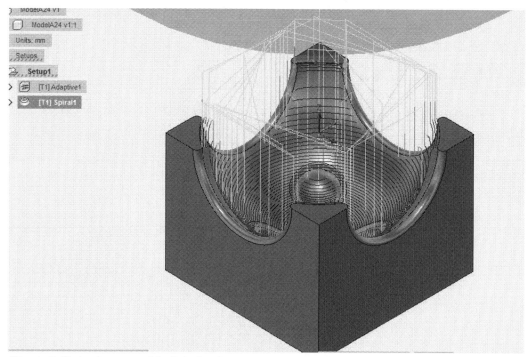

Figure-5. Toolpath generated for Spiral tool

Radial

The **Radial** tool is used to create toolpath along the radii of an arc. The toolpath created by radial is similar to the spokes of wheel which are then projected down on the surface. The procedure to use this tool is discussed next.

- Click on the **Radial** tool of **3D** drop-down from **Toolbar**; refer to Figure-6. The **RADIAL** dialog box will be displayed; refer to Figure-7.
- Click on the **Select** button of **Tool** section from **Tool** tab. The **Select Tool** dialog box will be displayed. Select the required tool.
- Click on the **Passes** tab of **RADIAL** dialog box. The **Passes** tab will be displayed; refer to Figure-8.
- Click in the **Angular Step** edit box of **Passes** tab and enter the angular value of step between radial passes.
- Click in the **Angle From** edit box of **Passes** tab and enter the value of radial starting angle measured from the X-axis.
- Click in the Angle To edit box of Passes tab and enter the value of radial ending value measured from the X-axis.
- The other options of the dialog box were discussed earlier.
- After specifying the parameters click on the **OK** button from **RADIAL** dialog box. The toolpath will be generated and displayed on the model; refer to Figure-9.

Figure-6. Radial tool

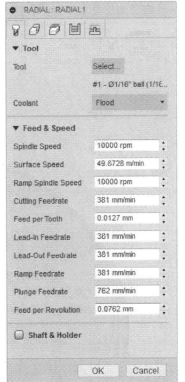

Figure-7. RADIAL dialog box

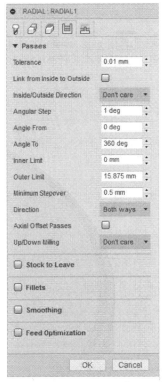

Figure-8. Passes tab of
RADIAL dialog box

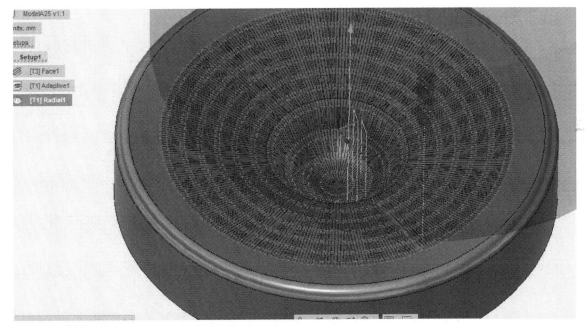

Figure-9. Toolpath generated for Radial tool

Morphed Spiral

The **Morphed Spiral** tool is mainly used to create toolpath of free-form surfaces. The procedure to use this tool is discussed next.

- Click on the **Morphed Spiral** tool of **3D** drop-down from **Toolbar**; refer to Figure-10. The **MORPHED SPIRAL** dialog box will be displayed; refer to Figure-11.

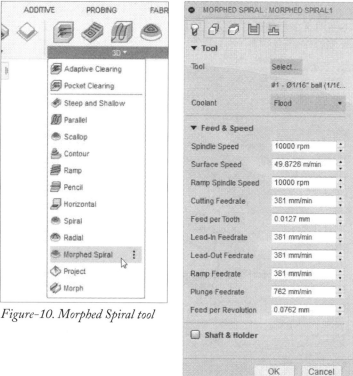

Figure-10. Morphed Spiral tool

Figure-11. MORPHED SPIRAL dialog box

- Click on the **Select** button of **Tool** section from **Tool** tab. The **Select Tool** dialog box will be displayed. Select the required tool.
- The other options of the dialog box are same as discussed earlier.
- After specifying the parameters, click on the **OK** button from **MORPHED Spiral** dialog box. The toolpath will be created and displayed on the model; refer to Figure-12.

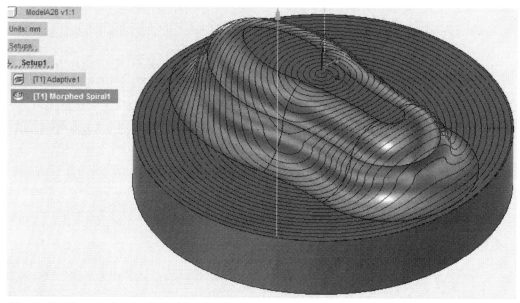

Figure-12. Generated toolpath for Morphed Spiral tool

Project

The **Project** tool is used to create a toolpath along the selected contour. The contour will be machined with the center of the tool. The procedure to use this tool is discussed next.

- Click on the **Project** tool of **3D** drop-down from **Toolbar**; refer to Figure-13. The **PROJECT** dialog box will be displayed; refer to Figure-14.

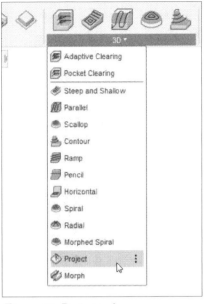

Figure-13. Project tool

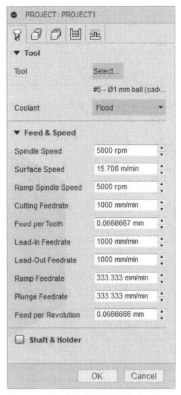

Figure-14. PROJECT dialog box

- Click on the **Select** button of **Tool** section from **Tool** tab. The **Select Tool** dialog box will be displayed. Select the desired tool.
- Click on the desired curve from the model.
- The other options of the dialog box are same as discussed earlier.
- After specifying the parameter, click on the **OK** button from **PROJECT** dialog box. The toolpath will be generated and displayed on the model; refer to Figure-15.

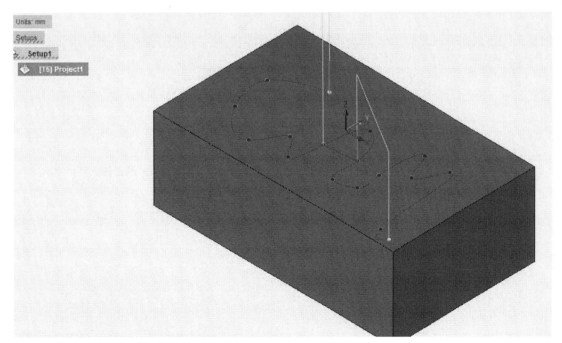

Figure-15. Generated toolpath for Project tool

Morph

The **Morph** tool is used to create the toolpath for machining shallow areas between selected contour. The procedure to use this tool is discussed next.

*   Click on the **Morph** tool of **3D** drop-down from **Toolbar**; refer to Figure-16. The **MORPH** dialog box will be displayed; refer to Figure-17.

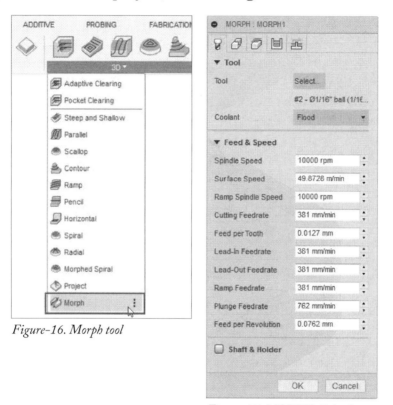

Figure-16. Morph tool

Figure-17. MORPH dialog box

*   Click on the **Select** button of **Tool** section from **Tool** tab. The **Select Tool** dialog box will be displayed. Select the required tool.
*   Select the curve as required from model; refer to Figure-18.

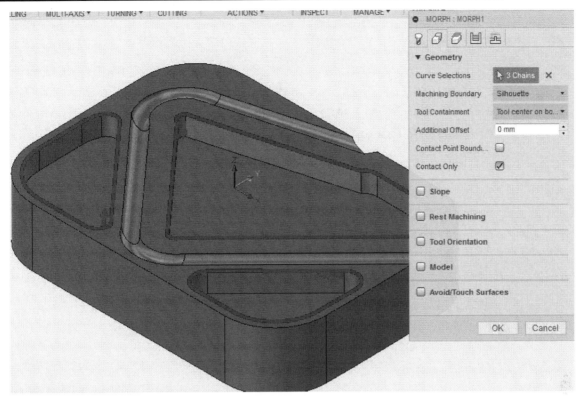

Figure-18. Selection of curve for Morph tool

- The options of the dialog box were discussed earlier.
- After specifying the various parameters, click on the **OK** button from **MORPH** dialog box. The toolpath will be generated and displayed on the model; refer to Figure-19.

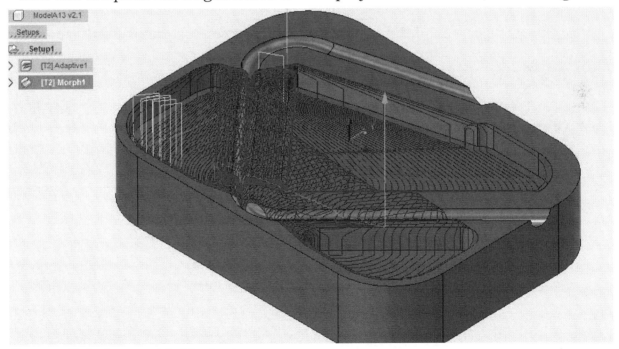

Figure-19. Toolpath generated for Morph tool

MULTI-AXIS TOOLPATH

Till now, we have discussed the procedure of creating 2D and 3D toolpath. In this section, we will discuss the procedure of creating the multi-axis toolpaths which are used to machine complex 3D shapes.

Creating Swarf Toolpath

The **Swarf** is a multi-axis toolpath which is used for side cutting of model. It is used for milling the beveled edges and tapered walls. The procedure to create this toolpath is discussed next.

• Click on the **Swarf** tool of **MULTI-AXIS** drop-down from **Toolbar**; refer to Figure-20. The **SWARF** dialog box will be displayed; refer to Figure-21.

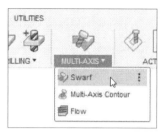

Figure-20. Swarf tool

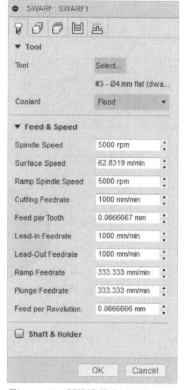

Figure-21. SWARF dialog box

• Click on the **Select** button of **Tool** section from **Tool** tab. The **Select Tool** dialog box will be displayed. Select the required tool.

Geometry

• Click on the **Geometry** tab of **SWARF** dialog box. The **Geometry** tab will be displayed; refer to Figure-22.

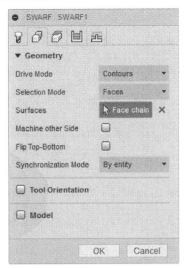

Figure-22. Geometry tab of
SWARF dialog box

- Select the **Contours** option from **Drive Mode** drop-down to select the contour from model.
- Select the **Surface** option from **Drive Mode** drop-down to select the faces from the model for generation of toolpath.
- Select **Faces** option from **Selection Mode** drop-down to select continuous faces from model for selection.
- Select **Contour Pairs** option from **Selection Mode** drop-down to select the upper and lower edges chain from the tapered face which will drive the swarf toolpath.
- Select **Manual** option from **Selection Mode** drop-down to select the individual surfaces from the model.
- The **Nothing** button of **Surfaces** section is active by default. You need to select the face, edges, or contour.
- Select the **Machine other Side** check box of **Geometry** section to force the toolpath to machine to the other side of the selected contour.
- Select the **Flip Top Bottom** check box of **Geometry** section to change the direction of tool by switching the lower and upper contour. This option will only be applied when **Contours pairs** option is not selected in the **Select Mode** drop-down.
- Click on the **Synchronization Mode** drop-down from **Geometry** tab and select the desired option if Contours option is selected in the **Drive Mode** drop-down.

Passes

Click on the **Passes** tab of **SWARF** dialog box. The options of **Passes** tab will be displayed; refer to Figure-23.

Figure-23. Passes tab of SWARF dialog box

- Click on the **Cutting Mode** drop-down of **Passes** tab and select the required option to specify how the tool will cut vertically.
- Click in the **Tool Offset** edit box of **Passes** tab and enter the value of tool offset along the tool axis relative to the bottom guide curve.
- Click in the **Top** of **Stock** edit box of **Passes** tab to specify the overall thickness of the stock.
- Select the **Repeat Finishing Passes** check box of **Passes** tab to perform an additional finishing pass with zero stock.
- Select the **Tangential Fragment Extension Distance** edit box of **Passes** tab to extends the cut tangentially at both ends of the pass.
- Select the **Minimize axial Motion** check box of **Passes** tab to minimize the motion of tool.
- Select the **Along Stock** check box of **Passes** tab to move the tool along stock for machining.
- Click in the **Pass Overlap** edit box of **Passes** tab and enter the value of distance to extend machining for a closed pass.
- Click on the **Maximum Fan Distance** edit box of **Passes** tab and specify the maximum distance over which to fan the tool axis.
- Click on the **Sideways tilt** edit box of **Passes** tab and specify the values in degrees the tool should be tilted sideways.
- Click on the **Maximum Segment Length** edit box of **Passes** tab and specify the value of maximum length for a single segment for the generated for toolpath.
- Click on the **Maximum Tool Axis Sweep** edit box of **Passes** tab and specify the maximum angle up to which tool can deviate about its axis while cutting.
- The other options of the dialog box were discussed earlier.
- After specifying the parameter, click on the **OK** button from **SWARF** dialog box. The toolpath will be generated and displayed on the model; refer to Figure-24.

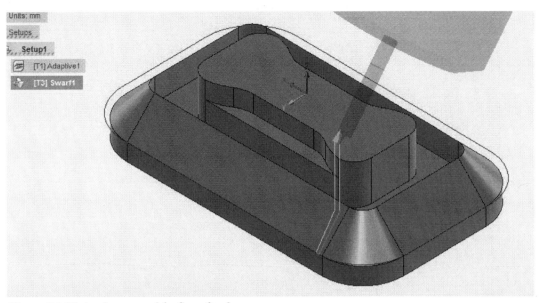

Figure-24. Toolpath generated for Swarf tool

Creating Multi-Axis Contour Toolpath

The **Multi-Axis Contour** tool is used for machining curves with the help of 5-Axis machining. These curves lie on the face of a model forming different 3D curvatures. The procedure to use this tool is discussed next.

*   Click on the **Multi-Axis Contour** tool of **Multi-Axis** drop-down from **Toolbar**; refer to Figure-25. The **MULTI-AXIS CONTOUR** dialog box will be displayed; refer to Figure-26.

Figure-25. Multi-Axis Contour tool

*   Click on the **Select** button of **Tool** section from **Tool** tab. The Select **Tool** dialog box will be displayed. Select the required tool.
*   Click on the curve from the model to select for machining. You can also select more than 1 curves for machining.
*   Click on the **Passes** tab of **MULTI-AXIS CONTOUR** dialog box. The **Passes** tab will be displayed; refer to Figure-27.

Figure-26. MULTI-AXIS CON-
TOUR dialog box

Figure-27. Passes tab of MULTI-
AXIS CONTOUR dialog box

- Click on the **Cutting Mode** drop-down from **MULTI-AXIS CONTOUR** dialog box and select the required option to specify the method for machining along a specific contact path.
- Click on the **Sideways Compensation** drop-down and select the required option.
- Click on the **Forward Tilt** edit box of **MULTI-AXIS CONTOUR** dialog box and enter the angular value for tool should be tilted forward.
- Click in the **Minimum Tilt** edit box of **MULTI-AXIS CONTOUR** dialog box and specify the minimum value if allowed tilt from the selected operation tool axis.
- Click in the **Maximum Tilt** edit box of **MULTI-AXIS CONTOUR** dialog box and specify the minimum value if allowed tilt from the selected operation tool axis.
- The other options of the dialog box were discussed earlier.
- After specifying the parameter, click on the **OK** button from **MULTI-AXIS CONTOUR** dialog box. The toolpath will be generated and displayed on the model; refer to Figure-28.

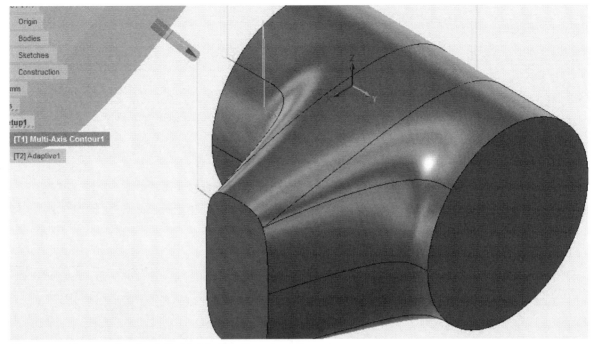

Figure-28. Generated toolpath for Multi-Axis Contour tool

Creating Flow Toolpath

The Flow Toolpath is used to machine round edges of the model using multi-axes strategy. Using this option will allow better finish at rounds. The procedure to create this toolpath is given next.

- Click on the **Flow** tool from the **MULTI-AXIS** drop-down in the **Ribbon**. The **Flow** dialog box will be displayed; refer to Figure-29.

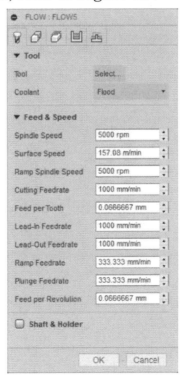

Figure-29. Flow dialog box

- Click on the **Select** button and select the desired fillet tool. Specify the desired feed and speed parameters.

- Click on the **Geometry** tab and select the round faces on which you want to apply flow toolpath; refer to Figure-30.

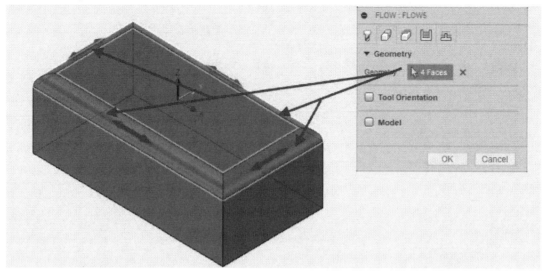

Figure-30. Faces selected for flow toolpath

- Click on the **Passes** tab in the dialog box. The options will be displayed as shown in Figure-31.

Figure-31. Passes tab for Flow dialog box

- Select the **Along u** option from **Isometric Direction** drop-down if you want to move the tool horizontally while cutting. Select the **Along v** option from the drop-down if you want to move the tool vertically while cutting.
- Specify the desired value of **Number of Stepovers** edit box to increase the finish of cut. Specified number of toolpath passes will be created along the selected face.
- Select the **Use Multi-Axis** check box to allow tilting of tool/workpiece bed to create multi-axis toolpath.

- Specify the other parameters as discussed earlier and click on the **OK** button. The toolpath will be created; refer to Figure-32.

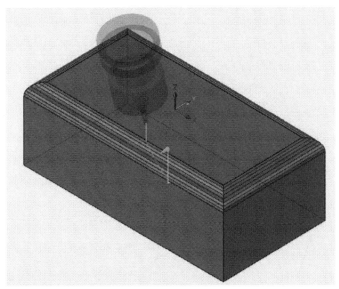

Figure-32. Flow toolpath created

CREATING DRILL TOOLPATH

The **Drill** tool is used to perform drilling at the specified locations. The procedure to use this tool is discussed next.

- Click on the **Drill** tool from **DRILLING** panel in the **Toolbar**; refer to Figure-33. The **DRILL** dialog box will be displayed; refer to Figure-34.

Figure-33. Drilling tool

Figure-34. DRILL dialog box

- Click on the **Select** button of **Tool** section from **Tool** tab. The **Select Tool** dialog box will be displayed. Select the required drill tool for drilling. Note that you can also select boring, threading, tapping, reaming, and probe tool if you are going to perform related operation.

Geometry

- Click on the **Geometry** tab of **DRILL** dialog box. The **Geometry** tab will be displayed; refer to Figure-35.

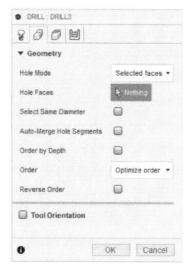

Figure-35. Geometry tab of DRILL dialog box

- Select the **Selected faces** option from **Hole Mode** drop-down to select the faces of hole from model for drilling. Select the **Selected points** option from **Hole Mode** drop-down to select the points of holes for drilling. Select the **Diameter range** option from drop-down if you want to select all the holes inside specified maximum & minimum diameter range.
- The **Nothing** button of **Hole Faces/Hole Points/Containment Boundary** option (based on your selection in **Hole Mode** drop-down) from **Geometry** tab is active by default. You need to click on the geometry from model; refer to Figure-36.

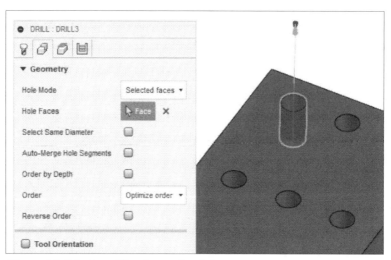

Figure-36. Selection of face for creating hole

- Select the **Select Same Diameter** check box of **Geometry** tab to select the hole of same diameter.
- Select the **Auto-Merge Hole Segments** check box of **Geometry** tab to include the neighboring segments automatically while drilling a hole with multiple segments.
- Select the **Optimize Order** check box of **Geometry** tab to minimize the ordering of hole by ordering the holes.
- Select the desired option from the **Order** drop-down to define order of drilling holes.

Cycle

- Click on the **Cycle** tab of **DRILL** dialog box. The **Cycle** tab will be displayed; refer to Figure-37.

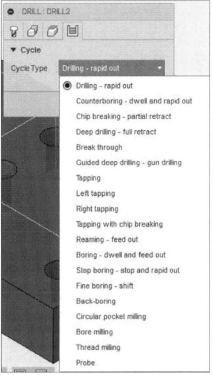

Figure-37. Cycle tab of DRILL dialog box

- Click on the **Cycle Type** drop-down of **Cycle** tab and select the required option.
- The other options of the dialog box are same as discussed earlier.
- After specifying the parameters, click on the **OK** button from **DRILL** dialog box. The toolpath will be generated and displayed on the model; refer to Figure-38.

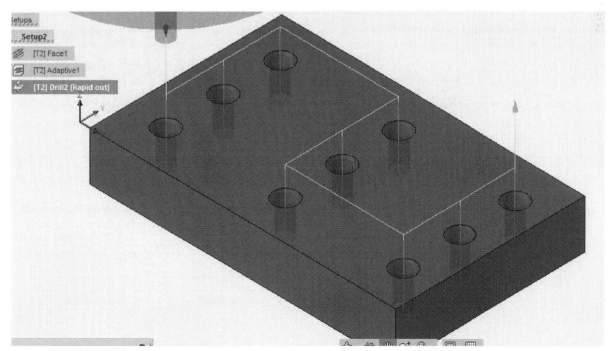

Figure-38. Toolpath generated for drill

TOOLPATH BY HOLE RECOGNITION

The **Hole Recognition** tool is used to create toolpath for drilling holes automatically based on recognized holes. The procedure to create toolpath is given next.

- Click on the **Hole Recognition** tool from the **DRILLING** panel in the **MILLING** tab of **Toolbar**. The **Hole Recognition** dialog box will be displayed with all the holes selected; refer to Figure-39.

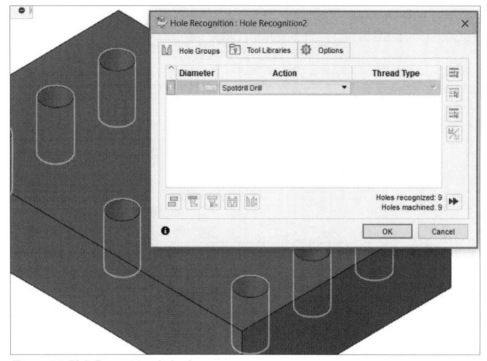

Figure-39. Hole Recognition dialog box

- Select the desired tool type from the drop-down in the **Action** column of **Hole Groups** tab in the dialog box like Simple Drill, Spot Drill, and so on.
- Click on the **Tool Libraries** tab in the dialog box and select check boxes for tools you want to use for drilling.
- Click on the **Options** tab in the dialog box. The options will be displayed as shown in Figure-40.

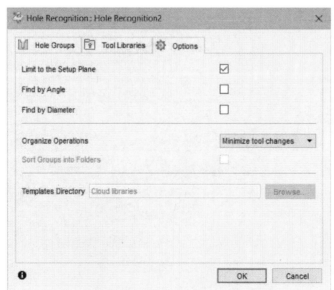

Figure-40. Options tab in Hole Recognition dialog box

- Select the **Limit to the Setup Plane** check box to limit search for holes to current active plane.
- Select the **Find by Angle** check box and specify the minimum-maximum angle limits recognizing holes.
- Select the **Find by Diameter** check box and specify the maximum diameter upto which you want to search for the holes.
- Select the **Minimize tool changes** option from the **Organize Operations** drop-down if you want selected cutting tool to complete all operations before the next tool is selected. Select the **Group by size** option from the drop-down if you want to complete all operations on first hole and then move to another hole.
- After setting desired parameters, click on the **OK** button from the dialog box. The toolpaths will be created automatically; refer to Figure-41.

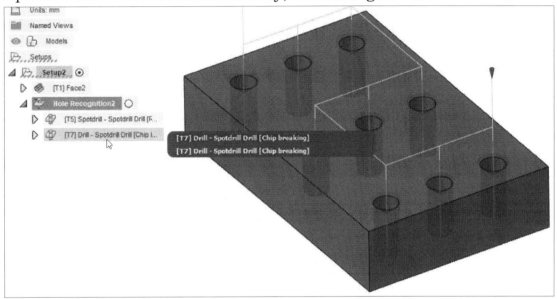

Figure-41. Toolpaths created for drilling

PRACTICAL

Create CAM program of the given model using 3D and 2D toolpaths; refer to Figure-42.

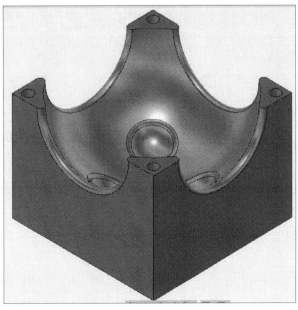

Figure-42. Practical 1

Adding Model to MANUFACTURE

- Create and save the part in **MANUFACTURE** workspace. The part file is available in the respective chapter folder of **Autodesk Fusion 360** resources.
- Click on the **MANUFACTURE** workspace from **Workspace** drop-down. The model will be displayed in the **MANUFACTURE** workspace.

Creating Stock

- Click on the **New Setup** tool of **SETUP** drop-down from **Toolbar**. The **SETUP** dialog box will be displayed along with the stock of model.
- Specify the parameters of **Setup** tab, **Stock** tab and **Post Process** tab of **SETUP** dialog box as shown in Figure-43.

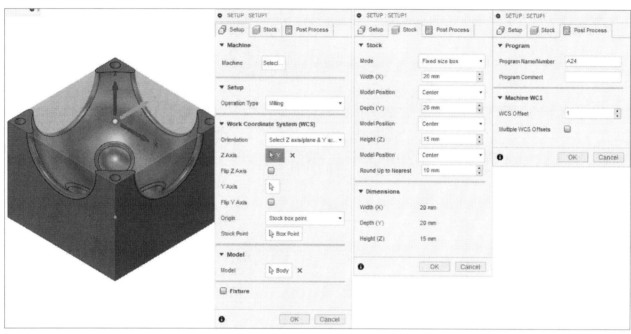

Figure-43. Specifying parameters for stock

- After specifying the parameters, click on the **OK** button from **SETUP** dialog box. The stock will be created and displayed on the model.

Generating Adaptive Clearing Toolpath

- Click on the **Adaptive Clearing** tool of **3D** drop-down from **Toolbar**. The **ADAPTIVE** dialog box will be displayed.
- Click on the **Select** button of **Tool** tab and select the tool from the record list of **Select Tool** dialog box as shown in Figure-44.
- If the tool is not available in the list then create a new ball mill tool. After selecting the tool, click on the **OK** button from **Select Tool** dialog box. The tool will be added in the **ADAPTIVE** dialog box.

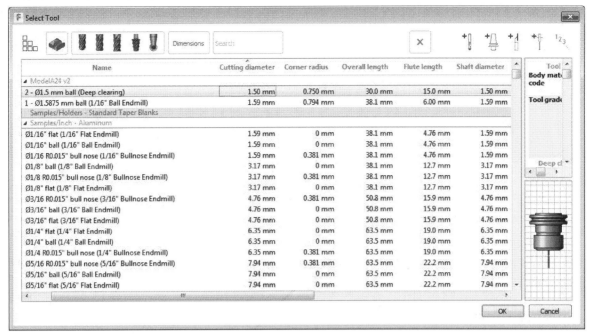

Figure–44. Selecting tool for adaptive clearing

- Specify the parameters of **Geometry** tab, **Passes** tab, and **Linking** tab of **ADAPTIVE** dialog box; refer to Figure-45.

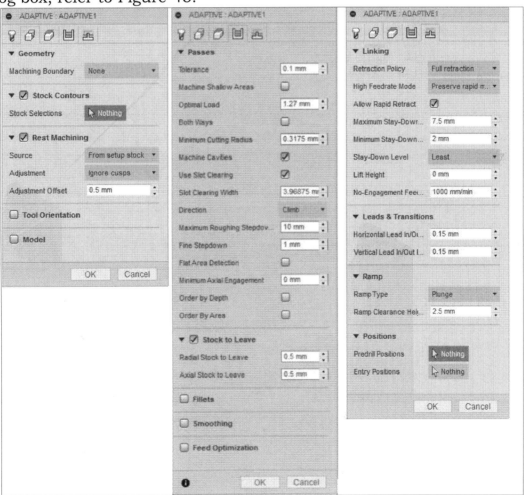

Figure–45. Parameters of Adaptive dialog box

- After specifying the parameters, click on the **OK** button from **ADAPTIVE** dialog box. The toolpath will be generated and displayed on the model; refer to Figure-46.

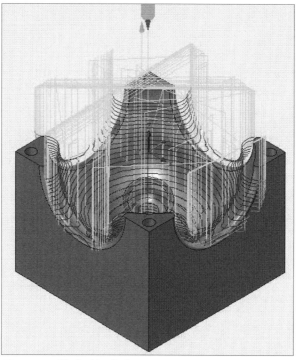

Figure-46. Toolpath of adaptive clearing

Generating Spiral Toolpath

- Click on the **Spiral** tool of **3D** drop-down from **Toolbar**. The **SPIRAL** dialog box will be displayed.
- Click on the **Select** button of **Tool** tab and select the tool from the record list of **Select Tool** dialog box as shown in Figure-47.

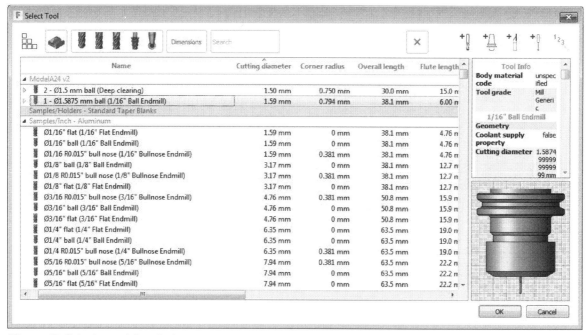

Figure-47. Selecting tool for spiral

- Specify the parameters of **Geometry** tab, **Passes** tab, and **Linking** tab of **SPIRAL** dialog box; refer to Figure-48.

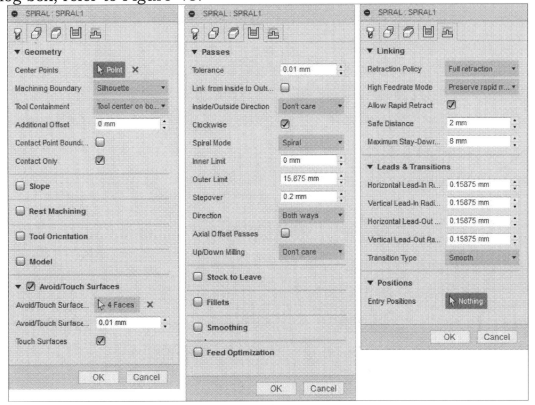

Figure–48. Specifying parameters for spiral

Generating Scallop Toolpath

- Click on the **Scallop** tool of **3D** drop-down from **Toolbar**. The **SCALLOP** dialog box will be displayed.
- Click on the **Select** button of **Tool** section and select the tool which is selected in last operation from **Select Tool** dialog box.
- Specify the parameters of **Tool** tab, **Geometry** tab, **Passes** tab, and **Linking** tab as shown in Figure-49.

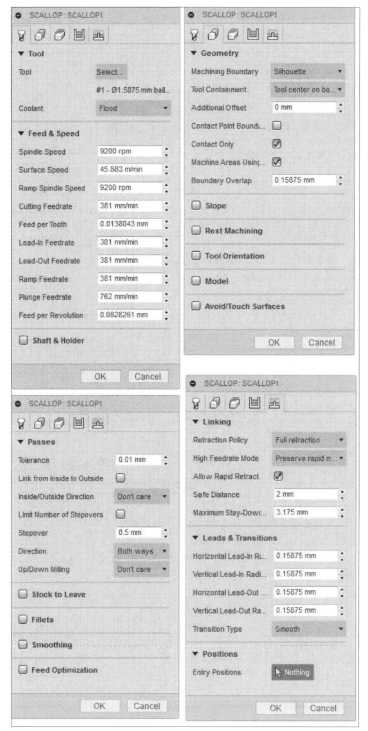

Figure–49. Parameters for Scallop tool

- After specifying the parameters, click on the **OK** button from **SCALLOP** dialog box. The toolpath will be created and displayed on the model; refer to Figure-50.

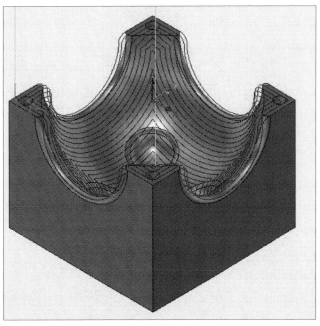

Figure-50. Toolpath generated for scallop

Generating Radial Toolpath

- Click on the **Radial** tool of **3D** drop-down from **Toolbar**. The **RADIAL** dialog box will be displayed.
- Click on the **Select** button of **Tool** section and select the tool which is selected in last operation from **Select Tool** dialog box.
- Click on the **Geometry** tab of the **RADIAL** dialog box. The **Geometry** tab will be displayed.
- Click on the **Machine Boundary** drop-down and select the **Selection** option.
- The **Nothing** button of **Machine Boundary** option is active by default. You need to select the chain for machining; refer to Figure-51.

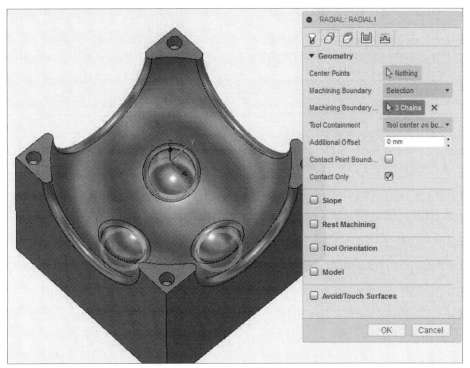

Figure-51. Selecting chains for machining

- Specify the parameters of **Passes** tab and **Geometry** tab as displayed in Figure-52.

Figure-52. Parameters for Radial dialog box

- After specifying the parameters, click on the **OK** button from **RADIAL** dialog box. The toolpath will be created and displayed on the model; refer to Figure-53.

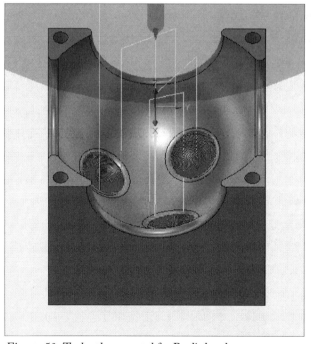

Figure-53. Toolpath generated for Radial tool

Generating Drill Toolpath

- Click on the **Drill** tool from **Toolbar**. The **DRILL** dialog box will be displayed.
- Click on the **Select** button of **Tool** section and select the tool from **Select Tool** dialog box as displayed in Figure-54.

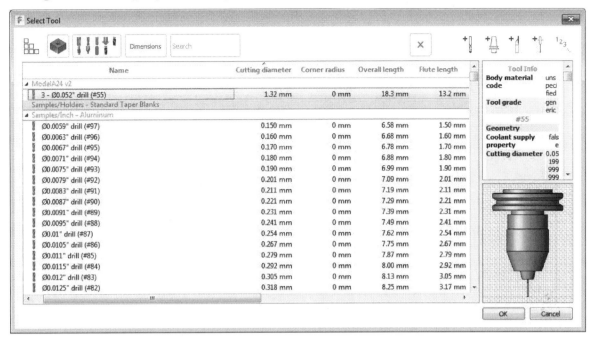

Figure-54. Selection of tool for drill

- After selecting the tool for drill, click on the **OK** button from **Select Tool** dialog box. The tool will we added in **DRILL** dialog box.
- Specify the parameters of **Geometry** tab from **DRILL** dialog box as displayed in Figure-55. Select the round face of one of the hole.

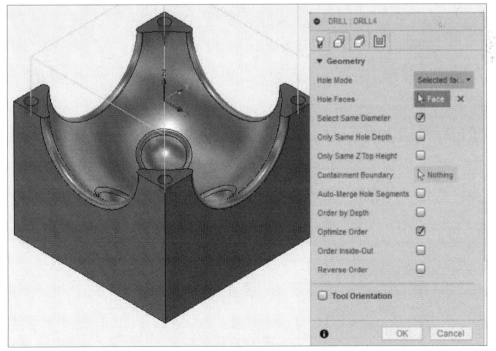

Figure-55. Sspecifying geometry tab of DRILL dialog box

- After specifying the parameters, click on the **OK** button from **DRILL** dialog box. The toolpath will be generated and displayed on the model; refer to Figure-56.

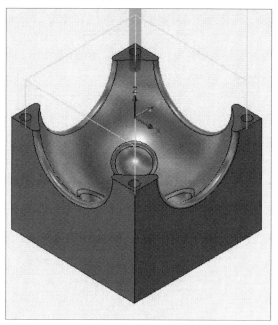

Figure-56. Generated toolpath for Drill tool

- Till now, we have applied the tools to create the required toolpath. Now, we will simulate the whole process to check whether the generated toolpath is working properly or there is a collision of tool with stock.
- Click on the **Simulate** button from shortcut menu of Setup. The **SIMULATE** dialog box will be displayed.
- Specify the parameters of **SIMULATE** dialog box as required and click on the **Play** button. The machining process will be started; refer to Figure-57. Make sure to create finishing

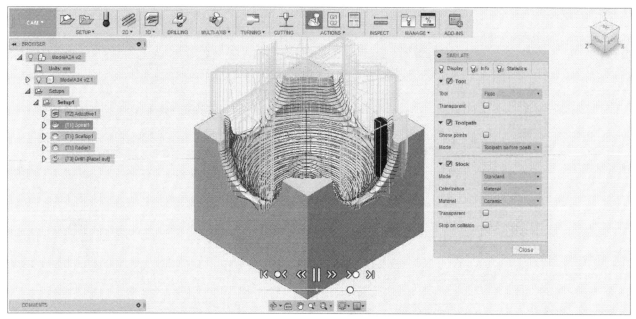

Figure-57. Simulating the generated toolpath

PRACTICE 1

Machine the stock of width as 148 mm, depth as 52 mm, height as 21 mm to create the part as shown in Figure-58. The part file of this model is available in the respective folder of **Autodesk Fusion 360**.

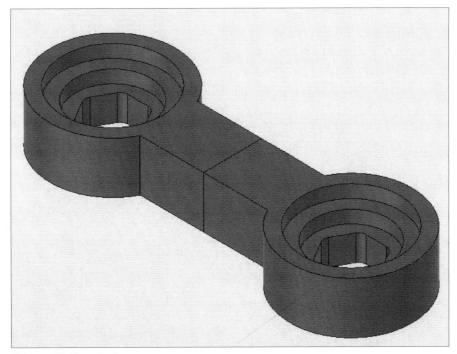

Figure-58. Practice 1

PRACTICE 2

Machine the stock of width as 102 mm, depth as 62 mm, height as 23 mm to create the part as shown in Figure-59. The part file of this model is available in the respective folder of **Autodesk Fusion 360**.

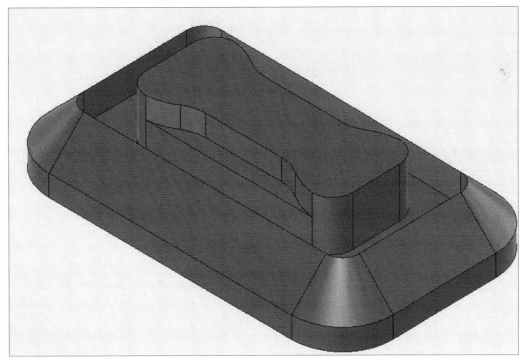

Figure-59. Practice 2

PRACTICE 3

Machine the stock of stock diameter as 80 mm, thickness as 7 mm and stock align to the center to create the part as shown in Figure-60. The part file of this model is available in the respective folder of **Autodesk Fusion 360**.

Figure-60. Practice 3

Chapter 18

Generating Turning and Cutting Toolpaths

Topics Covered

The major topics covered in this chapter are:

- *Turning Profile*
- *Turning Face*
- *Turning Chamfer*
- *Turning Thread*
- *Turning Groove*
- *Cutting Toolpaths*

GENERATING TURNING TOOLPATH

Till now, we have discussed the procedure of creating milling toolpaths with the help of various tools. In this section, we will discuss the tools used for creating the Turning toolpaths. You need to open a part for turning in Autodesk Fusion and create a machine setup of Turning machine as discussed earlier in Chapter 15 before working on this chapter.

Turning Profile Roughing

The **Turning Profile Roughing** tool is used for roughing the profile of model using various tools. The procedure to use this tool is discussed next.

*   Click on the **Turning Profile Roughing** tool of **TURNING** drop-down from **Toolbar**; refer to Figure-1. The **PROFILE ROUGHING** dialog box will be displayed; refer to Figure-2.

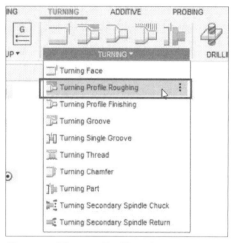

Figure-1. Turning Profile tool

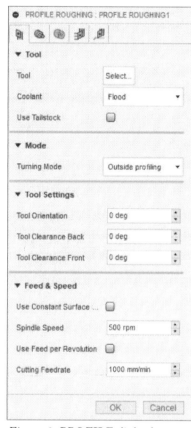

Figure-2. PROFILE dialog box

*   Click on the **Select** button of **Tool** option from **Tool** tab. The **Select Tool** dialog box will be displayed. Select the desired tool for profiling and click on the **OK** button. The tool will be added in the **PROFILE ROUGHING** dialog box.

Tool

*   Click on the **Coolant** drop-down of **Tool** tab and select the desired option.
*   Select the **Use Tailstock** check box of **Tool** tab to apply support to the part to be machined. When you have a long part for turning then you should use tail stock for support.
*   Select the **Outside profiling** option of **Turning Mode** drop-down from **Mode** section to retract the tool outside of the stock and machine axially depending on the direction setting.

- Select the **Inside Profiling** option of **Turning Mode** drop-down from **Mode & Direction** section to approach or retract the tool from the center-line and machines radially depending on the direction setting.
- Set the desired angle values in edit boxes of **Tool Settings** section to define orientation of the cutting tool.
- Select the **Use Constant Surface Speed** check box of **Feed & Speed** section from **Tool** tab to automatically adjust the spindle speed for maintaining a constant surface speed between tool and the workpiece.
- Click in the **Surface Speed** edit box of **Feed & Speed** section to enter the value of spindle speed expressed as the speed of the tool on the surface.
- Click in the **Maximum Spindle Speed** edit box of **Feed & Speed** section and enter the value of maximum allowed spindle speed when using constant surface speed.
- Select the **Use Feed Per Revolution** check box of **Feed & Speed** section to automatically adjust the feed rate based on the RPM of the spindle to maintain a constant chip load.
- Click in the **Cutting Feed Per Revolution** edit box of **Feed & Speed** section and specify the distance of tool advancement into the material for each 360 degree rotation of spindle when the tool is fully engaged.

Geometry

- Click on the **Geometry** tab of **PROFILE** dialog box. The **Geometry** tab will be displayed; refer to Figure-3.

Figure-3. Geometry tab of PROFILE dialog box

- Select the **Model** check box of **Geometry** tab to select a model contour for machining. The **Nothing** button of **Model Contour** option is active by default. You need to click on the contour of model to be used as profile for cutting.
- Select the desired option from **Front Mode** drop-down and define the reference for front confinement region. Confinement region is an imaginary space within which machining of part will be done.
- Click in the **Offset** edit box of **Front** section in **Geometry** tab and enter the value to specify the offset distance for front confinement plane from selected reference.
- Specify the value of extension in **Tangential Extension** edit box if you want the open profiles to be tangentially extended.
- Similarly, specify parameters for back plane of confinement region.

- Select the **Rest Machining** check box of **Geometry** tab to specify that only stock left after the previous operations should be machined.
- Click on the **Source** drop-down of **Rest Machining** check box and select the required option to specify the source from which the rest machining stock should be calculated.

Radii

Click on the **Radii** tab of **PROFILE** dialog box. The options of **Radii** tab will be displayed; refer to Figure-4.

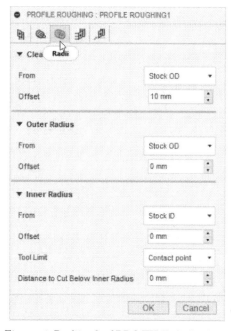

Figure-4. Radii tab of PROFILE dialog box

- Click on the **From** drop-down of **Clearance** section and select the required reference for clearance location.
- Click in the **Offset** edit box of **Clearance** section and enter the desired value.
- Click on the **From** drop-down of **Outer Radius** section and select the required reference for defining outer diameter of part.
- Click in the **Offset** edit box of **Outer Radius** section and enter the desired value.
- Click on the **From** drop-down of **Inner Radius** section and select the required reference for inner diameter of part.
- Click in the **Offset** edit box of **Inner Radius** section and enter the desired value.
- Select the desired option from the **Tool Limit** drop-down to define the reference to be used as tool point for creating toolpath.
- Click in the **Distance to Cut Below Inner Radius** edit box and specify the value of distance upto which the cutting tool should continue cutting when the tools has reached centerline of part during parting or facing operations.

Passes

Click on the **Passes** tab of **PROFILE** dialog box. The options of **Passes** tab will be displayed; refer to Figure-5.

- Select the desired option from the **Cycle** drop-down to define how tool will retract and come back for next cutting pass.

- Select the **Front to back** option of **Direction** drop-down from **Cycle and Direction** section to cut from the front side of the stock towards the back side.
- Select the **Back to Front** option of **Direction** drop-down from **Cycle and Direction** section to cut the material of stock from back side towards the front side.
- Select the **Both Ways** option of **Direction** drop-down from **Cycle and Direction** section to cut the stock from both direction.
- Click on the **Grooving** drop-down from **Cycle and Direction** section and select the desired option to define which type of grooving is allowed while cutting.
- Select the **Use Canned Cycle** check box to output cutting operation as canned cycle.
- Click in the **Tolerance** edit box of **Passes** tab and enter the value of tolerance for each cutting pass.
- Specify the maximum depth of cut allowed for each cutting pass in the **Depth of Cut** edit box.
- Select the **Make Sharp Corners** check box of **Passes** tab to specify that sharp corners must be forced.
- Select the **Use Pecking** check box if you have not selected the **Use Canned Cycle** check box to use multiple retractions along its path when tool is cutting material so that long chips are not formed while cutting. Specify the related depth and retraction value for pecking in respective edit boxes below the **Use Pecking** check box.
- Specify the desired values of material to be left for finishing toolpath in the edit boxes of **Finish Allowance** section of the dialog box.

Linking

Click on the **Linking** tab of **PROFILE ROUGHING** dialog box. The options of **Linking** tab will be displayed; refer to Figure-6.

- Select the desired option from the **High Feedrate Mode** drop-down to define when to use G01 code of rapid feed move and when to use G00 code of rapid retraction move if there is not cutting operation involved in the current step. Select the **Always use high feed** option when there are chances of collision at maximum rapid move speed and specify the desired speed in the **High Feedrate** edit box.
- Set the desired options in **Approach Z** and **Retract Z** drop-downs to define the respective safe Z locations.
- Select the **Override Setup Safe Z** check box if you want to override the value of Safe Z location and specify the related parameters.
- Specify the desired value of retraction distance from cutting pass in the **Retract Distance** edit box.
- The other options of the dialog box were discussed earlier in this book.
- After specifying the parameter, click on the **OK** button from **PROFILE ROUGHING** dialog box. The toolpath will be generated and displayed on the part; refer to Figure-7.

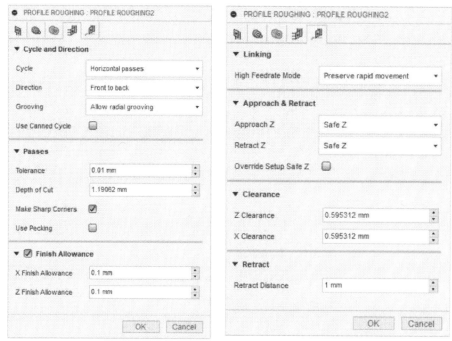

Figure-5. Passes tab of PROFILE ROUGHING dialog box

Figure-6. Linking Tab of PROFILE ROUGHING dialog box

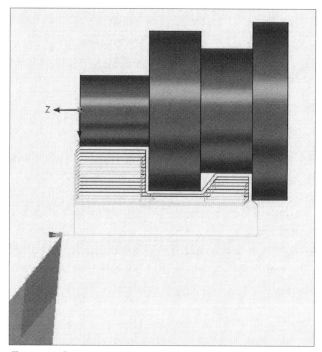

Figure-7. Generated toolpath for Turning Profile tool

Turning Profile Finishing

The **Turning Profile Finishing** tool is used for finishing the model profile with the use of various tools. The procedure to use this tool is discussed next.

• Click on the **Turning Profile Finishing** tool from the **TURNING** drop-down in the **TURNING** tab of **Toolbar**. The **PROFILE FINISHING** dialog box will be displayed as shown in Figure-8.

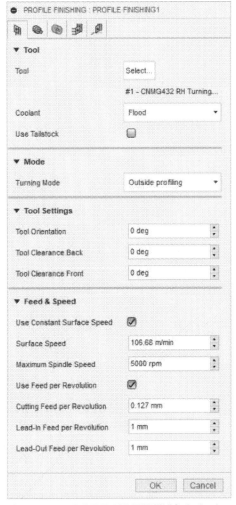

Figure-8. PROFILE FINISHING dialog box

Most of the options in this dialog box are same as discussed for **PROFILE ROUGHING** dialog box. The options which have not been discussed earlier are discussed next.

- Click in the **Tool Orientation** edit box of **Tool Settings** section and enter the angular value to specify the angle of tool for cutting process. This option is used when your lathe turret has a programmable B-Axis. This option will help in machining process by cutting the stock corners of part.
- Click in the **Tool Clearance Back** edit box of **Tool Settings** section and enter the angular value which is added to the tool angle to provide clearance behind the cutting edge.
- Click in the **Tool Clearance Front** edit box of **Tool Settings** section and enter the angular value which is added to the tool angle to provide clearance in front of the cutting edge.
- Click in the **Lead-In feed per Revolution** edit box of **Feed & Speed** section and specify the feed rate of tool in cutting mode before the tool approaches and initially enters the material.
- Click in the **Lead-Out feed per Revolution** edit box of **Feed & Speed** section and specify the feedrate of tool in cutting mode when the tool exists the material.
- Select the **Spring Pass** check box from the **Passes** section of **Passes** tab in the dialog box to create additional finishing pass with zero stock thickness for better finish.

- Select the **No Dragging** check box from the **Passes** section of **Passes** tab in the dialog box to allow changing of tool position when cutting direction is switched between axial and radial. In this way, less drag (stress) is applied on the tool while cutting.
- Specify the desired values for no drag parameters: **No Drag Limit**, **No Drag Clearance**, **No Drag Overlap** in their respective edit boxes. Refer to Figure-9.

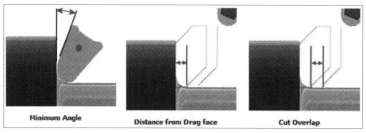

Figure-9. No Drag parameters

- Specify the desired parameters in **Leads & Transitions** section of **Linking** tab in the dialog box to define how cutting tool will enter the workpiece in first cutting pass and how tool will exit in last cutting pass.
- Specify the other parameters as discussed earlier and click on the **OK** button from the dialog box to generate the toolpath.

Turning Groove

The **Turning Groove** tool is used for roughing and finishing strategy to create the groove in the model. The procedure to use this tool is discussed next.

- Click on the **Turning Groove** tool of **TURNING** drop-down from **Toolbar**; refer to Figure-10. The **GROOVE** dialog box will be displayed; refer to Figure-11.

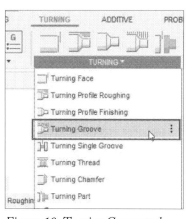

Figure-10. Turning Groove tool

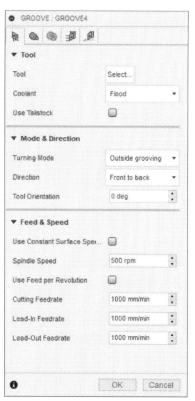

Figure-11. The GROOVE dialog box

- Click on the **Select** button of **Tool** section. The **Select Tool** dialog box will be displayed. Select the required tool and click on **OK** button. The tool will be added in the **GROOVE** dialog box.
- Click on the **Turning Mode** drop-down of **Mode & Direction** section from **TOOL** tab and select the required option according to your turning strategy.
- Click on the **Direction** drop-down of **Mode & Direction** section and select the required option according to the requirement.
- Set the containment of grooving as shown in Figure-12.

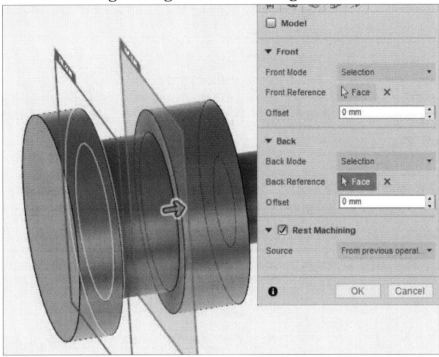

Figure-12. Selection of face for grooving

Passes tab

- Click on the **Passes** tab of **GROOVE** dialog box. The **Passes** tab will be displayed; refer to Figure-13.

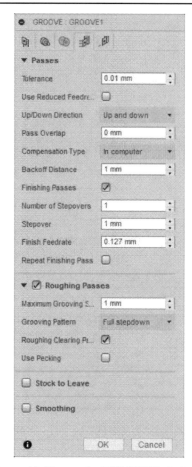

Figure-13. Passes tab of GROOVE dialog box

- Click on the **Tolerance** edit box of **Passes** tab and enter the value of tolerance value.
- Select the **Use Reduced Feedrate** check box of **Passes** tab to reduce the feedrate when grooving along the X-Axis.
- Click on the **Up/Down Direction** drop-down of **Passes** tab and select the required option to control the direction of finishing passes.
- Click in the **Pass Overlap** edit box of **Passes** tab to specify the overlap distance used for finishing pass split due to only up and only down machining directions.
- Click on the **Compensation Type** drop-down of **Passes** tab and select the required compensation type.
- Click in the **Backoff Distance** edit box of **Passes** tab and specify the distance to backoff from the stock before retracting.
- Select the **Finishing Passes** check box of **Passes** tab to remove the material from stock as a secondary finishing operation. This option is only available when **Roughing pass** option is enabled.
- Click in the **Number of Stepovers** check box of **Passes** tab and enter the value of number of finishing stepovers to apply.
- Click in the **Stepover** edit box of **Passes** tab and enter the value of distance which determine the amount of material initial toolpaths leave for the first finishing pass and for any subsequent finishing stepovers.
- Click in the **Finish Feedrate** edit box of **Passes** tab and enter the value of feed rates used for final finishing pass.
- Select the **Repeat Finishing Pass** check box of **Passes** tab to perform an additional finishing pass with zero stock.

- Select **Roughing Passes** check box to enable roughing of the part.
- Click on the **Full stepdown** option of **Grooving Pattern** drop-down from **Passes** tab to remove the stock material radially, before moving along the spindle axis to remove the next amount.
- Click on the **Partial stepdown** drop-down of **Grooving Pattern** drop-down to remove all the material along the spindle axis before starting to remove the material at the next depth which is specified by the Maximum Groove Stepdown value.
- Click on the **Sideways** with **Partial Stepdown** option of **Grooving Pattern** drop-down to remove the material from groove side by side. Due to this strategy the tool life is increased and it results in smaller chips formation.
- Select the **Use Pecking** check box of **Passes** tab to cut the material by a specified pecking depth using pecking force with the help of cutting tool. The gradual progressing down of tool to the cutting depth is required. The tool then retracts along its path by the specified pecking retract distance.
- The other tools of the dialog box were discussed earlier.
- After specifying the parameters, click on the **OK** button from **GROOVE** dialog box. The toolpath will be generated and displayed on the model; refer to Figure-14.

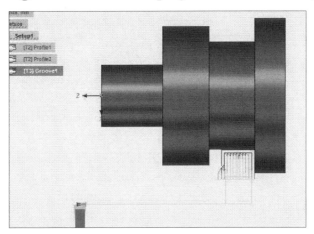

Figure-14. Generated toolpath Groove tool

Turning Face

The **Turning Face** tool is used for machining the front side of the part. The procedure to use this tool is discussed next.

- Click on the **Turning Face** tool of **TURNING** drop-down from **Toolbar**; refer to Figure-15. The **FACE** dialog box will be displayed; refer to Figure-16.

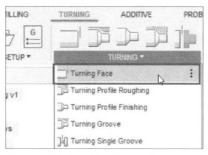

Figure-15. Turning Face tool

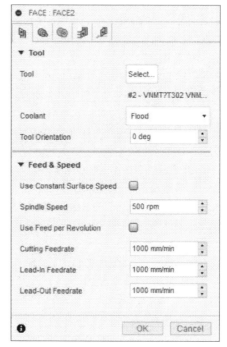

Figure-16. FACE dialog box

- Click on the **Select** selection button of **Tool** section. The **Select Tool** dialog box will be displayed. Select the required tool and click on **OK** button. The tool will be added in the **FACE** dialog box.
- Click on the **Tool Orientation** edit box of the **Tool** tab and enter the angular value to orient the tool as required.
- The options of the dialog box have already been discussed earlier.
- After specifying the parameters, click on the **OK** button from **FACE** dialog box. The toolpath will be generated and displayed on the model; refer to Figure-17.

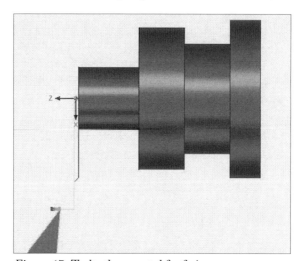

Figure-17. Toolpath generated for facing

Turning Single Groove

The **Turning Single Groove** tool is used for grooving at the selected position only. This tool will create a groove equal to the width of the tool. This is perfect for making a clearance groove behind the thread. The procedure to use this tool is discussed next.

- Click on the **Turning Single Groove** tool of **TURNING** drop-down from **Toolbar**; refer to Figure-18. The **SINGLE GROOVE** dialog box will be displayed; refer to Figure-19

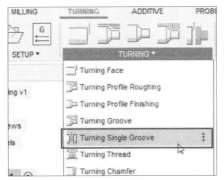

Figure-18. Turning Single Groove tool

Figure-19. SINGLE GROOVE dialog box

- Click on the **Select** button of **Tool** section. The **Select Tool** dialog box will be displayed. Select the required tool and click on **OK** button. The tool will be added in the **SINGLE GROOVE** dialog box.

Geometry

- Click on the **Geometry** tab of **SINGLE GROOVE** dialog box. The **Geometry** tab will be displayed; refer to Figure-20.

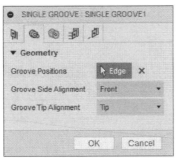

Figure-20. Geometry tab of
SINGLE GROOVE dialog box

- The **Nothing** button of **Groove Positions** option of **Geometry** tab is active by default. You need to click on the edge of groove to select.
- Click on the **Groove Side Alignment** drop-down of **Geometry** section and select the required option for tool side alignment.
- Click on the **Groove Tip Alignment** drop-down of **Geometry** section and select the required option for tip alignment.
- Select the **Dwell Before Retract** check box to give a pause of specified seconds before grooving tool comes out of the workpiece after cutting. Specify the desired dwell time in **Dwelling Period** edit box.

- Select the **Allow Rapid Retract** check box if you want to use G00 code for retraction of tool. By default, rapid feed rate is used for retraction.
- The other options of the dialog box are same as discussed earlier.
- After specifying the various parameters, click on the **OK** button from **SINGLE GROOVE** dialog box. The toolpath will be generated and displayed on the model; refer to Figure-21.

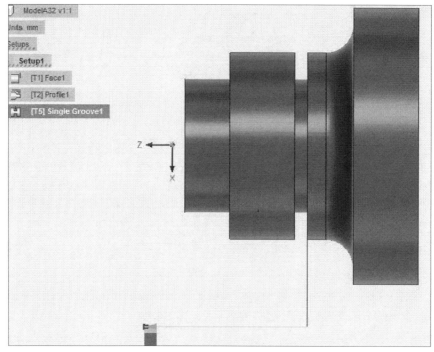

Figure-21. Toolpath generated for Single Groove tool

Turning Chamfer

The **Turning Chamfer** tool is used for chamfering the sharp corners that have not been chamfered in the design. The procedure to use this tool is discussed next.

- Click on the **Turning Chamfer** tool of **TURNING** drop-down from **Toolbar**; refer to Figure-22. The **CHAMFER** dialog box will be displayed; refer to Figure-23.

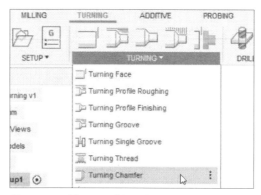

Figure-22. Turning Chamfer tool

Figure-23. The CHAMFER dialog box

- Click on the **Select button** of **Tool** section. The **Select Tool** dialog box will be displayed. Select the required tool and click on **OK** button. The tool will be added in the **CHAMFER** dialog box.
- Click on the **Turning Mode** drop-down of **Mode & Direction** section from **Tool** tab and select the required option according to the turning strategy.
- Click in the **Tool Orientation** edit box of **Mode & Direction** section from **Tool** tab and enter desired angle value to orient the tool.

Geometry

Click on the **Geometry** tab of **CHAMFER** dialog box. The **Geometry** tab will be displayed; refer to Figure-24.

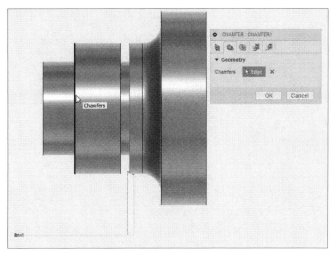

Figure-24. Geometry tab of CHAMFER dialog box

- The **Nothing** button of **Chamfers** option is active by default. You need to click on the edges from model to select.

Passes

Click on the **Passes** tab of **CHAMFER** dialog box. The **Passes** tab will be displayed; refer to Figure-25.

Figure-25. Passes tab of CHAMFER dialog box

- Click in the **Chamfer Width** edit box of **Passes** tab and enter the value of width of chamfer.
- Click in the **Chamfer Extension** edit box of **Passes** tab and enter the value by which to extend the chamfer cutting pass.
- Click in the **Chamfer Angle** edit box of **Passes** tab and enter the value of angle of the chamfer measured from the Z-Axis.
- The other options of the dialog box were discussed earlier in this book.
- After specifying the parameters, click on the **OK** button from **CHAMFER** dialog box. The toolpath will be generated and displayed on the model; refer to Figure-26.

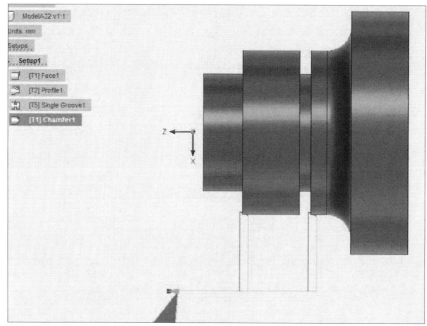

Figure-26. The generated toolpath for Chamfer tool

Turning Part

The **Turning Part** tool is used for cutting the part off with the bar. This tool is also known as cut off operation. The procedure to use this tool is discussed next.

- Click on the **Turning Part** tool of **TURNING** drop-down from **Toolbar**; refer to Figure-27. The **PART** dialog box will be displayed; refer to Figure-28.

Figure-27. Turning Part tool

Figure-28. PART dialog box

- Click on the **Select button** of **Tool** section. The **Select Tool** dialog box will be displayed. Select the required tool and click on **OK** button. The tool will be added in the **PART** dialog box.
- Select the **Edge Break** check box from the **Geometry** tab in the dialog box to define how edges will be conditioned while parting; refer to Figure-29.
- Select the **Chamfer** option from the **Edge Break Type** drop-down to create chamfer at the outer edge before cut off. Select the **Fillet** option from the **Edge Break Type** drop-down to create round at the outer edge before cut off. Specify the parameters related to the selected option in the edit boxes of **Edge Break** section.

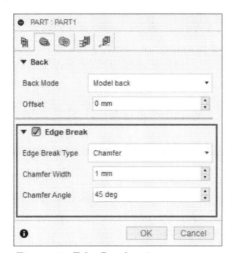

Figure-29. Edge Break options

- The other options of the dialog box are same as discussed earlier.
- After specifying the parameters, click on the **OK** button from **PART** dialog box. The toolpath will be generated and displayed on the model; refer to Figure-30.

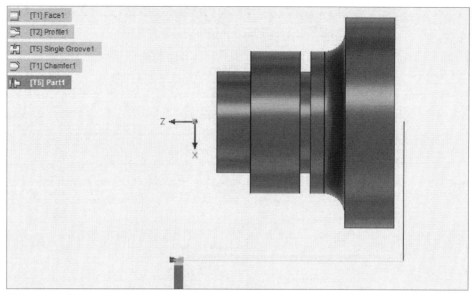

Figure-30. Generated toolpath for Turning Path tool

Turning Thread

The **Turning Thread** tool is used to create thread on cylindrical and conical surfaces. The procedure to use this tool is discussed next.

- Click on the **Turning Thread** tool of **TURNING** drop-down from **Toolbar**; refer to Figure-31. The **THREAD** dialog box will be displayed; refer to Figure-32.

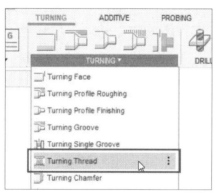

Figure-31. Turning Thread tool

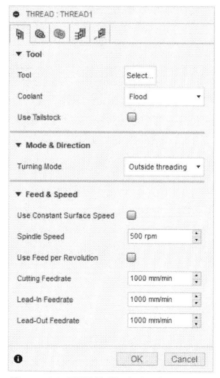

Figure-32. THREAD dialog box

- Click on the **Select** button of **Tool** section. The **Select Tool** dialog box will be displayed. Select the desired tool and click on **OK** button. The tool will be added in the **THREAD** dialog box.
- Click on the **Nothing** button of **Thread Faces** option from **Geometry** tab and select the round faces where you want to machine the thread; refer to Figure-33.

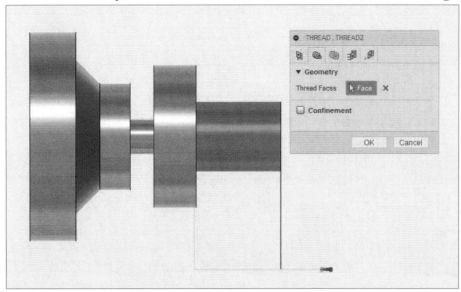

Figure-33. Selection of Face for thread

Passes

Click on the **Passes** tab of **THREAD** dialog box. The **Passes** tab will be displayed; refer to Figure-34.

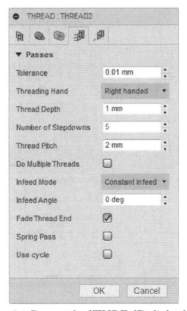

Figure-34. Passes tab of THREAD dialog box

- Click on the **Threading Hand** drop-down of **Passes** tab and select the required threading direction.
- Click in the **Thread Depth** edit box of **Passes** tab and enter the desired value to specify the depth of thread.
- Click in the **Number of Stepdown** edit box of **Passes** tab and specify the desired number of step downs.

- Click in the **Thread Pitch** edit box of **Passes** tab and specify the value of thread pitch.
- Select the **Do Multiple Threads** check box of **Passes** tab to enter the number of threads.
- Click on the **Infeed Mode** drop-down of **Passes** tab and select the required option.
- Click in the **Infeed Angle** edit box of **Passes** tab and enter the angular infeed value.
- Select the **Fade Thread End** check box of **Passes** tab to fade out the thread at the end.
- Select the **Spring Pass** check box of **Passes** tab to perform the final finishing pass twice to remove stock left due to tool deflection.
- Select the **Use cycle** check box of **Passes** tab to request output as canned cycle.
- The other options of the dialog box were discussed earlier.
- After specifying the parameters, click on the **OK** button from **THREAD** dialog box. The toolpath will be generated and displayed on the model; refer to Figure-35.

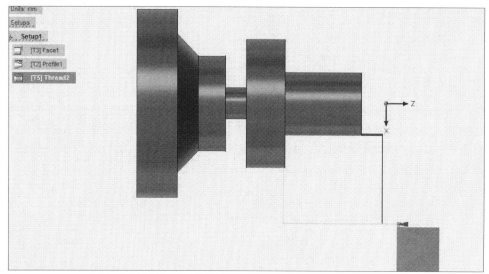

Figure-35. Toolpath generated for thread tool

- After simulating the thread toolpath, the model will be displayed as shown in Figure-36.

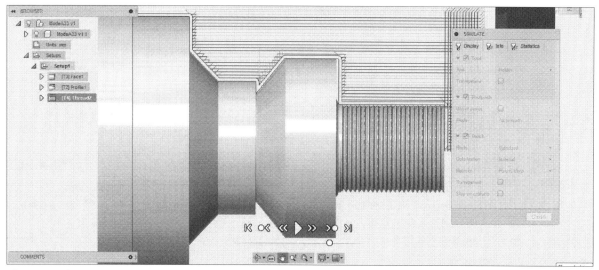

Figure-36. Simulating thread toolpath

Turning Secondary Spindle Chuck

The **Turning Secondary Spindle Chuck** tool is used to transfer stock from one chuck to another (Sub-spindle). This tool is useful when you want to machine back side of part after machining the front side. The procedure to use this tool is discussed next.

- Click on the **Turning Secondary Spindle Chuck** tool of **TURNING** drop-down from **Toolbar**; refer to Figure-37. The **SECONDARY SPINDLE CHUCK** dialog box will be displayed; refer to Figure-38

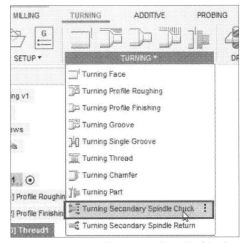

Figure-37. Turning Secondary Spindle Chuck tool

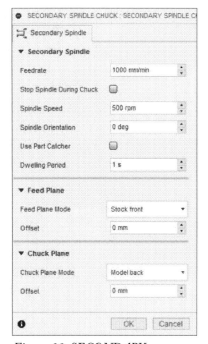

Figure-38. SECONDARY SPINDLE CHUCK dialog box

- Click in the **Feedrate** edit box of **Secondary Spindle** section from **SECONDARY SPINDLE CHUCK** dialog box and enter the value of feed rate.
- Select the **Stop Spindle During Chuck** check box of **Secondary Spindle** section to keep spindle stopped during operations.
- Click in the **Spindle Orientation** edit box of **Secondary Spindle** section and enter the angular value between primary and secondary axis.
- Select the **Use Part Catcher** check box of **Secondary Spindle** section to activate part catcher when available.
- Click in the **Dwelling Period** edit box of **Secondary Spindle** section and enter a time for the operation to dwell.
- Click in the **Feed Plane Mode** drop-down of **Feed Plane** section and select the desired option to specify the feed plane.
- Click in the **Offset** edit box of **Feed Plane** section and enter the offset value.
- Click in the **Chuck Plane Mode** drop-down of **Chuck Plane** section and select the required option to specify the chuck plane.
- Click in the **Offset** edit box of **Chuck Plane** section and enter the offset value.
- Click on the **OK** button from the dialog box. The operation will be created and displayed on the **BROWSER**. Note that there is no simulation for this operation. Only NC codes are generated for this operation based on selected machine.

Turning Secondary Spindle Return

The **Turning Secondary Spindle Return** tool is used for automatic stock return from secondary chuck to main chuck. No toolpath is associated with the strategy. The procedure to use this tool is discussed next.

- Click on the **Turning Secondary Spindle Return** tool of TURNING drop-down from **Toolbar**; refer to Figure-39. The **SECONDARY SPINDLE RETURN** dialog box will be displayed; refer to Figure-40.

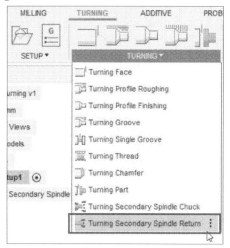

Figure-39. Turning Secondary Spindle Return tool

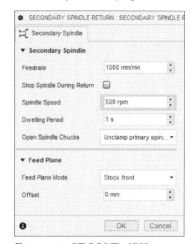

Figure-40. SECONDARY SPINDLE RETURN dialog box

- Click in the **Feedrate** edit box of **Secondary Spindle** section from **SECONDARY SPINDLE RETURN** dialog box and enter the value of feedrate.
- Select the **Stop Spindle During Return** check box of **Secondary Spindle** section to keep spindle stopped during operations.
- Click in the **Spindle Speed** edit box of **Secondary Spindle** section and enter the value of spindle speed in rpm for each machining operation.
- Click in the **Dwelling Period** edit box of **Secondary Spindle** section and enter a time for the operation to dwell.
- Click on the **Open Spindle Chucks** drop-down of **Secondary Spindle** section and select the required option to choose which spindle chucks to open before returning the secondary spindle.
- Click in the **Feed Plane Mode** drop-down of **Feed Plane** section and select the required option to specify the feed plane.

- Click in the **Offset** edit box of **Feed Plane** section and enter the offset value; refer to Figure-41.

Figure-41. Entering offset value

- After specifying the parameters, click on the **OK** button from **SECONDARY SPINDLE RETURN** dialog box. The operation will be added in the **Browser Tree**.

GENERATING CUTTING TOOLPATHS

Till now, we have discussed the procedure to use turning toolpaths and milling toolpaths. In this section, we will discuss the procedure of generating toolpaths for 2D profile cutting using machines like water jet, laser, and plasma cutters.

Cutting

The **2D Profile** tool is used to create toolpaths for cutting material with the help of Laser machine, Plasma cutters, and Water jet machines on a 2D Profile. The procedure to use this tool is discussed next.

- Click on the **2D Profile** tool from the **CUTTING** panel in the **FABRICATION** tab of **Toolbar**; refer to Figure-42. The **2D PROFILE** dialog box will be displayed; refer to Figure-43.

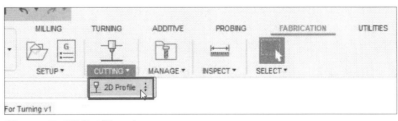

Figure-42. 2D Profile tool

Figure-43. The 2D PROFILE dialog box

- Click on the selection button for **Tool** section. The **Select Tool** dialog box will be displayed. Select the desired tool for cutting and click on **OK** button. The tool will be added in the **2D PROFILE** dialog box.
- Click on the **Cutting Mode** drop-down of **Tool** section and select the required option to set the appropriate cutting feeds for the material being cut. In some machines, there are internal quality tables to set the value.

Geometry

Click on the **Geometry** tab of **2D PROFILE** dialog box. The **Geometry** tab will be displayed; refer to Figure-44.

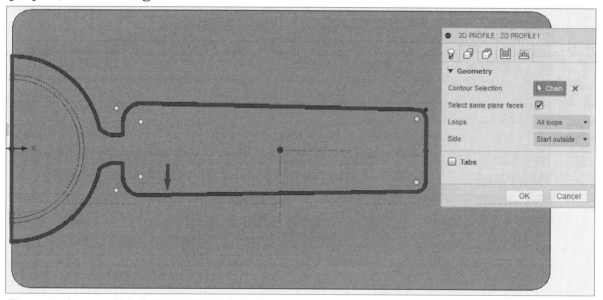

Figure-44. Geometry Tab of 2D PROFILE dialog box

- The **Nothing** button of **Contour Selection** option is active by default. You need to click on the closed contour from the model to cut.
- Select the **Select same plane faces** check box of **Geometry** tab to select all the faces created on the same plane, from all parts within the stock boundary.
- Click on the **Loops** drop-down of **Geometry** tab and select the required option to filter outer or inner chain.
- Click on the **Side** drop-down of **Geometry** tab and select the required option to offset selected edges or sketches.
- Select the **Tabs** check box and provide tabs as discussed earlier.

Linking

Click on the **Linking** tab of **2D PROFILE** dialog box. The **Linking** tab will be displayed; refer to Figure-45.

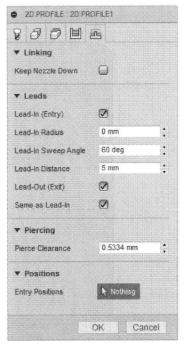

Figure-45. Linking Tab of 2D PROFILE dialog box

- Select the **Keep Nozzle Down** check box of **Linking** tab to avoid retracts and avoid previously cut areas. Set the desired parameters in **Linking** section which are displayed on selecting the **Keep Nozzle Down** check box.
- Select the **Lead-In (Entry)** check box of **Leads** section to enable a contour blend.
- Click in the **Lead-In Radius** edit box of **Leads** section and enter the value to specify the radius for lead in moves.
- Click in the **Lead-In Sweep Angle** edit box of **Leads** section and enter the value to specify the sweep angle of the lead-in arc.
- Click in the **Lead-In Distance** edit box of **Leads** section and enter the value to specify the length of the linear lead in the move.
- Select the **Lead-Out (Exit)** check box of **Linking** tab to enable a contour blend.
- Select the **Same as Lead-In** check box of **Linking** tab to set the lead-Out values be identical to the Lead-In values.
- Click in the **Pierce Clearance** edit box of **Piercing** section and enter the value to distance away from the part edge to start the cut.
- The **Nothing** button of **Entry Positions** option from **Positions** section is active by default. You need to click on the point from model to select.
- The other options of the dialog box are same as discussed earlier.
- After specifying the parameters, click on the **OK** button from **2D PROFILE** dialog box. The toolpath will be generated and displayed on the tool; refer to Figure-46.

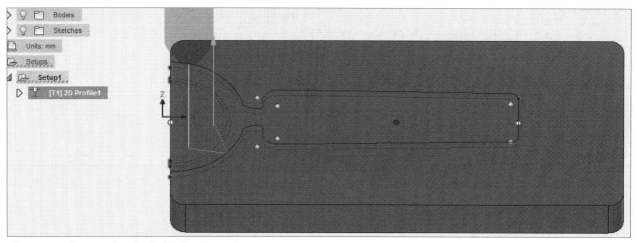

Figure-46. Generated toolpath for Cutting tool

PRACTICAL

Generate the toolpaths of the given model shown in Figure-47 using Turning tools.

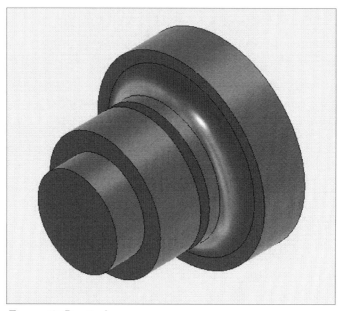

Figure-47. Practical

Adding Model to CAM

- Firstly, create and save the part in **DESIGN** workspace. The part file is available in the respective chapter folder of **Autodesk Fusion 360** folder in resources folder.
- Click on the **MANUFACTURE** workspace from **Workspace** drop-down. The model will be displayed in the **MANUFACTURE** workspace.

Creating Stock

- Click on the **New Setup** tool of **SETUP** drop-down from **Toolbar**. The **SETUP** dialog box will be displayed along with the stock of model.
- Specify the parameters of **Setup** tab and **Stock** tab of **SETUP** dialog box to create the stock; refer to Figure-48.

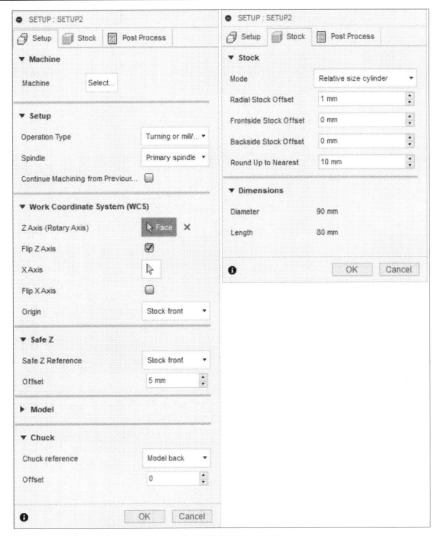

Figure–48. Specifying parameters for SETUP dialog box

- After specifying the parameters of **SETUP** dialog box, click on the **OK** button. The stock will be created and displayed on the model; refer to Figure-49.

Figure–49. Created stock for practical

Generating Face Toolpath

- Click on the **Turning Face** tool of **TURNING** drop-down from **Toolbar**. The **FACE** dialog box will be displayed.
- Click on the **Select** button of **Tool** option and select the facing tool from **Select Tool** dialog box as displayed in Figure-50.

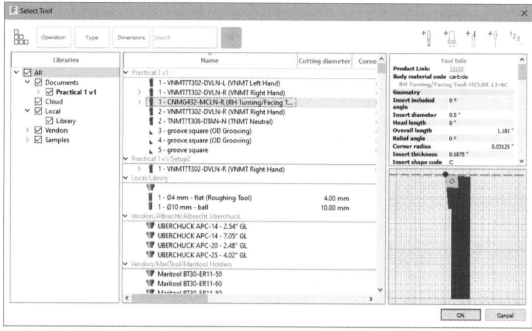

Figure-50. Selecting tool for turning

- After selecting the tool, click on the **OK** button from **Select Tool** dialog box. The tool will be added in the **Face** dialog box.
- Specify the parameters of **Tool** tab, **Geometry** tab, **Passes** tab and **Linking** tab of **FACE** dialog box as shown in Figure-51.

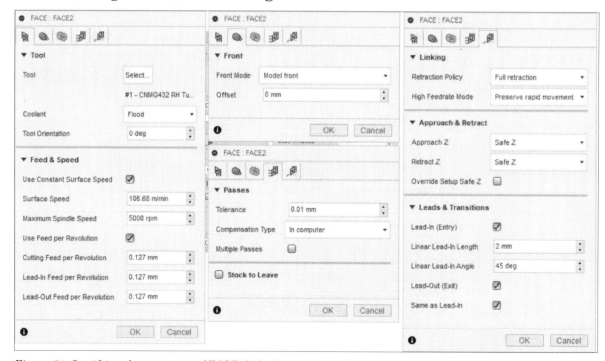

Figure-51. Specifying the parameters of FACE dialog box

- After specifying the parameters, click on the **OK** button from **FACE** dialog box to generate the toolpath. The toolpath will be generated and displayed on the model.

Generating Turning Profile Roughing Toolpath

- Click on the **Turning Profile Roughing** tool of **TURNING** drop-down from **Toolbar**. The **PROFILE ROUGHING** dialog box will be displayed.
- Click on the **Select** button of **Tool** option and select the required tool from **Select Tool** dialog box.
- Specify the parameters of **Tool** tab, **Geometry** tab, **Passes** tab and **Linking** tab of **PROFILE** dialog box as shown in Figure-52.

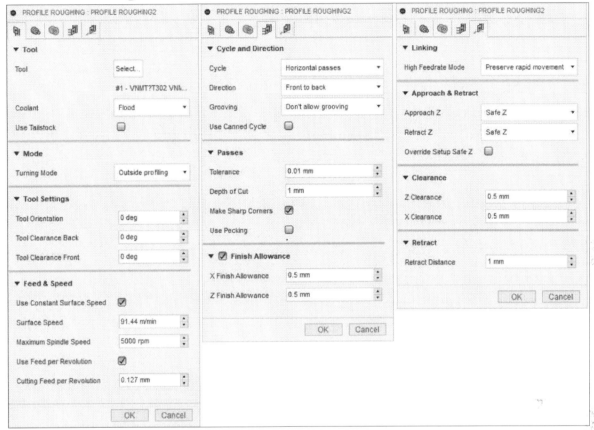

Figure-52. Specifying parameters for PROFILE dialog box

- After specifying the parameters, click on the **OK** button from **PROFILE** dialog box. The toolpath will be generated and displayed on the model; refer to Figure-53.

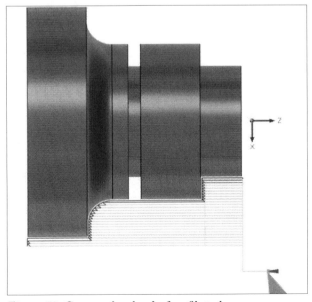

Figure-53. Generated toolpath of profile tool

Generating Turning Profile Finishing Toolpath

- Click on the **Turning Profile Finishing** tool of **TURNING** drop-down from **Toolbar**. The **PROFILE FINISHING** dialog box will be displayed.
- Click on the **Select** button of **Tool** option and select the required tool from **Select Tool** dialog box.
- Specify the parameters of **Tool** tab, **Geometry** tab, **Passes** tab and **Linking** tab of **PROFILE** dialog box as shown in Figure-54.

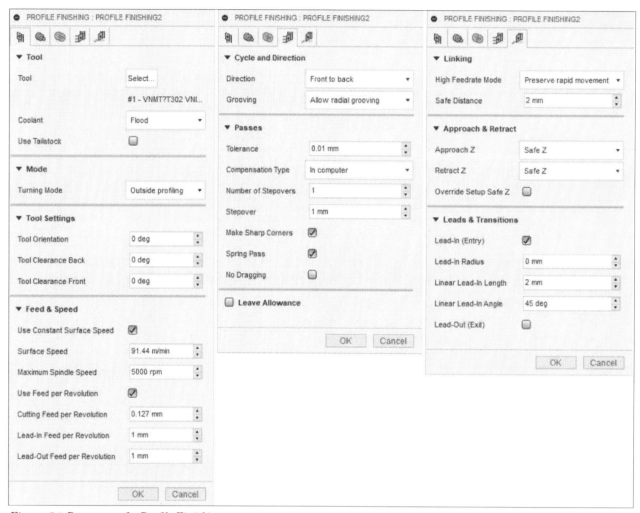

Figure-54. Parameters for Profile Finishing

- After setting the parameters, click on the **OK** button from the dialog box. The finishing toolpath for profile will be created.

Generating Turning Single Groove Toolpath

- Click on the **Turning Single Groove** tool of **TURNING** drop-down from **Toolbar**. The **SINGLE GROOVE** dialog box will be displayed.
- Click on the **Select** button of **Tool** option and select an OD groove square tool of insert thickness 4 mm from **Select Tool** dialog box.
- Specify the parameters of **Tool** tab, **Geometry** tab, **Passes** tab and **Linking** tab of **PROFILE** dialog box as shown in Figure-55.

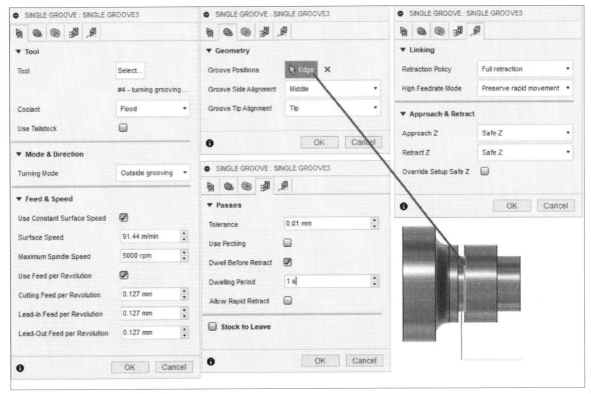

Figure-55. Specifying parameters for SINGLE GROOVE dialog box

- After specifying the parameters, click on the **OK** button from **SINGLE GROOVE** dialog box. The toolpath will be generated and displayed on the model; refer to Figure-56

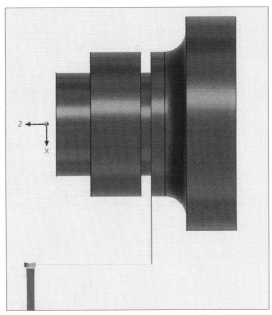

Figure-56. Generated toolpath for single groove

Generating Turning Part toolpath

- Click on the **Turning Part** tool from **TURNING** drop-down in **Toolbar**. The **PART** dialog box will be displayed.
- Click on the **Select** button of **Tool** option from **PART** dialog box and select the grooving tool of parameters shown in Figure-57.

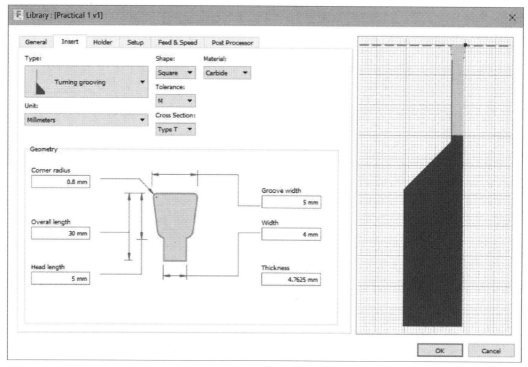

Figure-57. Selecting tool for part

- After selecting the tool of parameters displayed above, click on the **OK** button from **Select Tool** dialog box. The tool will be added in the **PART** dialog box.
- Specify the parameter of **Tool** tab, **Passes** tab, and **Linking** tab of **PART** dialog box as displayed in Figure-58.

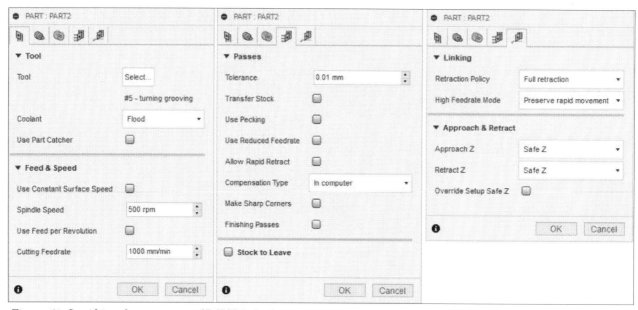

Figure-58. Specifying the parameters of PART dialog box

- After specifying the parameters, click on the **OK** button from **PART** dialog box. The toolpath will be generated and displayed on the model; refer to Figure-59.

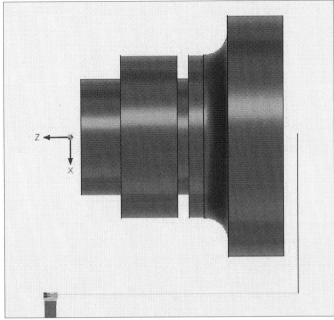

Figure-59. Generated toolpath of Part tool

Simulating the Toopath

- Right-click on the **Setup** from **Browser Tree** and click on the **Simulate** tool from the Marking menu. The **SETUP** dialog box will be displayed along with the model.
- Use the simulation keys to play the machining animation to check the errors occurred while machining process; refer to Figure-60.

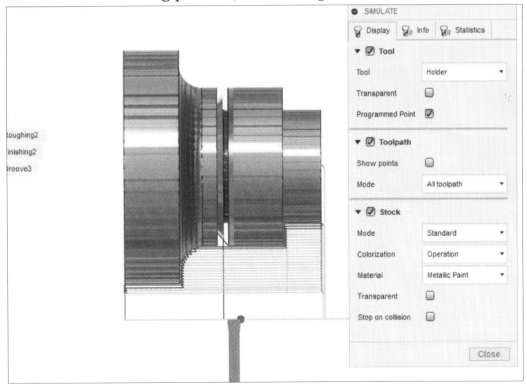

Figure-60. Simulation process

SELF ASSESSMENT

Q1. Which of the following tool is used to cut material from the profile of round part?

a. Turning Profile Roughing   b. Turning Groove
c. Turning Chamfer   d. Turning Part

Q2. You can specify maximum spindle speed parameter for cutting tool in Autodesk Fusion 360 only when you are using constant surface speed. (T/F)

Q3. What is the difference between Turning Groove and Turning Single Groove tool?

Q4. Which of the following tool is used to cut off a section of part?

a. Turning Part   b. Turning Single Groove
c. Turning Chamfer   d. Turning Thread

Q5. Which of the following tool is used to generate NC program for cutting material using water jet machine?

a. Turning Part   b. 2D Adaptive Clearing
c. 2D Profile   d. Trace

PRACTICE 1

Machine the stock of Diameter as 50 mm and Length as 62 mm to create the part as shown in Figure-61. The pat file of this model is available in the respective folder of **Autodesk Fusion 360**.

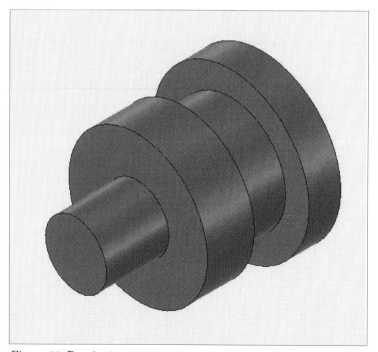

Figure-61. Practice 1

PRACTICE 2

Machine the stock of Diameter as 80 mm and Length as 130 mm to create the part as shown in Figure-62. The pat file of this model is available in the respective folder of **Autodesk Fusion 360**.

Figure-62. Practice

FOR STUDENT NOTES

Chapter 19

Probing, Additive Manufacturing, and Miscellaneous CAM Tools

Topics Covered

The major topics covered in this chapter are:

- *New Folder*
- *New Pattern*
- *Probing*
- *Inspecting Surface*
- *Simulating*
- *Generate Toolpath and Clear Toolpath*
- *Machining Time, Tool Library, and Task Manager*
- *Post Process*
- *Creating Form Mill tool*

INTRODUCTION

Till now, we have learned the procedure of generating Milling and Turning toolpath. In this chapter, we will discuss some of the other tools used to organize and manipulate the toolpaths.

NEW FOLDER

The **New Folder** tool is used for creating a folder to combine similar group operation. The procedure to use this tool is discussed next.

- Select the operations from **Browser Tree** by holding **CTRL** key and right-click on any of the selected operations. A shortcut menu will be displayed; refer to Figure-1.

Figure-1. Add to new folder tool

- Click on the **Add to New Folder** button from the menu. The selected operations will be added in a new folder. The folder will be displayed in the **BROWSER** with the name as **Folder**; refer to Figure-2.

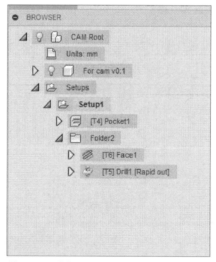

Figure-2. Moved operations

- If you want to rename the newly created folder then double-click on the folder with a pause between the click and enter the desired name.

There is an another method for creating the folder which is discussed next.

• Click on the **New Folder** tool of **SETUP** drop-down from **Toolbar**; refer to Figure-3. The folder will be created in the **BROWSER**.

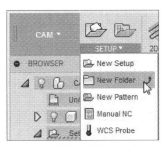

Figure-3. New Folder tool

• Select the operations by holding **CTRL** key from **BROWSER** and drag the operations into newly created folder. The operation will be added in the created folder.

NEW PATTERN

The **New Pattern** tool is used for duplicating a generated toolpath on the same model in **Linear**, **Circular**, **Mirror**, **Component**, and **Duplicate** pattern. The use of **New Pattern** tool can speed up your entire programming process since all changes to a pattern take effect immediately and no toolpath has to be updated. The procedure to use this tool is discussed next.

• Right-click on the operation(s) that you want to pattern. The shortcut menu will be displayed; refer to Figure-4.

Figure-4. The Add to New Pattern tool

• Click on the **Add to New Pattern** tool from the displayed menu. The **FOLDER : PATTERN** dialog box will be displayed; refer to Figure-5.

Figure-5. FOLDER PATTERN dialog box

Linear Pattern

In this section, we will discuss the procedure of creating linear pattern.

- Click on the **Liner Pattern** option of **Pattern Type** drop-down from **FOLDER : PATTERN** dialog box for creating linear pattern.
- The selection button of **Direction 1** section of **Pattern** tab is active by default. You need to click on the edge or face from model to select the direction.
- Select the **Flip Direction 1** check box of **Pattern** tab to flip the direction of pattern along selected edge or face.
- Click in the **Spacing for Direction 1** edit box of **Pattern** tab and enter the value of distance between two consecutive instances of the pattern.
- Click on the **Number of instances 1** edit box of **Pattern** tab and enter the number of instances required in the pattern along first direction.
- Select the **Additional Direction** check box of **Pattern** tab to use an additional direction for creating the pattern.
- Select the **Keep Original** check box of **Pattern** tab to keep the original pattern while applying a new pattern.
- Select the **Preserve Order** option of **Operation Order** drop-down from **Pattern** tab to machine all operations in each instance of the pattern before moving to the next instance.
- Select **Order by Operation** option of **Operation Order** drop-down from **Pattern** tab to machine all occurrences of each operation in the pattern before moving to the next operation.
- Select **Order by tool** option of **Operation Order** drop-down from **Pattern** tab to machines all operations in the pattern that use the current tool before changing tools.
- Select the **Reverse** check box to reverse the order of pattern.
- The other tools of the drop-down were discussed earlier in this book.
- After specifying the parameters, click on the **OK** button from **FOLDER : PATTERN** dialog box; refer to Figure-6. The pattern will be created and displayed in the **BROWSER**.

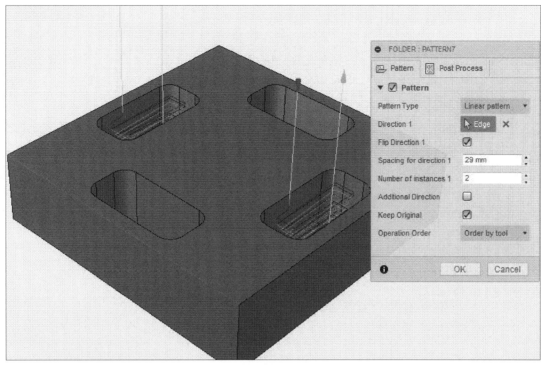

Figure-6. Applied linear pattern

Circular Pattern

In this section, we will discuss the procedure of creating the circular patter.

- Click on the **Circular Pattern** option of **Pattern Type** drop-down from **FOLDER : PATTERN** dialog box for creating circular pattern; refer to Figure-7.

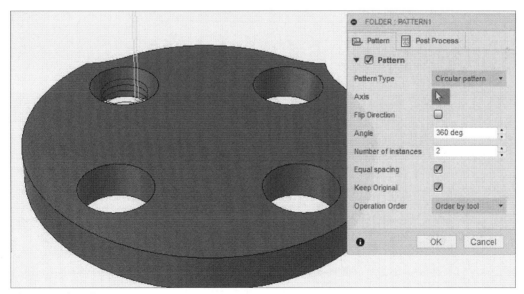

Figure-7. Circular pattern option

- The selection button of **Axis** section from **Pattern** tab is active by default. You need to click on the axis or edge from model to select; refer to Figure-8.

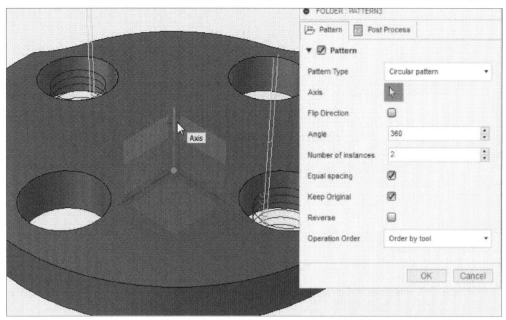

Figure-8. Selecting axis for pattern

- If you want to select the axis from origin to select then visible the origin from **Browser Tree** and select the required axis.
- Select the **Flip Direction** check box of **Pattern** tab to flip the direction of selected edge or axis.
- Click in the **Angle** edit box of **Pattern** tab and enter the angular value to place the pattern.
- Click on the **Number of instances** edit box of **Pattern** tab and enter the value to specify number of times the operation should be machined in the selected direction.
- Select the **Equal Spacing** check box of **Pattern** tab to equally distribute the selected patterns at a specified angle.
- Select the **Keep original** check box of **Pattern** tab to keep the original pattern while applying a new pattern.
- Select the **Reverse** check box to reverse the pattern order.
- The other tools of the drop-down are same as discussed earlier in this book.
- After specifying the parameters, click on the **OK** button from **FOLDER : PATTERN** dialog box; refer to Figure-9. The preview of pattern will be created and displayed on the model.

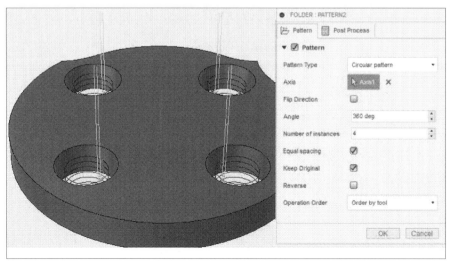

Figure-9. Preview of circular pattern

Mirror Pattern

In this section, we will discuss the procedure of creating the mirror pattern.

- Click on the **Mirror Pattern** option of **Pattern Type** drop-down from **FOLDER : PATTERN** dialog box for creating mirror pattern; refer to Figure-10.

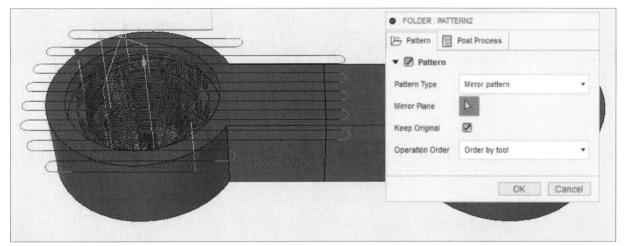

Figure-10. Mirror pattern option

- The selection button of **Mirror Plane** section from **Pattern** tab is active by default. You need to click on the plane or face from model to select.
- The other options of the dialog box are same as discussed earlier.
- After specifying the parameters, click on the **OK** button from **FOLDER : PATTERN** dialog box; refer to Figure-11. The preview of pattern will be created and displayed on the model.

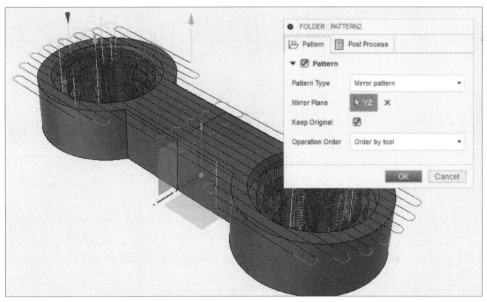

Figure-11. Completed mirror pattern

Duplicate Pattern

In this section, we will discuss the procedure of creating the duplicate pattern.

- Click on the **Duplicate Pattern** option of **Pattern Type** drop-down from **FOLDER : PATTERN** dialog box for creating duplicate pattern; refer to Figure-12.

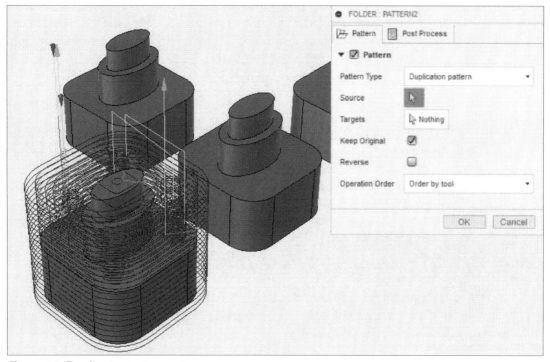

Figure-12. Duplication pattern option

- The selection button of **Source** section from **Pattern** tab is active by default. You need to click on the point from source model to select.
- The selection button of **Targets** section of **Pattern** tab is active by default. You need to click on the target points on the model on which you want to duplicate the toolpath.
- The other options of the dialog box have been discussed earlier.
- After specifying the parameters, click on the **OK** button from **FOLDER : PATTERN** dialog box; refer to Figure-13. The preview of duplicate pattern will be created and displayed on the model.

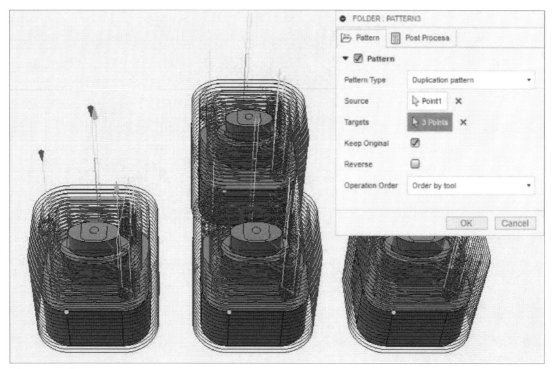

Figure-13. Selecting target body

Component Pattern

The component pattern is used to pattern the toolpaths created on one component onto the other component. Note that to use this pattern, you must have more that one components individually setup for machining in assembly. The procedure to use this option is given next.

- Select the **Component pattern** option from the **Pattern type** drop-down in the dialog box. The **FOLDER : PATTERN** dialog box will be displayed as shown in Figure-14.

Figure-14. Component Pattern option

- Clear the **Automatic** check box if you do not want to automatically select targets based on selected source components.
- Click on selection button of **Source** option and select the component on which you have created toolpaths already.
- Click on the selection button of **Targets** option and select the components on which you want to create pattern instances; refer to Figure-15.

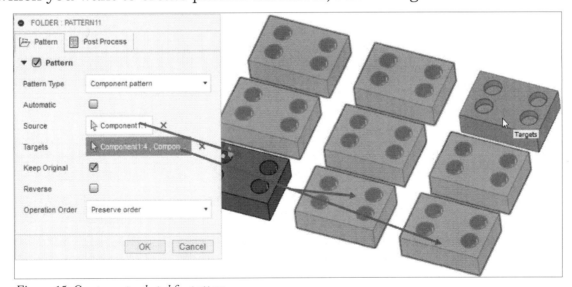

Figure-15. Components selected for pattern

- After specifying desired parameters, click on the **OK** button from the dialog box.

Manual NC

The **Manual NC** tool is used to insert special manual NC entries in the CAM browser. The procedure to use this tool is discussed next.

- Click on the **Manual NC** tool of **SETUP** drop-down from **Toolbar**; refer to Figure-16. The **MANUAL NC** dialog box will be displayed; refer to Figure-17.

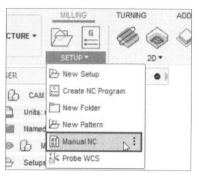

Figure-16. Manual NC tool

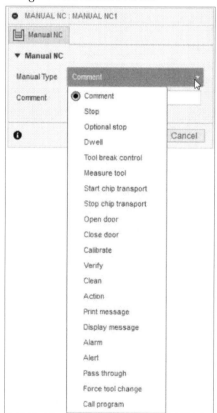

Figure-17. MANUAL NC dialog box

- Click on the **Manual Type** drop-down from **MANUAL NC** dialog box and select the required option to specify the type of manual NC operation.
- Click in the edit box below the drop-down and specify the desired text to be output during post processing.
- Click on the **OK** button from the dialog box. The manual nc code will be added in the **SETUP** node of **BROWSER**.

PROBING

Probing is used to measure the geometry of object by sensing various points of object using different types of probes. There are various types of probes like mechanical probes, optical probes, laser probes, and so on. The tools to create NC program for probing are available in **PROBING** tab of **Toolbar**; refer to Figure-18. Various tools in this tab are discussed next.

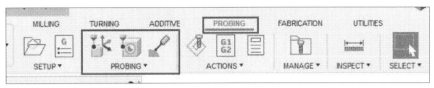

Figure-18. PROBING tab

WCS Probe

The **Probe WCS** tool is used to output the NC code for the probing cycles of your CMM. The procedure to use this tool is discussed next.

- Click on the **Probe WCS** tool of **SETUP** drop-down from **Toolbar**; refer to Figure-19. The **WCS PROBE** dialog box will be displayed; refer to Figure-20.

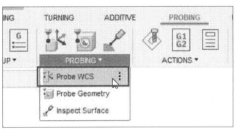

Figure-19. Probe WCS tool

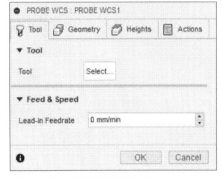

Figure-20. PROBE WCS dialog box

- Click on the **Select** button of **Tool** section from **Tool** tab. The **Select Tool** dialog box will be displayed; refer to Figure-21.

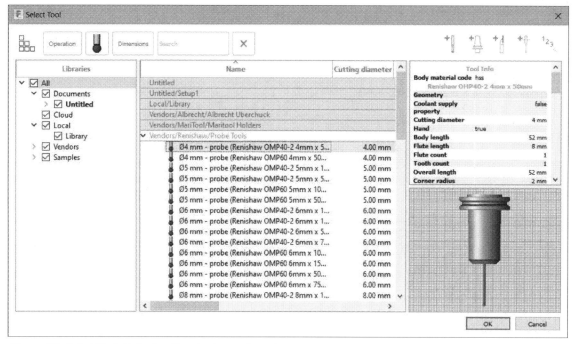

Figure-21. Select Tool dialog box for selecting probe tool

- Select the desired probing tool from the table and click on the **OK** button from **Select Tool** dialog box.
- Specify the desired lead-in feed rate for the probe in **Lead-In Feedrate** edit box.

Geometry

Click on the **Geometry** tab of **WCS PROBE** dialog box. The **Geometry** tab will be displayed; refer to Figure-22.

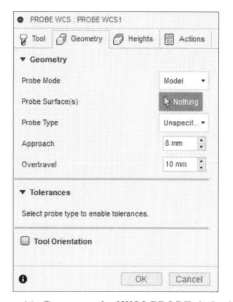

Figure-22. Geometry tab of WCS PROBE dialog box

- Click in the **Probe Mode** drop-down of **Geometry** tab from **WCS PROBE** dialog box and select the desired option to define whether you want to probe part or stock.
- The **Nothing** button of **Probe Surface(s)** section of **Geometry** tab is active by default. You need to click on the face of model to be checked by probe; refer to Figure-23.

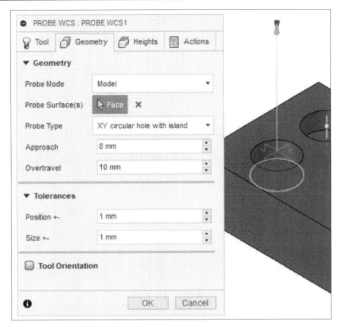

Figure-23. Selected face for probing

- Select the desired option from the **Probe Type** drop-down to define what type of probe you are using. If you have selected the **Z surface** option from the drop-down then **Use Selected Point** check box will be displayed. Select this check box if you want to use selected point as reference for probing on the surface.
- Specify the desired value of approach distance and over travel of probe in the respective edit boxes in the dialog box. The approach distance is the distance from selected point from where probe starts to measure. The over travel distance is the distance from selected point upto which probe can move past the selected point while measuring.
- Specify the desired tolerance values for position and size edit boxes in the **Tolerances** section of the dialog box.
- Click on the Actions tab of dialog box and select check boxes for actions to display messages in case of measurement error.
- The other options of the dialog box have been discussed earlier in this book.
- After specifying the parameters, click on the **OK** button from **PROBE WCS** dialog box. The operation will be created and displaced in the **BROWSER**.

The **Probing Geometry** tool works in the same way as **Probe WCS** tool.

Inspecting Surface

The **Inspect Surface** tool is used to probe multiple points on selected surface by using a machine. The procedure to use this tool is given next.

- Click on the **Inspect Surface** tool from the **PROBING** panel in the **PROBING** tab of **Toolbar**. The **INSPECT** dialog box will be displayed; refer to Figure-24.
- Select the desired tool and specify feed/speed parameters in the **Tool** tab of dialog box.
- Click on the **Geometry** tab of dialog box and click on the surface at desired locations to specify inspection points.
- Set the other parameters as discussed earlier and click on the **OK** button from the dialog box.

Simulate

The **Simulate** tool is used to review and simulate the created toolpaths. The procedure to use this tool is discussed next.

- Click on the **Simulate** tool of **ACTIONS** drop-down from **Toolbar**; refer to Figure-25. The **SIMULATE** dialog box will be displayed along with model and simulation keys; refer to Figure-26.

Figure-24. *INSPECT dialog box*

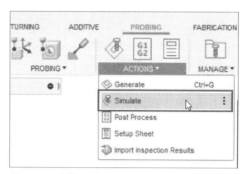

Figure-25. *Simulate tool*

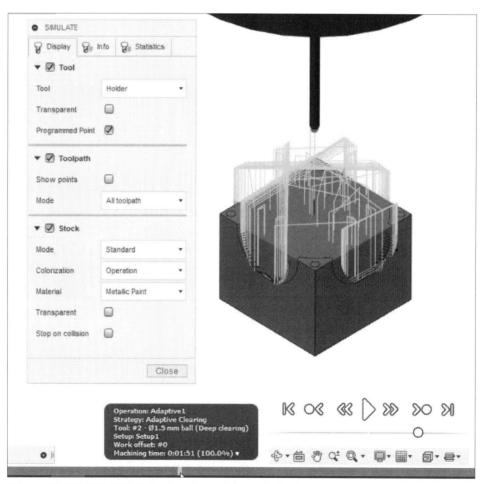

Figure-26. *SIMULATE dialog box along with simulation keys*

- There is also another way to select **Simulate** tool. Right-click on the specific operation or setup from **BROWSER**. A shortcut menu will be displayed; refer to Figure-27. Click on the **Simulate** tool from the menu. The **SIMULATE** dialog box will be displayed.

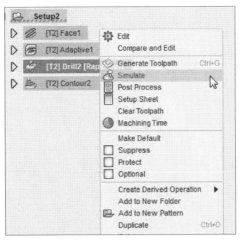

Figure-27. Simulate tool from shortcut menu

Display tab

- Select the **Tool** check box of **Display** tab from **SIMULATE** dialog box to view the tool and holder while machining animation process.
- Click on the **Tool** drop-down of **Display** tab and select the required option to tell software that which segment of the tool to show while machining.
- Select the **Transparent** check box of **Display** tab to make the tool transparent.
- Select the **Programmed Point** check box to display the points where changes occur in toolpath like change in toolpath curve, change in feed & speed, and so on.
- Select the **Toolpath** check box of **Display** tab to display the toolpath on the model. Clear the **Toolpath** check box to hide the toolpath.
- Select the **Show Points** check box of **Toolpath** node to display the points of toolpath on the model. Clear the **Show Points** check box to hide the points.
- Click on the **Mode** drop-down of **Toolpath** node from **Display** tab and select the required option to show the toolpath of the specific part.
- Select the **Stock** check box of **Display** tab to view the stock on the part. Clear the check box to hide the stock from part.
- Select the **Standard** option of **Mode** drop-down from **Stock** check box for simulation of any toolpath including 2D, 3-axis, 3-Axis indexing and multi axis toolpath.
- Select the **Fast (3-Axis only)** option of **Mode** drop-down from **Stock** check box for simulating faster toolpath in large toolpaths.
- Click on the **Colorization** option of **Stock** check box to select the required option to specify how the stock should be colorized.
- Click on the **Material** drop-down of **Stock** check box to specify the material used for visualization.
- Select the **Transparent** check box of **Stock** tab to transparent the stock of model.
- Select the **Stop on collision** option of **Stock** tab to stop the tool on collision with stock of model. When the tool or holder collides with stock then it shows red sign in the animation bar; refer to Figure-28

Info tab

Click on the **Info** tab of **SIMULATE** dialog box. The **Info** tab will be displayed; refer to Figure-29.

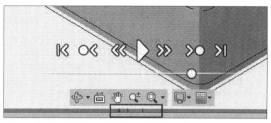

Figure-28. Holder collision with stock

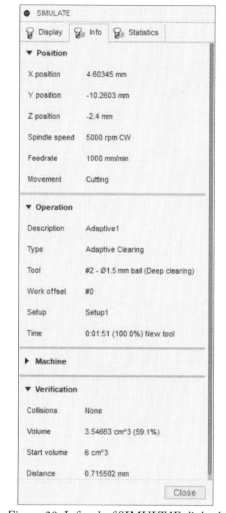

Figure-29. Info tab of SIMULTAE dialog box

• In this **Info** tab, the information related to stock, operation, spindle speed, volume, cursor position, and so on will be displayed.

Statistics

Click on the **Statistics** tab of **SIMULATE** dialog box. The **Statistics** tab will be displayed; refer to Figure-30.

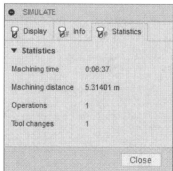

Figure-30. Statistics tab

• In the **Statistic** tab, the information like Machining time, Machining distance, Operations, and Tool change will be displayed.

Simulation Keys

The simulation keys are used to watch the animation of stock removal; refer to Figure-31.

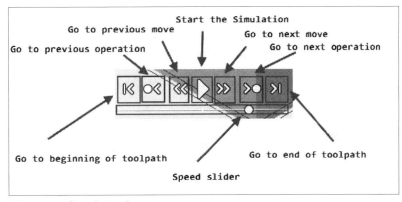

Figure-31. Simulation keys

Post Process

The **Post Process** tool is used to convert the machine-independent cutter location data into machine-specific NC code that can be run directly on CNC machines. The procedure to use this tool is discussed next.

- Click on the **Post Process** tab of **ACTIONS** tab from **Toolbar**; refer to Figure-32. The **Post Process** dialog box will be displayed; refer to Figure-33.

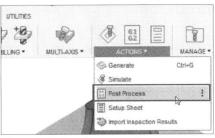

Figure-32. Post Process tool

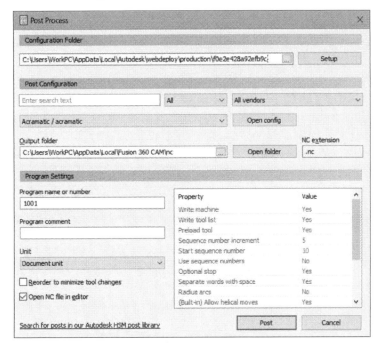

Figure-33. Post Process dialog box

- Click on the **Browse** button of **Configuration Folder** section from **Post Process** dialog box. The **Select post process configuration folder** dialog box will be displayed; refer to Figure-49.

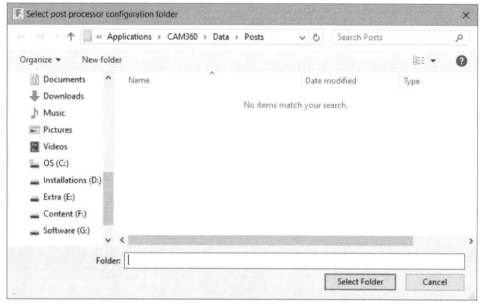

Figure-34. Select post processor configuration folder dialog box

- Create a new folder or select from the existing one to set the post processing configuration folder and click on the **Select Folder** button.
- Click on the **Setup** button of **Post Process** dialog box and select the desired option to reset the default post processor configuration.
- Select the desired machine type and vendor for the post processor from respective drop-downs in the **Post Configuration** section of the dialog box.
- Click on the **Open config** button of **Post Process** dialog box to open the post configuration in the default word processor application.
- Click in the **Browse** button for **Output folder** option to select the output folder for saving the NC file.
- Click on the **Open Folder** button of **Post Process** dialog box to open the output folder in windows explorer.
- Click in the **Program name or number** edit box of **Post Process** dialog box and enter the desired name or number of the output file.
- Click in the **Program comment** edit box of **Post Process** dialog box and enter the desired text related to the output file.
- Click in the **Unit** drop-down of **Post Process** tab and select the desired unit to specify the output unit. When unit of the output file is set to **Document unit** option then either inch or millimeter will be used.
- Select the **Reorder to minimize tool changes** check box of **Post Process** tab to record the operation between jobs to minimise the number of tool changes.
- Select the **Open NC file in editor** check box of **Post Process** dialog box to open the output NC file in editor.
- If you want to reset a single property or all the properties for output file then right-click on any property from **User defined property** box and select the required option. The property will be reset.
- After specifying the parameters, click on the **Post** button from **Post Process** dialog box. The **Post Process** output location folder will be displayed; refer to Figure-35.

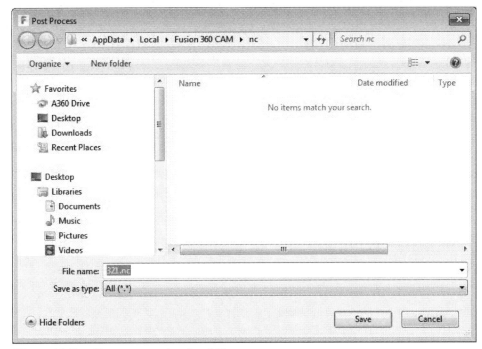

Figure-35. Post Process output location folder

- Click on the **Save** button to save the file. The output file will be save in specified folder.
- If you have selected the option to view the file in editor then the program will be displayed in default editor; refer to Figure-36.

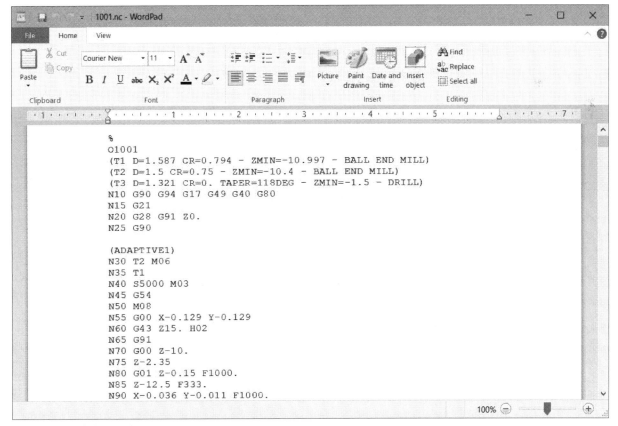

Figure-36. NC file in editor

- You can edit the codes as required by using the options of the editor.

Setup Sheet

The **Setup Sheet** tool is used to generate an overview for the NC program operator. Setup sheet provides the data related to stock, tool data, work piece position, and machine statistics. Before creating the setup sheet, you need to be sure that the proper setup is selected.

If you are on a network and the operator has access to a PC on the shop floor, you can save this to a folder that the operator can access. This will save paper and ensure the operator always has access to the most current setup information. The default **Setup Sheet** can be viewed in any standard web browser. The procedure to use this tool is discussed next.

*   Click on the **Setup Sheet** tool of **ACTIONS** panel from **Toolbar**; refer to Figure-37. The **Select Setup Sheet Output Folder** dialog box will be displayed; refer to Figure-38.

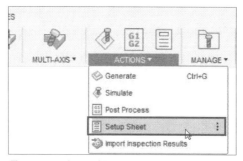

Figure-37. Setup Sheet tool

Figure-38. Select Setup Sheet Output Folder dialog box

*   Select the location folder as required and click on the **Select Folder** button from **Select Setup Sheet Output Folder** dialog box. The setup sheet will be created and open in the default internet browser; refer to Figure-39.

Figure-39. Created setup sheet

Generate Toolpath

The **Generate** tool is used to regenerate the toolpath of the selected operation whenever a feature of model is modified on which the operation depends. The procedure to use this tool is discussed next.

- Click on the operation for which you want to regenerate the toolpath from **Browser Tree**.
- Click on the **Generate** tool of **ACTIONS** drop-down from **Toolbar**; refer to Figure-40.
- You can also select the **Generate** tool from shortcut menu; refer to Figure-41.

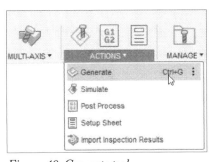

Figure-40. Generate tool

Figure-41. Selecting Generate tool from Shortcut menu

- The toolpath will be regenerated and displayed in **BROWSER**; refer to Figure-42.

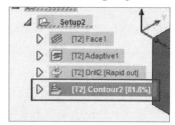

Figure-42. Regenerating toolpath

Clear Toolpath

The **Clear toolpath** tool is used to clear the toolpath of the selected operation. The procedure to use this tool is discussed next.

- Right-click on the required operation from **BROWSER** and select the **Clear Toolpath** tool; refer to Figure-43.

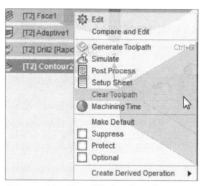

Figure-43. Clear Toolpath tool

- The tool path of selected operation will be deleted.

Machining Time

The **Machining Time** tool is used to measure and calculate the machining time for a selected operation with a high accuracy. The procedure to use this tool is discussed next.

- Right-click on the required operation from **Browser Tree** and select the **Machining Time** tool; refer to Figure-44.

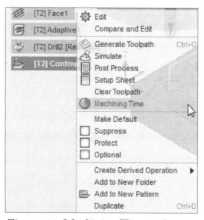

Figure-44. Machining Time tool

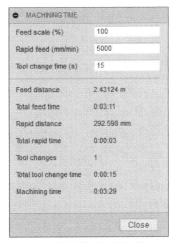

Figure-45. MACHINING TIME dialog box

- Click in the **Feed Scale(%)** edit box of **MACHINING TIME** dialog box and enter the desired value.
- Click in the **Rapid Feed(mm/min)** edit box of **MACHINING TIME** dialog box and enter the required value.
- Click in the **Tool change Time(s)** edit box of **MACHINING TIME** dialog box and enter the desired value.
- In the **MACHINING TIME** dialog box other information related to tool will be displayed.

Tool Library

The **Tool Library** tool displays the **Tool Library** dialog box where you manage all the tools like milling, lathe, and cutting tools for your individual documents and operations, as well as libraries of predefined tools.

- Click on the **Tool Library** tool of **MANAGE** drop-down from **Toolbar**; refer to Figure-45. The **CAM Tool Library** dialog box will be displayed; refer to Figure-46.

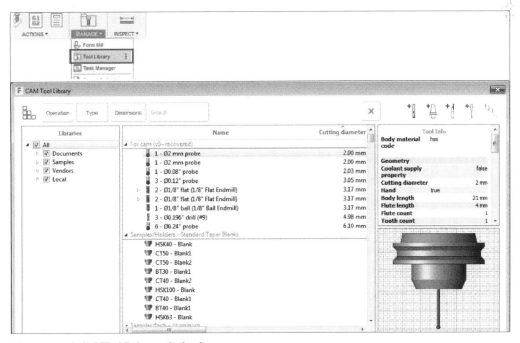

Figure-46. CAM Tool Library dialog box

• View or modify the tool as required from the **CAM Tool Library** dialog box. You can also perform common copy-paste functions in the library.

Task Manager

The **Task Manager** tool is used for controlling toolpath generation. CAM allows you to continue working inside Fusion 360 while generating toolpaths in the background. The main interface for controlling toolpath generation is the **CAM Task Manager**.

• Click on the **Task Manager** tool of **MANAGE** drop-down from **Toolbar**; refer to Figure-47. The **CAM Task Manager** dialog box will be displayed; refer to Figure-48.

Figure-47. Task Manager tool

Figure-48. CAM Task Manager dialog box

• Now, generate a toolpath of any operation and you can see the progress on the **CAM Task Manager**; refer to Figure-49.

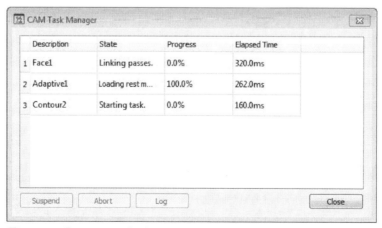

Figure-49. Running multiple operations simultaneously

Creating Form Mill Tool

The **Form Mill** tool in **MANAGE** drop-down is used to create a milling tool of desired shape. The procedure to use this tool is given next.

- Click on the **Form Mill** tool from the **MANAGE** drop-down in the **Toolbar**. The **FORM MILL** dialog box will be displayed; refer to Figure-50.

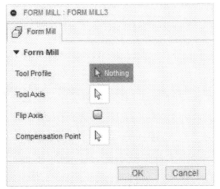

Figure-50. FORM MILL dialog box

- Select the desired sketch profile, axis and cutting point of the tool; refer to Figure-51.

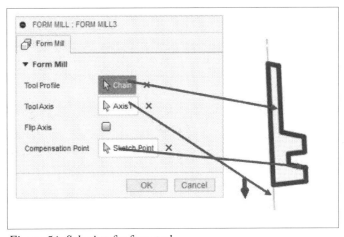

Figure-51. Selection for form tool

- Select the **Flip Axis** check box if you want to reverse the orientation of tool.
- Click on the **OK** button from the dialog box. The new tool will be added in the **CAM Tool Library** dialog box; refer to Figure-52.

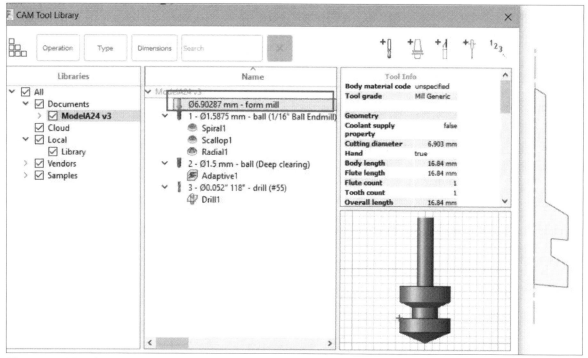

Figure-52. New form tool added in the CAM Tool Library dialog box

Select the **Export Defaults** tool from the **MANAGE** drop-down in the **Toolbar** to export all the defaults settings of manufacturing to a file. Select the **Import Defaults** tool from the **MANAGE** drop-down in the **Toolbar** to import settings of manufacturing from a file. Select the **Reset Defaults** option from the **MANAGE** drop-down in the **Toolbar** to reset settings to system defaults.

ADDITIVE MANUFACTURING

Additive manufacturing is a separate extension of Autodesk Fusion Manufacture workspace. You need to purchase it using credits from the **Extensions** dialog box; refer to Figure-53. So, make sure you have access to this extension. The procedure to activate tools for additive manufacturing is discussed next.

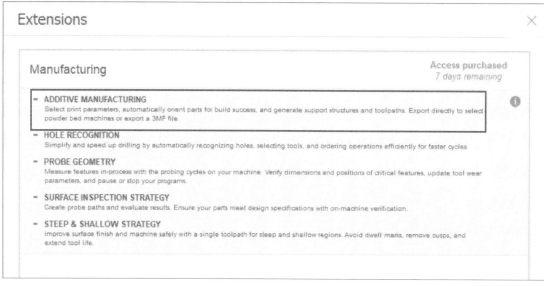

Figure-53. Extensions dialog box

- Click on the **New Setup** tool from the **SETUP** drop-down in the **Toolbar** of **MANUFACTURE** workspace. The **SETUP** dialog box will be displayed as discussed earlier.
- Select the **Additive** option from the **Operation Type** drop-down in the **Setup** tab of dialog box. The options will be displayed as shown in Figure-54.

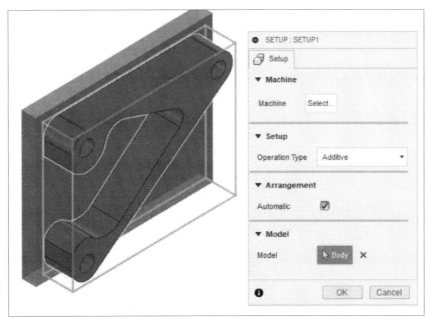

Figure-54. Options for Additive operation setup

- Click on the **Select** button and select desired machine 3D Printer machine.
- Click on the **OK** button from the **SETUP** dialog box to apply operation setup.

Now, click on the **ADDITIVE** tab in the **Toolbar**. The options for additive manufacturing will be displayed; refer to Figure-55.

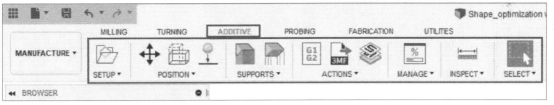

Figure-55. ADDITIVE tab in Toolbar

Most of the tools in this tab have been discussed earlier like Move, Task Manager, Measure and so on. Rest of the tools are discussed next.

Minimize Build Height

The **Minimize Build Height** tool is used to orient the part in such a way that it occupies minimum space on machine bed and more parts can be 3D printed on bed. The procedure to use this tool is given next.

- Click on the **Minimize Build Height** tool from the **POSITION** drop-down in the **ADDITIVE** tab of **Toolbar**. The **MINIMIZE BUILD HEIGHT** dialog box will be displayed; refer to Figure-56.

*Figure-56. MINIMIZE BUILD
HEIGHT dialog box*

- Select the component/components for 3D printing, specify the desired value of clearance from platform in the **Platform Clearance** edit box, and click on the **OK** button. The part will be oriented; refer to Figure-57.

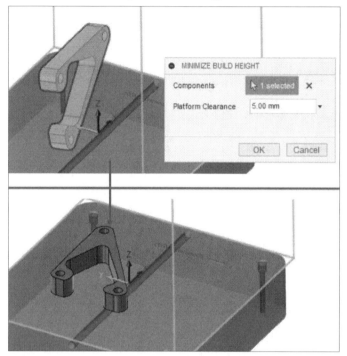

Figure-57. Setting orientation based on minimum build height

Automatic Orientation

The **Automatic Orientation** tool is used to place parts on the machine bed based on manufacturing requirements and minimum build height parameters. The procedure to use this tool is given next.

- Click on the **Automatic Orientation** tool from the **POSITION** drop-down in the **ADDITIVE** tab of **Toolbar**. The **AUTOMATIC ORIENTATION** dialog box will be displayed; refer to Figure-58.

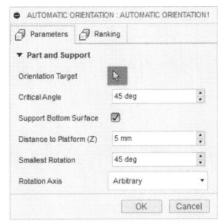

Figure-58. AUTOMATIC ORIENTATION dialog box

- Select the desired object to be reoriented and specify desired parameters in the dialog box like distance from platform, bottom surface, rotation axis.
- Click on the **Ranking** tab and select the ranking for various parameters to be considered based on priority level. For example, if you want to set minimum part height as priority then select the **Very high** option from the **Part Height** drop-down in the dialog box.
- Click on the **OK** button from the dialog box after setting desired parameters.

Place Parts on Platform

The **Place parts on platform** tool is used to place parts directly on platform or at some clearance distance from the platform. The procedure to use this tool is given next.

- Click on the **Place parts on platform** tool from the **POSITION** drop-down in the **ADDITIVE** tab of **Toolbar**. The **PLACE PARTS ON PLATFORM** dialog box will be displayed; refer to Figure-59.

Figure-59. PLACE PARTS ON PLATFORM dialog box

- Select the desired part and specify parameters as desired. If you select the Flat Face option from the Type drop-down then you can select the face to be directly placed on the platform.
- After specifying parameters, click on the **OK** button.

Interference Check

The Interference tool is used to check whether two components on machine bed are interfering. The procedure to use this tool is given next.

- Click on the **Interference** tool from the **POSITION** drop-down in the **ADDITIVE** tab of **Toolbar**. The **INTERFERENCE** dialog box will be displayed; refer to Figure-60.

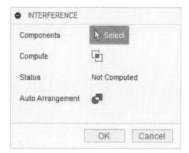

Figure-60. INTERFERENCE dialog box

- Select the components whose interference is to be checked and click on the **Compute** button. The status will be displayed. If there is an interference then you can click on the **Auto Arrangement** button to automatically arrange components.
- Click on the **OK** button to exit the dialog box.

Applying Supports

The tools in the **SUPPORTS** panel are used to apply different type of supports to component while 3D printing; refer to Figure-61.

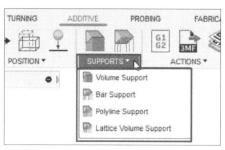

Figure-61. SUPPORTS dialog box

The procedure to use various tools is discussed next.

Creating Volume Support

The **Volume Support** tool is used to create support material for the components with specified structure. The procedure to create volume support is given next.

- Click on the **Volume Support** tool from the **SUPPORTS** drop-down in the **Toolbar**. The **VOLUME SUPPORT** dialog box will be displayed as shown in Figure-62.

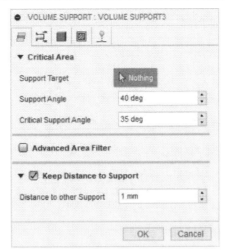

Figure-62. VOLUME SUPPORT dialog box

- By default, the **Support Target** selection button is active. Select the faces on which you want to apply volume supports.
- Specify the desired values of angles from horizontal line in **Support Angle** and **Critical Support Angle** edit boxes to define width of support structures in normal and critical areas respectively.
- If you do not want to select the faces individually and want to use a window selection then you can use the options in **Advanced Area Filter** section of the dialog box to refine your selected of faces.
- Specify the minimum distance between new support and older support beam in the **Distance to other support** edit box.
- Click on the **General** tab in the dialog box to define general shape of volume support structures; refer to Figure-63.

Figure-63. General tab in VOLUME SUPPORT dialog box

- Select the desired option from the **Filling Type** drop-down to define the general shape of volume support. Select the **Hollow** option from the drop-down to create hollow supports. If you want to create structure of wired wall, punch plate, or solid structure then select the **Structured** option from the drop-down.
- Set the desired parameters in various edit boxes of the tab.

- Click on the **Volume Properties** tab to modify parameters of support structure. The options will be displayed as shown in Figure-64. Note that this tab will be displayed only when **Structured** option is selected in the **Filling Type** drop-down.

Figure-64. Volume Properties tab

- Select the desired options from the **Pattern** and **Density** drop-downs to define shape and density of structure.
- Specify the desired values in **Top Connections** and **Bottom Connections** edit boxes of the **Thickening up Structures** section to increase/decrease thickness of structure for top or bottom connection points of the structure. If you want to increase or decrease thickness of the main structure then specify desired value in the **Main Structure** edit box.
- Similarly, you can specify parameters for fin structure in the **Fin Structures** section of the dialog box.
- Click on the **Raster and Contour** tab in the dialog box to modify parameters related to net structure of rasters and contours. The options will be displayed as shown in Figure-65.

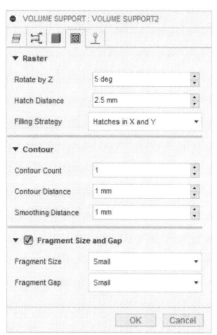

Figure-65. Raster and Contour tab

- Set the desired parameters in this tab and similarly, specify parameters related to different connection points in the **Connections** tab of dialog box.
- Click on the **OK** button from the dialog box to create support structure.

Creating Bar Support

The **Bar Support** tool is used to create bars of specified shape and size to support the printed structure. The procedure to use this tool is given next.

- Click on the **Bar Support** tool from the **SUPPORTS** panel in the **Toolbar**. The **BAR SUPPORT** dialog box will be displayed; refer to Figure-66.

Figure-66. BAR SUPPORT dialog box

- Select the faces that you want to be supported and specify desired parameters in the **Geometry** tab as discussed earlier.
- Click on the **General** tab to define density of base points of support, type of tree structure used for support, and projection angle for support structures in respective edit boxes; refer to Figure-67.

Figure-67. General tab in BAR SUPPORT dialog box

- Click on the **Bar Properties** tab in the dialog box and set the desired shape of bar in the dialog box.
- Click on the **OK** button from the dialog box. The support will be created; refer to Figure-68.

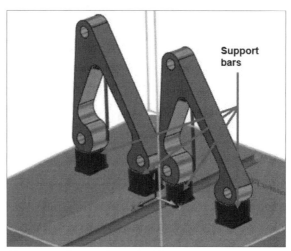

Figure-68. Support bars created

You can use the **Polyline Support** and **Lattice Volume Support** tools of **SUPPORTS** panel in **Toolbar** in same way as other support tools have been discussed.

Generating Toolpath for Additive Manufacturing

After setting desired parameters, click on the **Generate** button from the **ACTIONS** panel in the **ADDITIVE** tab of **Toolbar**. The toolpath will be generated and displayed in the **BROWSER**.

After creating toolpath, click on the **Simulate additive toolpath** tool from the **ACTIONS** panel and check the simulation as discussed earlier.

Exporting Toolpath and Printing Data

The **Export Toolpath** and **Export 3MF** tools in the **ACTIONS** panel are used to export the toolpath and printing setup for use by machines or other postprocessing software. Select the desired tool from the panel and specify location where you want to save the exported file.

SELF- ASSESSMENT

Q1. Which of the following tool is used to group together various cutting operations?

a. Setup Sheet   b. Add to New Pattern
c. Add to New Folder   d. Post Process

Q2. Which of the following pattern option is used to copy all the toolpaths created on one body onto another independent body?

a. Circular Pattern   b. Mirror Pattern
c. Duplicate Pattern   d. Component Pattern

Q3. Which of the following NC parameter is not available for Manual NC entry?

a. Start   b. Stop
c. Dwell   d. Optional Stop

Q4. What is the difference between the use of **Probe WCS** tool and **Inspect Surface** tool available in **PROBING** panel of **Toolbar** in **MANUFACTURE** workspace?

Q5. The **Simulate** tool is used to check how tools cuts through material in the form of an animation. (T/F)

FOR STUDENT NOTES

FOR STUDENT NOTES

Chapter 20

Introduction to
Simulation in Fusion 360

Topics Covered

The major topics covered in this chapter are:

- *Introduction.*
- *Types of Analyses performed in Fusion 360.*
- *FEA*
- *User Interface of Fusion 360 Simulation.*

INTRODUCTION

Simulation is the study of effects caused on an object due to real-world loading conditions. Computer Simulation is a type of simulation which uses CAD models to represent real objects and it applies various load conditions on the model to study the real-world effects. Fusion 360 is a CAD-CAM-CAE software package. In Fusion 360 Simulation, we apply loads on a constrained model under predefined environmental conditions and check the result (visually and/or in the form of tabular data). The types of analyses that can be performed in Autodesk Fusion are given next.

TYPES OF ANALYSES PERFORMED IN FUSION 360 SIMULATION

Fusion 360 Simulation performs almost all the analyses that are generally performed in Industries. These analyses and their uses are given next.

Static Analysis

This is the most common type of analysis we perform. In this analysis, loads are applied to a body due to which the body deforms and the effects of the loads are transmitted throughout the body. To absorb the effect of loads, the body generates internal forces and reactions at the supports to balance the applied external loads. These internal forces and reactions cause stress and strain in the body. Static analysis refers to the calculation of displacements, strains, and stresses under the effect of external loads, based on some assumptions. The assumptions are as follows.

- All loads are applied slowly and gradually until they reach their full magnitudes. After reaching their full magnitudes, load will remain constant (i.e. load will not vary against time).
- Linearity assumption: The relationship between loads and resulting responses is linear. For example, if you double the magnitude of loads, the response of the model (displacements, strains and stresses) will also double. You can make linearity assumption if:

1. All materials in the model comply with Hooke's Law that is stress is directly proportional to strain.
2. The induced displacements are small enough to ignore the change is stiffness caused by loading.
3. Boundary conditions do not vary during the application of loads. Loads must be constant in magnitude, direction, and distribution. They should not change while the model is deforming.

If the above assumptions are valid for your analysis, then you can perform **Linear Static Analysis**. For example, a cantilever beam fixed at one end and force applied on other end; refer to Figure-1.

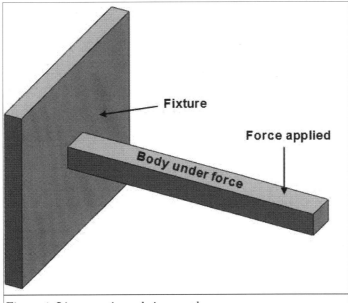

Figure-1. Linear static analysis example

If the above assumptions are not valid, then you need to perform the **Non-Linear Static analysis**. For example, force applied on an object attached with a spring; refer to Figure-2.

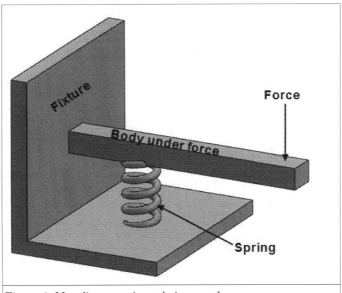

Figure-2. Non-linear static analysis example

Modal Analysis (Vibration Analysis)

By its very nature, vibration involves repetitive motion. Each occurrence of a complete motion sequence is called a "cycle." Frequency is defined as so many cycles in a given time period. "Cycles per second" or "Hertz". Individual parts have what engineers call "natural" frequencies. For example, a violin string at a certain tension will vibrate only at a set number of frequencies, that's why you can produce specific musical tones. There is a base frequency in which the entire string is going back and forth in a simple bow shape.

Harmonics and overtones occur because individual sections of the string can vibrate independently within the larger vibration. These various shapes are called "modes".

The base frequency is said to vibrate in the first mode, and so on up the ladder. Each mode shape will have an associated frequency. Higher mode shapes have higher frequencies. The most disastrous kinds of consequences occur when a power-driven device such as a motor, produces a frequency at which an attached structure naturally vibrates. This event is called "resonance." If sufficient power is applied, the attached structure will be destroyed. Note that armies, which normally marched "in step," were taken out of step when crossing bridges. If the beat of the marching feet align with a natural frequency of the bridge, then it could fall down. Engineers must design in such a way that resonance does not occur during regular operation of machines. This is a major purpose of Modal Analysis. Ideally, the first mode has a frequency higher than any potential driving frequency. Frequently, resonance cannot be avoided, especially for short periods of time. For example, when a motor comes up to speed it produces a variety of frequencies. So, it may pass through a resonant frequency.

Thermal analysis

There are three mechanisms of heat transfer. These mechanisms are Conduction, Convection, and Radiation. Thermal analysis calculates the temperature distribution in a body due to some or all of these mechanisms. In all three mechanisms, heat flows from a higher-temperature medium to a lower temperature one. Heat transfer by conduction and convection requires the presence of an intervening medium while heat transfer by radiation does not.

There are two modes of heat transfer analysis.

Steady State Thermal Analysis

In this type of analysis, we are only interested in the thermal conditions of the body when it reaches thermal equilibrium, but we are not interested in the time it takes to reach this status. The temperature of each point in the model will remain unchanged until a change occurs in the system. At equilibrium, the thermal energy entering the system is equal to the thermal energy leaving it. Generally, the only material property that is needed for steady state analysis is the thermal conductivity. This type of analysis is available in Fusion 360.

Transient Thermal Analysis

In this type of analysis, we are interested in knowing the thermal status of the model at different instances of time. A thermos designer, for example, knows that the temperature of the fluid inside will eventually be equal to the room temperature(steady state), but designer is interested in finding out the temperature of the fluid as a function of time. In addition to the thermal conductivity, we also need to specify density, specific heat, initial temperature profile, and the period of time for which solutions are desired. Till the time of writing this book, the transient thermal analysis was not available in Fusion 360.

Thermal Stress Analysis

The Thermal Stress Analysis is performed to check the stresses induced in part when thermal and structural loads act on the part simultaneously. Thermal Stress Analysis is important in cases where material expands or contracts due to heating or cooling of the part to certain temperature in irregular way. One example where thermal stress analysis finds its importance is two material bonded strip working in a high temperature environment.

Structural Buckling Analysis

Slender models tends to buckle under axial loading. Buckling is defined as the sudden deformation which occurs when the stored membrane (axial) energy is converted into bending energy with no change in the externally applied loads. Mathematically, when buckling occurs, the stiffness becomes singular. The Linearized buckling approach, used here, solves an eigenvalue problem to estimate the critical buckling factors and the associated buckling mode shapes.

In a laymen's language, if you press down on an empty soft drink can with your hand, not much will seem to happen. If you put the can on the floor and gradually increase the force by stepping down on it with your foot, at some point it will suddenly squash. This sudden scrunching is known as "buckling."

Event Simulation

The Event Simulation analysis is used to study the effect of object velocity, initial velocity, acceleration, time dependent loads, and constraints in the design. The results of this analysis include displacements, stresses, strains, and other measurements throughout a specified time period. You can perform this analysis when you need to check the effect of throwing a phone from some height or similar cases where motion is involved.

Shape Optimization

The Shape Optimization in Fusion 360 is not an analysis but a study to find the shape of part which utilizes minimum material but sustains the applied load up to required factor of safety.

Till this point, you have become familiar with the analyses that can be performed by using Fusion 360. But, do you know how the software analyze the problems. The answer is FEA.

FEA

FEA, Finite Element Analysis, is a mathematical system used to solve real-world engineering problems by simplifying them. In FEA by Fusion 360, the model is broken into small elements and nodes. Then, distributed forces are applied on each element and node. The cumulative result of forces is calculated and displayed in results. Note that Fusion 360 uses **Linear Tetrahedron** element with 4 nodes, Parabolic Tetrahedron element with 10 nodes and Parabolic Tetrahedron elements with Curved Edges having 10 nodes to mesh 3D solids. The **Line** element for bolt connectors (only available in Fusion 360 Ultimate). 2D and Planar (shell) elements are not supported in Autodesk Fusion 360 till the time we are writing this book.

As we are ready with some basic information about simulation in Fusion 360. Let's get started with initiating the simulation environment of Fusion 360.

STARTING SIMULATION IN FUSION 360

In Fusion 360, every workspace is available in a seamless manner. To start simulation in Fusion 360, click on the **Change Workspace** drop-down and select the **SIMULATION** option; refer to Figure-3. The **Simulation Workspace** will become active; refer to Figure-4. Also, the **New Study** dialog box will be displayed asking you to select the analysis type you want to perform.

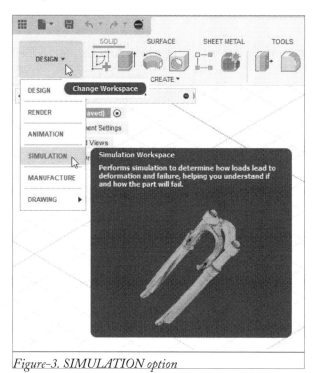

Figure-3. SIMULATION option

Figure-4. Simulation Workspace of Fusion 360

PERFORMING AN ANALYSIS

The static stress analysis is performed when the load is stable and the object deforms according to Hooke's Law. The procedure to start static stress analysis is given next. You can apply the same procedure for starting other analyses too.

• Double-click on the **Static Stress** button from the **New Study** dialog box. The tools required to perform static stress analysis will be displayed in the **Toolbar**; refer to Figure-5.

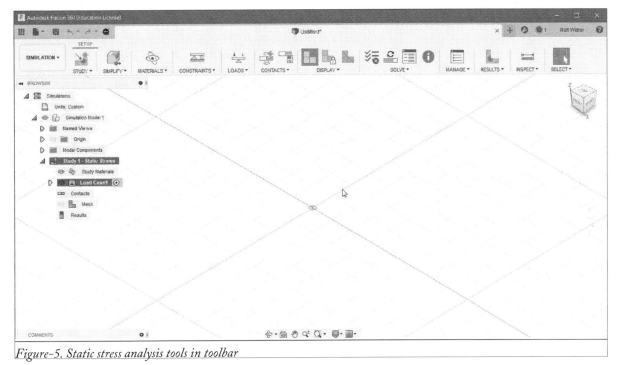

Figure-5. Static stress analysis tools in toolbar

Various tools and options of **Toolbar** in Simulation environment are discussed next.

STARTING NEW SIMULATION STUDY

While you are working on an analysis if you need to start another analysis then you can do so by using the **New Simulation Study** button. The procedure is given next.

• Click on the **New Simulation Study** tool from **STUDY** panel in the **Toolbar**; refer to Figure-6. The **New Study** dialog box will be displayed as discussed earlier.

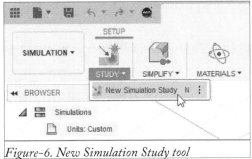

Figure-6. New Simulation Study tool

• Double-click on the desired button to perform respective analysis.

SIMPLIFYING MODEL FOR ANALYSIS

Most of the parts and assemblies have features that are irrelevant to analysis. These features hardly affect the result of analysis but take too much of processing resources. Such features should be removed before performing analysis. Examples of these features can be chamfers, fillets, unnecessary components which have no role in analysis. In Autodesk Fusion, there is a simple way to simplify your model using **Simplify** tool.

• Click on the **Simplify** tool from **SIMPLIFY** panel in the **Toolbar**; refer to Figure-7. The **SIMPLIFY Toolbar** will be displayed; refer to Figure-8.

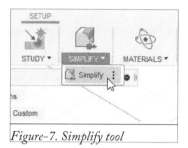

Figure-7. Simplify tool

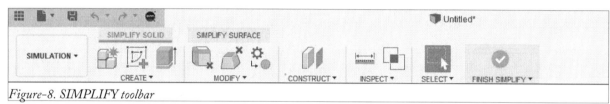

Figure-8. SIMPLIFY toolbar

If you go through various drop-downs and panels in this **Toolbar** then you will find that most of the tools are same as discussed for Modeling and Surface designing in earlier chapters. So, we will skip those tools and discuss the other tools.

Removing Features

The **Remove Features** tool is used to remove selected feature from the model in Simulation environment only. The procedure to use this tool is given next.

• Click on the **Remove Features** tool from **MODIFY** drop-down in the **SIMPLIFY** toolbar; refer to Figure-9. The **REMOVE FEATURES** dialog box will be displayed; refer to Figure-10.

Figure-9. Remove Features tool

Figure-10. REMOVE FEATURES dialog box

- Select the bodies whose extra features are to be removed for performing analysis. The features being removed based on your selection in the **REMOVE FEATURES** dialog box, will be highlighted; refer to Figure-11.

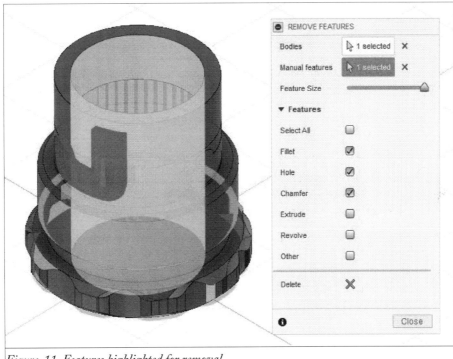

Figure-11. Features highlighted for removal

- Select the desired check boxes from the dialog box to remove respective features.
- Move the **Feature Size** slider left or right to consider smaller or larger features, respectively for removal.
- Although most of the features get selected automatically based on specified conditions in the dialog box but if you want to manually add/remove the features then click on the **Select** button of **Manual features** option in the dialog box and select the desired features.
- After selecting the features, click on the **Delete** button (✖) at the bottom of the dialog box and close the dialog box; refer to Figure-12.

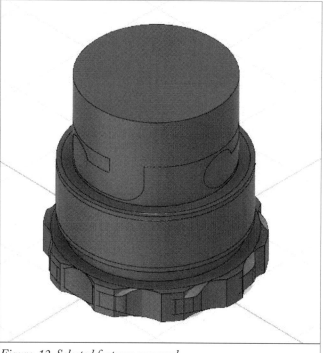

Figure-12. Selected features removed

Removing Faces

The **Remove Faces** tool is used to remove selected faces from the model. The procedure to use this tool is given next.

• Click on the **Remove Faces** tool from **MODIFY** drop-down in the **SIMPLIFY** toolbar; refer to Figure-13. The **REMOVE FACES** dialog box will be displayed; refer to Figure-14.

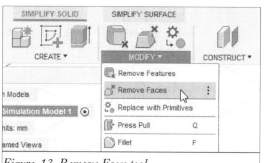

Figure-13. Remove Faces tool

Figure-14. REMOVE FACES dialog box

• The **no selection** button of **Select Faces** section is active by default. Click on the face to be remove; refer to Figure-15.

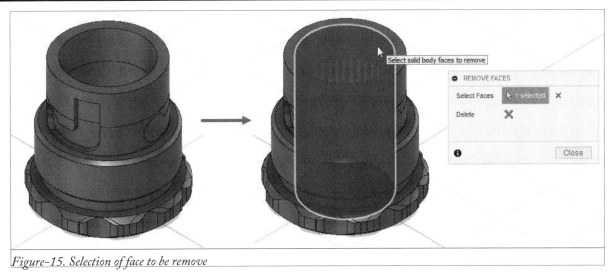

Figure-15. Selection of face to be remove

- Click on the **Delete** button from the dialog box. The selected faces will be deleted; refer to Figure-16.

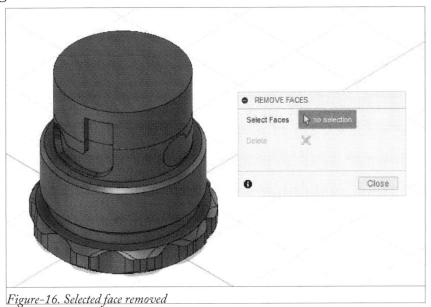

Figure-16. Selected face removed

- Click on **Close** button to exit the tool.

Replace With Primitives

The **Replace with Primitives** tool is used to replace selected body/component by primitive shapes like box, cylinder, and sphere. The procedure to use this tool is given next.

- Click on the **Replace with Primitives** tool from the **MODIFY** drop-down in the **SYMMETRY** toolbar; refer to Figure-17. The **REPLACE WITH PRIMITIVES** dialog box will be displayed; refer to Figure-18.

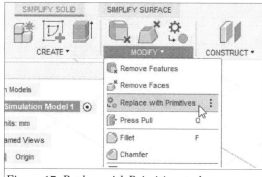

Figure-17. Replace with Primitives tool

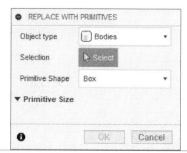

Figure-18. REPLACE WITH PRIMITIVES dialog box

- Select the desired object type from the **Object type** drop-down.
- Select the **Bodies** option if you want to replace bodies with primitives and select the **Components** option if you want to replace assembly components with primitives for analysis.
- The **Select** button of **Selection** section is active by default. Click on the body/component to be selected; refer to Figure-19.

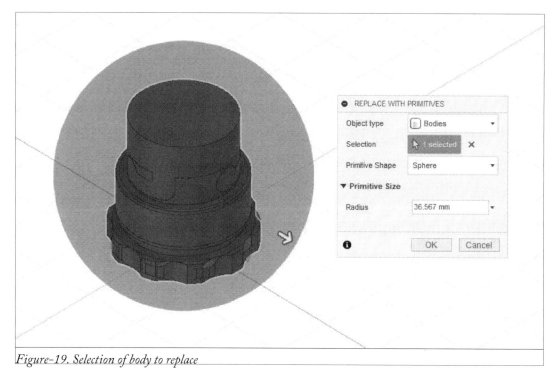

Figure-19. Selection of body to replace

- Select the desired shape from **Primitive Shape** drop-down and specify the related size parameters in the edit boxes of dialog box.
- Click on the **OK** button from the dialog box to replace the body/component; refer to Figure-20.

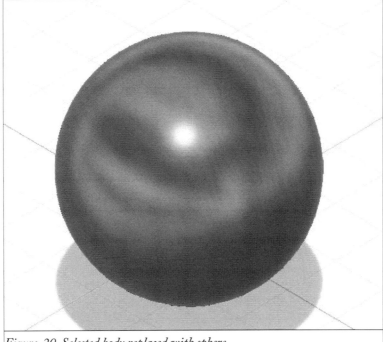

Figure-20. Selected body replaced with sphere

After performing desired simplification operations, click on the **FINISH SIMPLIFY** button from the **Toolbar** to exit Simplify mode.

STUDY MATERIAL

Study material is the material applied to model with all the physical properties so that you can check the effect of load on actual material conditions. The tools related to study material are available in the **MATERIALS** drop-down of the **Toolbar**; refer to Figure-21. These tools are discussed next.

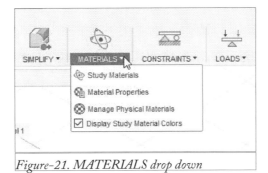

Figure-21. MATERIALS drop down

Applying Study Material

Study material is applied to assign physical properties of material to the model. The procedure to apply study material is given next.

*   Click on the **Study Materials** tool from the **MATERIALS** drop-down in the **Toolbar**; refer to Figure-22. The **Study Materials** dialog box will be displayed; refer to Figure-23.

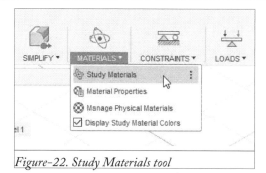

Figure-22. Study Materials tool

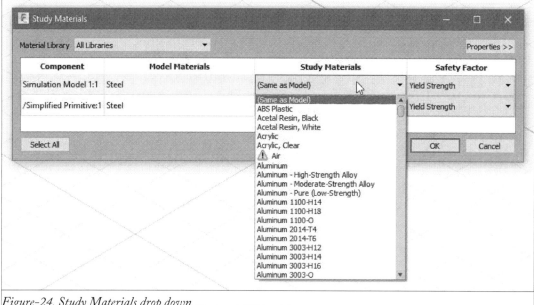

Figure-23. Study Materials dialog box

- Click in the drop-down of **Study Materials** column in the dialog box for the current component and select the desired material; refer to Figure-24.

Figure-24. Study Materials drop down

- Select the desired safety factor criteria from the drop-down in **Safety Factor** column of the dialog box. There are two options in this drop-down; **Yield Strength** and **Ultimate Tensile Strength**. Yield Strength is the point where metal starts to permanently deform. Ultimate Tensile Strength is the point after which the metal becomes so weak that it can break.
- After specifying all the desired parameters, click on the **OK** button. The material will be applied.

Displaying Material Properties

All the properties of different materials in material library can be checked by using the **Material Properties** button. The procedure is discussed next.

- Click on the **Material Properties** tool from the **MATERIALS** drop-down in the **Toolbar**; refer to Figure-25. The **Material Properties** dialog box will be displayed; refer to Figure-26.

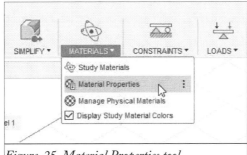

Figure-25. Material Properties tool

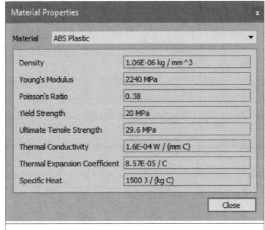

Figure-26. Material Properties dialog box

- Select the material from the **Material** drop-down at the top in the dialog box to check the material properties.
- Click on the **Close** button to exit the dialog box.

Managing Physical Material

The **Manage Physical Materials** tool is used to manage physical properties of material. If you want to edit any parameter of material before using it in analysis then you can do so by using this tool. The procedure is given next.

- Click on the **Manage Physical Materials** tool from the **MATERIALS** drop-down in the **Toolbar**; refer to Figure-27. The **Material Browser** dialog box will be displayed; refer to Figure-28.

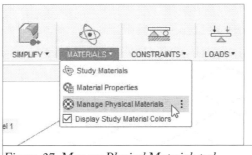

Figure-27. Manage Physical Materials tool

Figure-28. Material Browser dialog box

- Select the desired material library and category from the left area of the **Material Browser** dialog box.
- Hover the cursor on the material you want to edit from the right area and click on the **Adds material to favorites and displays in editor** button; refer to Figure-29. The editing options will be displayed at the right in dialog box; refer to Figure-30.

Figure-29. Adding material to edit

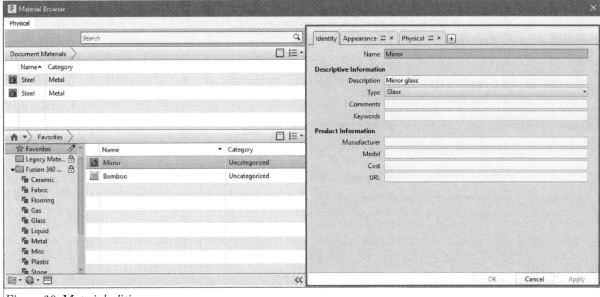

Figure-30. Material editing area

- Click at the desired tab in the right area of the dialog box and specify the parameters related to material.
- Click on the **Apply** button from the right area to apply the changes and then click on the **OK** button to exit the **Material Browser** dialog box.

Creating New Material

If you want to create a new material then follow the procedure given next.

- Click on the **Create New Library** tool from the **Creates, opens, and edits user-defined libraries** drop-down at the bottom left corner of the **Material Browser** dialog box; refer to Figure-31. The **Create Library** dialog box will be displayed; refer to Figure-32.

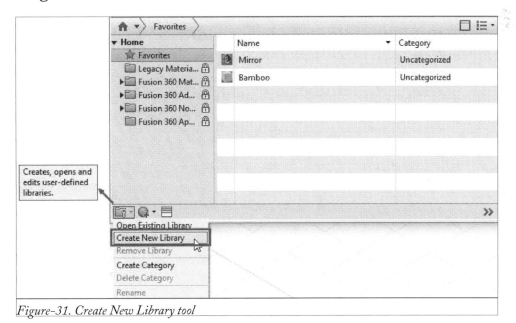

Figure-31. Create New Library tool

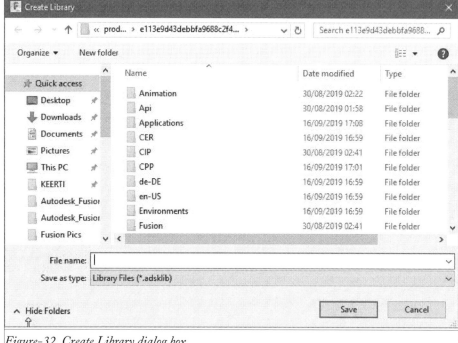

Figure-32. Create Library dialog box

- Specify the desired name of the library in **File name** edit box and click on the **Save** button to save the library file at desired location. A new library will be added.
- Select the newly added library and click on the **Create Category** tool from the **Creates, opens, and edits user-defined libraries** drop-down at the bottom left corner of the **Material Browser** dialog box; refer to Figure-33. A new category will be added to the library. Right-click on the category and select **Rename** if you want to rename it as desired.

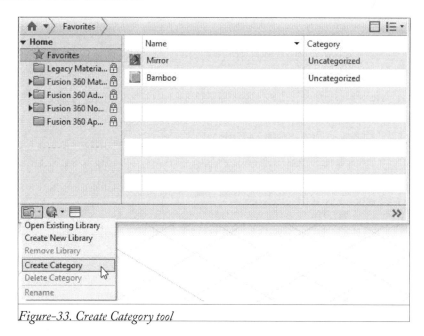

Figure-33. Create Category tool

- Click on the **Create New Material** tool from the **Creates and duplicates materials** drop-down at the bottom in the dialog box as shown in Figure-34. The **Select Material Browser** dialog box will be displayed along with editing options in the **Material Browser** dialog box; refer to Figure-35.

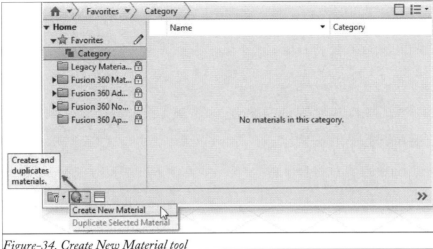
Figure-34. Create New Material tool

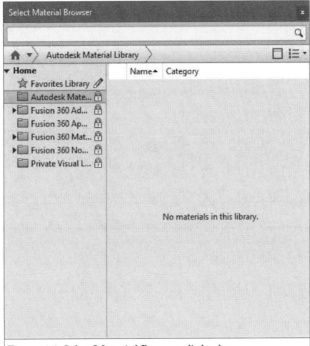
Figure-35. Select Material Browser dialog box

- Close the **Select Material Browser** dialog box and specify the desired parameters of material in the right area.
- To apply physical or appearance properties to material, click on the **+** sign next to **Identity** tab in the editing area of the dialog box. A drop-down will be displayed; refer to Figure-36.

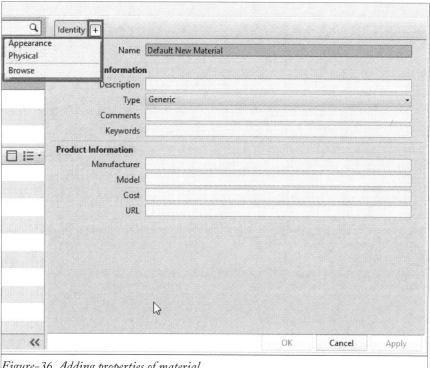

Figure-36. Adding properties of material

- Select the desired option from the drop-down (like, we have selected the **Physical** option). The **Asset Browser** dialog box will be displayed; refer to Figure-37.

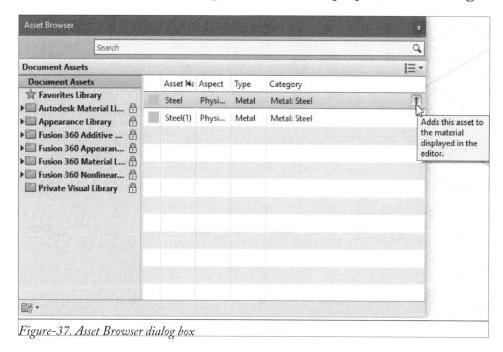

Figure-37. Asset Browser dialog box

- Click on the **Adds this asset to the material displayed in the editor** button as shown in Figure-37 to copy the physical properties of material.
- Close the **Asset Browser** dialog box. The physical properties have been assigned to the new material. Modify the values as required.
- Click on the **Apply** button. The material will be added in the library.
- Add more materials as required and then close the dialog box.

Displaying Study Material Colors

By default, appearance assigned to the part in the **Design workspace** is displayed in the **Simulation workspace**. If you want to display appearance of study material then select the **Display Study Material Colors** check box from the **MATERIALS** drop-down; refer to Figure-38.

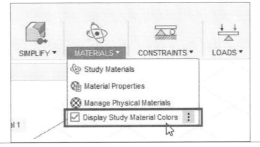

Figure-38. Display Study Material Colors check box

APPLYING CONSTRAINTS

Constraints are used to restrict motion of part when load is applied to form equilibrium. The tools to apply constraints are available in **CONSTRAINTS** drop-down in the **Toolbar**; refer to Figure-39.

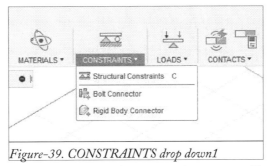

Figure-39. CONSTRAINTS drop down1

The procedure to apply different type of constraints are discussed next.

Applying Structural Constraints

The structural constraints are used to apply different type of structural constraints like fixed, pin, frictionless and so on. The procedure to apply structural constraint is given next.

- Click on the **Structural Constraints** tool from the **CONSTRAINTS** drop-down in the **Toolbar**; refer to Figure-40. The **STRUCTURAL CONSTRAINTS** dialog box will be displayed; refer to Figure-41.

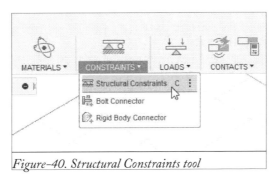

Figure-40. Structural Constraints tool

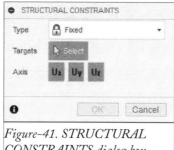

Figure-41. STRUCTURAL CONSTRAINTS dialog box

Fixed Constraint

- Select **Fixed** option from **Type** drop-down in the **STRUCTURAL CONSTRAINTS** dialog box if you want to fix selected faces/edges/vertices of the part.
- Select the face/edge/vertex that you want to be fixed.
- Select the desired axis button from the **Axis** section. Like, select the **Ux** button if you want to restrict movement along X axis. By default, all the three buttons are selected and hence the movement along all the three axes is restricted. Refer to Figure-42.

Figure-42. Faces selected for fixed constraint

- Click on the **OK** button from the dialog box to fix the selected geometries.

Pin Constraint

The Pin constraint is used to restrict radial, axial, and tangential movement of a cylindrical part. The procedure to use this constraint is given next.

- Select the **Pin** option from the **Type** drop-down in the **STRUCTURAL CONSTRAINTS** dialog box. The options in the dialog box will be displayed as shown in Figure-43.

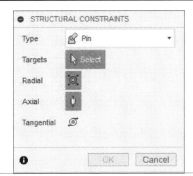

Figure-43. STRUCTURAL CONSTRAINTS
dialog box with Pin option selected

• Select the cylindrical face on which you want to apply pin constraint; refer to Figure-44.

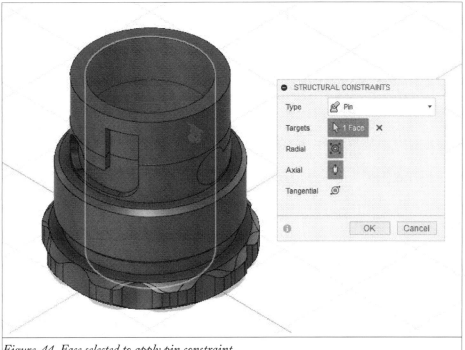

Figure-44. Face selected to apply pin constraint

• Select the desired buttons to restrict the respective motion. For example, select the **Radial** button to restrict radial motion.
• Similarly, specify the other parameters as required and click on the **OK** button to complete the process.

Frictionless Constraint

The Frictionless constraint is used to restrict the movement of object perpendicular to selected face. However, the object is free to move in the plane. The procedure to apply this constraint is given next.

• Select the **Frictionless** option from the **Type** drop-down in the **STRUCTURAL CONSTRAINTS** dialog box. The options in the dialog box will be displayed as shown in Figure-45.

Figure-45. STRUCTURAL CONSTRAINTS
dialog box with Frictionless option selected

• Select the desired face on which you want to apply the frictionless constraint.

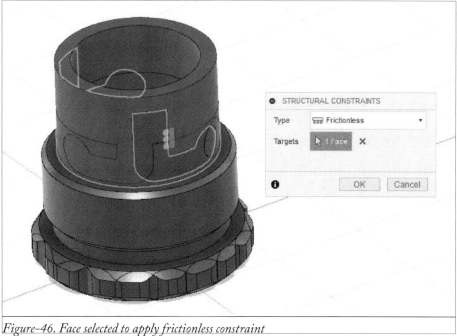

Figure-46. Face selected to apply frictionless constraint

• Click on the **OK** button to exit.

Prescribed Displacement Constraint

The **Prescribed displacement** constraint is used to apply fixed constraint at specified displacement. The procedure to use this constraint is given next.

• Select the **Prescribed Displacement** option from **Type** drop-down in the **STRUCTURAL CONSTRAINTS** dialog box. The options in the dialog box will be displayed as shown in Figure-47. You will be asked to select the face/edge/vertex.

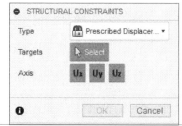

Figure-47. STRUCTURAL CONSTRAINTS dialog
box with Prescribed Displacement option selected

• Select the desired geometry. The **STRUCTURAL CONSTRAINTS** dialog box will be updated; refer to Figure-48.

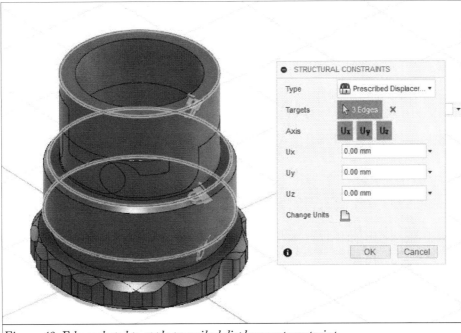

Figure-48. Edges selected to apply prescribed displacement constraint

- Specify the desired parameters and click on the **OK** button to exit the tool.

Applying Bolt Connector Constraint

Bolt connector is used to apply connection similar to bolt fastener connection in assemblies. Note that bolt connector represents the nut-bolt connection or threaded nut connection mathematically. The procedure to apply bolt connector is given next.

- Click on the **Bolt Connector** tool from the **CONSTRAINTS** drop-down in the **Toolbar**; refer to Figure-49. The **BOLT CONNECTOR** dialog box will be displayed; refer to Figure-50.

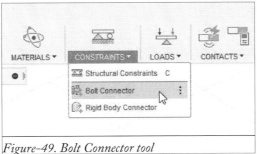

Figure-49. Bolt Connector tool

Figure-50. BOLT CONNECTOR dialog box

- The **Select** button of **Location for Bolt Head** option is active by default.
- Select the round edge of the part where you want the bolt head to be placed. The **BOLT CONNECTOR** dialog box will be updated; refer to Figure-51.

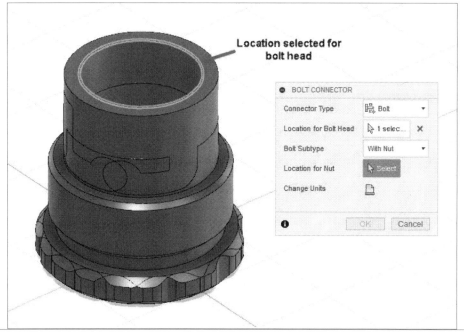

Figure-51. Updated BOLT CONNECTOR dialog box after selecting location for bolt head

Bolt Fastener with Nut

- Select the **With Nut** option from the **Bolt Subtype** drop-down if you want to create a bolt-nut fastener constraint. You will be asked to select the round edge where nut will be placed.
- Select the desired edge. The **BOLT CONNECTOR** dialog box will be updated with preview of bolt-nut fastener; refer to Figure-52.

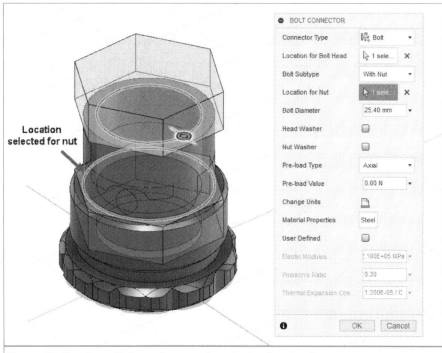

Figure-52. Preview of bolt nut fastener after selecting location for nut

- Specify the parameters like bolt diameter, bolt washer, nut washer, pre-load etc. and click on the **OK** button to create the constraint.

Bolt with Threaded Hole

- Select the **Threaded Hole** option from the **Bolt Subtype** drop-down if you want to create threaded bolted connection. You will be asked to select face to be threaded.
- Select the desired face. Preview of the bolt will be displayed; refer to Figure-53.

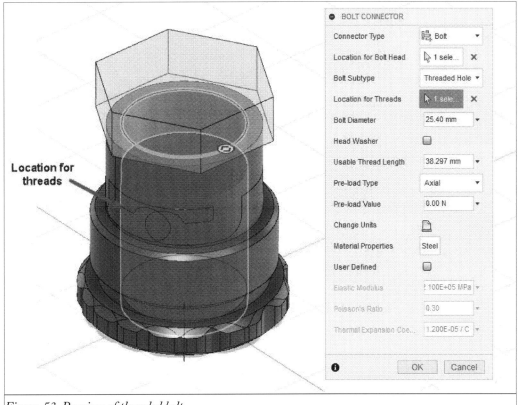

Figure-53. Preview of threaded bolt

- Specify the parameters as required and click on the **OK** button to exit the tool.

Rigid Body Connector Constraint

The Rigid Body Connector constraint is used where a vertex of one component is to be rigidly connected with face, edge, or vertex of other body. The procedure to use this constraint is given next.

- Click on the **Rigid Body Connector** tool from the **CONSTRAINTS** drop-down in the **Toolbar**; refer to Figure-54. The **RIGID BODY CONNECTOR** dialog box will be displayed; refer to Figure-55.

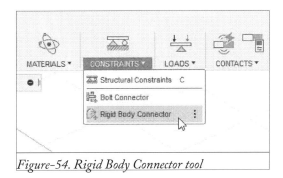

Figure-54. Rigid Body Connector tool

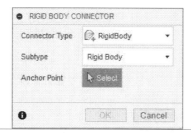

Figure-55. RIGID BODY CONNECTOR dialog box

- Select the desired vertex that you want to be anchor point for connection on the first body/component. You will be asked to select the dependent entities.
- Select the points/faces/edges that are dependent on the anchor point for movement; refer to Figure-56.

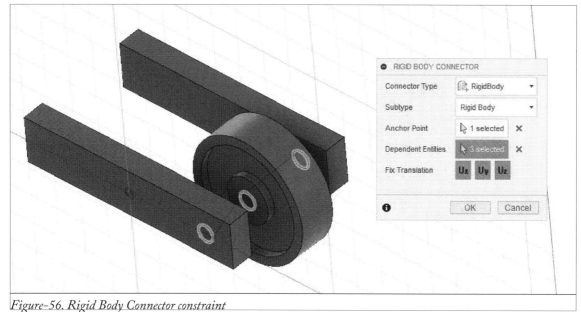

Figure-56. Rigid Body Connector constraint

- Similarly, you can use the **Interpolation** option from the **Subtype** drop-down to create rigid connection with translational and rotational constraining.

APPLYING LOADS

Loads in Fusion 360 are the representation of forces and loads applied on the part in real application. The tools to apply loads are available in the **LOADS** drop-down in the **Toolbar**; refer to Figure-57. Various tools in this drop-down are discussed next.

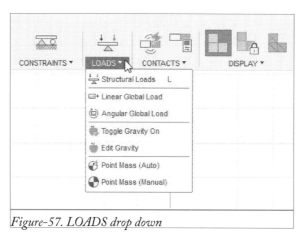

Figure-57. LOADS drop down

Applying Structural Loads

There are various structural loads that can be applied on the object like force, pressure, moment, remote force, bearing load, and hydrostatic pressure. The procedure to apply different loads are discussed next.

- Click on the **Structural Loads** tool from the **LOADS** drop-down in the **Toolbar**. The **STRUCTURAL LOADS** dialog box will be displayed; refer to Figure-58.

Figure-58. STRUCTURAL LOADS dialog box

Applying Force

- By default, **Force** option is selected in the **Type** drop-down of **STRUCTURAL LOADS** dialog box. If not selected then select the **Force** option from the **Type** drop-down. You will be asked to select face/edge/point on which force is to be applied.
- Select the desired face/edge/point. The options in the **STRUCTURAL LOADS** dialog box will be modified according to geometry selected; refer to Figure-59.
- Select the desired **Direction Type** button from the dialog box. If you have selected the **Normal** button 🔲 then force will be applied perpendicular to the selected face. You can use the **Flip** 🔀 button below it to reverse direction of force; refer to Figure-60.

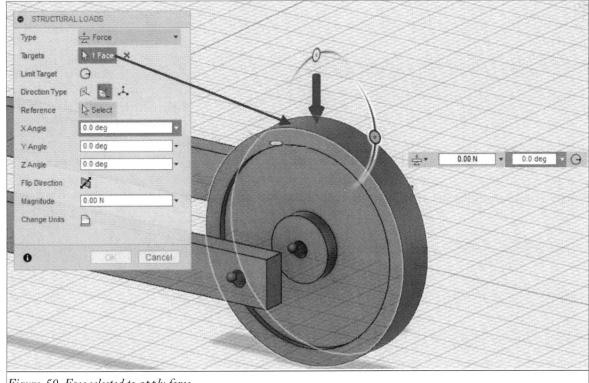

Figure-59. Face selected to apply force

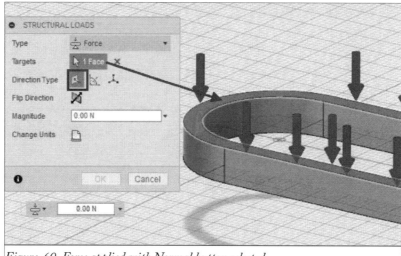

Figure-60. Force applied with Normal button selected

- Select the **Angle (delta)** button ⬚ from the **Direction Type** section of the dialog box if you want to apply force at some angle; refer to Figure-59. Specify the desired angle values in the **X Angle**, **Y Angle**, and **Z Angle** edit boxes. Select the **Flip Direction** button to reverse the direction if required. Note that the **Limit Target** button is also available in the dialog box. Select this button and specify the radius range in which the force will be applied.
- Select the **Vectors** button from the **Direction Type** section if you want to specify force value along each vector direction.
- To change the unit of load, click on the **Change Units** button if you want to change the unit for load.
- Click on the **OK** button from the dialog box to apply the load.

Applying Pressure

- Select the **Pressure** option from the **STRUCTURAL LOADS** dialog box. You will be asked to select the faces to apply pressure.
- Select the face(s) to apply pressure force. The options in the dialog box will be displayed as shown in Figure-61.

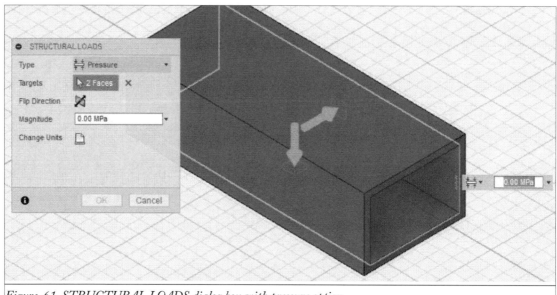

Figure-61. STRUCTURAL LOADS dialog box with pressure option

- Specify the desired value of pressure in the **Magnitude** edit box. If you want to change the unit then select the **Change Units** button and specify the desired value in the edit box displayed.
- Click on the **OK** button from the dialog box to apply the pressure load.

Applying Moment

- Select the **Moment** option from the **STRUCTURAL LOADS** dialog box. You will be asked to select the faces to apply moment.
- Select the desired face. The options in the dialog box will be updated; refer to Figure-62.

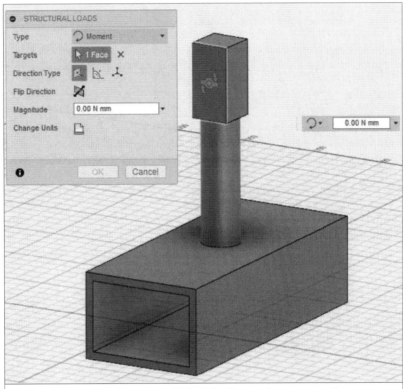

Figure-62. STRUCTURAL LOADS dialog box with moment option

- Set the desired value of moment in the **Magnitude** edit box.
- Set the other parameters as discussed earlier and click on the **OK** button to apply moment load.

Applying Bearing Load

Bearing load is the force exerted by bearing on round face of the part. The procedure to apply bearing load is given next.

- Select the **Bearing Load** option from the **Type** drop-down in the **STRUCTURAL LOADS** dialog box. You will be asked to select the round face on which bearing load is to be applied.
- Select the desired face. The options in the dialog box will be displayed as shown in Figure-63.

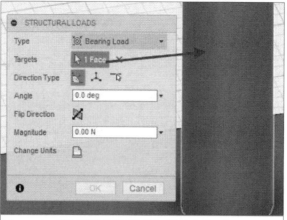

Figure-63. STRUCTURAL LOADS dialog box with Bearing Load option

- Specify the desired parameters as discussed earlier. Note that bearing load is a directional force and applicable on only half of the full 360 cylindrical face.
- After specifying the parameters, click on the **OK** button to apply bearing load.

Applying Remote Force

The remote force is used to represent effect of load applied at different location on the selected location; refer to Figure-64. The procedure to apply load is given next.

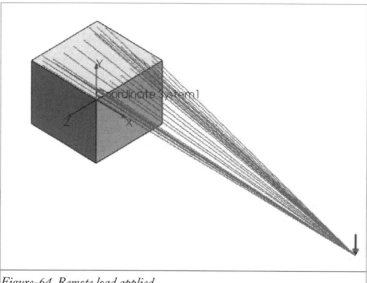

Figure-64. Remote load applied

- Select the **Remote Force** option from the **Type** drop-down in the **STRUCTURAL LOADS** dialog box. You will be asked to select a location to apply force.
- Select the desired face/edge/point. The options in the dialog box will be displayed as shown in Figure-65.

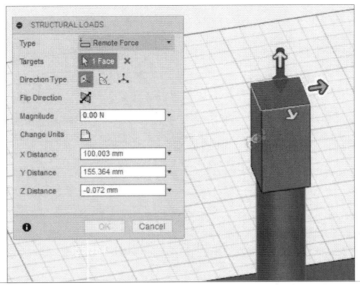

Figure-65. STRUCTURAL LOADS dialog box with Remote Force option

- Set the X, Y, and Z distances of the load location in the **X Distance**, **Y Distance**, and **Z Distance** edit boxes of the dialog box, respectively.
- Specify the other parameters as discussed earlier.
- Click on the **OK** button to apply remote force.

Applying Hydrostatic Pressure

Hydrostatic pressure is a linearly varying pressure exerted by fluid on the surface of part. This force is applicable when the part is in contact with high volume of fluid. The procedure to apply this load is given next.

- Select the **Hydrostatic Pressure** option from the **Type** drop-down in the **STRUCTURAL LOADS** dialog box.

Note that if you are applying hydrostatic pressure for the first time then a message box will be displayed prompting you to activate gravity. Activate the gravity by clicking on the **OK** button.

- The **Hydrostatic Pressure** option will be selected in the dialog box. You will be asked to select the face(s)to apply hydrostatic pressure.
- Select the desired face(s). The options in the dialog box will be displayed as shown in Figure-66.

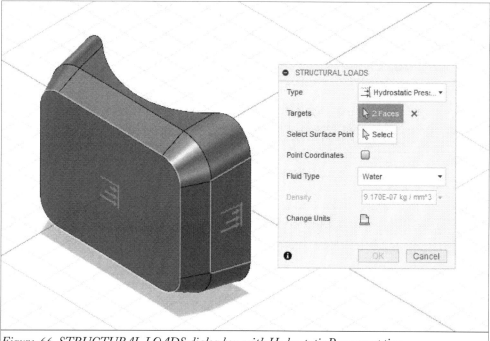

Figure-66. STRUCTURAL LOADS dialog box with Hydrostatic Pressure option

- Click on the **Select** button for **Select Surface Point** section in the dialog box and select the desired point up to which the fluid is filled in the system.
- Specify the desired offset value for fluid surface point in the **Offset Distance** edit box.
- Select the desired fluid type from the **Fluid Type** drop-down. If you have a different fluid that the options available then select the **Custom** option and specify the density of fluid in the **Density** edit box.
- Click on the **OK** button after specifying the desired values to apply load.

Applying Linear Global Load (Acceleration)

Linear Global Load is the applied when the whole system is under acceleration like an object placed in an accelerating car. The procedure to apply linear global load is given next.

- Click on the **Linear Global Load** tool from the **LOADS** drop-down in the **Toolbar**. The **LINEAR GLOBAL LOAD** dialog box will be displayed as shown in Figure-67 and you will be asked to select a reference for acceleration direction.

Figure-67. LINEAR GLOBAL LOAD dialog box

- Select the desired face/edge to specify the direction of acceleration; refer to Figure-68.

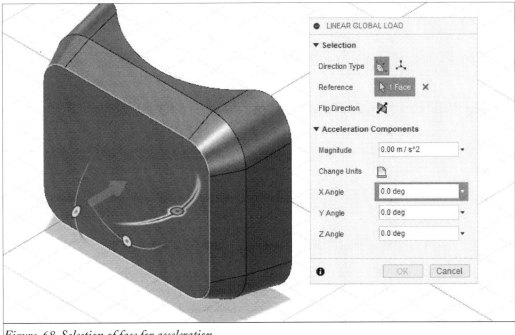

Figure-68. Selection of face for acceleration

- Specify the desired value of acceleration in the **Magnitude** edit box.
- Similarly, specify the desired angle value for X, Y, and Z in the **X Angle**, **Y Angle**, and **Z Angle** edit boxes.
- Specify the other parameters as required and click on the **OK** button to apply the linear global load.

Applying Angular Global Load

The Angular Global Load is applied to give angular velocity or angular acceleration to the system. The procedure to apply angular global load is given next.

- Click on the **Angular Global Load** tool from the **LOADS** drop-down in the **Toolbar**. The **ANGULAR GLOBAL LOAD** dialog box will be displayed; refer to Figure-69.

Figure-69. ANGULAR GLOBAL LOAD dialog box

- The **Select** button of **Location Reference** section is active by default. Select the desired location for applying velocity or acceleration. The input boxes will be displayed to apply angular velocity and specify the location of the exerting point along X direction.
- Click on the **Select** button from the **Direction Reference** section and select the face to define axis for angular velocity/acceleration.
- Specify the other parameters as discussed earlier.
- Click on the **Acceleration** button if you want to specify the acceleration also from the **Acceleration Components** rollout in the dialog box. Specify the related parameters as discussed earlier.
- Click on the **OK** button to apply angular velocity/acceleration.

Toggling Gravity On/Off

Anyone who has passed high school should be knowing what is gravity!! The procedure to activate and de-activate gravity is given next.

- Click on the **Toggle Gravity On** button from the **LOADS** drop-down in the **Toolbar** if the gravity is off and you want to activate it.
- Click on the **Toggle Gravity Off** button from the **LOADS** drop-down in the **Toolbar** if the gravity is on and you want to de-activate it; refer to Figure-70.

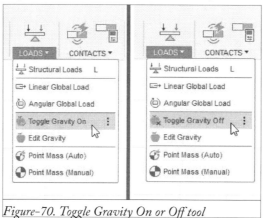

Figure-70. Toggle Gravity On or Off tool

Editing Gravity

The **Edit Gravity** tool is used to edit the value and direction of gravity acting the system. The procedure is given next.

- Click on the **Edit Gravity** tool from the **LOADS** drop-down in the **Toolbar**. The **EDIT GRAVITY** dialog box will be displayed; refer to Figure-71.

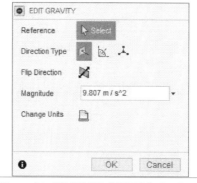

Figure-71. EDIT GRAVITY dialog box

- The **Select** button of **Reference** section is active by default. Select the desired direction reference (face/edge) to specify the direction of gravity.
- Specify the desired value of gravity in the **Magnitude** edit box.
- Click on the **OK** button to apply the edited Gravity.

Apply Point Mass (Auto)

The **Point Mass (Auto)** tool is used to replace the real component with a point mass. This phenomena is used to simplify simulation calculations. The procedure to use this tool is given next.

- Click on the **Point Mass (Auto)** tool from the **LOADS** drop-down in the **Toolbar**. The **POINT MASS (AUTO)** dialog box will be displayed; refer to Figure-72.

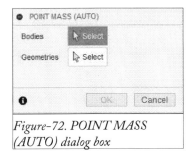

Figure-72. POINT MASS (AUTO) dialog box

- The **Select** button of **Bodies** section is active by default. Select the object that you want to be replaced by point mass.
- Click on the **Select** button for **Geometries** section and select the face on which you want to place the mass.
- Specify the desired mass value in the **Mass** edit box of the dialog box; refer to Figure-73.

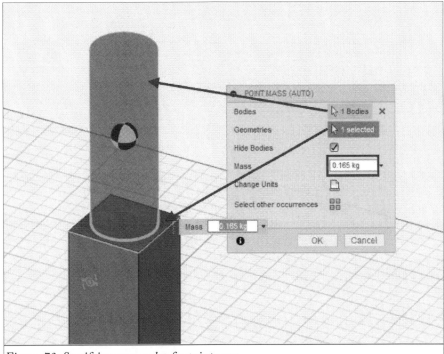

Figure-73. Specifying mass value for point mass

- Specify other parameters as required and click on the **OK** button to apply point mass.

Apply Point Mass (Manual)

The **Point Mass (Manual)** tool works in the same way as **Point Mass (Auto)**. The only difference between the two is that in case of **Point Mass (Manual)** tool, you do not need to select a body to be replaced by mass.

APPLYING CONTACTS

Contacts are applied when there are two or more bodies/components in contact with each other and load is transferred between them during simulation. The tools to apply contact are available in the **CONTACTS** drop-down; refer to Figure-74. These tools are discussed next.

Figure-74. CONTACTS drop down

Applying Automatic Contacts

If you are performing analysis on an assembly with multiple components then applying automatic contact is a very important steps. Without applying automatic contact, you can not perform analysis of assembly in Fusion 360. The procedure to apply automatic contact is given next.

*   Click on the **Automatic Contacts** tool from the **CONTACTS** drop-down in the **Toolbar**. The **AUTOMATIC CONTACTS** dialog box will be displayed; refer to Figure-75.

Figure-75. AUTOMATIC CONTACTS dialog box

*   Specify the desired value of tolerance in **Solids** edit box of the **AUTOMATIC CONTACTS** dialog box. The tolerance specified here is the maximum gap up to which the software will apply contacts. If the gap between two components is more than the specified value then Fusion will not apply any contact automatically.
*   Click on the **Generate** button. The contacts will be generated automatically.

Modifying Contacts

Automatic Contacts tool applies the same contact to the components in the assembly. The procedure to check and modify automatically applied contacts is given next.

- To check the automatically applied contacts, click on the **Edit** button displayed on hovering the cursor over **Contacts** node of the **BROWSER**; refer to Figure-76. The **CONTACTS MANAGER** dialog box will be displayed; refer to Figure-77. Here, you can check the contacts automatically applied.

Figure-76. Contacts Edit button

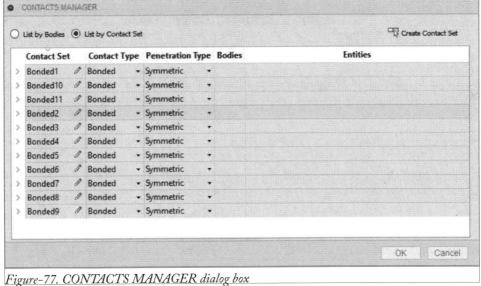

Figure-77. CONTACTS MANAGER dialog box

- Select the contact that you want to edit from the **Contact Set** column in the **CONTACTS MANAGER** dialog box. The contact will be highlighted in the model.
- To modify the contact, click in the **Contact Type** column for the selected contact. List of different available contacts will be displayed; refer to Figure-78.

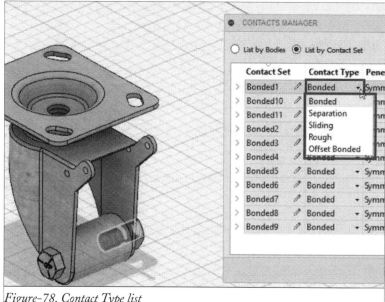

Figure-78. Contact Type list

- Select the desired contact type to change. Various contact types are discussed next.

Bonded Contact Type

The bonded contact is used when there is no relative displacement between two connected solid bodies is required. This type of contact is used to glue together different solids of an assembly. The two surfaces that are in contact are classified as master and slave. Every node in the slave surface(slave nodes) is tied to a node in the master surface(master node) by a constraint. You will learn about master surface and slave surface in the next topic.

Separation Contact Type

The separation contact is applied when separation between parts is allowed but prohibits part penetration.

Sliding Contact Type

The sliding contact is a type of contact which allows displacement tangential to the contacting surface but no relative movement along the normal direction. This type of contact constraint is used to simulate sliding movement in the assembly. The two surfaces that are in contact are classified as master and slave. Every node in slave surface(slave nodes) is tied to a node in the master surface(master node) by this constraint.

Rough Contact Type

The rough contact is used when two parts cannot slide over each other as friction between them is very high. Note that the parts cannot penetrate in each other if this contact type is selected.

Offset Bonded Contact Type

The offset bonded contact is used when two parts are at a distance in assembly but you want them to be bonded as bonded contact type.

Applying Manual Contacts

Applying automatic contacts is the first step for performing analysis on the assembly but **Automatic Contacts** apply the same contact to all the assembly joints which can be changed by using **CONTACTS MANAGER**. But what to do if automatic contacts are not generated for required faces. The **Manual Contacts** tool is used to apply these contacts. The procedure to use this tool is given next.

- Click on the **Manual Contacts** tool from the **CONTACTS** drop-down in the **Toolbar**. The **MANUAL CONTACTS** dialog box will be displayed as shown in Figure-79. Also, you will be asked to select the master body.

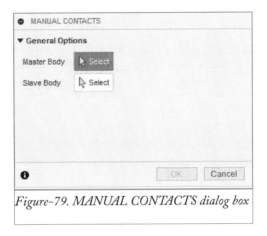

Figure-79. MANUAL CONTACTS dialog box

- The **Select** button of **Master Body** section is active by default. Select the first body. You will be asked to select the slave body.
- Select the second body. You will be asked to select the face/edge on the first body.
- Select the desired face/edge at which the body is in contact with other body.
- Click on the **Select** button of **Selection Set 2** section in the dialog box and select the contacting face/edge on the second body. The options in the dialog box will be displayed as shown in Figure-80.

Figure-80. Options in MANUAL CONTACTS dialog box

- Select the desired contact type from the **Contact Type** drop-down in the dialog box.
- Select the desired option from the **Penetration Type** drop-down. If you have selected the **Symmetric** option then both master component and slave component cannot penetrate into each other. If the **Unsymmetric** option is selected then the master component can penetrate the slave component.
- Specify the desired maximum activation distance in the **Max. Activation Distance** edit box. This parameter is useful when parts are not coincident and a small gap is present between them. Choose a small value to prevent conflicting contact interactions.
- Similarly, specify the other parameters as required.
- Click on the **OK** button to create the contact.

Manage Contacts Tool

The **Manage Contacts** tool in the **CONTACTS** drop-down is used to edit contacts earlier applied. On clicking this tool, the **CONTACTS MANAGER** will be displayed. The options in the **CONTACTS MANAGER** have already been discussed.

SOLVING ANALYSIS

Once you have applied all the information required to perform analysis, you need to perform a check whether you have specified the required information or not. Once the system says, it has the required information then you are good to go for analysis. The tools to perform pre-check and analysis are available in the **SOLVE** drop-down of the **Toolbar**; refer to Figure-81. These tools are discussed next.

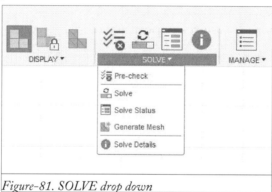

Figure-81. SOLVE drop down

Performing Pre-check

Pre-checking is an important step before performing analysis. Although the tool will not tell you that you have specified load at wrong place or other design faults but the tool will warn you that you have not specified load, constraint, contact like parameters which need to be specified before performing analysis. The procedure to perform pre-check is given next.

- Click on the **Pre-check** tool from the **SOLVE** drop-down in the **Toolbar**. If there is any parameter left to be specified then **Cannot Solve** dialog box will be displayed; refer to Figure-82.

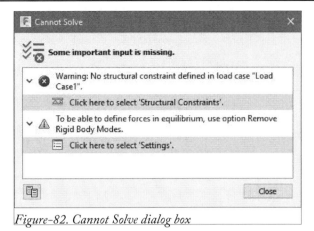

Figure-82. Cannot Solve dialog box

- Apply the parameters which are not specified. If all the parameters are specified then **Ready to Solve** dialog box will be displayed; refer to Figure-83.

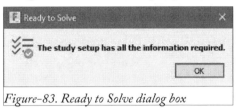

Figure-83. Ready to Solve dialog box

- Click on the **OK** button and perform meshing.

Meshing

Meshing is the base of FEM. Meshing divides the solid/shell models into elements of finite size and shape. These elements are joined at some common points called nodes. These nodes define the load transfer from one element to other element. Meshing is a very crucial step in design analysis. The automatic mesher in the software generates a mesh based on a global element size, tolerance, and local mesh control specifications. Mesh control lets you specify different sizes of elements for components, faces, edges, and vertices.

The software estimates a global element size for the model taking into consideration its volume, surface area, and other geometric details. The size of the generated mesh (number of nodes and elements) depends on the geometry and dimensions of the model, element size, mesh tolerance, mesh control, and contact specifications. In the early stages of design analysis where approximate results may suffice, you can specify a larger element size for a faster solution. For a more accurate solution, a smaller element size may be required.

Meshing generates 3D tetrahedral solid elements and 1D beam elements. A mesh consists of one type of elements unless the mixed mesh type is specified. Solid elements are naturally suitable for bulky models. Shell elements are naturally suitable for modeling thin parts (sheet metals), and beams and trusses are suitable for modeling structural members.

The procedure to create the mesh of the solid is given next.

- Click on the **Generate Mesh** tool from the **SOLVE** drop-down in the **Toolbar**. The system will start creating mesh and progress bar will be displayed. Once the operation is complete. The mesh will be displayed; refer to Figure-84.

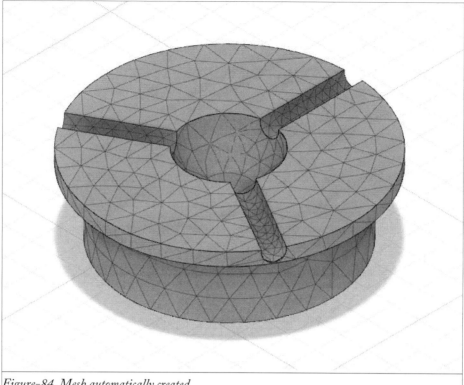

Figure-84. Mesh automatically created

- If you want to change the automatic mesh settings then click on the **Edit** button displayed on hovering the cursor over **Mesh** in the **BROWSER**; refer to Figure-85. The **Mesh Settings** dialog box will be displayed; refer to Figure-86.

Figure-85. Edit button of mesh

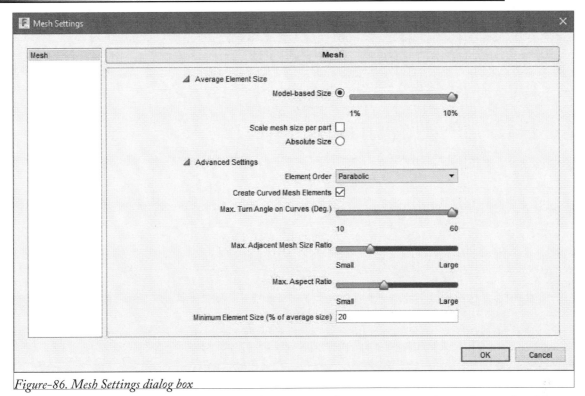

Figure-86. Mesh Settings dialog box

- Move the slider towards left to decrease the average size of mesh. Note that decreasing the size will increase the analysis solution time.
- Select the **Scale mesh size per part** check box if you want to system to scale mesh size of each individual part in assembly based on its size. In other words, if there are 10 parts in assembly with different sizes then mesh elements of each part will have different size.
- If you want to specify a value for all mesh element sizes then select the **Absolute Size** radio button and specify the desired value for element size in the edit box next to it.
- Select the desired element order from the **Element Order** drop-down in the **Advanced Settings** node of the dialog box. Select the **Parabolic** option element order for complex parts which require higher degree of elements. For simple parts, select the **Linear** option from the drop-down.
- Select the **Create Curved Mesh Elements** check box if you want the mesh elements to follow curvature of round/curved faces of the part.
- Similarly, specify the other parameters in the **Advanced Settings** node and click on the **OK** button to apply the mesh settings.

Applying Local Mesh Control

Local mesh control is used when you need to increase or decrease the size of elements in a finite area of the part. The procedure to apply local mesh control is given next.

- Click on the **Local Mesh Control** tool from the **MANAGE** drop-down in the **Toolbar**; refer to Figure-87. The **LOCAL MESH CONTROL** dialog box will be displayed; refer to Figure-88. You will be asked to select a face/edge.

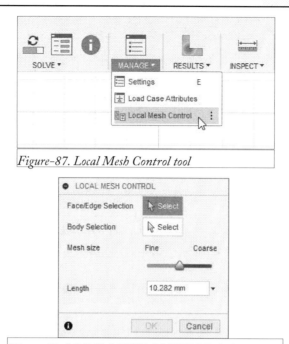

Figure-87. Local Mesh Control tool

Figure-88. LOCAL MESH CONTROL dialog box

- The **Select** button of **Face/Edge Selection** section is active by default. Select the face/edge(s) for which you want to increase/decrease the element size. If you are working on an assembly then you can select the body after clicking on the **Select** button from **Body Selection** section of the dialog box.
- After selecting the desired geometries, move the slider towards coarse or fine to change the mesh size.
- Click on the **OK** button to apply the change.

Note that changes in mesh will not be reflected automatically. To update mesh, right-click on the **Mesh** in the **Browser** and select the **Generate Mesh** option from the shortcut menu; refer to Figure-89.

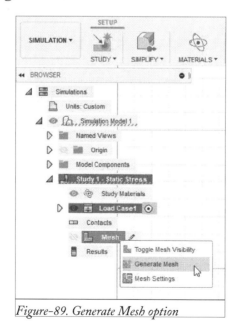

Figure-89. Generate Mesh option

Adaptive Mesh Refinement

Adaptive mesh refinement is used when dynamic refinement of mesh is required at the stress-strain locations to increase accuracy. The procedure to apply adaptive mesh refinement is given next.

- Click on the **Settings** tool from the **MANAGE** drop-down in the **Toolbar**. The **Settings** dialog box will be displayed. Click on the **Adaptive Mesh Refinement** option in the left side of the **Settings** dialog box. The **Adaptive Mesh Refinement** page will be displayed; refer to Figure-90.

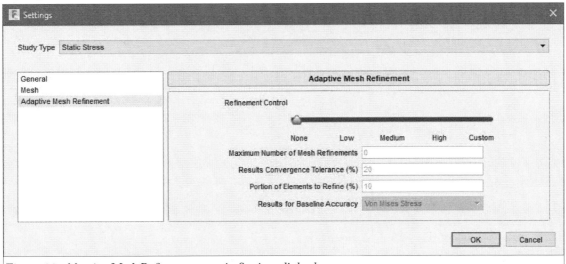

Figure-90. Adaptive Mesh Refinement page in Settings dialog box

- Move the **Refinement Control** slider towards right to increase refinement level of meshing at stress/strain areas.
- Click on the **OK** button to apply refinement.

Solving Analysis

Once you have specified all the parameters then it is time to solve the analysis. The procedure to do so is given next.

- Click on the **Solve** tool from the **SOLVE** drop-down in the **Toolbar**. The **Solve** dialog box will be displayed; refer to Figure-91.

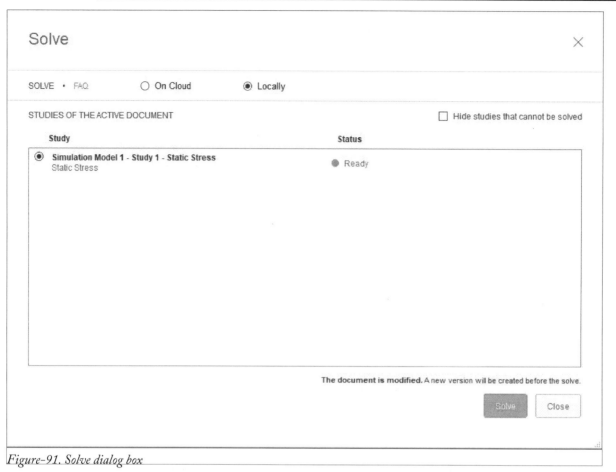

Figure-91. Solve dialog box

- Make sure **Ready** is displayed in the **Status** column of the study to be performed. Click on the **Solve** button. The results will be displayed; refer to Figure-92.

Figure-92. Results displayed after solving analysis

To check the strongest areas of design, click on the **Show strongest areas of design** button from the **RESULTS DETAILS** dialog box. The strongest areas of design will be displayed; refer to Figure-93.

Figure-93. Strongest area results

Move the sliders on scale to change the threshold to be counted as weak area.

Preparing and Manipulating the Results

Once the analysis is complete, the next step is to prepare and manipulate the results as required. The tools to prepare results are available in the **RESULT TOOLS** drop-down from **RESULTS** tab in the **Toolbar**; refer to Figure-94. The tools in this drop-down are discussed next.

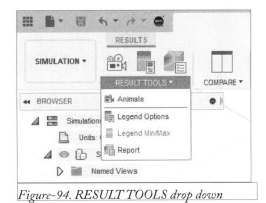

Figure-94. RESULT TOOLS drop down

Animating the Results

Animation is used to represent the analysis results in dynamic motion. The procedure to animate the analysis result is given next.

- Click on the **Animate** tool from the **RESULT TOOLS** drop-down in the **Toolbar**. The **ANIMATE** dialog box will be displayed; refer to Figure-95.

Figure-95. ANIMATE dialog box

- Select the **One-way** check box or **Two-way** check box to repeat the animation.
- Set the other parameters as required and click on the **Play** button.
- Click on the **OK** button to exit the dialog box.

Legend Options

The **Legend Options** tool is used to modify the appearance of legends displayed in the results. The procedure to use this tool is given next.

- Click on the **Legend Options** tool from the **RESULT TOOLS** drop-down in the **Toolbar**. The **LEGEND OPTIONS** dialog box will be displayed; refer to Figure-96.

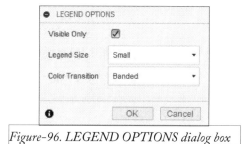

Figure-96. LEGEND OPTIONS dialog box

- Select the desired legend size and color transition method from the **Legend Size** drop-down and **Color Transition** drop-down respectively.
- Click on the **OK** button to apply changes.

Generating Reports

Once you find the analysis results as expected, it is the time to generate reports. The procedure to generate report is given next.

- Click on the **Report** tool from the **RESULT TOOLS** drop-down in the **Toolbar**. The **Report** dialog box will be displayed; refer to Figure-97.

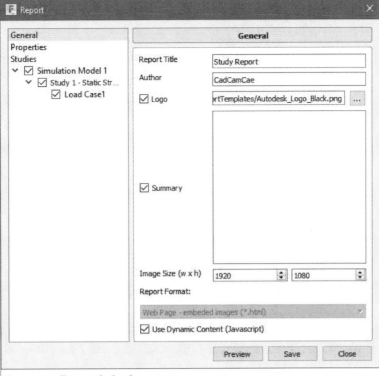

Figure-97. Report dialog box

- Click on the **Save** button to save the report. The **Save Report As** dialog box will be displayed; refer to Figure-98.

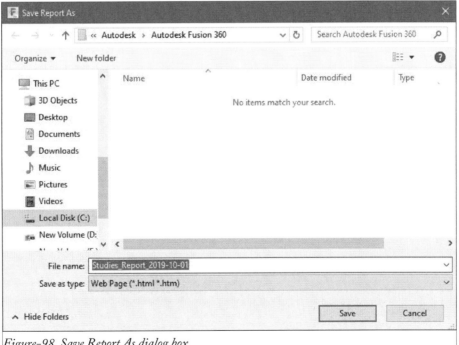

Figure-98. Save Report As dialog box

- Specify the desired name of the report and click on the **Save** button. The file will be saved and displayed in the web browser.

DEFORMATION Drop-down

The options in the **DEFORMATION** drop-down are used to scale up or scale down the deformation caused in the part due to load in the results. By default, the deformation scale is set to **Adjusted**. To change the scale, select the desired option from the **DEFORMATION** drop-down; refer to Figure-99.

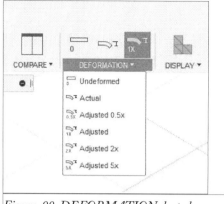

Figure-99. DEFORMATION drop down

DISPLAY Options

The **DISPLAY** options are used to switch between desired display of your model. The display commands are accessible through the **DISPLAY** panel in the **Toolbar**; refer to Figure-100.

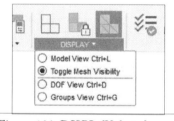

Figure-100. DISPLAY drop down

- The **Toggle Mesh Visibility** tool is used to enable or disable the display of the mesh in results.
- The **Toggle Wireframe Visibility** tool is used to toggle the wireframe display of the model in results.
- Select the **DOF View** radio button to check whether the model is fully fixed, partially fixed or free. The model will be displayed in respective color code; refer to Figure-101.

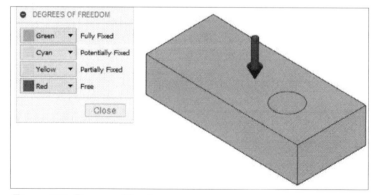

Figure-101. Degrees of freedom

- Select the **Groups View** radio button from the drop-down if you want to display components of different groups in different colors.

In this chapter, we have worked on a Static Stress analysis. We have also gone through the basic process of analysis in Fusion 360. In the next chapter, we will work through the other types of analysis available in Autodesk Fusion 360.

SELF-ASSESSMENT

Q1. An analysis fulfills following conditions:

• All loads are applied slowly and gradually until they reach their full magnitudes. After reaching their full magnitudes, load will remain constant (i.e. load will not vary against time).
• Linearity assumption: The relationship between loads and resulting responses is linear. For example, if you double the magnitude of loads, the response of the model (displacements, strains and stresses) will also double.

Which of the following analyses should be used to check the design?

a. Linear Static Analysis   b. Non-linear Static Analysis
c. Linear Dynamic Analysis   d. Buckling Analysis

Q2. What is the different between steady state thermal analysis and transient thermal analysis?

Q3. Which of the following analysis is used to study the effect of object velocity, initial velocity, acceleration, time dependent loads, and constraints in the design in Autodesk Fusion 360?

a. Shape Optimization   b. Structural Buckling Analysis
c. Event Simulation   d. Modal Analysis

Q4. Which of the following is not an element type for 3D objects in Autodesk Fusion 360 simulation?

a. Linear Tetrahedron   b. Parabolic Tetrahedron
c. Parabolic Tetrahedron with Curved edges   d. Wedge

Q5. Which of the following tool is used to apply pin constraint?

a. Structural Constraint   b. Bolt Connector
c. Rigid Body Connector   d. Joint Origin

Q6. A linearly varying pressure exerted by fluid on surface of a part is called ....

Q7. The **Pre-check** tool is used to warn if constraint is applied on wrong face of model. (T/F)

FOR STUDENT NOTES

Chapter 21

Simulation Studies
in Fusion 360

Topics Covered

The major topics covered in this chapter are:

- *Introduction*
- *Nonlinear Static Stress Analysis*
- *Modal Frequencies Analysis*
- *Buckling Analysis*
- *Thermal Analysis*
- *Event Simulation*
- *Shape Optimization*

INTRODUCTION

In the previous chapter, you have learned about the basics of the analysis. In this chapter, you will learn the procedure of applying different analyses on the part.

NONLINEAR STATIC STRESS ANALYSIS

Non-linear static stress analysis is used to check the effect of load on part when three common forms of nonlinearity like material, geometric, and boundary conditions nonlinearity are applicable in analysis. The procedure to apply non-linear static stress analysis is given next.

- Click on the **New Simulation Study** button from **STUDY** drop-down in the **Toolbar**. The **New Study** dialog box will be displayed.
- Double-click on the **Nonlinear Static Stress** button from the dialog box. The analysis environment will be displayed.
- Click on the **Settings** button from the **MANAGE** drop-down in the **Toolbar**; refer to Figure-1. The **Settings** dialog box will be displayed; refer to Figure-2.

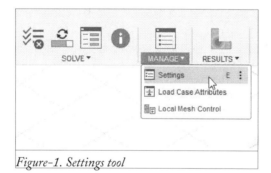

Figure-1. Settings tool

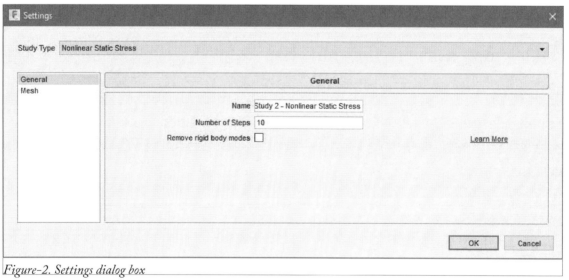

Figure-2. Settings dialog box

- In the **Number of Steps** edit box, specify the desired number of steps in which the total load will be applied.
- Select the **Remove rigid body modes** check box to exclude linear component of force effects. Click on the **OK** button to apply the parameters.
- Apply the elastic material, load, and constraint as required on the model; refer to Figure-3. Note that elastic materials are displayed with a graph sign in **Study Materials** drop-down of **Study Materials** dialog box.

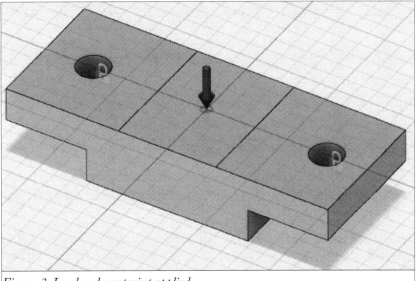

Figure–3. Load and constraint applied

- Click on the **Solve** button from the **SOLVE** drop-down in the **Toolbar**. The **Solve** dialog box will be displayed.
- Click on the **Solve** button from the dialog box. Make sure **Cloud** radio button is selected while solving the analysis. The result will be displayed in the screen; refer to Figure-4.

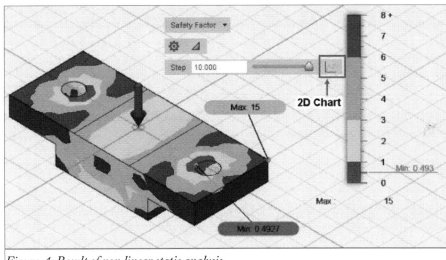

Figure–4. Result of non linear static analysis

- Click on the **2D Chart** button ⌐ in the results to check the transient behavior. The **TRANSIENT RESULTS PLOT** dialog box will be displayed with the results; refer to Figure-5.

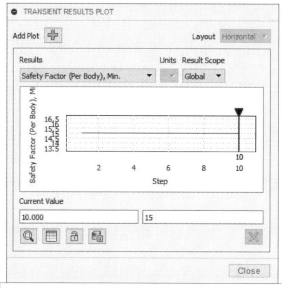

Figure-5. TRANSIENT RESULTS PLOT dialog box

- Move the slider in the graph to check the results of load at different steps. Select the desired result type from the **Results** drop-down in the dialog box.

You can generate the report as discussed earlier.

STRUCTURAL BUCKLING ANALYSIS

Slender models tend to buckle under axial loading. Buckling is defined as the sudden deformation which occurs when the stored membrane (axial) energy is converted into bending energy with no change in the externally applied loads. Mathematically, when buckling occurs, the stiffness becomes singular. The Linearized buckling approach, used here, solves an eigenvalue problem to estimate the critical buckling factors and the associated buckling mode shapes.

A model can buckle in different shapes under different levels of loading. The shape the model takes while buckling is called the buckling mode shape and the loading is called the critical or buckling load. Buckling analysis calculates a number of modes as requested in the Buckling dialog. Designers are usually interested in the lowest mode (mode 1) because it is associated with the lowest critical load. When buckling is the critical design factor, calculating multiple buckling modes helps in locating the weak areas of the model. The mode shapes can help you modify the model or the support system to prevent buckling in a certain mode.

A more vigorous approach to study the behavior of models at and beyond buckling requires the use of nonlinear design analysis codes. In a laymen's language, if you press down on an empty soft drink can with your hand, not much will seem to happen. If you put the can on the floor and gradually increase the force by stepping down on it with your foot, at some point it will suddenly squash. This sudden scrunching is known as "buckling."

Models with thin parts tend to buckle under axial loading. Buckling can be defined as the sudden deformation, which occurs when the stored membrane (axial) energy is converted into bending energy with no change in the externally applied loads. Mathematically, when buckling occurs, the total stiffness matrix becomes singular.

In the normal use of most products, buckling can be catastrophic if it occurs. The failure is not one because of stress but geometric stability. Once the geometry of the part starts to deform, it can no longer support even a fraction of the force initially applied. The worst part about buckling for engineers is that buckling usually occurs at relatively low stress values for what the material can withstand. So they have to make a separate check to see if a product or part thereof is okay with respect to buckling.

Slender structures and structures with slender parts loaded in the axial direction buckle under relatively small axial loads. Such structures may fail in buckling while their stresses are far below critical levels. For such structures, the buckling load becomes a critical design factor. Stocky structures, on the other hand, require large loads to buckle, therefore buckling analysis is usually not required.

Buckling almost always involves compression. In civil engineering, buckling is to be avoided when designing support columns, load bearing walls and sections of bridges which may flex under load. For example an I-beam may be perfectly "safe" when considering only the maximum stress, but fail disastrously if just one local spot of a flange should buckle! In mechanical engineering, designs involving thin parts in flexible structures like airplanes and automobiles are susceptible to buckling. Even though stress can be very low, buckling of local areas can cause the whole structure to collapse by a rapid series of 'propagating buckling'.

Buckling analysis calculates the smallest (critical) loading required for buckling a model. Buckling loads are associated with buckling modes. Designers are usually interested in the lowest mode because it is associated with the lowest critical load. When buckling is the critical design factor, calculating multiple buckling modes helps in locating the weak areas of the model. This may prevent the occurrence of lower buckling modes by simple modifications.

USE OF BUCKLING ANALYSIS

Slender parts and assemblies with slender components that are loaded in the axial direction buckle under relatively small axial loads. Such structures can fail due to buckling while the stresses are far below critical levels. For such structures, the buckling load becomes a critical design factor. Buckling analysis is usually not required for bulky structures as failure occurs earlier due to high stresses. The procedure to use buckling analysis in Fusion 360 is given next.

- Open/create the part on which you want to perform buckling analysis. Click on the **New Simulation Study** button from **STUDY** drop-down in the **Toolbar**. The **New Study** dialog box will be displayed.
- Double-click on the **Structural Buckling** tool from the **New Study** dialog box. The analysis environment will be displayed.
- Apply material, constraint, load, and other parameters as required and solve the study as discussed earlier. The results of buckling will be displayed; refer to Figure-6.

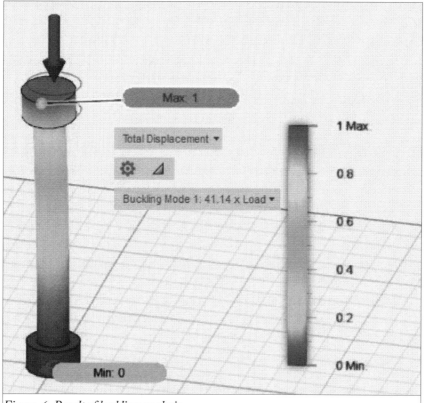

Figure-6. Result of buckling analysis

- Click in the **Buckling Mode** drop-down in the results and select the desired buckling mode to check the effect; refer to Figure-7.

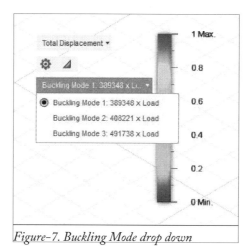

Figure-7. Buckling Mode drop down

MODAL FREQUENCIES ANALYSIS

Every structure has the tendency to vibrate at certain frequencies, called **natural or resonant frequencies**. Each natural frequency is associated with a certain shape, called **mode shape**, that the model tends to assume when vibrating at that frequency. When a structure is properly excited by a dynamic load with a frequency that coincides with one of its natural frequencies, the structure undergoes large displacements and stresses. This phenomenon is known as **Resonance**. For undamped systems, resonance theoretically causes infinite motion. **Damping**, however, puts a limit on the response of the structures due to resonant loads.

A real model has an infinite number of natural frequencies. However, a finite element model has a finite number of natural frequencies that are equal to the number of degrees of freedom considered in the model. Only the first few modes are needed for most purposes.

If your design is subjected to dynamic environments, static studies cannot be used to evaluate the response. Frequency studies can help you design vibration isolation systems by avoiding resonance in specific frequency band. They also form the basis for evaluating the response of linear dynamic systems where the response of a system to a dynamic environment is assumed to be equal to the summation of the contributions of the modes considered in the analysis.

Note that resonance is desirable in the design of some devices. For example, resonance is required in guitars and violins.

The natural frequencies and corresponding mode shapes depend on the geometry, material properties, and support conditions. The computation of natural frequencies and mode shapes is known as modal, frequency, and normal mode analysis.

When building the geometry of a model, you usually create it based on the original (undeformed) shape of the model. Some loads, like the structure's own weight, are always present and can cause considerable effects on the shape of the structure and its modal properties. In many cases, this effect can be ignored because the induced deflections are small.

Loads affect the modal characteristics of a body. In general, compressive loads decrease resonant frequencies and tensile loads increase them. This fact is easily demonstrated by changing the tension on a violin string. The higher the tension, the higher the frequency (tone).

You do not need to define any loads for a frequency study but if you do their effect will be considered. By having evaluated natural frequencies of a structure's vibrations at the design stage, you can optimize the structure with the goal of meeting the frequency vibro-stability condition. To increase natural frequencies, you would need to add rigidity to the structure and (or) reduce its weight. For example, in the case of a slender object, the rigidity can be increased by reducing the length and increasing the thickness of the object. To reduce a part's natural frequency, you should, on the contrary, increase the weight or reduce the object's rigidity.

Note that the software also considers thermal and fluid pressure effects for frequency studies.

The procedure to perform the frequency analysis is given next.

- Open/create the part on which you want to perform modal analysis. Click on the **New Simulation Study** button from **STUDY** drop-down in the **Toolbar**. The **New Study** dialog box will be displayed.
- Double-click on the **Structural Buckling** tool from the **New Study** dialog box. The analysis environment will be displayed.

- Click **Settings** tool from the **MANAGE** drop-down in the **Toolbar**. Select **Modal Frequencies** option from **Study Type** drop-down in the dialog box. The **Settings** dialog box for **Modal Frequencies** option will be displayed; refer to Figure-8.

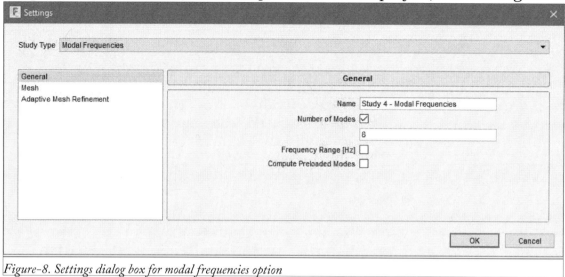

Figure-8. Settings dialog box for modal frequencies option

- Select the **Number of Modes** check box and specify the total number of frequencies that you want to test for resonance.
- Select the **Frequency Range (Hz)** check box to specify the minimum & maximum frequencies within which the natural frequencies are to be found.
- Select the **Compute Preloaded Modes** check box if you include the effect of structural loads in modal frequency analysis.
- Select the desired calculation method from the **Extraction Method** drop-down in the dialog box. **LANCZOS** is used when a large number of modes are being solved (greater than 20). **SUBSPACE** has high computing time when solving for a large number of modes so it is better used for low number of modes.
- After specifying all the parameters, click on the **OK** button.
- Apply material, constraint, load, and other parameters as required and solve the study as discussed earlier. Note that you can perform modal analysis without applying any load but if you apply a load then its effects will also be counted in the results if **Compute Preloaded Modes** check box is selected in the **Settings** dialog box. The results of buckling will be displayed; refer to Figure-9.

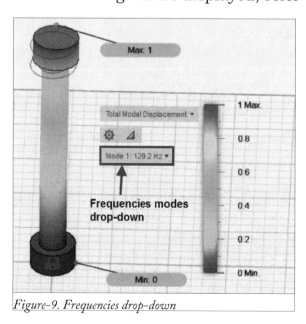

Figure-9. Frequencies drop-down

- Click on the **Mode** drop-down in **Results** area to check different natural frequencies of the model.

THERMAL ANALYSIS

Thermal analysis is a method to check the distribution of heat over a body due to applied thermal loads. Note that thermal energy is dynamic in nature and is always flowing through various mediums. There are three mechanisms by which the thermal energy flows:

- Conduction
- Convection
- Radiation

In all three mechanisms, heat energy flows from the medium with higher temperature to the medium with lower temperature. Heat transfer by conduction and convection requires the presence of an intervening medium while heat transfer by radiation does not.

The output from a thermal analysis can be given by:
1. Temperature distribution.
2. Amount of heat loss or gain.
3. Thermal gradients.
4. Thermal fluxes.

This analysis is used in many engineering industries such as automobile, piping, electronic, power generation, and so on.

Important terms related to Thermal Analysis

Before conducting thermal analysis, you should be familiar with the basic concepts and terminologies of thermal analysis. Following are some of the important terms used in thermal analysis:

Heat Transfer Modes

Whenever there is a difference in temperature between two bodies, the heat is transferred from one body to another. Basically, heat is transferred in three ways: Conduction, Convection, and Radiation.

Conduction

In conduction, the heat is transferred by interactions of atoms or molecules of the material. For example, if you heat up a metal rod at one end, the heat will be transferred to the other end by the atoms or molecules of the metal rod.

Convection

In convection, the heat is transferred by the flowing fluid. The fluid can be gas or liquid. Heating up water using an electric water heater is a good example of heat convection. In this case, water takes heat from the heater.

Radiation

In radiation, the heat is transferred in space without any matter. Radiation is the only heat transfer method that takes place in space. Heat coming from the Sun is a good example of radiation. The heat from the Sun is transferred to the earth through radiation.

Thermal Gradient

The thermal gradient is the rate of increase in temperature per unit depth in a material.

Thermal Flux

The Thermal flux is defined as the rate of heat transfer per unit cross-sectional area. It is denoted by q.

Bulk Temperature

It is the temperature of a fluid flowing outside the material. It is denoted by Tb. The Bulk temperature is used in convective heat transfer.

Film Coefficient

It is a measure of the heat transfer through an air film.

Emissivity

The Emissivity of a material is the ratio of energy radiated by the material to the energy radiated by a black body at the same temperature. Emissivity is the measure of a material's ability to absorb and radiate heat. It is denoted by e. Emissivity is a numerical value without any unit. For a perfect black body, e = 1. For any other material, e < 1.

Stefan–Boltzmann Constant

The energy radiated by a black body per unit area per unit time divided by the fourth power of the body's temperature is known as the Stefan-Boltzmann constant. It is denoted by s.

Thermal Conductivity

The thermal conductivity is the property of a material that indicates its ability to conduct heat. It is denoted by K.

Specific Heat

The specific heat is the amount of heat required per unit mass to raise the temperature of the body by one degree Celsius. It is denoted by C.

PERFORMING THERMAL ANALYSIS

- Click on the **New Simulation Study** button from **STUDY** drop-down in the **Toolbar**. The **New Study** dialog box will be displayed.
- Double-click on the **Thermal** button from the dialog box. The thermal analysis environment will be displayed.
- Apply the desired material to the mode as discussed earlier.

- Click on the **Thermal Loads** tool from the **LOADS** panel in the **Toolbar**; refer to Figure-10. The **THERMAL LOADS** dialog box will be displayed; refer to Figure-11.

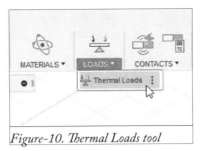

Figure-10. Thermal Loads tool

Figure-11. THERMAL LOADS dialog box

- Select the desired thermal load type from the **Type** drop-down in the **Load** section of the dialog box. Select the **Applied Temperature** option from the drop-down and enter the desired temperature if you want to apply a fix temperature to the selected geometry. Select the **Heat Source** option if you want to specify the amount of heat energy to be applied on selected geometry. Select the **Radiation** option if heat is transferred through radiation to the selected face. Select the **Convection** option if heat is transferred through convection. Select the **Internal Heat** option from the drop-down if heat is generated inside the model.
- Select the face/edge/vertex on which you want to apply thermal load. If you want to select a body then click on the **Bodies** button from the **Object Type** section of the dialog box and then select the body.
- Specify the desired values of thermal load in edit boxes as per the option selected in the **Type** drop-down.
- Click on the **OK** button from dialog box to apply the settings.
- Specify the contacts as discussed earlier for heat flow between different components of the assembly.
- Click on the **Settings** button from the **MANAGE** drop-down in the **Toolbar**. The **Settings** dialog box will be displayed. Specify the desired value of atmospheric temperature in the **Global Initial Temperature** edit box. Set the other parameters as discussed earlier. Click on the **OK** button from the dialog box to apply settings.
- After specifying all the parameters, click on the **Solve** button. The **Solve** dialog box will be displayed. Click on the **Solve Study** button in the dialog box. The results of analysis will be displayed; refer to Figure-12.

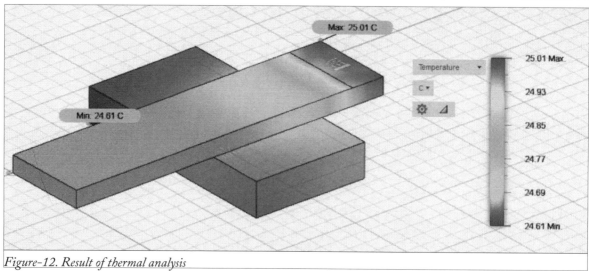

Figure-12. Result of thermal analysis

THERMAL STRESS ANALYSIS

The thermal stress analysis is used to check the effect of thermal and structural loads on the model. The procedure to perform the analysis same as discussed earlier for thermal and stress analyses.

EVENT SIMULATION

Event Simulation is used to study the effect of motion/load on different parts/bodies in model. This analysis is similar to dynamic non-linear analysis you may have studied in engineering. Note that event simulation is in the preview mode while we are writing this book. It may get new features in the later versions. In this example, we will simulate the collision of a ball on the plate. The procedure to perform event simulation is given next.

- Click on the **New Simulation Study** button from **STUDY** drop-down in the **Toolbar**. The **New Study** dialog box will be displayed. Double-click on the **Event Simulation** button from the dialog box. The environment to solve event simulation will be displayed.
- Specify the material, constraints, and load as applied earlier.
- Click on the **Prescribed Translation** tool from **CONSTRAINTS** drop-down in the **Toolbar**; refer to Figure-13 and specify the displacement, velocity, or acceleration of the selected body as required; refer to Figure-14.

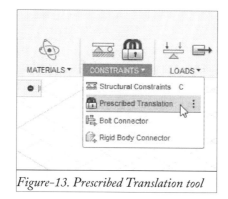

Figure-13. Prescribed Translation tool

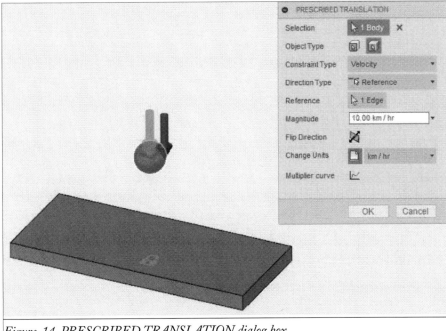

Figure-14. PRESCRIBED TRANSLATION dialog box

- Click on the **Solve** tool from **SOLVE** drop-down in the **Toolbar** and then click on the **Solve** button from the dialog box displayed. The results of analysis will be displayed. Set the slider to desired step to check the analysis result at intermediate steps.

SHAPE OPTIMIZATION

The Shape optimization study is used to reduce the mass of part while satisfying all the design requirements of the part. The procedure to use shape optimization is given next.

- Create/open the model on which you want to perform shape optimization study. Click on the **New Simulation Study** tool from **STUDY** drop-down in the **Toolbar**. The **New Study** dialog box will be displayed.
- Double-click on the **Shape Optimization** button from the dialog box. The environment to perform shape optimization will be displayed.
- Set the material, constraint, load, and contacts as required.

Preserve Region

- Click on the **Preserve Region** tool from the **SHAPE OPTIMIZATION** drop-down in the **Toolbar**; refer to Figure-15. The **PRESERVE REGION** dialog box will be displayed; refer to Figure-16.

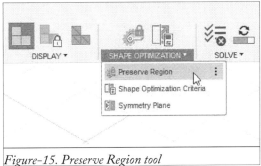

Figure-15. Preserve Region tool

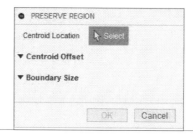

Figure-16. PRESERVE REGION dialog box

- Select the face that you want to be preserved after shape optimization. The options for preserving region based on selected faces will be displayed in the dialog box.
- Set the desired options like if you have select a cylindrical face then specify the radius up to which you want to preserve the region; refer to Figure-17.
- Click on the **OK** button from the dialog box to apply the parameters.

Figure-17. PRESERVE REGION dialog box with cylindrical face selected

Setting Shape Optimization criteria

- Click on the **Shape Optimization Criteria** tool from the **SHAPE OPTIMIZATION** drop-down in the **Toolbar**; refer to Figure-18. The **SHAPE OPTIMIZATION CRITERIA** dialog box will be displayed; refer to Figure-19.

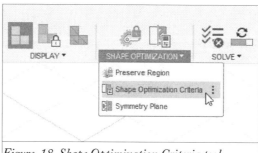

Figure-18. Shape Optimization Criteria tool

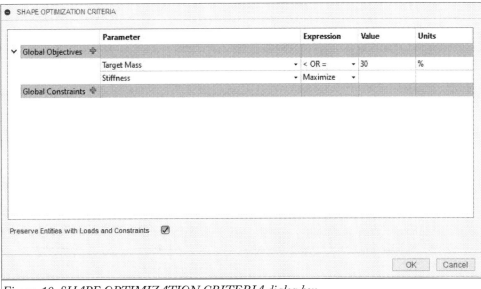

Figure-19. SHAPE OPTIMIZATION CRITERIA dialog box

- Set the desired conditions in the dialog box like, Target Mass less than or equal to 40%.
- Click on the **OK** button to apply the settings.
- Create desired load and constraint conditions for the model.
- Click on the **Solve** tool from **SOLVE** drop-down in the **Toolbar**. The **Solve** dialog box will be displayed.
- Click on the **Solve** button. The result will be displayed; refer to Figure-20.

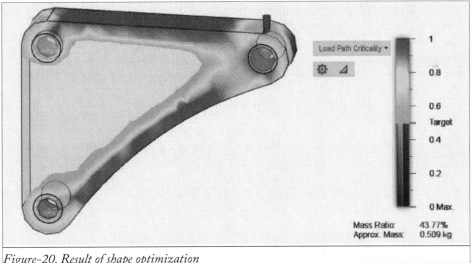

Figure-20. Result of shape optimization

Generating Mesh Body of Result

- Click on the **Promote** tool from **RESULT TOOLS** drop-down in **Toolbar**; refer to Figure-21. The **PROMOTE** dialog box will be displayed; refer to Figure-22.

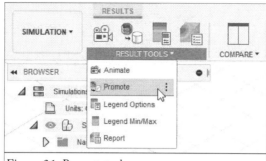

Figure-21. Promote tool

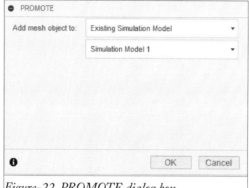

Figure-22. PROMOTE dialog box

- Select the **Model Workspace** option from the **Add mesh object to** drop-down to generate mesh model as mesh object in model. Select the **Existing Simulation Model** option from the drop-down to add the mesh object in selected simulation model. Select the **Clone Current Simulation Model** option to create a copy of simulation model with mesh body. Select the **Clone Studies** check box while making copy to also copy simulation study parameters.
- Click on the **OK** button from the dialog box. The mesh body will be displayed which can be used to modify the part; refer to Figure-23.

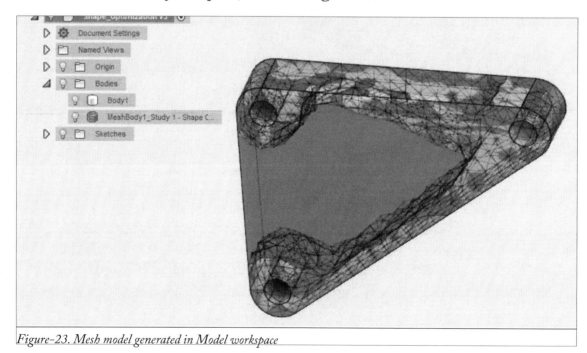

Figure-23. Mesh model generated in Model workspace

SELF ASSESSMENT

Q1. Which of the following is not a parameter of non linearity for non-linear static analysis?

a. Material   b. Geometry
c. Load   d. Time

Q2. Using transient results plot, you can check the effect of load with respect to time. (T/F)

Q3. When the stored membrane (axial) energy is converted into bending energy with no change in the externally applied loads then you can perform structural buckling analysis. (T/F)

Q4. The buckling mode displays shape of model under buckling load. (T/F)

Q5. When a structure is properly excited by a dynamic load with a frequency that coincides with one of its natural frequencies, the structure undergoes large displacements and stresses. (T/F)

Q6. The phenomena by which a structure goes large deformation when excited at natural frequency is called ....

Q7. Which of the following is a parameter does not apply for structural analysis?

a. Film Coefficient   b. Pressure
c. Density   d. Force

PRACTICE 1

Consider a rectangular plate with cutout. The dimensions and the boundary conditions of the plate are shown in Figure-24. It is fixed on one end and loaded on the other end. Under the given loading and constraints, plot the deformed shape. Also, determine the principal stresses and the von Mises stresses in the bracket. Thickness of the plate is 0.125 inch and material is **AISI 1020**.

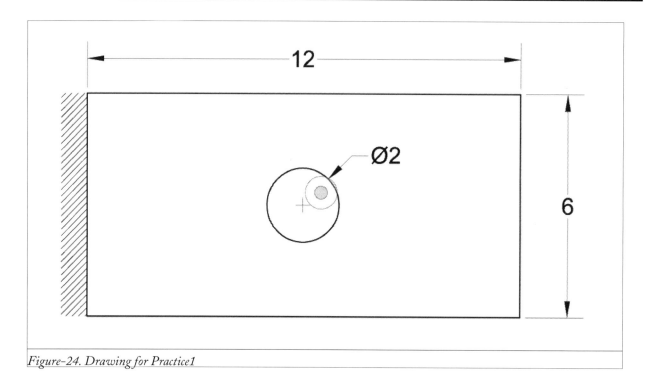

Figure-24. Drawing for Practice1

PRACTICE 2

Open the model for this exercise from the resource kit and perform the static analysis using the conditions given in Figure-25. Find out the **Factor of Safety** for the model.

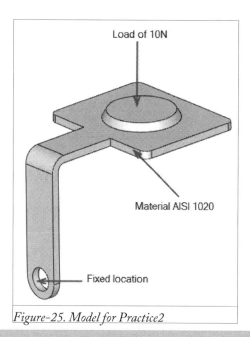

Figure-25. Model for Practice2

PRACTICE 3

Check out what happens to the fork under the conditions specified in Figure-26. Note that the material of fork is **Alloy Steel** and it is in the hands of a nasty kid. (You know kids!! they don't exert linear forces.)

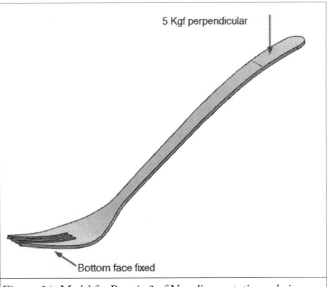

Figure-26. Model for Practice3 of Non-linear static analysis

PROBLEM 1

A metal sphere of diameter d = 35mm is initially at temperature Ti = 700 K. At t=0, the sphere is placed in a fluid environment that has properties of T∞ = 300 K and h = 50 W/m2-K. The properties of the steel are k = 35 W/m-K, ρ = 7500 kg/m3, and c = 550 J/kg-K. Find the surface temperature of the sphere after 500 seconds.

PROBLEM 2

A flanged pipe assembly; refer to Figure-27, made of plain carbon steel is subjected to both convective and conductive boundary conditions. Fluid inside the pipe is at a temperature of 130°C and has a convection coefficient of hi = 160 W/m²-K. Air on the outside of the pipe is at 20°C and has a convection coefficient of ho = 70 W/m²-K. The right and left ends of the pipe are at temperatures of 450°C and 80°C, respectively. There is a thermal resistance between the two flanges of 0.002 K-m²/W. Use thermal analysis to analyze the pipe under both steady state and transient conditions.

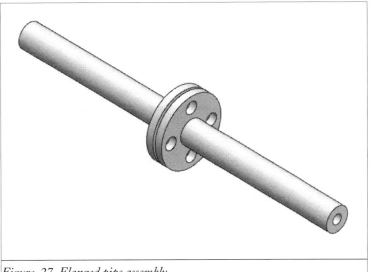

Figure-27. Flanged pipe assembly

FOR STUDENT NOTES

FOR STUDENT NOTES

Chapter 22

Sheetmetal Design

Topics Covered

The major topics covered in this chapter are:

- *Introduction*
- *Sheetmetal Rules*
- *Flange*
- *Unfold*
- *Flat Pattern*
- *Practical*
- *Practice*

INTRODUCTION

Sheet metal is used when you need a component of thickness in the range of 0.16 mm to 12.70 mm and do not require conventional cutting machines. The components that can be created by Punch-press and bending machines are designed in Sheet Metal environment. In Autodesk Fusion, the tools to design sheet metal components are available in **SHEET METAL** tab of **DESIGN** workspace; refer to Figure-1. Various tools and parameters of **SHEET METAL** tab are discussed next.

Figure-1. SHEET METAL toolbar in DESIGN Workspace

SHEET METAL RULES

The Sheet Metal rules are used to specify various parameters related to sheet metal design like, bend radius, corner conditions, K Factor, thickness of sheet and so on. The procedure to set sheet metal rules in Autodesk Fusion are discussed next.

*   Click on the **Sheet Metal Rules** tool from the **MODIFY** drop-down in **Toolbar**; refer to Figure-2. The **SHEET METAL RULES** dialog box will be displayed; refer to Figure-3.

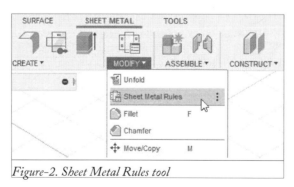

Figure-2. Sheet Metal Rules tool

Figure-3. SHEET METAL RULES dialog box

- Expand the desired category from the dialog box to check the parameters; refer to Figure-4.

Figure-4. Properties of steel in SHEET METAL RULES dialog box

- Hover the cursor on the name of property. Two buttons will be displayed next to it as shown in Figure-4.

Modifying the rules

- Click on the **Edit Rule** button for desired sheet metal rule from **SHEET METAL RULES** dialog box; refer to Figure-5, if you want to modify the property. The **Edit Rule** dialog box will be displayed; refer to Figure-6.

Figure-5. Edit Rule button

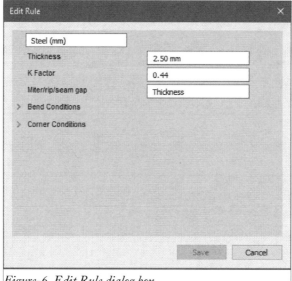
Figure-6. Edit Rule dialog box

- Specify the desired name for the rule in the **Rule Name** edit box.
- Set the other parameters like sheet thickness, K factor, seam gap etc. in their respective edit boxes.
- Click on the **Save** button after setting parameters to save the rule.

Creating New Sheet Metal Rule

- Click on the **New Rule** button from **SHEET METAL RULES** dialog box if you want to create a new sheet metal rule; refer to Figure-7. The **New Rule** dialog box will be displayed; refer to Figure-8.

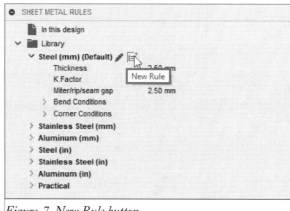
Figure-7. New Rule button

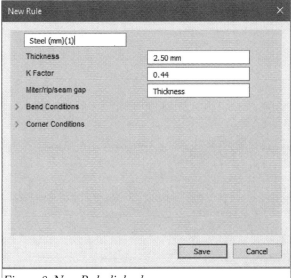

Figure-8. New Rule dialog box

- Set the desired parameters as discussed earlier and click on the **Save** button to save new sheet metal rule.

CREATING FLANGES

Flanges are the building blocks of sheet metal parts. Flanges act as base and walls of sheet metal parts. The procedure to create flange is given next.

- Click on the **Flange** tool from the **CREATE** drop-down in the **Toolbar**; refer to Figure-9. The **FLANGE** dialog box will be displayed; refer to Figure-10. You will be asked to select a sketch or edge to create flange.

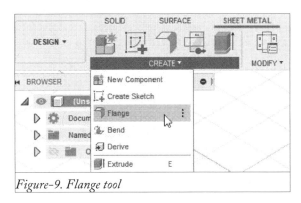

Figure-9. Flange tool

Figure-10. FLANGE dialog box

- Select the desired sketch or edge. Preview of the flange will be displayed; refer to Figure-11 and Figure-12.

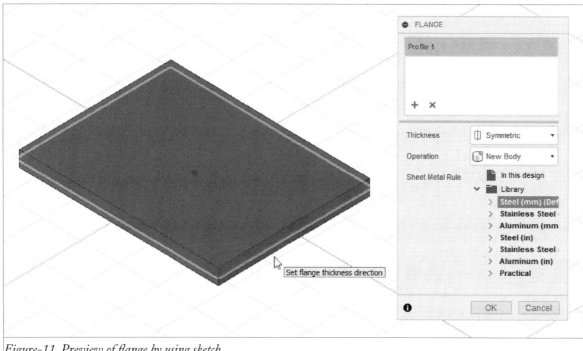

Figure-11. Preview of flange by using sketch

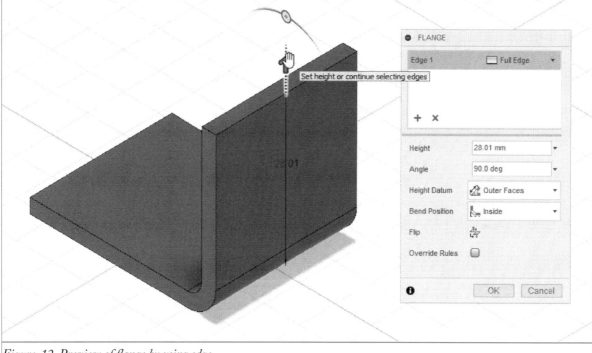

Figure-12. Preview of flange by using edge

- If you have used a closed sketch to create flange then set the direction thickness direction in the **Thickness** drop-down.
- If you have selected an edge to create flange then the options of the dialog box will be displayed as shown in Figure-12. Set the desired **Height** and **Angle** values in the respective edit boxes in the dialog box.
- Select the desired option from the **Height Datum** drop-down. Select the **Inner Faces** option if you want to set the height of flange from the inner face. Select the **Outer Faces** option if you want to set the height of flange from the outer face.

Select the **Tangent To Bend** option if you want to set the height from the edge of bend created by flange.

- Select the **Inside** option from the **Bend Position** drop-down if you want the bend to be created starting from the inner edge of the flange. Select the **Outside** option if you want the bend to be created from outer edge of the flange. Select the **Adjacent** option if you want to create bend ahead of the outer edge of bend equal to the thickness of sheet. Select the **Tangent** option if you want the bend to start tangent to the face of the selected flange.
- To flip the direction of flange, click on the **Flip** button.
- By default the bend rules are applied on the flange to be created but if you want to change any of the rule specific to the flange then select the **Override Rules** check box. The options below it will be displayed; refer to Figure-13.

Figure-13. Override Rules options in FLANGE dialog box

- Select the desired check box and change the parameter as required.
- Click on the **OK** button to create the flange.

Creating Contour Flange

Using the **Flange** tool, you can also create contour flanges. The procedure is given next.

- Create a sketch of desired shape and size for contour flange; refer to Figure-14.

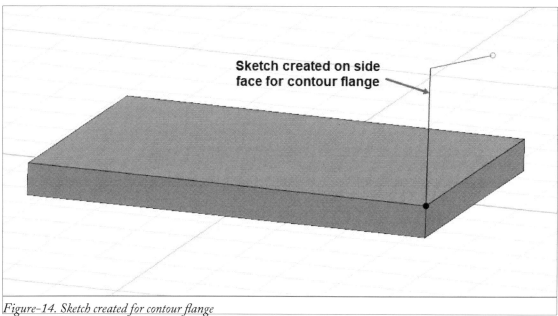

Figure-14. Sketch created for contour flange

- Click on the **Flange** tool from the **CREATE** drop-down in the **Toolbar** and select the newly created sketch for creating contour flange; refer to Figure-15.

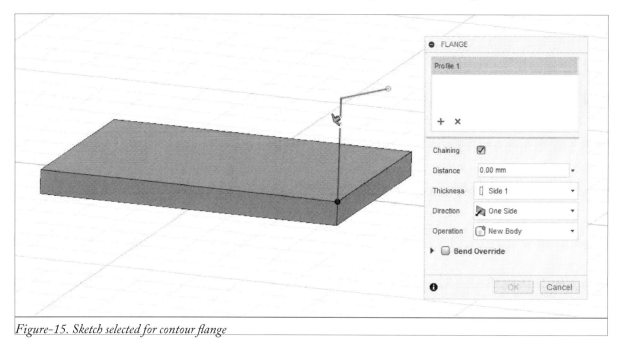

Figure-15. Sketch selected for contour flange

- Now, select all the edges one by one by clicking **Add New Selection** button from **FLANGE** dialog box to define shape of flange. Preview of the contour flange will be displayed; refer to Figure-16.

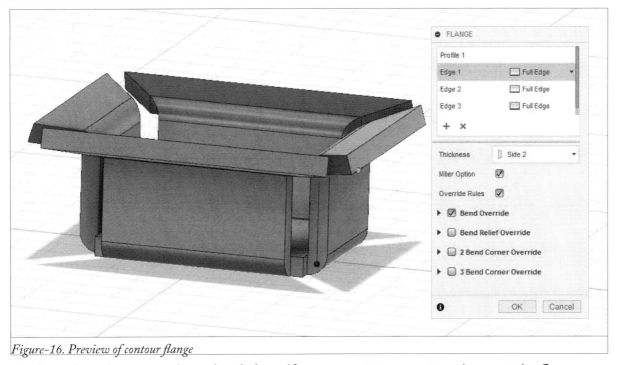

Figure-16. Preview of contour flange

- Select the **Miter Option** check box if you want to create miter cut in flanges.
- Click on the **OK** button from the dialog box to create the flanges.

UNFOLDING SHEETMETAL PART

The **Unfold** tool is used to unbend all the selected bends of the part. The procedure to unfold is given next.

- Click on the **Unfold** tool from **MODIFY** drop-down in the **Toolbar**; refer to Figure-17. The **UNFOLD** dialog box will be displayed; refer to Figure-18.

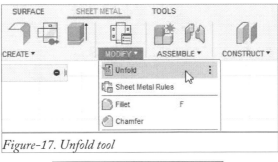

Figure-17. Unfold tool

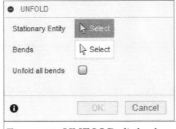

Figure-18. UNFOLD dialog box

- Select the desired face to be made stationary. All the bends will be highlighted; refer to Figure-19.

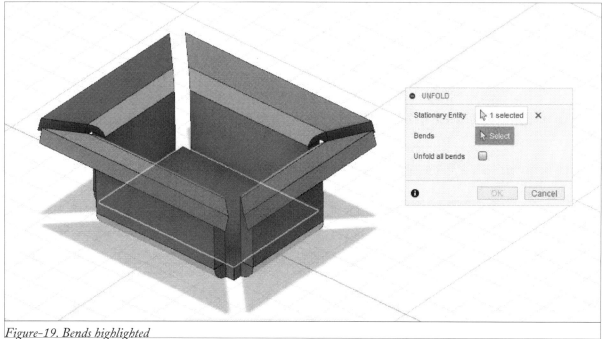

Figure-19. Bends highlighted

- Select the bends that you want to be unfolded. Preview of unfolding will be displayed; refer to Figure-20.

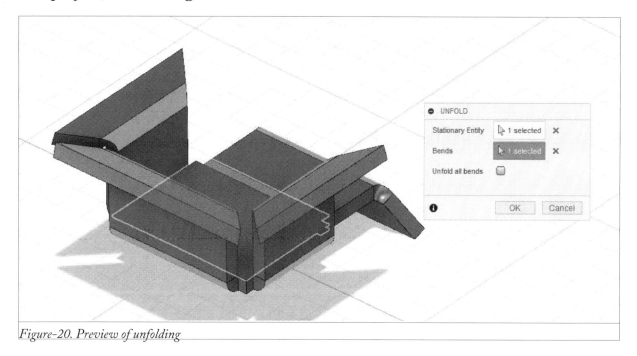

Figure-20. Preview of unfolding

- If you want to unfold all the bends then select the **Unfold all bends** check box.
- Click on the **OK** button to create the unfold feature.

Refolding Faces

The **Refold** tool is used to refold the unfolded faces. To do so, click on the **Refold** tool from **REFOLD FACES** drop-down in the **Toolbar**; refer to Figure-21. The **Refold** tool will become active when the faces are being unfolded.

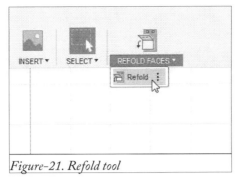
Figure-21. Refold tool

Some people may ask why to unfold and refold the faces of sheet metal parts. The answer is editing between unfolding and refolding steps. After unfolding, you can create holes or other modifications at the bend locations and then you can refold them.

CONVERT TO SHEET METAL

The **Convert to Sheet Metal** tool is used to convert a thin part into sheet metal part. The procedure to use this tool is given next.

- Click on the **Convert to Sheet Metal** tool from the **CREATE** panel in the **SHEET METAL** tab of **Toolbar**; refer to Figure-22. The **CONVERT TO SHEET METAL** dialog box will be displayed; refer to Figure-23 and you will be asked to select a thin part created as solid.

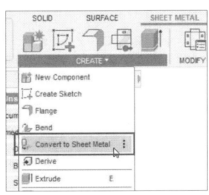
Figure-22. Convert to Sheet Metal tool

Figure-23. CONVERT TO SHEET METAL dialog box

- Click on the face of part to be converted into sheet metal. The updated **CONVERT TO SHEETMETAL** dialog box will be displayed; refer to Figure-24.

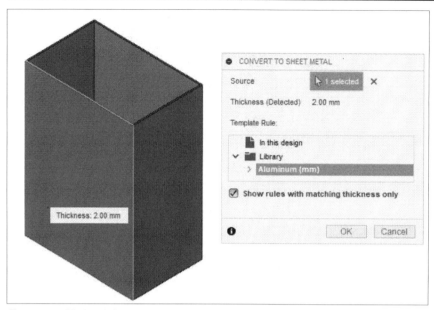

Figure-24. Updated CONVERT TO SHEET METAL dialog box

- By default the **Show rules with matching thickness only** check box is selected and hence only the rules that match with the model thickness are displayed. Clear this check box to select other rules.
- Click on the **OK** button from the dialog box. The part will be converted to a sheet metal part.

FLAT PATTERN

The **Flat Pattern** tool is used to create flat pattern using the sheet metal part so that the part can be cut from the sheet and bent to form desired product. The procedure to use this tool is given next.

- Click on the **Create Flat Pattern** tool from **CREATE** drop-down in the **Toolbar**; refer to Figure-25. The **CREATE FLAT PATTERN** dialog box will be displayed; refer to Figure-26.

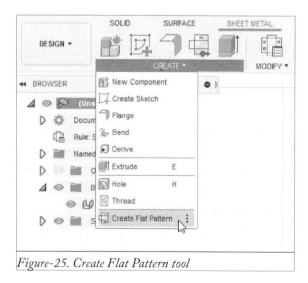

Figure-25. Create Flat Pattern tool

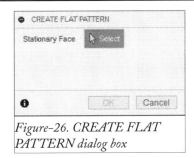

Figure-26. CREATE FLAT PATTERN dialog box

- Select the face that you want to be stationary and click on the **OK** button. The flat pattern will be created; refer to Figure-27.

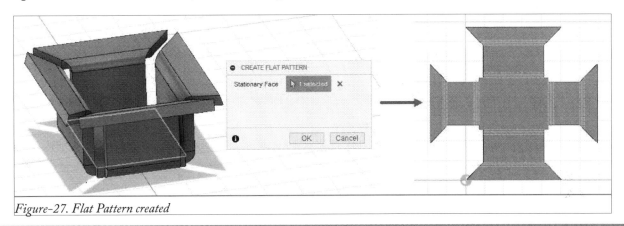

Figure-27. Flat Pattern created

EXPORTING DXF

The **Export Flat Pattern as DXF** tool is used to export the created flat pattern. The procedure is given next.

- Click on the **Export Flat Pattern as DXF** tool from **EXPORT** panel in the **Toolbar** after creating the flat pattern; refer to Figure-28. The **EXPORT FLAT PATTERN AS DXF** dialog box will be displayed; refer to Figure-29.

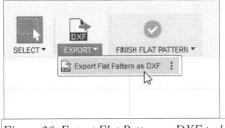

Figure-28. Export Flat Pattern as DXF tool

Figure-29. EXPORT FLAT PATTERN AS DXF dialog box

- Select the **Convert Splines to Polylines** check box if you want to convert all splines in the flat pattern to polylines. Specify the **Tolerance** value in the edit box as desired. This option is useful when your laser cutting machine do not support splines.
- Click on the **OK** button from the dialog box. The **Save As DXF** dialog box will be displayed; refer to Figure-30.

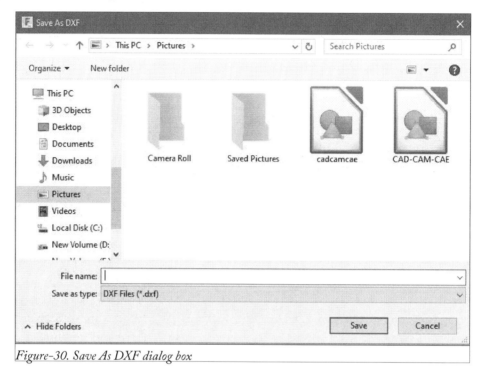

Figure-30. Save As DXF dialog box

- Specify the desired name and save the file at desired location.

PRACTICAL

Create the sheet metal model as shown in Figure-31. Dimensions are given in Figure-32. Also create flat pattern and annotate the drawing.

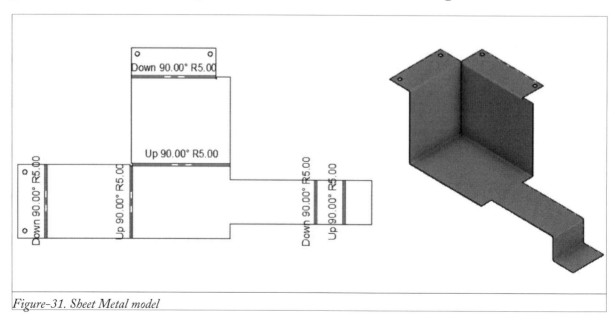

Figure-31. Sheet Metal model

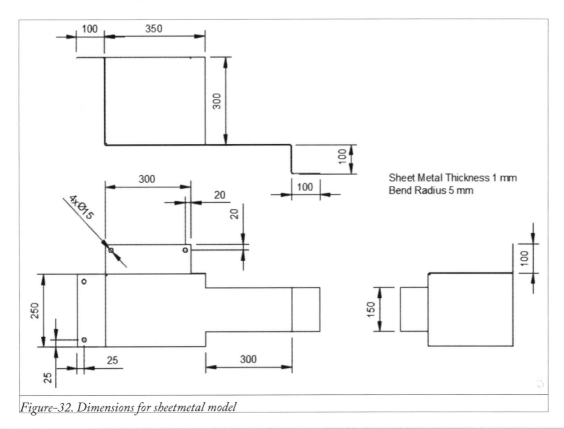

Figure-32. Dimensions for sheetmetal model

Starting Sheet Metal and Creating Base Sheet

- Start Autodesk Fusion and select the **SHEET METAL** tab in **DESIGN** workspace. The tools related to Sheet Metal design will become active.
- Click on the **Create Sketch** tool from **CREATE** drop-down in the **Toolbar** and create a sketch on the **XY** plane as shown in Figure-33.

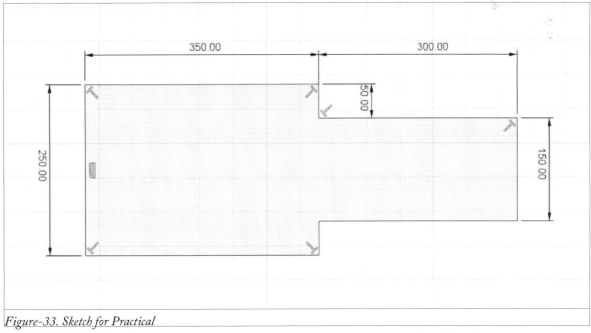

Figure-33. Sketch for Practical

- Click on the **FINISH SKETCH** tool from the **Toolbar** to exit the sketching environment.

Setting Sheet Metal Rules

- Click on the **Sheet Metal Rules** option from **MODIFY** drop-down in the **Toolbar**. The **SHEET METAL RULES** dialog box will be displayed.
- Select any of the sheet metal rule and click on the **New Rule** button. The **New Rule** dialog box will be displayed.
- Specify the name of rule as **Practical** in the **Rule Name** edit box. Click in the **Thickness** edit box and specify the value as **1 mm**.
- Expand the **Bend Conditions** node and specify the **Bend radius** as **5 mm**.
- Click on the **Save** button and **Close** the dialog box.

Creating Flanges

- Click on the **Flange** tool from **CREATE** drop-down in the **Toolbar** and select the newly created sketch.
- Select the **Practical** option from the **Sheet Metal Rule** area of the dialog box; refer to Figure-34 and click on the **OK** button.

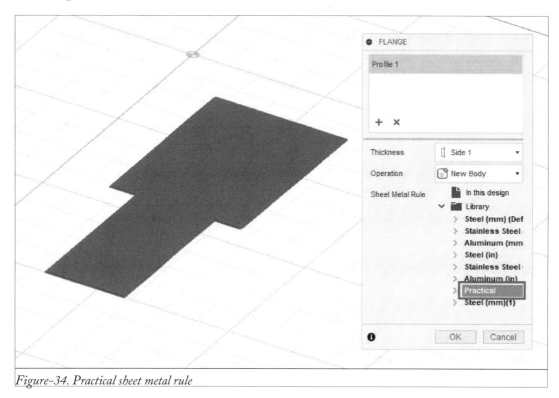

Figure-34. Practical sheet metal rule

- Click on the **Flange** tool from **CREATE** drop-down in the **Toolbar**. Select the edges as shown in Figure-35 and specify the height as **300**.

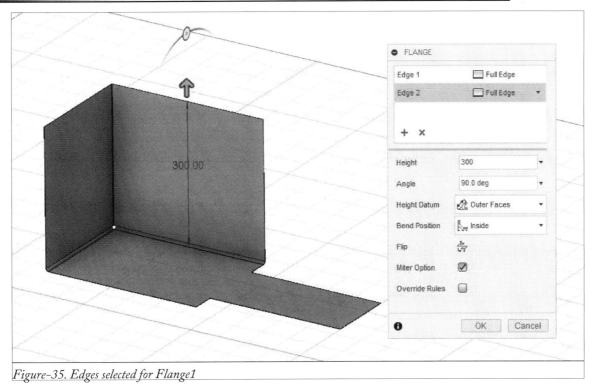

Figure-35. Edges selected for Flange1

- Click on the **OK** button to create vertical flanges.
- Click again on the **Flange** tool and select the outer edges of the newly created vertical flanges.
- Set the height of flanges as **100** mm and clear the **Miter Option** check box. Preview of the flanges will be displayed; refer to Figure-36.

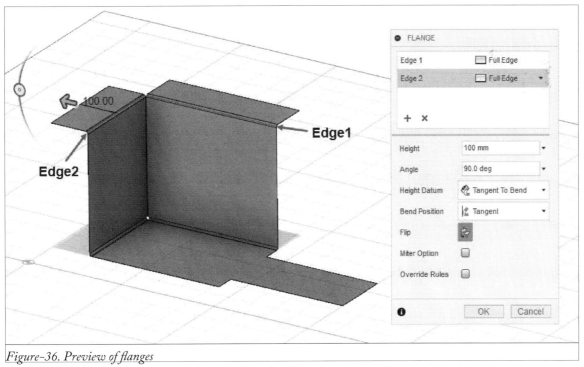

Figure-36. Preview of flanges

- Click on the **Full Edge** option of Edge 1 in the selection box and select the **Two Offset** option. Now, you will be able to edit the length of flange.
- Move the drag handle to **50** mm backward; refer to Figure-37.

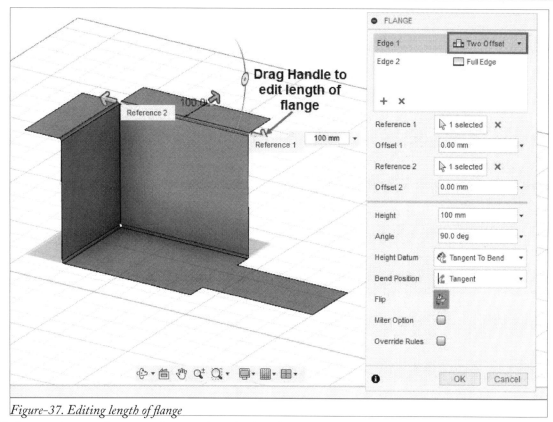

Figure-37. Editing length of flange

- Click on the **OK** button from the dialog box. Similarly, you create other flanges to form a part as shown in Figure-38.

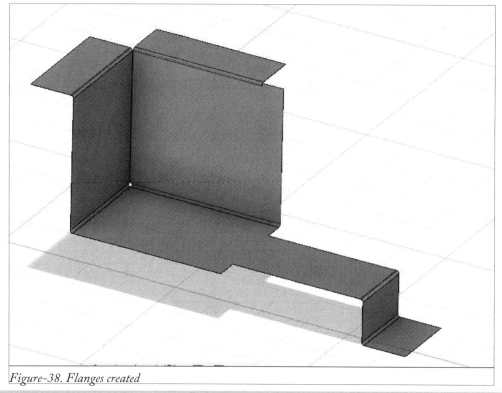

Figure-38. Flanges created

Creating Holes

- Click on the **Create Sketch** tool from **CREATE** drop-down in the **Toolbar**. You will be asked to select a face/plane.

- Select the face as shown in Figure-39. Create four points as shown in Figure-40 and exit the sketching environment.

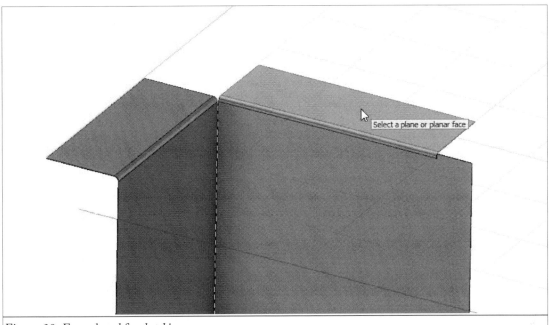

Figure-39. Face selected for sketching

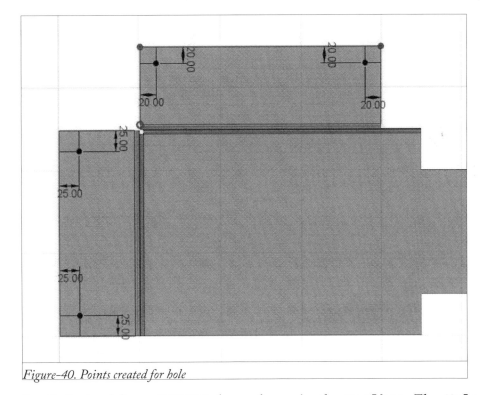

Figure-40. Points created for hole

- Click on the **Hole** tool from **CREATE** drop-down in the **Toolbar**. The **Hole** dialog box will be displayed.
- Select the **From Sketch (Multiple Holes)** button from **Placement** section in the dialog box. You will be asked to select the sketch points.
- Select all the sketch points created earlier and specify depth as 5 mm and diameter as 15 mm in the respective edit boxes of the dialog box. Preview of the holes will be displayed; refer to Figure-41.

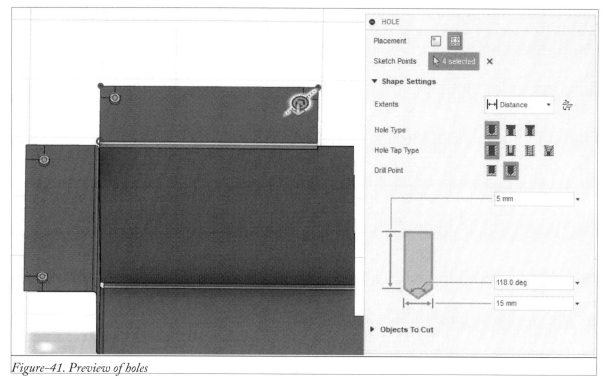

Figure-41. Preview of holes

- Click on the **OK** button from the dialog box to create the holes. The final part will be created.

Click on the **Create Flat Pattern** tool from **CREATE** drop-down in the **Toolbar**. You will be asked to select a stationary face. Select the base flange and click on the **OK** button. The flat pattern will be displayed; refer to Figure-42.

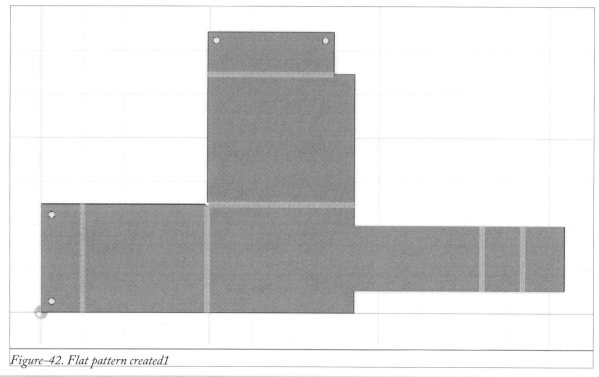

Figure-42. Flat pattern created1

Creating Drawing for Flat Pattern

- Click on the **From Design** tool from **DRAWING** cascading menu in the **Change Workspace** drop-down. The **Save** dialog box will be displayed.

- Specify desired name and location and then click on the **Save** button. The **CREATE DRAWING** dialog box will be displayed.
- Set the desired parameters and click on the **OK** button. You will be asked to place the drawing view.
- Set the desired parameters in the **DRAWING VIEW** dialog box and place the **TOP** view of flat pattern; refer to Figure-43.

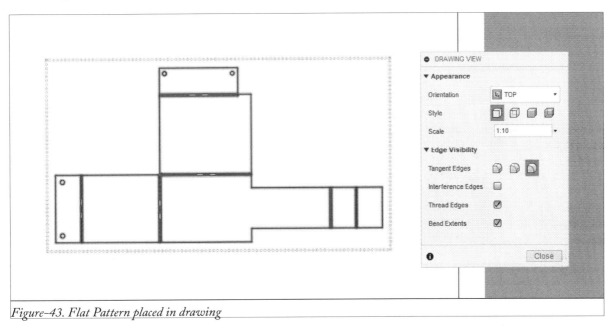

Figure-43. Flat Pattern placed in drawing

Annotating Flat Pattern in Drawing

- Click on the **Leader** tool from **TEXT** drop-down in the **Toolbar**. You will be asked to select the edges to be annotated.
- One by one, select the center lines of all the bends in the flat pattern. The annotations will be displayed as shown in Figure-44. You can also use bend identifiers with table to annotate bends in a sheet metal part.

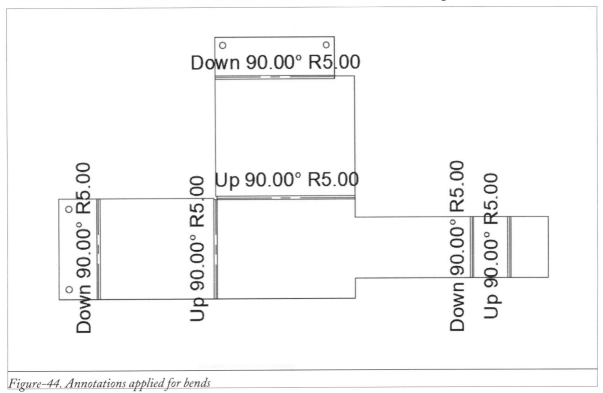

Figure-44. Annotations applied for bends

- Apply the other dimensions and create the other views as discussed earlier in the book.

PRACTICE

Create the sheet metal model as shown in Figure-45. Dimensions are given in Figure-46.

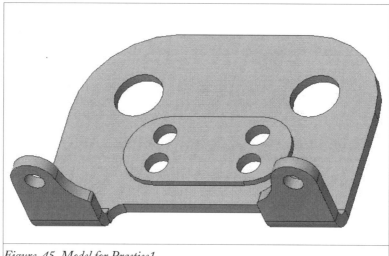

Figure-45. Model for Practice1

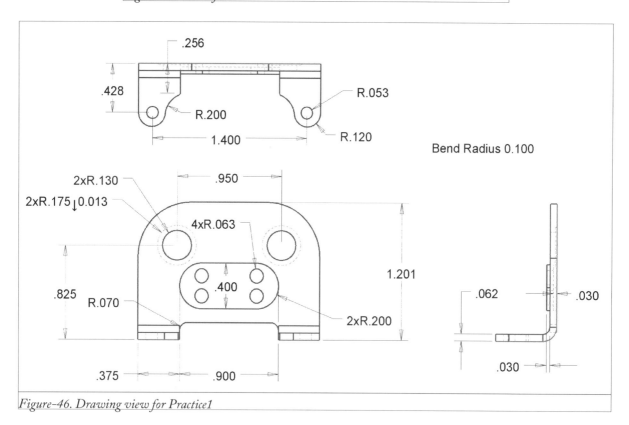

Figure-46. Drawing view for Practice1

Index

Ethics of an Engineer

- Engineers shall hold paramount the safety, health and welfare of the public and shall strive to comply with the principles of sustainable development in the performance of their professional duties.

- Engineers shall perform services only in areas of their competence.

- Engineers shall issue public statements only in an objective and truthful manner.

- Engineers shall act in professional manners for each employer or client as faithful agents or trustees, and shall avoid conflicts of interest.

- Engineers shall build their professional reputation on the merit of their services and shall not compete unfairly with others.

- Engineers shall act in such a manner as to uphold and enhance the honor, integrity, and dignity of the engineering profession and shall act with zero-tolerance for bribery, fraud, and corruption.

- Engineers shall continue their professional development throughout their careers, and shall provide opportunities for the professional development of those engineers under their supervision.